MOBILE

MOBILE

The New History of Alabama's First City

Edited by Michael V. R. Thomason

Foreword by Joe Langan

The University of Alabama Press • *Tuscaloosa and London*

Manufactured in Hong Kong by C & C Offset Printing Co., Ltd.

9 8 7 6 5 4 3 2 1
09 08 07 06 05 04 03 02 01

Designer: Michele Myatt Quinn
Typeface: AGaramond

Published in cooperation with the Mobile Tricentennial Commission

∞

The paper on which this book is printed meets the minimum requirements of American National Standard for Information Science–Permanence of Paper for Printed Library Materials, ANSI Z39.48–1984.

Library of Congress Cataloging-in-Publication Data

Mobile: the new history of Alabama's first city / edited by Michael V. R. Thomason; foreword by Joe Langan.

p. cm.

Includes bibliographical references and index.

ISBN 0-8173-1065-7 (alk. paper)

1. Mobile (Ala.)—History. 2. Mobile (Ala.)—History—Pictorial works. I. Thomason, Michael.

F334.M6 M63 2001

976.1'22—dc21

00-011125

British Library Cataloguing-in-Publication Data available

Contents

Foreword

Histories are written to record the past. They are also written so that the present generation may learn from the experiences of the past and thus have a brighter, richer, and more bountiful future. As Mobile celebrates its tricentennial it would be well for all of us to look back over our three hundred year history to determine where we came from and what we are today and to learn what and who made our city what it is. This book affords us the opportunity to review the history of the city of Mobile and to learn of its successes and failures, its triumphs and defeats, its joys and sorrows. In doing so, we can strive for the best future for our city and all its citizens.

Every community has limited resources in leadership and trained personnel, in natural and manufactured resources, and in economic and capital resources, and the more they are fragmented and split into various factions with different and even opposing agendas, the less will be accomplished for the community's overall welfare. The development of any community is determined to some extent by extraneous events and conditions, but the major factor in the growth of a city is its own resources and how they are utilized.

The greatest asset or resource of a city is its people, but they can also be its greatest liability. To become a vibrant and outstanding community there must be leaders among the people who are willing to place the common good above their personal gain and who can convince citizens to make personal sacrifices in order to provide for the community's infrastructure, services, and facilities so as to enrich the lives of all. Mobile needs educated and trained people to provide a work force attractive to business and industry; therefore, it must be willing to provide and support a quality educational system. We must also have healthy and industrious people. To assure that we do, this community must provide adequate health services and facilities along with clean water and air and sanitary conditions for all. Still, people can also retard their community's growth by not being willing to assume leadership roles; by seeking their own parochial interests rather than the overall good; or by tolerating an uneducated or undereducated and untrained population and sickly and listless people with a poor work ethic, willing to live in an unhealthy and unsanitary environment.

Mobile's natural and manufactured resources have always played an important role in its history. The founding of the city was brought about because of the natural resources of a port, an extensive river system, and forests and game to support trade in deerskins and furs. Unfortunately, during the one hundred years of Mobile's colonial period very little development occurred. It remained a military outpost and a center for Indian trade. The original 63 inhabitants who founded the city in 1702 had increased to only 405 living in ninety wooden houses by 1813. While France, England, and Spain governed Mobile, none of them was willing to provide the necessary human and economic resources to develop a city. All were content to let it remain an Indian trading post and military garrison.

Although the American takeover changed Mobile forever, throughout the nineteenth and most of the twentieth centuries Mobile has suffered from a shortage of capital resources. The community's divisions also impeded its growth because many leaders sought primarily to further their own parochial interests. Ethnic divisions were often exploited, and a "status quo" mentality dominated the minds of Mobilians. Even as late as the mid-twentieth century, fiscal shortcomings stemming from the Great Depression and the challenges of World War II meant that the city's government was just recovering from twenty years of barely making ends meet.

In 1953 a new era began with the election of three new city commissioners, Charles Hackmeyer, Henry Luscher, and me. We faced many challenges because we simply did not have the revenue to pay city employees to undertake municipal paving, drainage, and recreational projects that were long overdue. We raised taxes on a variety of items and then used that money to tackle these jobs over the next decade and beyond. No one likes to pay taxes, but when they result in new parks, expanded library and museum services, a new university, upgraded fire and police protection, and many other beneficial innovations, people understand. All over the city, citizens could see their hometown moving forward, both materially and on the human relations front. We were optimistic about our future and willing to work together, even across racial lines, far more than many of our neighboring southern cities. The city government handled its money honestly and used its expanding resources to build the foundation for even more growth.

To insure that we did not lose our most precious resource, our people, we undertook a program of annexation that tripled the city's area from its thirty-three square miles in 1953. By 1960 Mobile reached its population zenith with 203,000 people. Despite the subsequent closing of Brookley Field, Mobile was not only a bigger but a better city. We had used our resources for our community's benefit.

If the Mobile community is to continue to have a vibrant and progressive future with the amenities of the good life for all its citizens, I believe one of three things must take place. The Alabama legislature should enact a North Carolinian type of annexation law to allow the city to expand its area even further; the city and county governments should be consolidated; or the county should be given full municipal authority so that it can provide all municipal services to its citizens. In the latter case the cities should be dissolved, and the county should take over their functions with a mayor-council form of government.

As the authors of this fine book have shown us, Mobile's history has largely been a product of the efforts of all its diverse people, most impressively when people with political and economic power and vision have stepped forward to give the community real leadership. There are never enough of these people in this or any community, but in the past when leaders realized that our people are the city's greatest asset, good things have happened, and I am sure they will again and again.

JOE LANGAN
Former Mayor of Mobile

Acknowledgments

There are a great many people to thank for their work on this project. The chapter authors themselves deserve our recognition for the quality of their work and their willingness to do it—not for money but for you, the readers. In addition, Sheila Flanagan provided special help with the chapter on civil rights. Elisa Baldwin spent many painstaking hours choosing the illustrations, finding many new ones for this volume. We owe many of the fine photographs of contemporary Mobile to Catt Sirten. Others were graciously provided by Mike Marshall, editor of the *Mobile Register,* and the paper's photo staff. John Sledge and Devereaux Bemis of the Mobile Historic Development Commission also provided contemporary photographs of historic structures. Each of these people enabled us to round out the visual side of this book. Hope Byrd copied old photographs or printed original negatives, working long hours in the darkroom of the University of South Alabama Archives. She kept our spirits up and did her work well. Eugene Wilson did the excellent maps that, with Ms. Baldwin's illustration selections, enliven the text so very much. Helga McCurry did much of the clerical work and kept track of the status of each author's contribution. Sylvia Ash, Heather Harper, and Carol Ellis worked many long hours copy editing and typing. After Sylvia had to leave the project, Heather and Carol worked particularly hard. It is not possible to convey how much work is involved in this or how cheerfully supportive all three were! Ms. Ellis also did the index, again spending long hours doing so, and saved me from a task I just could not face.

Other individuals and institutions in our community provided valuable help that we are happy to acknowledge also. Velma Croom, Ulysses Miller, and Dean Mosher certainly assisted. The following Mobile institutions also deserve a special "thank you" above and beyond that provided by a credit line. They are the University of South Alabama Center for Archaeological Studies, the Mobile Public Library's Local History Division, the Mobile County Probate Court, the Historic Mobile Preservation Society, the Museum of Mobile, the Mobile Art Museum,

AmSouth Bank, Bellingrath Gardens and Home, the Archdiocese of Mobile, and the University of South Alabama Archives.

All of the work these people and institutions have contributed would have been in vain were it not for the Mobile Tricentennial Commission, led initially by Jay Higginbotham and later by Ann Bedsole. The commission was unwavering in its support. When it became evident that a large financial subvention would be necessary to bring out a top quality volume at a reasonable price, the commission did not hesitate. Its financial backing and moral support for the project were wonderful, and all Mobilians are in its debt. The staff of the University of Alabama Press, especially Kathy Swain and Nicole Mitchell, have also been a pleasure to work with throughout the process.

Like Mobile's history, one can see that this book has been a communal effort.

MOBILE

Introduction

Writing history can be a daunting proposition. This is especially true when you are writing about an old community that takes its past as seriously as does Mobile. Over the years there have been histories written about the city, some lighthearted, some scholarly, and others infused with romantic notions about one or another era. Perhaps the most famous of these histories is Peter Hamilton's *Colonial Mobile,* which is still read and quoted after more than a century. That volume, which is remarkably modern in its approach, came out on the eve of our community's bicentennial and was the inspiration for this book.

Encouraged by Jay Higginbotham and others, I wanted to produce a history of Mobile written for a general audience by the best scholars available. There was not much time if the volume was to be out for our tricentennial celebration beginning in 2001. Nor was there one author who could do justice to the whole of the city's history. After all, Hamilton had written only about the colonial era and had taken nearly six hundred pages to do that! The solution was to recruit the best historians of Mobile, or of the period of Mobile's history they would write about, and build a book. Fortunately, most of the people asked to participate were enthusiastic about the challenge. A few were unavailable, but the scholars who said yes make up a remarkable array, and we all owe them a sincere vote of thanks for their work. We corresponded and talked about the overall nature of the book and of each particular chapter, but it was left to each author to determine how best to handle his or her period. After all, if you have the best people to do the job, you do not have to tell them how to do it.

Nevertheless, I was apprehensive that we would have a collection of essays instead of a flowing narrative history. As the chapters came in it was clear that this would be far better than a collection of essays; it would be a history, and a history with a theme running through it. That theme is both simple and profound: Mobile is the product of all the people who have lived here, black, white, southern, northern, native born, immigrant, rich and poor, young and old, male and female.

Mobile is the product of the interaction of diverse peoples, but it was no utopian experiment. The interaction was born in necessity and perpetuated by success. So, some will sneer that ours is a "multicultural, politically correct history," when in truth it is an honest effort to record the contributions of all sorts of people in good times and bad for three centuries.

Except during the Civil War, Mobile has never been surrounded by a wall protecting it from the hostile world outside. From Bienville's day on, it has been an open city, conservative yes, but not closed. Although some newcomers and new ideas have been more welcome than others, it has never lived in isolation. At one time or another Mobile has needed all of its people to survive, whether it admitted it at the time or not.

This history of Mobile is hardly perfect. As long as the tale is, some subjects have gotten short shrift. There is not much on military or architectural history; many political leaders, famous in their own day, are left out. Some of our most cherished legends are passed over in silence: the Boyington Oak, the Copeland Gang, Lafayette's appreciation of the beauty of local women, and so on, largely because they are untrue, unverifiable, or irrelevant. (Two outstanding architectural histories and several detailed treatments of the city's military record are available.) We were trying to break new ground and synthesize a modern history. Let old legends die. Many have blinded us to the truths this book's authors have tried to show us.

Also, this is a history of Mobile, both of early efforts by Europeans to explore and exploit the area and of the settlement begun in 1702. A great deal of good work has been and is being done by archaeologists on the precontact world of the Americas. Nonetheless, Mobile's is the story of what happened as a result of the European discovery of our continent. Although Native Americans lived in this area for millennia before 1702, they did not start this city. Their important role in Mobile's development is explored in the first chapters, but it remains true that if people of European origin had not come here there would not be a Mobile at all. So, we refer interested readers to the works of archaeologists for an analysis of the Americas before contact with Europe. We have tried to focus on other subjects that have not been adequately explored and that are clearly in the purview of historians.

One wonders whether this volume will even be remembered when our descendants celebrate the quadricentennial in 2102. I leave that answer to the future itself. If readers in our own day appreciate how many different kinds of people have made Mobile what it is, our task will have been worthwhile. If we build on that knowledge the city's fourth century is bound to be a success.

MICHAEL V. R. THOMASON

CHAPTER I

Discovery, Exploration, and Colonization of Mobile Bay to 1711

Jay Higginbotham

The estuary known today as Mobile Bay, so distinct on early Spanish maps of the Gulf of Mexico, was not always so perceptible. When first the bay began assuming its present form during one of the distant ice ages, little life existed in the area—and it was not intelligent life; not even more advanced forms of animal life were present.

In the course of revolving ice ages, during which the gulf waters epochally advanced and retreated, inundating the coastal plain and then returning to sea again, the bay took its current shape, witnessing the gradual infusion of life of all forms. Over the millennia, as the great masses of water alternately froze and melted, leaving in their wake fertile marshes and tidal streams, a teeming variety of land and sea life—including deer, bear, and muskrat—developed, feeding on the infinite food resources of sea mammals, whelk, and mussel.

Even before Mobile Bay attained its present dimensions (some thirty-five miles deep, eight to twenty miles wide), however, the region was discovered and colonized by beings walking upright, moving in from every direction, particularly from the north and northwest. These ancient explorers, descendants of wandering Siberians, came hunting and gathering. They eventually grouped themselves into small village settlements, venturing deep into the gulf some sixty miles beyond the present Mobile Point, the shoreline at that time being much farther south. Around this bay and far beyond the present shoreline, these Paleo-Indians of the later Pleistocene epoch lived for millennia, gradually being forced back toward the hills surrounding the bay as the ice caps melted and the gulf waters flooded their former village sites.[1]

From 7000 B.C. to the present, Mobile Bay has slowly stabilized, steadily assuming its present shape and condition. Terminus for the next-to-largest river basin sys-

Indian shell mound at Dauphin Island, circa 1910.

Erik Overbey Collection, University of South Alabama (USA) Archives.

tem in North America, the bay gradually developed as a rich feeding ground for wild game and fish. With a humid, nearly subtropical climate and surroundings of rich southern pine forests, it was inviting both to humans and to other animals, the rich precipitation and fairly mild temperatures offering a haven for varied forms of life.[2]

At what point in prehistory the first pair of human eyes gazed on Mobile Bay cannot be precisely determined, but it seems fairly certain that sometime in the distant Pleistocene epoch, through the mists surrounding the newly formed inlet, small groups of Paleo-Indians were drawn to the bay. Approaching its shores many thousands of years before the sixteenth-century European invaders, they adapted themselves permanently to its shorelines, bayous, and marshes.

Principally hunter-gatherers on their arrival, the original bay peoples gradually developed more complex ways of living. They used oyster beds, perfected new fishing methods, and constructed fiber-tempered ceramic complexes. Over the years, they developed canoes and boats to exploit estuarine resources better.[3]

At the time of the golden age of Greece, Mobile Bay's natives were making occasional contact with other cultures. Evidence suggests some contact with natives from the Olmec and other Meso-American cultures, as well as with those from the Mississippi Valley and the upper Mobile River system. Through this long era the population slowly increased. The land was green, there was enough food for all, and there was little cause for strife between the unnamed (and virtually unknown) groups of settlers. Few were aggressive or territorial, there being no scarcity of usable, fruitful lands. Cooperation and sharing were much more productive modes of behavior in such a wilderness.[4]

By the beginning of the late prehistoric culture, the natives of the Mobile Bay regions were still living much as they had lived for thousands of years: hunting, for-

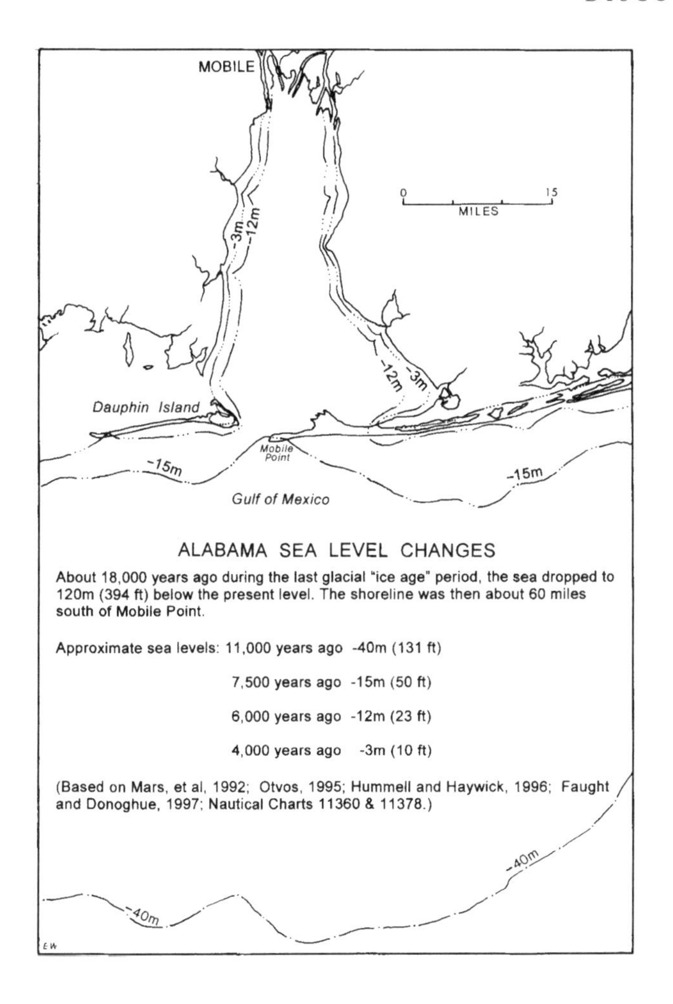

Alabama sea level changes.
Map by Eugene Wilson.

aging, and shell fishing. Change during this late prehistoric period did not appear at once, but gradually a more complex society began to emerge, stemming partly from contact with other societies in North and Central America. From such alien contacts came watercraft technologies and ceremonial mounds such as the noted Bottle Creek mound in the heart of the Mobile Bay delta. But were such contacts confined to North America and perhaps Central America, or did they extend further—to the Amazon? To Canada or Greenland? Perhaps even to Egypt? Did the mound-building zeal come from Mayan culture contacts, and did the Mayan influence originate in the valley of the Nile?[5]

Out of these exotic possibilities arose numerous legends and myths. One of the most persistent has been the African thesis: that thousands of years before Columbus, Egyptians predating Nefertiti or Tutankhamen sailed across the Atlantic (in reed boats, as Thor Heyerdahl once demonstrated was possible) to South America and perhaps even to North America. Such legends have persisted since the early days of Spanish exploration, but only in the 1800s was anything resembling scien-

A shell-tempered figure of a human head from the Mississippian period found in a midden on Dauphin Island.

Museum of Mobile. Photograph by Michael Thomason.

tific inquiry made. Since then the theories and supposed evidence have multiplied, including the appearance of New World alkaloids in Egyptian mummies; remarkable resemblances between New and Old World sculptures, art designs, and inscriptions; and similarities between New and Old World pyramids and their supposed influence on the mound builders of the Mobile River basin.[6]

Although the Egyptian thesis has not produced conclusive archaeological evidence, it has brought attention to new possibilities. That ancient Egyptians actually were in the Gulf of Mexico thousands of years before Columbus (or before Khufu, even) is a somewhat plausible theory, although not likely. What seems more probable is that even if occasional boatmen from Africa or Europe (or even rafters from Australia) made their way to the New World, they had no major cultural influence on New World societies. Equally probable is that the major groups of original discoverers and inhabitants of Mobile Bay first migrated from Asia across the Bering land mass some thirteen thousand to sixty thousand years ago and then moved down to the coastal areas.

After Egyptian theories, the next most persistent myth is the fable of Prince Madoc of Wales. According to legend, Madoc ab Owain Gwynedd, younger son of Owain the Great, Regent of Gwynedd in North Wales, sailed to the New World in 1170 A.D. Medieval poets described vividly Prince Madoc's heroic, adventurous voyages, but none ever mentioned where he landed, only that he sailed.

In the century after Columbus, however, as word of the Spanish discoveries spread across Europe, the legend was born of Madoc's having sailed across the Atlantic and landed in North America. In the late sixteenth century, Welsh scholar

John Dee entered Wales as a contender for New World territory by claiming not only that Madoc had sailed but also that he had installed a colony in La Florida after crossing the Atlantic in the twelfth century. Other writers, notably David Powel and Richard Hakluyt, added a detail or two to the epic story, so that in time the legend took on the aspect of historical fact. It was Sir Thomas Herbert, however, who first steered Madoc to the Gulf of Mexico, the far-reaching result being that, much later, writers of the nineteenth and twentieth centuries reported Madoc making contact with the white (Welsh) Indians of Kentucky, building stone forts in what are now Tennessee and Alabama after sailing up Mobile Bay, and then ascending the Coosa River to its source.[7]

Although widespread in Europe, the legend was thought by skeptics to be mere propaganda in order to afford England material to support the claims it was making in North America. Today the story of Madoc, especially the description of Madoc sailing up Mobile Bay three hundred years before Columbus, is treated as legend by serious historians, who, searching the literature, have never been able to find support for the story. The possibility exists that mariners of northern Europe, Scandinavia, and Iceland occasionally wandered along the Atlantic coast and perhaps even into the Gulf of Mexico in the centuries between Christ and Columbus, but no account has been documented other than in fable and song.[8]

In addition to such pre-Columbian mythical voyages, other legends followed, some of which included Columbus himself leaving Cuba and making a hasty cruise of the northern shores of the gulf. Because most of Columbus's movements have been carefully documented, however, few take this story seriously or that of Amerigo Vespucci's having sailed into Mobile Bay after mooring briefly at Dauphin Island.

Vespucci's voyage supposedly occurred in 1497, and part of the reason for belief in such an improbable venture is that maps began appearing in the early 1500s indicating certain Gulf Coast landmarks before records existed of any mariner or cartographer making surveys. The only answer is the rather plausible theory of unknown navigators. Whether or not Vespucci or Columbus ever sailed from Cuba to the mainland, it is almost certain that numerous early adventurers left the ancient ports of Puerto Real, San Cristóbal, and Verapaz and returned glowing reports to eager mapmakers. Aside from tales of gold-laden hills and fountains of everlasting youth, the reports described a marvelous bay somewhere on the northern Gulf Coast, a fabulous harbor capable of sheltering innumerable ships.[9]

Reporting to mapmakers and officials, these early adventurers pictured in glowing but general terms a fabulous bay they referred to as *Bahía del Espíritu Santo* (Bay of the Holy Spirit). It was deep and wide, opening from a narrow entrance to a vast expanse of calm water, capable of protecting innumerable vessels from the treacherous winds of the gulf, its banks and bluffs swarming with exotic creatures. Some of these early navigators had actually been to Mobile Bay, and others had visited Pensacola Bay or Galveston Bay. Which of these was the true Bay of the Holy Spirit cannot now be determined for certain. In some sense, they were all deserving of the name.[10]

In addition to the unknown navigators, other more famous sailors were rumored to have made voyages along the northern gulf, some perhaps even to the bay of Mobile. Among them was Juan Ponce de León, who in the early 1500s, before his fatal attack at the hands of coastal Florida natives, explored westward along the northern coastline for unknown distances. A more probable pre-Narváez cruise to reach Mobile Bay was the expedition of Diego de Miruelo, a daring Spanish pilot who in the year 1516 skirted the northern gulf shoreline on a trading voyage from Havana. On this cruise Miruelo certainly discovered Pensacola Bay (early maps of that bay even bear his name), encountering friendly natives, initiating trading ventures with them, and likely also exploring the bay of Mobile.[11]

Not long after the voyage of Miruelo, a new effort was made by Francisco de Garay, governor of Jamaica, who ordered Alonso Álvarez de Pineda to skirt the northern gulf from Ponce de León's bay to the Pánuco River. Setting out with four ships in the year 1519, Pineda returned the following year with much new information on the northern Gulf Coast. It was the most elaborate official reconnoitering expedition yet sent to the mysterious coastline. No doubt Pineda visited both Pen-

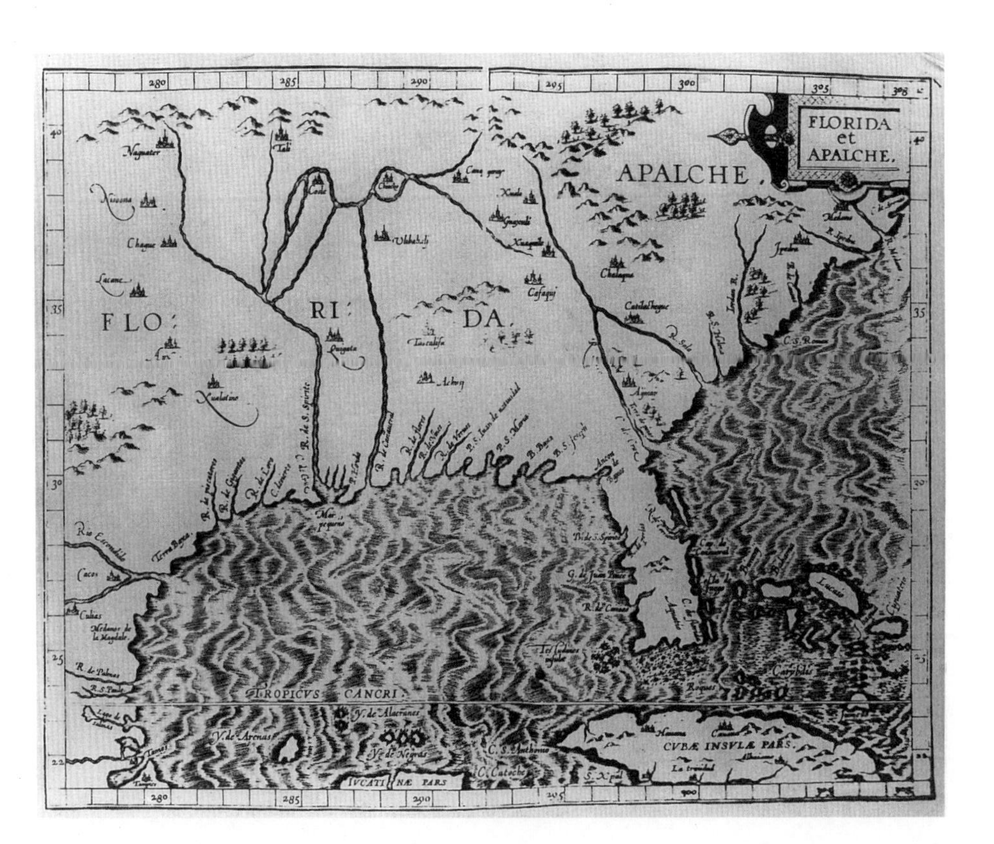

Late-sixteenth-century map of *La Florida.*

Corneille Wytfliet, *Descriptionis Ptolemaicae Augmentum* (1597).

sacola Bay and Mobile Bay (as well as Galveston Bay), but it is impossible to say for certain which he meant by the appellation Bahía del Espíritu Santo. What is more certain is that he and his men spent forty days in a large Indian village near the Gulf Coast and found the inhabitants friendly and eager to trade.[12]

Pineda's explorations, though disappointing in failing to locate a water route to the Pacific, did arouse more interest in future exploration of the Gulf Coast, particularly the fabled Bahía del Espíritu Santo. Not long after Pineda's return and the circulation of his reports along with another map made on an expedition sent out by Fernando Cortés, new interests were aroused, and further expeditions set out to explore the northern coast and the mythical bay. Among these explorers was Pánfilo de Narváez, who, after a disastrous confrontation in central Florida, drifted by the mouth of Mobile Bay in a makeshift vessel and encountered local natives who were not so friendly. After two such encounters, recorded by the journalist Álvar Núñez, Cabeza de Vaca, during which the natives seized a Greek named Doroteo Torodeo and a black slave, Narváez moved on westward, later to perish at sea.[13] Despite Narváez's disasters, Cabeza de Vaca returned to Spain full of enthusiasm for a new Florida enterprise. He also published a journal describing his experiences in detail.[14]

In Spain at the moment was Hernando de Soto, one of the New World's most successful soldiers of fortune. Soto, after brilliant successes in Nicaragua and Peru, was busy organizing an expedition to La Florida, having only recently secured approval from the crown. From his headquarters in Havana, where he served as governor and captain-general of Cuba, he departed for La Florida in 1539. From the province of Apalache near modern Tallahassee, Soto sent out ships under Francisco Maldonado to search for the mythical Bahía del Espíritu Santo, then embarked inland after making estimations of the distance between St. Joseph's Bay and the sought-after inlet. After a strenuous journey across the Deep South, searching desperately for the type of mines he had found in Central and South America, Soto spent a month in the rich chiefdom of Coosa and then headed south toward the long-sought bay where Maldonado should have been waiting.[15]

While following a major river somewhere in the distant highlands above Mobile Bay, Soto was greeted by a representative of the native headman, Tascalusa, who then led Soto to the village of Athahachi, head town of Tascalusa's paramount chiefdom. In this village Tascalusa and Soto met for the first time, after hearing the many rumors of each other's presence in the area for some weeks before.

Each leader, at first, seemed respectful of the other, yet Soto only shortly after meeting Tascalusa began making demands, notably for women, food, services, labor, and information—demands to which Tascalusa objected but agreed to fulfill because he believed he had not the wherewithal to resist. Promising to deliver the requested items at Mauvila, a small, fortified village downstream, Tascalusa led

Soto and his expeditioners down the Alabama River before crossing that stream at the village of Piachi and arriving at Mauvila early on the morning of October 18, 1540.

What followed was one of the most decisive encounters in the history of North America. Tascalusa, his wariness rising steadily, had become increasingly suspicious of Soto's carrot-and-stick strategies and his bravado in brandishing his power. He retreated to a nearby cabin even before the first meal had been served. Alarmed at being left alone with thousands of warriors skulking about, Soto tried frantically to lure Tascalusa back to the gathering, but Tascalusa, hoping that Soto would soon leave if nothing were provided him, could not be budged. When no plea was heeded, Luis de Moscoso, Soto's *maestre de campo;* Cristóbal de Espíndola, his captain of the guard; and Baltasar de Gallegos, his captain of infantry, attempted to enter Tascalusa's cabin but were met at the cabin door by the chief's guards. The Spanish intruders were being shoved back when Gallegos, in a fit of temper, struck one of the guards a mortal blow. This bloodletting sent the natives scurrying. Rushing

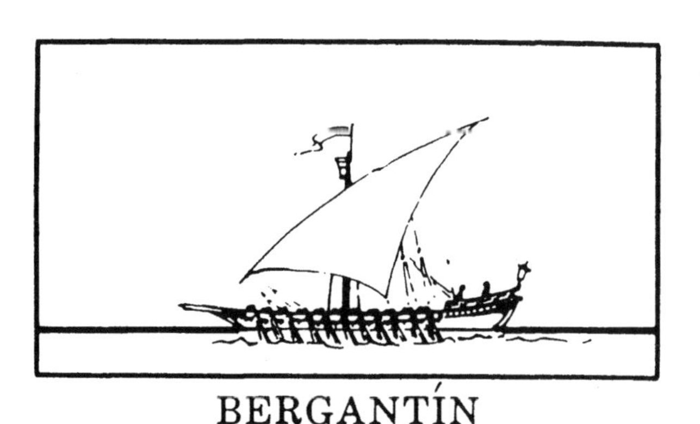

BERGANTÍN

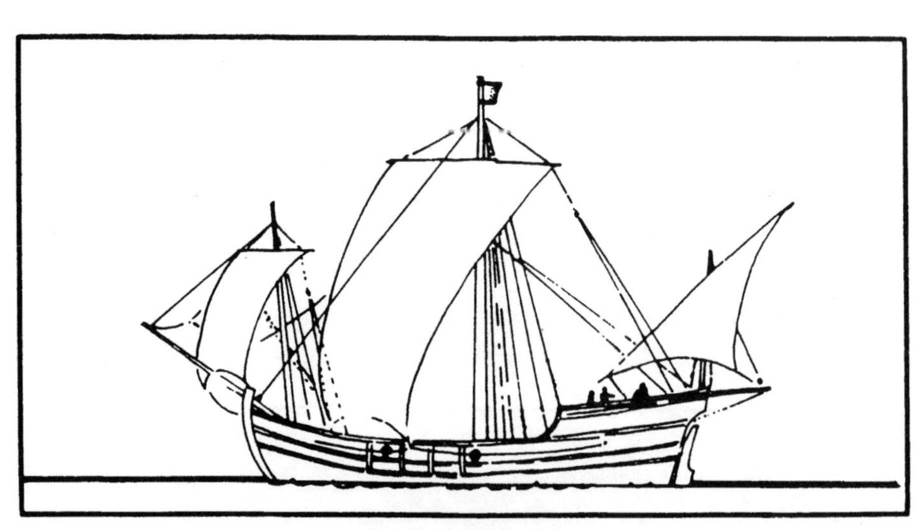

CARAVELA

Early Spanish explorers used highly responsive caravels, built for seaworthiness rather than cargo capacity, to cross the Atlantic Ocean. Smaller, partially decked, flat-bottom bergantines enabled them to explore in the shallows of the coastline and rivers.

Drawings by Roger C. Smith, *Gulf Coast Historical Review.*

Hernando de Soto.

Museum of Mobile.

from the cabins, hundreds of warriors attacked every Spaniard in sight and drove Soto and his chief lieutenants onto the plain outside of town. Despite the efforts of both Tascalusa and Soto to eschew open warfare, a major battle erupted.[16]

Outside the palisades of Mauvila, Soto regrouped, then launched a major assault on the town from all sides. The nearly six hundred Spaniards charged the stockade from all angles, the cavalry surrounding the town to help prevent escape, and then set fire to nearly every building within. As Mauvila burned, the hysterical natives broke in all directions, fighting as they fled. Many were killed on a battleground outside the stockade, and several hundred escaped into the forest, but the majority of some three thousand natives died in the flames, consumed by smoke and fire. As for Tascalusa, the possibility exists that he died in the fire, but his body was never identified. More likely he escaped into the forests.[17]

In spite of Soto's apparent triumph, the Spanish won a Pyrrhic victory. Aside from more than twenty fighting men killed outright, the expedition suffered numerous disabling injuries, including several of Soto's principal caballeros and captains of foot. They needed more than a month for recovery. The conquerors also lost much of their equipment and valuables, including more than two hundred pounds of pearls being brought from Cofachiqui. Moreover, morale was crushed, and mutiny and dissension threatened to fragment the expedition. In consequence of the battle of Mauvila (in addition to his expedition's material losses, Soto also lost his guides, women, and carriers), the *adelantado* (governor) felt forced to alter

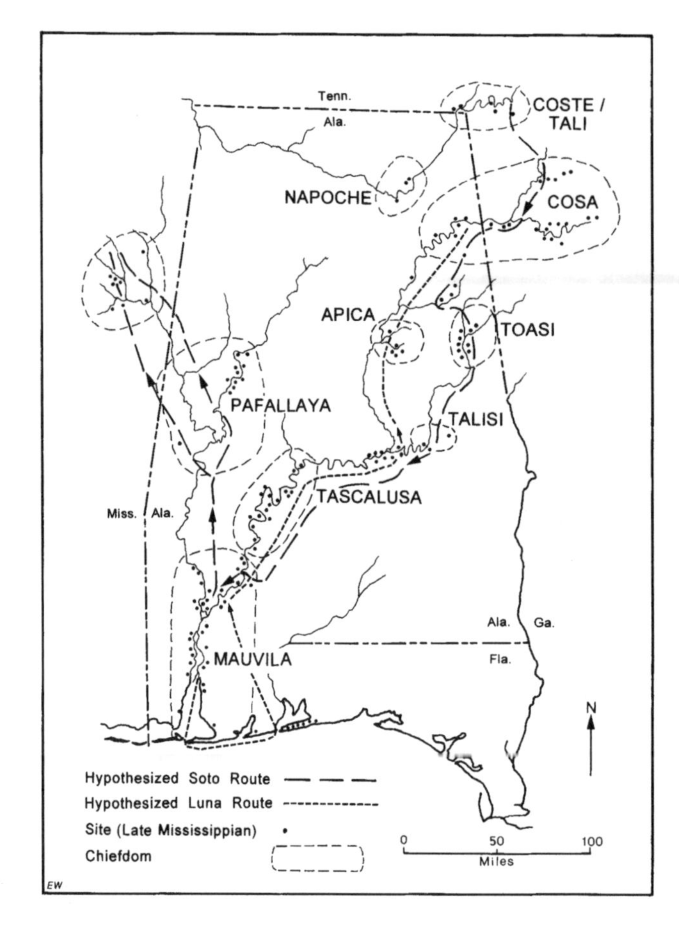

Current hypotheses of Spanish routes and Indian chiefdoms.

Map by Eugene Wilson based on Caleb Curran, *The Mauvila Project* (1992).

his strategy. Rather than continuing on to his Gulf Coast rendezvous with Maldonado to take on additional supplies from Havana, Soto changed course and fled to the north, a decision that was to cost him his life and two hundred of his men. Also abandoned was his strategy to promote access to the interior by establishing a base that would help open a pathway from the Bay of Ochuse to the Atlantic coast.[18]

Also as a result of the massacre at Mauvila, Soto's legacy lingered for years among the area's natives. François Le Maire, ministering in Mobile in the early 1700s, claimed that survivors of the ancient Mauvilians still remembered through their ancestors the carnage of a century and a half before.[19]

Two decades after Mauvila, Don Luis de Velasco, viceroy of New Spain, commissioned Tristán de Luna to explore further the lands that Soto and Maldonado had visited and to establish colonies at the most favorable sites, namely at Ochuse, Coosa, and Santa Helena.

After an exploratory voyage by Guido de Las Bazares, who had been sent to sound the various bays of the Gulf Coast, and specifically to locate the Bay of Ochuse, Las Bazares's pilot, Bernaldo Peloso, a former member of Soto's expedition, reached the Gulf Coast in September 1558. He made landfall at Ship Island twelve nautical miles southwest of Pascagoula Bay, which he called *Bahía de Bajos* (Shallow Bay). Finding this bay too shallow, he sailed east some twenty-seven nautical miles to the mouth of Mobile Bay (which he described with great accuracy, including Dauphin Island) and named it *Bahía Filipina* for Felipe II of Spain.[20]

In June 1559 Luna embarked from Veracruz with more than one thousand colonists, some Indians from Mexico, and nearly five hundred men under arms in the grandest attempt yet made to colonize La Florida. With a fleet of thirteen ships, Luna and his expedition arrived on the Gulf Coast in mid-July. Unloading many of his men and all his horses at Mobile Bay, Luna shortly thereafter set sail for a bay farther east thought by Peloso and other Soto veterans to have been Maldonado's Ochuse.

Five days after Luna's arrival in Pensacola Bay a fierce hurricane struck the Gulf Coast near Santa Rosa Island, sinking nine ships and destroying most of the food supplies. With no way to feed his colonists, Luna began to search for friendly natives. Pensacola Bay (Soto's Ochuse, which Luna had named *Bahía Filipina del Puerto de Santa María*) was uninhabited, however, and Luna was pressed to search inland for food supplies. In late September, a search party of nearly two hundred men, led by Mateo del Sauz, marched northward for forty leagues through rugged terrain to a village called Nanipicana on the river of Piachi, which Soto had crossed on his way to Mauvila. Finding food supplies at this village, Luna moved practically the entire colony to Nanipicana, where his people survived for nearly a year.[21]

The natives of Nanipicana were a bit more fearful than the peoples Soto had encountered on the Alabama River in 1540. Not only had their friendliness declined; their prosperity and numbers had also decreased, suffering as they had for two decades from the carnage, diseases, and damage that Soto and his men had wreaked upon their unsuspecting populations. Luna was to pay dearly for Soto's cruelty because the natives were now both less willing and less able to assist their foreign visitors. The further Luna's men probed the forests—some of them all the way to the once magnificent Coosa—the worse conditions became, until there seemed but one alternative left: to pack up and move back to the coast where at least the beleaguered colonists could survive on shellfish and small game.

With a heavy heart, then, Luna and his expeditioners returned to the gulf, this time back down the Alabama River to the bay where they had first made landfall, to the Bahía Filipina of the Las Bazares expedition. Here, on the lower east side of Mobile Bay, near where he had first unloaded his men and horses, Luna attempted another settlement. With no hurricanes threatening for several months, Luna remained at Mobile Bay, but he faced other difficulties. He could enlist aid from only a few natives, and the starving colonists soon grew restless. Few could envision any future in this trackless land. Bitter strife gradually developed, culminating in near mutiny and finally driving a desperate and defeated Luna (like others before him) to abandon his dreams of fame and fortune and sail back to Spain via Havana.[22]

The Luna and Soto expeditions had been both grandiose and disastrous, but each also produced important knowledge of the Mobile Bay area. Yet the lack of material success by the Spanish adventurers—the failure to find gold or silver mines or even thriving native chiefdoms—engendered a notable pessimism among the authorities in Spain, Mexico, and Cuba and among prospective adventurers. The northern Gulf Coast saw no official expeditions for well over a century after Luna, although infrequent vagabond journeys were no doubt made by freewheeling adventurers because it was possible to sail from Havana to La Florida in a single day. What galvanized the Spanish into action once again in the late 1600s was not new dreams of gold and jewels but the international political rivalry among France, Spain, and England.

After establishing New France along the St. Lawrence River in the early 1600s, Versailles was looking southward by midcentury. Such men as Pierre Le Sueur, Jacques Marquette, and Louis Joliet were leading the exploration of the Great Lakes region, gradually moving down the Mississippi River. Also active in the gulf were roving bands of French pirates, but not until the voyage to the mouth of the Mississippi by Cavelier de La Salle in 1682, during which he claimed the entire Mississippi Valley for France, did the struggle for control of the northern gulf began to simmer anew.

Even before La Salle's follow-up mission in 1684 had ended in disaster, Spain reacted by sending out a new expedition to search for his colony, in effect to rediscover and reclaim the fabled gulf ports of Mobile and Pensacola before the French could occupy them. By early February 1686, Juan Jordán de Reina, the future founder of the Pensacola fortress in 1698, was at Mobile and Pensacola Bays. The expedition of the *Nuestra Señora de la Concepción y San José,* although it failed to discover La Salle's lost colony, did renew official Spanish interest in the northern gulf entryways into the interior.[23]

The next year, on May 22, 1687, another expedition arrived at Mobile Bay, led by Martín de Rivas and Antonio de Iriarte. Even before it was able to return to Havana, however, another was commissioned, this one by Viceroy Conde de Monclova, who ordered the embarkation of Captains Francisco López de Gamarra and Andrés de Pez of the Armada de Barlovento from Veracruz. Pez's expedition was no more successful than its predecessor in locating La Salle's colony, but it did even more reconnaissance on the bays along the northern gulf. Reaching Mobile Bay on August 11, 1687, Pez recorded a greater water depth than did the Jordán de Reina expedition the previous year yet was unable to enter Pensacola Bay.[24]

As a result of these and subsequent expeditions in search of La Salle, however, the Spanish became determined to fortify at least one of the bays on the gulf. Following numerous discussions and months of serious debate during the years 1690 to 1692, King Carlos II commissioned the renowned cartographer, Carlos de Sigüenza y Góngora, to make a final and thorough investigation of Mobile and Pensacola Bays to determine which was more suitable to fortify. In 1693 Sigüenza y Góngora arrived on the Gulf Coast to make his maps and recommendations. A thorough survey of Mobile Bay convinced Sigüenza that Pensacola Bay would make a better site for a fort because of its greater depth and narrower entrance way. Carlos II ordered the Conde de Moctezuma, viceroy of New Spain, to occupy Pensacola Bay and build a presidio fortress. The officials proceeded quickly to carry out their orders.[25]

All such Spanish activity at Mobile and Pensacola Bays, in proximity as it was to the mouth of the Mississippi, did not go undetected by the French. Reports of the expeditions drifted back to the court of Louis XIV and aroused the extreme interest of not only French imperialists but also the religious and the crown. In truth, although La Salle had been spurred on to claims in the Mississippi Valley by Jean Talon and Louis de Buade, Comte de Frontenac, France was not overanxious to spread its empire to either North or South America. Once La Salle had made his claims, however, provoking reaction from the Spanish, there was no turning back. France was honor bound, at the very least, to protect its vast Mississippi Valley and Gulf Coast interests, which soon were to extend from the Perdido River to Matagorda Bay. The race for the Gulf Coast port to control this region was on.[26]

Although Mobile Bay was closer to the mouth of the Mississippi and slightly better known than other bays on the coast, Pensacola Bay had a better reputation

Spanish colonial coins found at the Old Mobile site.

University of South Alabama Center for Archaeological Studies, on loan to the Museum of Mobile. Photograph by Catt Sirten.

Pierre Le Moyne d'Iberville, painting by Maltby Sykes, 1944, from a steel engraving.

Alabama Department of Archives and History, Montgomery, Alabama.

among both Spanish and French cartographers as a site for a fortification and a possible colony. It was, as Sigüenza had reported, the "crown jewel of the empire." As intelligence kept filtering into Versailles concerning these Spanish surveys, the French became increasingly aware of Pensacola Bay's merit. When Pierre Le Moyne d'Iberville, New France's greatest naval hero, fresh from triumphs over the English in the Hudson Bay region, was commissioned to "reconnoiter the mouth of the Mississippi and fortify the entrance to it," he left without delay from the port of Brest in France to the Gulf of Mexico.[27]

On this first of three voyages to the gulf, Iberville arrived at Pensacola Bay in late 1698, only to find the Spanish already lodged firmly at the bay's entrance, although they had only been there a matter of weeks. Rebuffed at Pensacola, Iberville went on to explore Dauphin Island (which he named Massacre Island because of the great number of bones found in ceremonial mounds) and the entrance to Mobile Bay before moving on farther west to clear lands for his own fort, first on the Pascagoula River and finally at the bay of Biloxi.[28]

Weather permitting, Iberville would surely have discovered the harbor between Massacre and Pelican Islands that, though lacking the anchorage of Pensacola, was sufficient for his purpose. He would doubtless have sailed then to Ship Island, from which point he would have found entrance to the Mississippi before returning to

Mobile Bay to construct his initial fortress. Not finding sufficient anchorage at Massacre Island, however, Iberville moved on to Biloxi Bay, built Fort Maurepas, then sailed back to France, leaving his most capable lieutenant, Jean de Sauvole, in command.[29]

Iberville returned to the gulf in the spring of 1700, and by the time he left Fort Maurepas he had gained a clearer picture of the situation and how best to protect France's interests in the area. Biloxi Bay, although scenic and serene, offered no long-range strategic values; it could harbor no great number of ships, and there was no large river affording access into the interior. These advantages Mobile Bay offered: the river basin, thoroughly explored by Charles Levasseur in 1700 under orders from Sauvole, allowed entrance far into the interior to the sources of the Alabama and Tombigbee Rivers and their various tributaries, affording easy access to such strategic native groups as the Mobile, the Alabama, and the Grand and Little Tomeh, all villages that could be useful in helping stem the tide of the English from Carolina as well as the Spanish from Florida. Moreover, in the summer of 1701, it was duly decided in the French court (now under the heavy influence of the new minister of marine, Jérôme Phélypeaux de Maurepas de Pontchartrain) that colonization of Louisiana was now feasible and would henceforth be a policy objective. Only by colonizing the land it claimed could France long secure her vital interests in the Mississippi Valley.[30]

Thus, when Iberville departed La Rochelle on September 29, 1701, he had clear orders from the court: transfer fortifications from Biloxi Bay to the Mobile River, establish an actual town site for use as the capital, and prepare for extensive colonization. Decidedly ill on landfall at Pensacola, Iberville learned that Jean de Sauvole had perished a few months earlier at Fort Maurepas. With little delay, he ordered his younger brother, Jean Baptiste Le Moyne de Bienville, to begin making preparations to transfer his men and supplies from Fort Maurepas to Massacre Island.

On January 13, 1702, Bienville, Levasseur, and Iberville and Bienville's brother Joseph Le Moyne de Sérigny, all native Canadians, sailed up the Mobile River some thirty-eight miles from its mouth to the village of the Mobilians, making notes on the way of a beautiful bluff on the west side of the river. Levasseur had been shown this site by the Mobile natives in 1700. The Mobile village was located a few miles upstream, just below Nannahubba Bluff, and the Grand Tomeh and Little Tomeh were situated some miles above the village of the Mobile.

After making notes, Bienville dispatched them to Iberville along with a sketch of the bluff drawn by Levasseur. Still recovering at Pensacola when he received the notes and sketch, Iberville ordered Bienville to proceed immediately with building the fort, which was to be similar in size and shape to Fort Maurepas. It was to be called Fort Louis, after the Sun King. Bienville commenced to do this on January

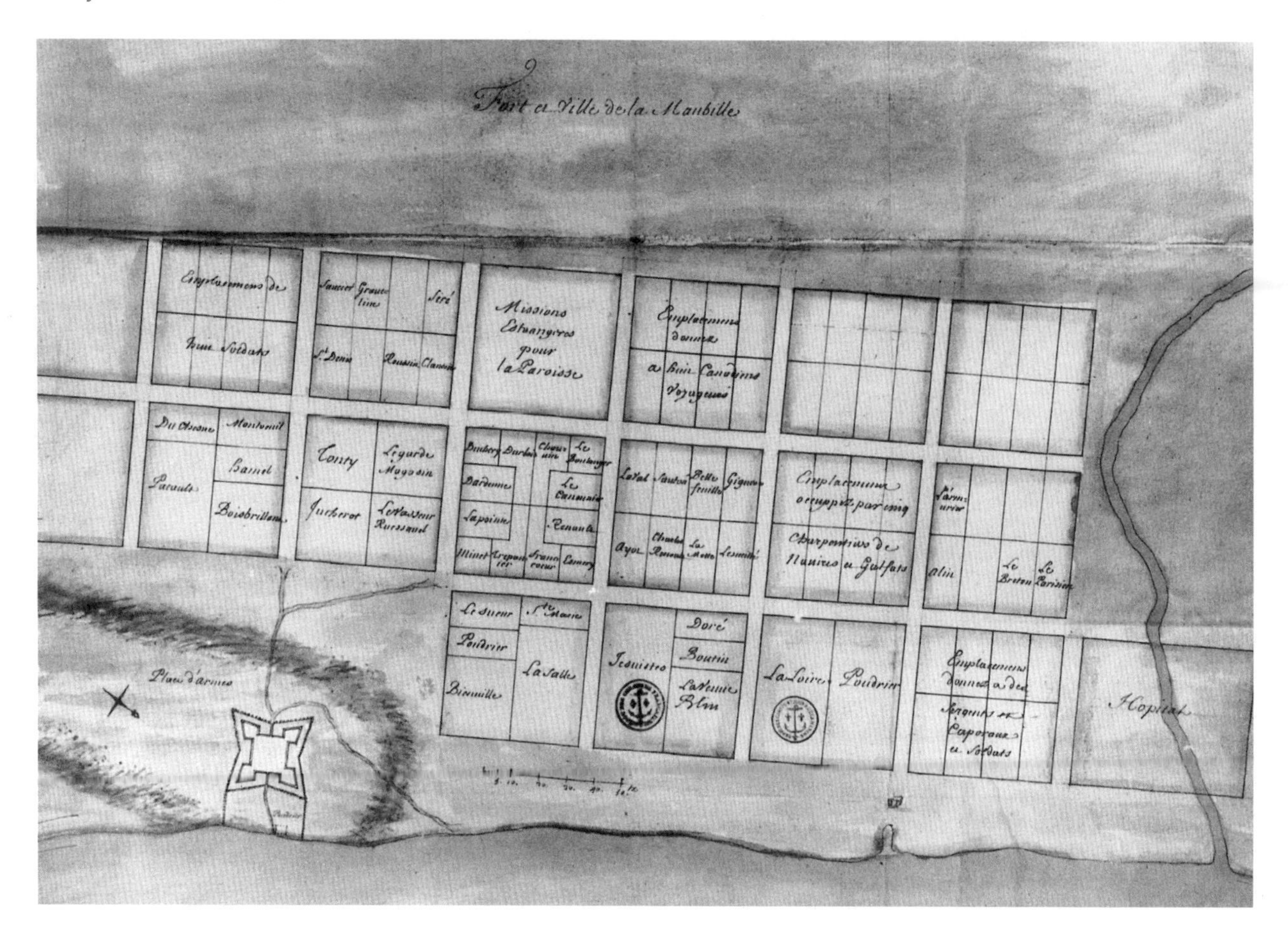

Map of Old Mobile, 1702, probably drawn by Charles Levasseur.

Archives Nationales, DFC 119A.

20. By the time Iberville arrived at Mobile in early March after having inspected two other settlements on the way (the port at Massacre Island and a warehouse at Dog River), he noted that the fort and stockade were nearing completion.[31]

Iberville remained at Fort Louis for nearly a month after his arrival, inspecting the streets being laid out and the houses being constructed by the Canadians and craftsmen from La Rochelle. Before he left to return to France via Massacre Island, he participated in a ceremony he regarded almost as crucial as the task of founding a capital for Louisiana: a peace conference involving leaders of the Choctaw and Chickasaw peoples, two of the most formidable chiefdoms in the southeast, without whose cooperation, Iberville reckoned, it would be difficult to succeed in defending France's claims against her more powerful European rivals.

The mission for a *Pax Gallica* (state of peace) was a risky venture. It involved sending into unexplored territory Iberville's most experienced and most respected lieutenant, Henri de Tonti. Tonti was born of Neapolitan parents but had served France in the wildernesses of North America for more than two decades. He was formerly a chief lieutenant of Cavelier de La Salle and had been at La Salle's side during the epic 1682 voyage down the Mississippi. His experience in wilderness travel and native diplomacy made Tonti an ideal candidate for the mission. After a three-week journey through both Choctaw and Chickasaw villages, he was able to entice the most important of the chieftains he encountered back to Mobile, arriving at Fort Louis on March 26. The next day, in a public conference, Iberville showed the markings of a skilled diplomat as well as those of a military man. After vigorous speeches, in which he alternately coaxed and threatened the leaders of both nations and offered them generous gifts of rifles, knives, and hatchets, the peace alliance appeared sealed, and the English, at least for the time being, more likely to be kept at bay.[32]

A few days later, as Iberville began preparing to return to France, he could rest more assured, confident he was leaving Mobile on sound footing both materially and diplomatically. Mobile, surrounded by friendly buffer villages, was well supplied and developing each day into a larger, more sophisticated town. After leaving instructions with his brother Bienville (the twenty-two-year-old commandant of Fort Louis, who would now be the chief authority in the nascent colony), Iberville left for France in April aboard the *Renommée.*

Bienville's problems as commandant of Fort Louis and leader of the new colony did not immediately surface in the months after Iberville left. Yet gradually the diminishing food and supplies began to cause difficulties. Backstairs trading agreements were made with the Spanish at Pensacola, and missions to Havana and Veracruz helped provide foodstuffs. It was discovered early, however, that wheat would not grow well in Mobile's subtropical climate, nor did agriculture on any large scale seem to be a profit-making venture. More support from France than was first anticipated would be needed.

Moreover, factional strife soon began, even before Iberville arrived back in La Rochelle. On one side were the Bienvillists, consisting largely of the Le Moyne brothers (Bienville, Sérigny, and Châteaugué [Antoine Le Moyne de Châteaugué]) and the great majority of the Canadians, the most seasoned and influential of the settlers, backed by the Jesuit religious order.[33] Opposing Bienville was Nicolas de La Salle, a haughty French bureaucrat whose demeanor and jealous guarding of the storehouse irked Bienville severely. It was especially annoying because La Salle boasted long experience in Louisiana, having served with Cavelier de La Salle as early as 1681. As commissary of the capital, he also had the support of the court, as well as of the seminary priests, who were shortly to move into the area after the bishop of Quebec, Jean-Baptiste de La Croix de Chevrières de Saint-Vallier, added Mobile on July 20, 1703, as a new parish to his North American diocese.[34] Soon after creating his Mobile parish, Bishop Saint-Vallier nominated a forceful pastor from the diocese of Bayeux, Henri Roulleaux de La Vente, who shortly after arriving in Louisiana sided with Commissary La Salle and other Frenchmen and seminary priests.

Saint-Vallier's interest in Mobile extended to peopling the colony as well as to providing for the health of souls. For some time, the colony had planned on receiving a shipload of females who would sail to Louisiana to be married and bear the colony's first children. Bishop Saint-Vallier, in Paris in 1703, accepted a suggestion by Pontchartrain, minister of marine, to help select the marital prospects for Mobile's bachelors. Screening candidates in Parisian convents and orphanages, such as the Couvent des Filles de St.-Joseph, Saint-Vallier eventually approved twenty girls "reared in virtue and piety . . . who are accustomed [also] to labor and diligence" to come to the new colony. Added to these were three other girls from Paris, daughters of habitant-to-be Étienne Burelle, for a total of twenty-three eligible mates. The girls left France in the spring of 1704 aboard a captured Dutch vessel called the *Pélican,* which also carried as passengers the newly appointed pastor, La Vente, and the noted Mississippi River explorer Pierre Le Sueur, who was to serve as Mobile's first judge.[35]

All went well on this memorable voyage until the *Pélican* entered the harbor of Havana and encountered the dreaded yellow fever. After nearly a week in port, the *Pélican* once more set sail for Mobile, this time without Le Sueur, who had been left behind, gravely ill. As the *Pélican* crossed the Gulf of Mexico, the fever contracted by many in Havana began to break out among the passengers. By the time the long-awaited vessel reached Massacre Island on July 22, it was a distressed ship indeed. Several members of the crew died soon after disembarking, and most of the rest became feverish and delirious.[36]

Upon arriving at Fort Louis at the beginning of August, most of the *Pélican*'s assemblage were still sick or just beginning to recover, except for one of the so-called *Pélican* girls, Louise- Françoise Lefevre, who died on August 2. By the end of the month, a strange phenomenon had occurred. All who had arrived ill on the *Pélican* were now recovered, but most of the settlers who had greeted them in good health were now ill, some fatally so. Among those who took sick and soon died were Henri de Tonti, Charles Levasseur, and Étienne Cantinteau. News also came shortly that Pierre Le Sueur had died in Havana a week after the *Pélican* had left port.

The fever that struck the colonists so hard worked even more viciously against the natives, who had little immunity. The fever was certainly deadly for the newly arrived natives from Florida—the Chato, Escambe, and Talimali groups—whom Bienville had enticed to Mobile Bay to serve as buffer villages but who only weeks after arriving began to succumb. Nor were the local natives spared: the Mobile, the Little Tomeh, and the Grand Tomeh all suffered greatly.

The marriages, so long anticipated by the court and settlers, were made during difficult times, but the results of these unions were the beginnings of some of the Gulf Coast's most prolific families: the Rivards, the Sauciers, the Trépaniers, the

Trudeaus, and the Alexandres, among others. The next summer saw the first of the new progeny appear, a development that only increased in 1706 and 1707. Moreover, with the arrival of several supply ships from France and New Spain (one bringing the first black slaves from Haiti), with the absence of any major diseases or epidemics, and with improved relations with Pensacola, Mobile's fortunes seemed to be steady, even rising.

Then, with great dismay, the colony suffered its greatest shock since the deaths of Tonti and Levasseur. Iberville, founder of Mobile and first governor of French Louisiana, had been planning for several years to return to the colony, this time with a large quantity of new supplies. Stopping by Havana in July, however, on his way to Mobile, Iberville, like Le Sueur before him, succumbed to yellow fever in the Cuban capital and was buried in the Plaza de Armas in the Church of San Cristóbal.[37]

It was October before Iberville's younger brother Châteaugué brought the news to Bienville that the governor had died. The death of Iberville was not only a personal tragedy for the brothers Le Moyne and other friends and relatives at Mobile but also a devastating setback for the colony because Louisiana had lost her governor and strongest voice at the court of Louis XIV. In addition, the long-awaited aid Iberville had been bringing did not arrive on time, and even when it did it was not as abundant as expected.

Old Mobile, 1702–11.

Painting by David Riall, Museum of Mobile.

The diminishing supplies and attendant hardships made many colonists increasingly restless, especially the Canadians, who were not used to dwelling idly in town. The worsening conditions also sparked new animosities between the Bienvillists and those siding with La Salle and La Vente. The pastor claimed that Bienville was subtly using the company storehouse to reward his friends and punish his enemies, and Bienville accused La Vente of impudence and virtual treason by lodging his complaints with the Spanish authorities in Pensacola. La Salle's charges against Bienville went even deeper. The young commandant, according to the commissary, was not only incompetent but also corrupt, working wily schemes with the colony's merchandise at the Massacre Island and Dog River warehouses. What infuriated Bienville was that both La Salle and La Vente were using every opportunity to send their complaints against the commandant back to France by any means possible. Bienville suspected that every ship that left the Mobile settlement and every traveler who journeyed to Pensacola carried indictments bound for the authorities in Paris or Rochefort.

Eventually, of course, such complaints did reach the court, arousing the suspicions of both king and minister. By the time the respected Jesuit Jacques Gravier arrived in Paris in 1707, Bienville was already in need of a skilled apologist. A special commission had by this time been at work nearly a year seeking to ferret out the accomplices in Iberville's final campaign against the English, a scheme that already had implicated two of the Le Moyne brothers as well as several of their close associates. Although the inquests were to drag on for a quarter-century, by the spring of 1707 Pontchartrain had come to believe that both Iberville and Sérigny had acted to the detriment of the colony. Although the extent of their guilt was not yet determined, the minister was assured that their conduct had been both insidious and baneful.[38] The fact that two senior officials were now lodging similar complaints against such a brash young commandant who was another of the Le Moyne family was too much for the court to ignore. Pontchartrain, as minister of marine, believed he should act, and act quickly, to maintain order and morale.

The logical answer was to send a new governor to replace the deceased Iberville, but one not of the Le Moyne clan. Pontchartrain's choice fell to Nicolas Daneau De Muy, former town-major of Quebec and recent recipient of the Cross of Saint-Louis. De Muy appeared to be an excellent compromise, being a nonpartisan who would favor neither Jesuit nor seminary priest. Accompanying the new governor would be a young man of twenty-four, formerly a part of the impressment service (as commissary of classes) at Bayonne, a bureaucrat of a noble family named Jean-Baptiste Martin Dartaguiette d'Iron. In addition to auditing the account books, Dartaguiette was to assist De Muy in an impartial investigation of Mobile's major disputes.[39]

On the way to Mobile, however, aboard the same ship Iberville had been sailing the year before (the *Renommée*), Governor De Muy fell ill and died just outside Havana's harbor. Incredibly, Louisiana had lost its first two governors within an eighteen-month period and both at the port of Havana.

Dartaguiette's position was not nearly as authoritative now that De Muy no longer commanded, yet Dartaguiette was greeted with respect by both La Salle and Bienville (especially by Bienville) when he arrived to carry out his investigation. The commandant immediately informed Dartaguiette of his awareness of the charges against him and offered to provide the young commissary any information and cooperation he needed.

Although Bienville made a favorable impression on Dartaguiette at the outset, the commissary still began his inquest soon after arriving. Within days he began calling witnesses, interviewing such respected Bienvillists as Joseph Chauvin, *dit* Léry, and François Trudeau, as well as Bienville antagonists René Boyer and Guillaume Boutin. The investigation, both lengthy and thorough, went on for days, yet when completed was indecisive. Dartaguiette, who had no power to arrest, or even to indict, could only investigate and report. Ultimately, Dartaguiette was impressed strongly by Bienville's attitude and leadership in the colony and, realizing he would be stranded there himself for at least the next few years, doubtless thought it best to maintain the status quo, especially because the majority of colonists seemed to support Bienville.[40]

After dispatching his preliminary reports back to France by the first ship leaving Mobile, Dartaguiette relaxed. The situation at the fort regarding the colony's local authorities seemed momentarily settled: both La Salle and Bienville would continue in office, with the hope that they would be kept in check by the young man from Bayonne now acting as co-commissary and in some measure as co-commandant. For the moment, the dispute was put on hold.

Although Dartaguiette had seemingly settled the issue of authority, he was unable to solve other, more material questions. Two years earlier, Bienville had received orders to strike the Canadians from the king's payroll. This Bienville could not bring himself to do and had delayed even mentioning it. Dartaguiette, however, brought a direct order from Pontchartrain that ordered Bienville to dismiss the Canadians immediately.

The unmarried Canadians vigorously objected, but they had no choice but to move out from the capital in search of new ways to earn a living. The individuals involved included some of the more prominent names in the colony. Zacharie Drapeau moved upriver nearer the Little Tomeh village; Charles Rochon had already transferred to the *Oignonets* (site of the later Fort Condé); Joseph Simon, *dit* La Pointe, and Jean-Baptiste Baudreau de Graveline moved to Massacre Island before later moving to Pascagoula; and Nicolas Bodin and Vincent Alexandre moved to the Fowl River area. Others went to the Mississippi River near present-day New Orleans, and a few, including Philippe Minette, drifted across Mobile Bay. Some even went to Pensacola, all in search of good lands to till or of other ways of making a living.[41]

After the *Renommée* returned to France in 1708, the tenor of life in the colony began to moderate. "We are a little more tranquil than we have been in the past," La Vente wrote Pontchartrain, "because of the presence of M. Dartaguiette, who inspires in us a little more reserve than is ordinary."[42]

Although factional strife had moderated, however, other problems began to surface. Several priests died, including the Jesuit Jacques Gravier, who was another of the veterans of Cavelier de La Salle's epic 1682 voyage as well as Bienville's closest associate among the religious. Moreover, a surprise attack by Alabama headmen on the Mobilian village just above the fort was enough to jolt the sleepy village upright. The Alabama, no doubt goaded by English traders in the area of the future Fort Toulouse, attacked and burned the Mobilian village, took several captives, and retreated upriver. Greatly outnumbered, the Mobile managed to defend themselves but only because of the muskets and ammunition supplied them by the French.

The attack on the Mobile Indians reminded Bienville of the need for additional security, including the renovation of Fort Louis. Only a few years after the fort had been built, rotting stakes and logs made extensive repair necessary. Now, in 1709, it was decomposing again, and Bienville was anxious to rebuild it, this time using brick and mortar. The need for repairing the fort brought to a head a basic issue that had been clouding the horizon since the colony's inception: that of the town's location. At the outset, Mobile Bay had been chosen as the general site for the capital because of the access into the interior it provided by its extensive river system. As to the particular site, the location twenty-six miles upstream from the river's mouth had been selected because of its proximity to the Indian village whose leaders had been most receptive to the French. Now that the issue was reappearing, La Salle felt constrained to offer another reason for changing its location: Mobile had been placed too far up the river from Massacre Island and the Dog River warehouse. Supplies unloaded at Massacre Island had to travel great distances to Dog River and Fort Louis. This offered more opportunity for theft and embezzlement than if the distances were shorter. La Salle thought the solution was simple: move Mobile to the mouth of the river within sight of the Dog River supply depot only nine miles away. This would help lessen the poaching and peculations and also allow the fort to protect better the port at Massacre Island, which had only recently been ransacked by English pirates from Jamaica. Moreover, La Salle claimed, the environment at Fort Louis was unhealthy, surrounded as it was by swamps, which caused poor drainage. During heavy rains, when the river rose, some of the houses even flooded. Furthermore, difficulties would arise should the town need to expand. The more elevated lands around the site where Fort Louis stood were limited; the rest would constantly be subject to poor drainage.[43]

Bienville had consistently opposed any move downstream. After all, he had been instrumental in selecting the present site himself. On his recommendations, Iberville had given the order to locate there. After years of debating the matter with La Salle and La Vente, however, Bienville was forced to reconsider. By late 1710 he was aware that Dartaguiette had instituted a system of accounts that could virtually eliminate the possibilities of fraud, but he still strongly believed that the future of Mobile lay in developing river plantations upstream and that this would hardly be promoted best by moving the capital in the opposite direction.

The crucial point in the swirling controversy came in April 1711, a few months after La Salle died and La Vente had returned to France. The spring rains fell incessantly, continuing even into May, swelling the streams that ran behind and to the northwest of the fort. The overflowing waters, unable to escape, filled the low places behind the bluff on which the fort stood. By the first week of May they had risen even higher than had the waters of 1707 and 1710. "The waters have ascended so greatly this spring," Dartaguiette wrote, "and with so much force, that most of the houses in this village were submerged to the ridgepole in five or six days; this lasted almost a month." Dartaguiette, at this point, felt compelled to confront Bienville with the complaints of the inhabitants and to present him with the hard fact that the town must be moved immediately.[44]

Faced with Dartaguiette's forceful statements, Bienville had little alternative but to acquiesce. Mutually agreeing to fortify the port at Massacre Island, Bienville and Dartaguiette also agreed to relocate the town to the site where Bienville had originally relocated the Chato Indians from Florida in 1704, that is, at the *Oignonets,* near the mouth of the river where the Canadians Charles Rochon, Claude Parent, and Gilbert Dardenne had resided since 1706. The Chato were removed to points farther down the bay and up Dog River as the project to move the town downriver commenced in late May of 1711.[45]

Along with the capital town, other Indian buffer villages were also moved. The Talimali repaired to Chickasabogue, and the Tawasa went to Bayou Sara, both streams but a few miles north of the new townsite. Having staked out the new location, Bienville and Dartaguiette returned to Fort Louis to inform the settlers of their moving plans, leaving Jacques Barbazant de Pailloux in charge of the new site. Barbazant and his aides began at once to lay out the town according to the general specifications given: the new Fort Louis was to be just back from the edge of the marsh on the first high rise of ground. The new town was also to be more regularly shaped than the former one. Except for larger lots given to Bienville and the seminary priests, the individual assignments had practically the same dimensions as the old ones—approximately 80 x 160 feet.[46]

Back at Old Mobile, the settlers were delighted to learn that the removal was to proceed immediately, but the complexities of moving an entire town were considerable. Transportation especially posed a problem, but fortunately the distance was fairly short, and all of it was downriver.

During the last week in May, the settlers began to dismantle their houses and float them downriver in pirogues and other small boats. After depositing their shipments at the new landing, the movers returned upstream for additional loads until, after numerous exhausting trips, they completed the transfer of their notched timbers and, in some cases, foundation bricks. Then began the task of reassembling the old structures.

The work of removal was cumbersome and tedious, but it went remarkably well. By June 20, 1711, Bienville could report to Pontchartrain that "the labor was proceeding nicely" and that the inhabitants were all reconstructing their houses at the new location. By early fall most of the town had been transferred, and the settlers had time to worry about the dwindling supplies. At just that time, however, the *Renommée* appeared at Massacre Island (soon to be renamed Île Dauphine, after Marie-Adélaïde de Savoye, Dauphine of France), the biggest event in the life of the colony since the ship's last arrival in 1708. In addition to the new supplies were some needed officers and men, including an engineer, Guillaume-Philbert Chevillot, who would aid in the construction of the new Fort Louis and the fortifications at Île Dauphine.[47]

Soon after the mooring of the *Renommée,* Barbazant de Pailloux returned from Veracruz, bringing additional supplies that, added to those brought by the *Renommée,* placed the capital on the soundest footing it had yet enjoyed in its decade-long history. Its mission accomplished, the *Renommée,* the most important ship in the young colony's history (having made the founding voyage in 1702, as well as those of 1708 and 1711), prepared to return to France after an overextended stay in port.

During the third week in October Bienville went down to Île Dauphine to see the famous ship off, along with Dartaguiette d'Iron, who was returning to Rochefort after a three-year stay in Mobile. Dartaguiette was at this point the man of the moment, the most effective official in the colony. He had come to Mobile at the crucial juncture when the settlement was near its lowest ebb, both materially and spiritually. By his 1711 departure, however, he and Bienville had resolved the colony's more pressing problems, and Mobile, now in a new location, was ready to begin a new chapter in its history.

Surveying the establishment on Île Dauphine now, Bienville felt hopeful about

Mobile in 1711. Like the Twenty-seven Mile Bluff site, the new site was initially a cluster of wooden buildings defended by an earth and palisade fort.

Erik Overbey Collection, USA Archives.

the future of that revitalized port. Industrious entrepreneurs such as Graveline, La Source, and La Pointe would soon develop profitable trading ventures on the island, and with the completion of fortifications, the port would be defensible.

Sailing back to the bay's head, Bienville could find optimism too in the labor of the colonists on their homes and gardens. The fields surrounding the new Fort Louis were now virtually cleared. Although no church had yet been constructed, Bienville felt confident that the seminary in France would soon show more interest in supporting its Mobile mission as the European war came to an end and the colony began to prosper. In spite of the difficult early years, the dogging poverty, the dissension among authorities, the aboriginal threats, the diseases, and the meager support from France, Bienville believed brighter days were dawning in Mobile. Some eminently stalwart and resourceful individuals were at work in the colony—men such as Trudeau, Graveline, La Loire, Trépanier, Saucier, the brothers Chauvin, and Des Prés Derbanne, men who would challenge the worst the wilderness had to offer, men who, whatever obstacles might lie ahead, would move the fortunes of Mobile and the Louisiana colony forward.

Suggestions for Further Reading

Clayton, Lawrence A., Vernon James Knight Jr., and Edward C. Moore, eds. *The De Soto Chronicles.* 2 vols. Tuscaloosa: University of Alabama Press, 1993. New translations of the Soto narratives supported by the most recent scholarship.

Galloway, Patricia, ed. *The Hernando de Soto Expedition: History, Historiography, and "Discovery" in the Southeast.* Lincoln: University of Nebraska Press, 1997. New insights into the Soto expedition by leading contemporary specialists.

Giraud, Marcel. *Histoire de La Louisiane Française: Le Regne de Louis XIV, 1698–1715.* Paris: Presses Universitaires de France, 1953. The first study of Louisiana's institutions based exclusively on archival research.

Higginbotham, Jay. *Old Mobile: Fort Louis de la Louisiane, 1702–1711.* Tuscaloosa: University of Alabama Press, 1991. A detailed account of the beginnings of French Louisiana.

McWilliams, Richebourg G., ed. *Fleur de Lys and Calumet.* Baton Rouge: Louisiana State University Press, 1953. The classic translation of Louisiana's most romantic observer.

Milanich, Jerald T. *Archeology of Precolumbian Florida.* Gainesville: University Press of Florida, 1994. A recent and scholarly treatment of Gulf Coast prehistory.

O'Neill, Charles Edwards. *Church and State in French Colonial Louisiana: Policy and Politics to 1732.* New Haven: Yale University Press, 1966. A prescient observation of the church's role in early French Louisiana

Spies, Gregory C. *Retracing the Bounds of Old Mobile.* Mobile: Archaeotechnics Publishing Co., 1993. A detailed analysis of the Old Mobile site based on studied examination.

Waselkov, Gregory A. *Old Mobile Archaeology.* Mobile: Center for Archaeological Studies, University of South Alabama, 1999. A brief, illustrated description of Old Mobile based on recent archaeological investigation.

Weddle, Robert S. *Spanish Sea: The Gulf of Mexico in North American Discovery, 1500–1685.* College Station, Tex.: Texas A & M University Press, 1985. A highly readable yet scholarly account of the discovery and explanation period.

CHAPTER 2

Colonial Mobile, 1712–1813

Richmond F. Brown

France launched its Louisiana enterprise in 1699 in hopes of containing English expansion into the Mississippi Valley and gaining a favorable position for penetrating Spanish American trade and territory. Despite these ambitions, French activity in Louisiana displayed a thoroughgoing reluctance. French rulers were reluctant to establish the colony and just as reluctant to sustain it. French commercial interests were reluctant to invest in its development—they were "not in the colonizing business."[1] The French church was reluctant to send missionaries, and the French people were reluctant to emigrate. Such attitudes created and reinforced a sad state of affairs. "In truth," says Gwendolyn Midlo Hall, "Louisiana had little to offer. The colony was poor, unhealthy, dangerous, and uninviting."[2]

Nevertheless, for better than six decades, France managed to hold the region or preserve the fiction that it did so. Mobile played an important role in this endeavor. For nearly two decades after its founding in 1702, Mobile was the capital of colonial Louisiana. After the transfer of the capital seat to New Orleans, Mobile remained the principal meeting place of French and Indian in the southeast. Lacking sufficient population or military resources of their own, the French relied on Indian allies to deter English expansion. Each year, Choctaw and other Indian emissaries ventured to Mobile to exchange deerskins for muskets, powder, clothing, and tools and to renew the friendship with gifts and mutual displays of respect, a practice inaugurated by Iberville and expanded by Bienville. While the wealth and population of the town stagnated and the fort rotted, the Indians came. They were the key to French power in the Lower Mississippi Valley.

Meanwhile, Mobile's inhabitants developed a distinctive way of life using the scarce resources available to them. The hardy settlers of frontier Mobile and its hinterland fashioned a society and economy based on cultural exchange. Their

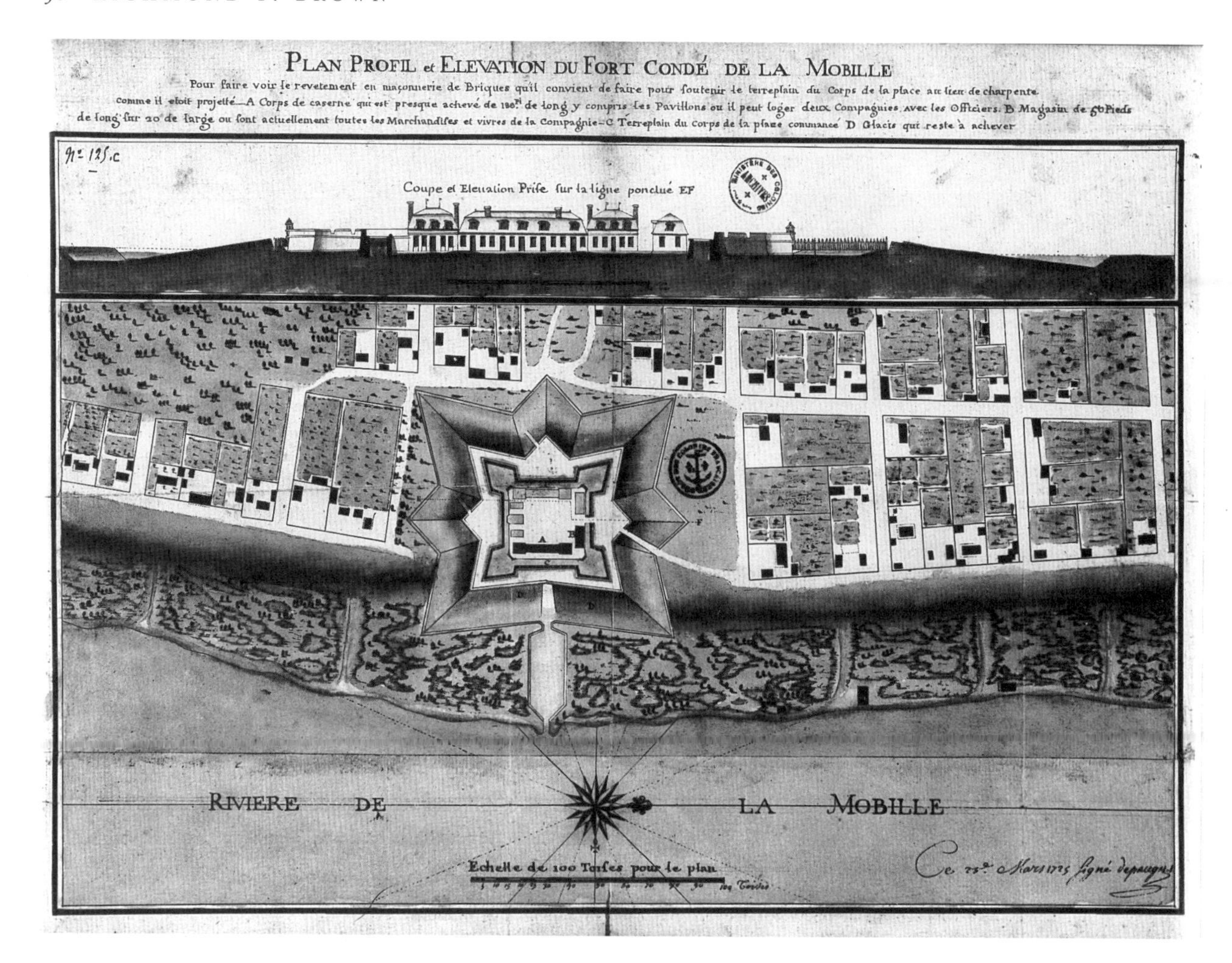

Plans for Fort Condé, drawn in 1725 by de Pauger, engineer-in-second of Louisiana.

USA Archives.

behavior seldom pleased colonial authorities who were bent on developing a plantation economy or reproducing European ways. Frequently neglected and chronically beset by disease and the forces of nature, Mobile nevertheless persevered. Native Americans, Africans, Europeans, and their descendants created a way of life that remained largely intact beyond the end of French control in 1763, through the seventeen years of British rule (1763–1780), and into the three decades of Spanish governance (1780–1813). Multicultural, frontier Mobile was ultimately overtaken only with the coming of the Americans, the removal of the Indians, and the rise of King Cotton.

French Mobile, 1712–1763

In September 1712, a French government strapped by the demands of the War of the Spanish Succession (1702–1713) and eager to be relieved of the costs and responsibilities of colonizing Louisiana, leased the infant colony to the wealthy French financier Antoine Crozat for fifteen years. He was granted a trade monopoly with Louisiana and was expected to use his own resources to develop it. He hoped to find silver or gold and to pursue trade with Mexico and Cuba. Antoine de la Mothe Cadillac, who had founded Detroit in 1701, became governor.

Cadillac supplanted the rugged Canadian Jean Baptiste Le Moyne de Bienville, a talented linguist and astute diplomat who had been in charge of the struggling colony since the death of his brother Iberville in 1706. Arriving in Mobile in 1713, the new governor was not impressed. "Here there is nothing more than the piled up dregs of Canada, jailbirds who escaped the rope, without any subordination to Religion or to Government, steeped in vice, principally in their concubinage with savage women, whom they prefer to French girls." He declared, "If God give me the health I shall attempt to put this colony on a firm foundation; at the moment it is not worth a straw."[3]

Nevertheless, the few emigrants recruited by Crozat and Cadillac did little to alter the raucous ambience of the frontier post or to put it on a sounder economic or military footing. Cadillac carried out a modest contraband trade with Pensacola and established French settlements to the west. In founding Nachitoches and Natchez he sought not only to expand the French presence in the gulf region but also to keep Bienville occupied with dangerous frontier missions. In 1717 Fort Toulouse was established at the confluence of the Coosa and Tallapoosa Rivers near present-day Wetumpka. Its purpose was to interdict English trade among the Choctaw and Upper Creeks. French settlement in the Lower Mississippi Valley would never extend into the interior beyond a fragile archipelago of isolated forts and trading posts. No mineral wealth appeared, and there was precious little trade with Mexico. Cadillac hampered French relations with Indians by abandoning the Le Moynes' policy of securing Choctaw support against the English (and their Chickasaw allies) through gifts and trade, encouraging instead fratricidal war to open land for French settlement that never materialized.

After the death of Louis XIV in 1715 and the subsequent removal of Minister of Marine Pontchartrain, the French government had even less enthusiasm for Louisiana than before. Losing money, Crozat was similarly disillusioned. In August 1717 the Crown accepted his resignation and awarded Louisiana to Scottish financier John Law.

Law's Company of the West received a monopoly of the Louisiana trade for twenty-five years, gaining exclusive ownership of lands and mines and the right to build fortifications and to nominate colonial officials. The king assumed the responsibility of maintaining forts and garrisons and providing presents for the Indians, renewing the policy of trade-based diplomacy. The company soon acquired other colonial charters for Africa, the Far East, and the Caribbean and became the Company of the Indies in 1720.[4]

Louisiana's jurisdiction expanded to include the Illinois country as well. The tarnished but invaluable Bienville was promoted to commandant general and awarded the Cross of St. Louis.[5] Looking for a base to establish more effective control over the Mississippi River, Bienville founded the eventual capital of New Orleans in 1718.

The one significant moment of military excitement for early Mobile came not in hostilities with Britain but in the war between France and Spain in 1719. In April 1719 Bienville received orders to capture Pensacola, the Spanish base founded in 1698, with whom Mobile enjoyed generally friendly relations. These neglected outposts of France and Spain had sustained each other in the harsh early years through illegal trade and occasional naval assistance.

In May Bienville captured Pensacola with a force of thirteen ships and five hundred men (mostly Choctaw). The company decided to transfer the base of its operations to Pensacola to take advantage of its superior port potential. In early August, however, two thousand Spanish troops reclaimed Pensacola, along with huge quantities of supplies the French had recently brought there. The French retreated to Mobile Bay, and at the end of August some nine hundred French, Indians, and blacks held off a siege at Dauphin Island. French reinforcements arrived, and Bienville and his largely Choctaw allies captured Pensacola once again in late September. Bienville recovered the company's provisions, burned the forts at both Pensacola and Santa Rosa Island, and returned victorious to Mobile. After the end of hostilities in 1720, Pensacola was quietly returned to Spain.[6]

In December 1720 Law was dismissed in France, and the Company of the Indies was reorganized. Bienville was retained as commandant general, to be headquartered in New Orleans. An administrative code and a colonial council were established for Louisiana in 1721. Implicated in illegal trade, Bienville was removed in 1724. In 1726 the company appointed Étienne de Périer, a longtime company employee, as commandant general.

Périer's tenure proved disastrous. Reflecting company plans to develop commercial agriculture, Périer encouraged the spread of tobacco in the fertile Natchez area. "Tobacco," he said, "must constitute the principal object of the colony." French encroachments on Natchez land and demands for labor led to tragedy. The Natchez leader, Tattooed Serpent, predicted the coming confrontation shortly before his death in 1725: "Before the arrival of the French we were living as men who know how to survive with what they have, in place of this, today we are walking as slaves."[7] On November 28, 1729, the Natchez assaulted Fort Rosalie, killed the hated Sieur de Chepart and slaughtered 145 men, 36 women, and 56 children—one-tenth of the white population of French Louisiana. The French retaliated brutally. The Natchez were virtually destroyed, and many were sold into West Indian slavery. Natchez refugees and their Chickasaw allies began raids against natives and white settlers near New Orleans and Mobile. Périer's disastrous policy and his incompetent conduct of the ensuing war convinced the company to get out of Louisiana. They returned control of Louisiana to the French government in July 1731.

French Minister of Marine Maurepas turned once again to Bienville. In power from 1733 to 1742, Bienville made strides in reforming colonial society and extending the French presence in the interior.[8] He established Fort Tombecbe in the 1730s to trade with the Choctaw on the Tombigbee River. Of most note, he conducted two major, and unsuccessful, campaigns against the Chickasaw, who had befriended both the Natchez and the British. After four decades of heroic and controversial service in Louisiana, the Canadian's career came to a poignant end with his futile efforts to destroy the hated Chickasaw. Bienville left in 1743 to live out the remainder of his life in France.

He was replaced by Pierre de Rigaud, Marquis de Vaudreuil, son of a former governor of Canada. As governor of Louisiana from 1743 until 1752, Vaudreuil ruled during the War of the Austrian Succession (1744–1748). With Louisiana practically cut off from French contact, Vaudreuil continued the campaign against the Chickasaw and increased pressure on his Choctaw allies to destroy them. The shortage of French goods (and the abundance of British merchandise) strained the alliance and opened divisions among the Choctaw themselves. A brutal civil war raged between the Eastern and Western Choctaws from 1747 to 1751.

The war entailed a "vicious cycle of raids and counteraids" that threatened Mobile and New Orleans. Vaudreuil insisted that the Choctaw raiders be punished.

Excavations at Port Dauphin and Old Mobile have revealed structures similar to those pictured in John Law's concession camp at New Biloxi, 1720.

Drawing by Le Bouteaux. Edward E. Ayer Collection, The Newberry Library, Chicago.

"During the winter of 1748–49, he received from the Choctaw at Mobile more than a hundred scalps and the heads of three men, allegedly chiefs responsible for starting the revolt. At the next annual meeting held in April 1750, he received another 130 scalps and the heads of three English traders." Rebel villages were destroyed at his insistence.[9]

Shortly thereafter Vaudreuil was named governor of Canada and was replaced by Louis Billouart de Kerlerec (1752–1762). Kerlerec governed during the overlapping French and Indian War and Seven Years' War (1754–1763) that ultimately ended French rule in North America. Somehow, the Choctaw alliance held until the end. The wars themselves had little impact on Louisiana. Their settlement in 1763, however, ended the French era, partitioned Louisiana between Spain and Britain, and transferred Mobile to British rule.

Throughout the French period, Mobile preserved its central role in Indian trade and diplomacy, even after it lost its designation as capital. Perhaps this was because the practice was well established, or perhaps Bienville and his company sponsors did not want New Orleans disturbed by periodic invasions of Indian emissaries. Mobile thus remained an important military outpost. The engineer Adrien de Pauger, who laid out New Orleans, stressed that Mobile was "crucial to the defense of Louisiana from the Spanish to the east at Pensacola, from the English to the northeast and from the Choctaw if they should ever choose to attack." Fort Louis was described in 1723 as "a pitiful structure, offering as much protection as an open park." By early 1728, when Périer visited Mobile to meet with Choctaw leaders, Mobile was growing, and the renamed Fort Condé was being strengthened, although construction was often interrupted by shortages of labor and money. By 1729 the stockade and three of the four bastions had been completed. The brick fort had a stone foundation, as Pauger envisioned, but most of the buildings were of wood.[10]

French control of the Lower Mississippi Valley, such as it was, depended on its relations with the larger Indian nations, especially the Choctaw. The Choctaw numbered about fifteen thousand people in the early 1700s, comprising some forty to fifty villages of farmers who also hunted deer and bear. French assistance helped the Choctaw defend themselves from British, Chickasaw, and Creek aggressions. The Chickasaw population was around four thousand. They were more mobile and more warlike than their Choctaw neighbors and more dependent on hunting. Armed with English weapons, the Chickasaw fought rival tribes and sold their captives into the English slave trade. Another major group generally linked to the British were the Creeks, who comprised some nine thousand people in present-day Alabama, northern Florida, and Georgia.[11]

The larger tribes of the southeast—the Choctaw, Chickasaw, Cherokee, and the Upper and Lower Creeks—established relatively formal relations with competing

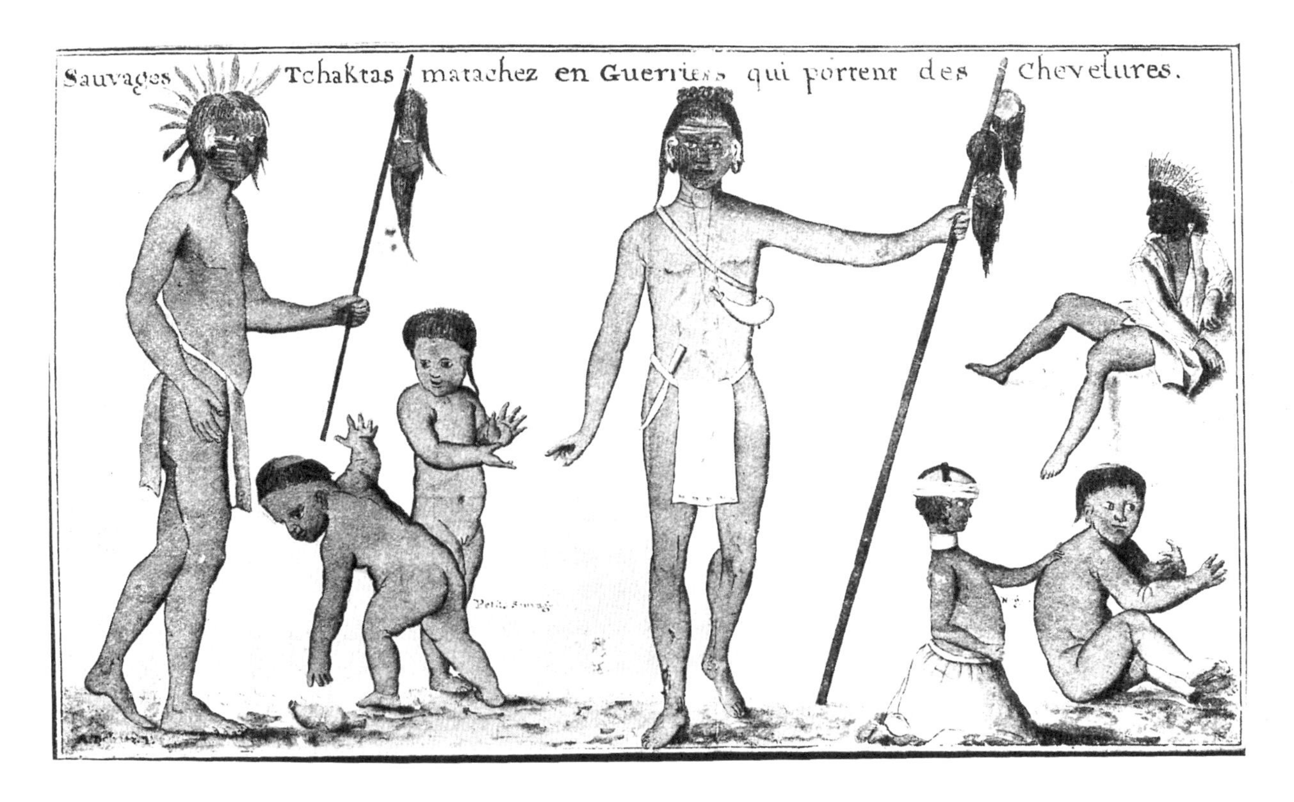

Choctaw Indians drawn by A. de Batz, 1732–35.

Museum of Mobile.

European powers, balancing diplomacy and trade. Less conspicuous were the smaller groups, the "petites nations." By the mid-1720s some ten Indian villages, inhabited collectively by some seventeen hundred people, were clustered around Mobile and Biloxi. The Biloxi, Grand Tomeh, Little Tomeh, Mobilian, Pascagoula, and Pensacola communities were indigenous to the area. They were joined by refugees from other areas—the Apalache, Tawasa, and Chato from Florida and the Taensa from Mississippi, who had moved to be nearer the colonial populations. The petites nations provided valuable goods and services to the colony: venison, corn, and other supplies. "Women sold herbs, foodstuffs, and baskets," and men earned wages "rowing pirogues, carrying trade merchandise, and delivering messages between posts."[12] They lived on the margins of colonial society but interacted closely with colonists while maintaining a substantial degree of cultural and political autonomy.

The French provided European goods valued by the Indians and upon which they eventually became dependent. Cotton replaced deerskin loin clothes and tunics; iron pots replaced earthenware pottery; and knives, pickaxes, and hoes replaced bones to clean hides and till the soil. The French reproduced Indian jewelry, furnished glass beads, and provided the Indians with combs, pipes, and buttons. Above all, the French supplied muskets to replace the bow and arrow for hunting and war. The Choctaw depended especially on the French for their supply of powder. Some of the trade items came to be produced in the colony itself. Hatchets and pickaxes were made in Mobile. In the winter of 1731–32, some nine hundred Native Americans traveled there to have their muskets repaired.[13]

The fur trade provided the most sustained enterprise in French Louisiana, and Mobile was its principal entrepôt. The prices for deerskins were fixed in 1721. At the same time the French promised Choctaw warriors "one gun, one pound of powder and two pounds of bullets for each Chickasaw scalp and eighty livres of merchandise for each Chickasaw slave."[14] By 1725 more than thirty thousand hides had been received from the Indians of Louisiana, nearly one-third of them from the Choctaw and the Chickasaw. The number of skins exported from Louisiana between 1720 and 1780 averaged fifty thousand per year. After a typical hunting season, Bienville reported in February 1743 that "the trade in deerskins amounts at present to more than one hundred thousand pounds." At midcentury, peltry accounted for one-third of the total value of commodities being exported from Louisiana. (Tobacco and indigo comprised 40 percent, and timber, pitch, and tar accounted for most of the rest.) Interruptions in the supply of trade goods and the difficulty of preserving the hides at Mobile, however, hampered the business.[15]

By the 1730s trade patterns were well established. Traders left for the villages after Choctaw delegations completed their annual ceremonial visits to Mobile. Indians from one of the small nations around Mobile, or some of the Choctaw themselves, accompanied the traders to the villages. When a trader arrived, he was taken to see the village chief. He would enter the chief's house in silence, taking the pipe offered him. The chief would acknowledge his presence, and the trader would proceed to describe his goods. The following day, the chief presented the trader to the villagers, who dealt with him individually. The sales trips would take two to three months. If a trader knew the language well (Mobilian became the lingua franca among the southeastern Indians), he could earn profits of perhaps 200 percent.[16]

Colonial officials dominated the deerskin trade. Bernard Dartaguiette d'Iron, the brother of Jean-Baptiste Martin Dartaguiette d'Iron, the company director and the commandant of Mobile, gained exclusive trading rights with the Choctaw under the Company of the Indies. He was challenged, however, by Étienne de Périer and Jacques de La Chaise, who tried to seize the pelt trade for New Orleans. When Louisiana became a royal colony in 1731 the trade was opened to all the people of Louisiana. Yet a visitor to Mobile in 1759 reported that the fur trade was "entirely in the hands of the officers, contrary to the King's wishes." Prices were regulated to keep French goods competitive with English goods. Nevertheless, difficulties persisted. In 1731 during the Natchez War, only 4,067 buckskins were received at Mobile. French merchandise often was in short supply. The *St. Anne* arrived in November 1731 to find only eleven pieces of material in the Mobile store for Indian trade and gifts.[17]

The annual arrival of Native American emissaries in Mobile certainly must have awakened the somnolent coastal village and shaped its social calendar. By the 1740s the Choctaw delegations would comprise more than one hundred men, including "a tribal chief, three district chiefs, war chiefs, dozens of village chiefs, and all their military and ceremonial assistants." They arrived before the planting season or after the harvest and received gifts worth as much as fifty thousand livres, often presented by the French governor himself. The Mobilian Indian village served as a way station for the visitors. From there they would proceed to Mobile with an interpreter, and each member of the delegation would greet the French leader. They smoked a pipe, made speeches, and then made camp outside the town as their gifts were collected and their guns were repaired. When the exchange was completed, another group would follow. The parade of visitors could last up to six weeks, severely straining the resources of the commandant, who was expected to fete the most distinguished Indian leaders at his own table. In early 1744 Vaudreuil welcomed more than three thousand members of the Choctaw tribe to Mobile. In 1753 members of all fifty Choctaw villages came to Mobile to meet with Kerlerec. He received more than two thousand Choctaw emissaries in the fall of 1754.[18]

In contrast to the impressive scale of Indian trade, efforts to populate Louisiana with European settlers and African slaves floundered. When Antoine Crozat turned Louisiana over to Law's Company of the West in 1717, the French population of Louisiana totaled only some four hundred men, women, and children. It proved difficult to entice French people to emigrate freely, so the company turned to force. Deportation to Louisiana became a common sentence in France from 1717 to 1720. Criminals (petty and otherwise), deserters, vagabonds, and the destitute were shipped off to the colony. Most of the women immigrants were in their thirties and had been convicted of minor offenses ranging from blasphemy to prostitution. One female deportee, however, had been accused of fifteen murders. Popular protest against the deportation policy, most notably a prison riot in January 1720, led the French king to suspend the practice in May of that year.[19]

The company sponsored the only substantial effort to populate Louisiana. Between October 1717 and May 1721, it sent forty-three ships to Louisiana carrying more than seven thousand colonists. These included 122 officers; 977 soldiers; 43 company officials and 302 company workers; 119 land grantees; 2,462 indentured servants; 1,278 salt smugglers and other exiles; 1,215 women; and 502 children. Their reception was a harsh one. In the winter of 1718–19, for example, "the forlorn inhabitants stranded at the coastal posts of Dauphin Island, Mobile and Biloxi lacked either the knowledge or the energy to gather fish and other available food sources, one group reduced instead to eating weevil-infested seed wheat." Of the seven thousand white settlers who came between 1717 and 1721, at least half of them either died or departed Louisiana before 1726.[20]

Port Dauphin, or Port Massacre, was of greatest importance to the French from 1702 until 1717 when the harbor entrance was closed by a storm.

Veue de l'Isle Dauphine dans la province de la Louisiane, circa 1718. Bibliothèque Nationale.

In addition to French immigrants, and consonant with its plans to develop plantation agriculture, the company initiated a major effort to bring in African slaves. The slaves came from West Africa, and most were Malinke-speaking captives from the interior, but some were members of coastal ethnic groups such as the Wolof and Sereer.[21] The approximately seven thousand blacks transported to Louisiana on slave ships between 1718 and 1731 experienced a mortality rate similar to the white immigrants. An inhospitable environment, unsanitary conditions, epidemic diseases, chronic food shortages, and poor medical knowledge and care doomed many of the newcomers.

By 1726 French Louisiana had a population of 3,784 Europeans, Africans, and Indian slaves (not including the free Indian populations). Mobile's population was 547 (compared with 901 for New Orleans). Two hundred sixty-one were ordinary "habitants" (free, nonlandholders), including 93 men, 72 women, and 96 children. There were 194 slaves, including 144 black slaves and 50 Indian slaves. There were seven *engagés* (indentured servants) and eighty-five soldiers.[22]

After the Natchez massacre, the Louisiana population crisis deepened. Many whites left, and few new colonists arrived. In 1733 a vicious hurricane and a smallpox epidemic added to Mobile's difficulties. "Our planters and merchants here are dying of hunger," wailed Mobile commander Dartaguiette d'Iron. "Some are clamoring to return to France; others secretly run away to the Spaniards at Pensacola. The colony is on the verge of being depopulated."[23] By about 1740 the white population of Louisiana had been reduced to less than twelve hundred, including troops and settlers. There was something of a recovery by 1746, when Louisiana had 4,100 slaves, 3,300 settlers, and 600 soldiers. Mobile in 1746 had some 150 white settlers (not including women and children) and 200 black slaves. It had seen little growth, if any, in two decades.

Efforts to convert French Louisiana into a flourishing plantation society never succeeded. The population was too small (and disinterested), and the necessary resources to develop it were never forthcoming. Imperial interests in the West Indies discouraged the creation of a competitor. The most notable effort to establish plantations had ended in the tragic Natchez War. Merchants and planters tied to agricultural exports thus never established effective control of society or the economy.

Instead, the elite of French Louisiana was a "military-bureaucratic clique" who depended on the Indian trade and legal and extralegal overseas commerce. This began with the Le Moyne brothers, who skirted and occasionally traversed the bounds of legality and decency. They were accused repeatedly of profiteering while colonists and soldiers suffered.[24]

Some French officials enjoyed a life of comfort and relative wealth. The Chevalier Montault de Montberaut was a former commander of Fort Toulouse who became an important landowner in the Mobile area. Among his many properties was Lisloy on the Fowl River. Enclosed by rail fences, the estate had a manor house, barns, gardens, dairies, stables, and parks. Worked by twenty-six slaves, Lisloy was stocked with five hundred cattle and fifty horses, as well as flocks of sheep and pigs. Montberaut had a boat to allow him easy access to Mobile, where he owned townhouses. He complained, however, that "life is very costly in Mobile." At his estate, he could "go about simply dressed." In town, the "expense is more than three or four times greater, especially because of having to treat daily with the Indians who respect a person according only to the brilliance of his dress."[25]

This cottage, formerly on the corner of Conti and Conception Streets, with its roof flaring out over the surrounding gallery, was typical of early French dwellings along the Gulf Coast.

Drawing by Roderick D. MacKenzie, 1887. Elizabeth Gould Papers, USA Archives.

Of course most inhabitants of the Mobile area had no such concerns. Most settlers were farmers or herders or lived by hunting, gathering, and fishing or by trading or providing military or transportation services.[26] A 1759 visitor to Mobile observed that "the industrious inhabitants trade with the Spaniards, who come from the presidio of Pensacola nearby to get salt, beef, fowl, corn, rice, and other staples. The inhabitants of Mobile are also in the tar business."[27] The settlement was chronically short on artisans, skilled workers, and professionals.

Given Mobile's strategic role, soldiers made up a significant segment of the colonial town's population. Military men comprised about 30 percent of Louisiana's white male population at midcentury. Mobile had some 141 soldiers in 1754. They, too, led a harsh existence. They were poorly and infrequently paid—a particular hardship for those dependent on wages. Many became deeply indebted to local merchants or even turned to theft. In 1741 Mobile's Major Beauchamp chided the minister of marine for the serious shortage of mattresses and blankets at Fort Condé: "I am quite convinced that your intention is not that the soldiers should be made to sleep like dogs." Disease, desertion, and death were common. Vulnerable to smallpox epidemics after campaigns, soldiers also faced more endemic maladies such as malaria, scurvy, dysentery, pneumonia, and syphilis. Mobile's climate was especially harsh on new recruits, where summer greeted them with "heat, humidity, and mosquitoes." Rebellious and recalcitrant, few soldiers settled permanently in the colony. In 1751 Vaudreuil complained that "very few have an inclination to marry, but a much smaller number have enough ambition and strength to undertake to clear a tract of land."[28]

Besides soldiers, other groups lived in Mobile largely against their will. Mobile had some fifty Indian slaves in 1726. Many of the Indians living in Louisiana households were women, and colonial officials were divided over the reality of concubinage and the legality or desirability of marriages between Indians and French or Canadian settlers. The arrival of European women partly resolved the question. Ultimately, fears of Indian and African slaves uniting against Europeans discouraged Indian slavery. By 1732 Louisiana had fewer than one hundred Indian slaves.[29]

The African slaves of Louisiana fulfilled numerous tasks. At Mobile in 1733, twelve government slaves manned the boat that plied the waters between that port and Fort Tombecbe, Fort Toulouse, and New Orleans. The shortage of population and the lack of skilled workers in the frontier town tended to minimize racial distinctions. In 1720 the company exchanged three African slaves for Bienville's "negro named Laurent who is a good blacksmith." Blacks participated widely in the colonial economy and society in many occupations. They became intimately acquainted with whites on many levels. Some were able to purchase their freedom. Interracial unions were prevalent, with white men taking Indian and black women as common-law wives or mistresses, further eroding efforts to divide society rigidly by race.[30]

Mobile defied efforts to re-create European life on the gulf. It housed a motley populace who among them spoke French, German, Mobilian and other Indian languages, and a variety of West African languages that, along with French, became the basis of Louisiana Creole. No schools, presses, or newspapers existed. Although French women tried to replicate Parisian society in Louisiana, their influence was limited by their small numbers and their failure to reproduce. Most colonists were apathetic or hostile toward the church establishment. Never during the French period did a majority of parishioners within commuting distance of chapels attend "compulsory" weekly services.[31]

As a rule, France valued Louisiana more for its military uses than as a colony to be developed in its own right. Population remained sparse and ties with the mother country tenuous. The limited efforts to establish plantation agriculture floundered. Instead, the inhabitants of Mobile and the rest of Louisiana forged an economy based on frontier exchange. This economy involved all the constituent groups in colonial Louisiana: whites, blacks, Indians, the free and the enslaved, men and women. Although disruptive to traditional Indian life, the exchange of deerskin and corn for European manufactures could be accommodated without devastating cultural change. As long as the settlers remained confined to the coastal towns and scattered trading posts in the interior, Indian ways could survive, albeit in modified form.

Petites nations took advantage of provisioning opportunities and European protection, while larger nations such as the Choctaw furnished corn and deerskin in exchange for trade goods. Settlers and slaves depended on Indians and each other for sustenance. Poor whites, free people of color, and even slaves engaged in petty trade with each other and with Indian inhabitants—whether petites nations or larger tribes. Female Indian and African American peddlers predominated in urban markets. African slaves peddled the goods of their owners and their own surpluses in an urban atmosphere that allowed substantial liberties. The diverse Louisianians borrowed from each other in food and in food ways. Indian uses of corn, persimmon, fruits, and nuts; African knowledge of rice culture; and European preferences for beef, pork, and fowl blended in a cultural and culinary gumbo.[32] They created a way of life that survived the partition of Louisiana in 1763.

British Mobile, 1763–1780

Mobile passed to British hands in 1763 by virtue of the Treaty of Paris ending the Seven Years' War. Evicted from Canada and Louisiana, France had earlier ceded western Louisiana, along with the "island" of New Orleans, to Spain. In the 1763 treaty Spain granted its Florida holdings to the British in exchange for the return of Havana, captured in the war. Mobile now became part of British West Florida, whose boundaries stretched from the Mississippi River to the Chatahoochee (Apalachicola) River and from the Gulf of Mexico to the thirty-first parallel. In 1764 the northern boundary alongside the Mississippi River was moved to the junction of the Yazoo and Mississippi Rivers to encompass the Natchez area.

Mobile was formally transferred in October 1763. Fresh from victory in Havana, Major Robert Farmar of the British Thirty-fourth Regiment of Foot arrived to receive the town. Born in New Jersey and schooled in England, Farmar was a veteran of wars in North America, Europe, and the West Indies. With his forces stranded on a sand bar in Mobile Bay, on October 18 Farmar was rowed to Fort Condé to meet with French commander De Velle, who had asked him to delay the transfer of the town until the completion of an Indian congress scheduled to begin in November. Irritated by French delays and concerned for his men, who had been confined to ships for most of the past three months, Farmar insisted on an immediate turnover. The grenadier companies of the Thirty-fourth and the Twenty-second raised the Union Jack on Thursday, October 20. The French troops departed two days later. It took more than a month for Farmar to get all of his troops ashore and even longer to unload his supplies.[33]

He renamed the post Fort Charlotte and exercised de facto control over West Florida for the next year. Mobile was essentially its capital during that time. Pensacola then became the capital and soon overtook Mobile in numbers and importance. Governor George Johnstone arrived in Pensacola in October 1764. Described as a "brawling Scot" with a "belligerent and overbearing manner," Johnstone was constantly at odds with military and civil officials, and his presence "kept the colony in turmoil until he left Pensacola in 1767."[34] Farmar had several confrontations with Johnstone, which eventually led to lengthy court-martial proceedings. Following an expedition to establish British rule in the Illinois country and his exoneration in the court-martial, Farmar retired to life as a planter in the present-day Stockton area on the Tensaw River.[35]

After Johnstone's departure, Montfort Browne served as interim governor until John Elliot arrived in April 1767. Elliot committed suicide one month after he got to West Florida, and the unpopular Browne was temporarily reinstated. He was replaced by yet another interim governor, Elias Durnford. Finally, Peter Chester arrived in West Florida in August 1770. Chester remained in office until the surrender of the province to Spain in 1781. Perhaps unfairly described as "a man of mediocre talents," he brought new stability to his post.[36] After a difficult beginning plagued by sickness and political confrontations, British West Florida enjoyed impressive growth under Chester's direction.

At the time of the transfer Mobile had some 350 townspeople, with some 90 French families in the surrounding countryside. By contrast, when the Spanish garrison left Pensacola, so did the Spanish civilians. The numerous petites nations sur-

George Johnstone.
Public Records Office, London.

rounding Mobile also left. Groups of the Alibamas, Apalaches, Biloxis, Chatos, Mobilians, Pacanas, Pascagoulas, and Taensas migrated from the Gulf Coast and Alabama River area to Spanish Louisiana.[37] The temporary abandonment of Pensacola and the permanent loss of valuable Indian provisioners removed two long-term supports for Mobile and perhaps played a role in bringing on the harsh conditions of the early years of British occupation.

In 1763 Mobile was "a scattering of one-story houses that barely adhered to any street plan and impinged upon the approaches to the fort." The rechristened fort was in a state of serious decay. The brickwork was crumbling, and "the ramparts were covered with weeds and bushes." The barracks needed rebuilding and expanding, "the wooden palisades on the glacis were rotten," and the gates were in bad shape, with "the main gate practically off its hinges." Farmar began repairs to the fort, but they proceeded slowly. He meant for his men "not be exposed to the inconvenience daily of being plundered by the savages, who have ever been used to come in and out as they pleased."[38]

The town itself was not in much better condition. Farmar wrote in 1764 that "this place at present carries the appearance of a little hamlet formed of Negro Hutts, rather than a well peopled town in Canada." Johnstone exclaimed in January 1765 that "the state of the town in filth, nastiness & brush wood running over the houses is hardly to be credited."[39]

Mobile became infamous for its deadly climate. Summers were particularly devastating. Troops arriving in the late summer found it difficult to adapt, discomfort was universal, and the mortality rate was frightfully high. One Mobile soldier deemed West Florida "good for nothing but destroying Englishmen."[40] The situation improved with cooler weather and the delay of the arrival of new men until the fall, but the town retained its deadly reputation.

Eager to keep useful populations, the British sought to convince the French inhabitants to stay in Mobile. They promised religious toleration and gave them three months to take an oath of allegiance or eighteen months in which to dispose of their property and depart. Ultimately 112 French Mobilians took the oath within a year of British military occupation.[41]

West Florida faced potential threats not only from its Spanish and Indian neighbors but also from the English immigrants who were in Johnstone's view "the refuse of the jails of the great cities and the overflowing scum of empire."[42] The first immigrants to reach Mobile after the British occupation were Indian traders and their employers. From Georgia and Carolina mainly, they were a rowdy lot. Robert Farmar incurred their hostility when he prohibited trade with New Orleans and punished them for defrauding Indians.[43]

To attract a better class of settler the British publicized the virtues of West Florida and extended generous offers of land. Although officials were cautioned to make grants only to those with serious intentions to settle, large land grants were given to royal favorites. Montfort Browne, for example, received a grant of twenty thousand acres of his choosing and proceeded to give Dauphin Island to his brother.

Officials contemplated transporting convicts to the new colony, but no such plans materialized. Browne engaged in a scheme to transport French Huguenot and Irish indentured servants, whom he planned either to use himself or sell to others. They met a harsh fate. A visitor to Mobile in July 1766 described them as "a number of men, women, and children laying and strolling about the streets, some dead, some dying, some unsuccessfully begging, and others shaking in an ague, or burning in a raging fever."[44]

The town's population grew slowly. In 1766, according to one observer, the Mobile district had "140 houses and plantations and a total population of 860, of whom 360 were black." By 1774 the colonial population of West Florida had grown to nearly four thousand whites and fifteen hundred blacks. The Reverend William Gordon estimated the town of Mobile's population in 1774 at 330 whites and 416 blacks.[45]

The American Revolution gave a great boost to the population of West Florida. In November 1775 Governor Chester proclaimed West Florida as a sanctuary for loyalists. He sweetened the offer of asylum with grants of free land to those who suffered losses on behalf of the Crown. By the next spring loyalists were arriving in the colony in large numbers. British West Florida grew to some seven thousand inhabitants before it fell to the Spanish during the American Revolution. Many of the new immigrants seem to have been wealthier than earlier settlers of West Florida, and many brought slaves and servants. The new arrivals headed almost exclusively to the western regions of the province, settling on the Mississippi River and giving impetus to the rise of plantation agriculture there.[46]

The naturalist William Bartram visited Mobile in 1778, noting that it extended about half a mile from the river. It was smaller than in earlier days, with many homes "vacant and mouldering to the earth." Yet he found "a few good buildings inhabited by French gentlemen, English, Scotch and Irish, and emigrants from the Northern British Colonies." The dominant Indian traders, Swanson and McGillivray, had made "extraordinary improvements in the buildings."[47]

Nonetheless, even town life was rustic. One resident's property near Fort Charlotte contained "eighteen sheep, five lambs, a cow and calf, a sow, and six dozen chickens." Neither Mobile nor the rest of British West Florida offered much in the way of intellectual stimulus. There were still no newspapers or printing presses. Rudimentary education took place in "makeshift schools and churches." A large segment of the population were bachelors. Religious activity was minimal, and most of the colony's population, free and slave alike, was illiterate.[48]

Life for slaves appeared to grow harsher with British rule, at least on paper. In November 1766 the newly established British West Florida Assembly approved a motion for a slave bill. The statute was enacted in January 1767. Manumission was expensive, and punishments for blacks were severe. The 1767 statute made color "the badge of slavery" and sought to enforce a rigid system of white supremacy. A second slave act in June 1767 was even stricter. Drumming and feasting were outlawed. Rewards for capturing runaways were increased, and dismemberment was added to the list of possible punishments. Slaves were prohibited from meeting in numbers on Sundays and holidays and from playing games of chance. The regulations appear to have been strictly enforced. The slaves of West Florida carried out the most demanding tasks on the plantations. Other slaves served as domestics in planter households, and still others worked in towns as craftsmen or at other tasks. Some obtained their freedom; in 1774 William Gordon found twenty-three freed blacks and mulattos in Mobile.[49]

Despite the stricter regulations, frontier conditions in West Florida made flight a tempting possibility for some slaves. At the same time, however, colonial authorities quickly realized their mutual interests in pursuing and returning fugitives across colonial boundaries. Slaves who sought refuge in neighboring colonies often found themselves in prison instead. Johnstone told Louisiana governor Charles-

Phillipe Aubry that he would not deliver "the Negroes, Deserters from New Orleans, now in custody at Mobile" until Aubry offered "reciprocal justice." Two runaway slaves of Mobile's John McGillivray were among the runaways then held captive in New Orleans.[50]

Merchants who were involved in trafficking slaves across colonial borders also played a role in retrieving runaways. In 1769 John Fitzpatrick of Manchac took custody of a slave woman and her child on behalf of Mobile merchant Daniel Ward, who had just moved from New Orleans. The woman did not want to leave her husband, who was a black silversmith in New Orleans. In 1771 "Fitzpatrick reported to another merchant at Mobile that two Negro men had run away from a planter at Pointe Coupee 'some time ago' and were reportedly seen living among the Negroes on a plantation near Mobile."[51]

In an effort to spur the colony's economic development, Governor Johnstone promoted British West Florida as the future "Emporium of the New World." He transported wine growers from Madeira to establish vineyards and brought in black divers to hunt for pearls in Mobile Bay. Neither scheme amounted to much, and prosperity remained elusive.[52]

The story of Charles Strachan illustrates the economic difficulties. A Scottish-born merchant, Strachan arrived in Mobile in 1764 as a factor of the Savannah firm of Johnson and Wylie. He established his own enterprise while representing the Georgia merchants, who supplied him with English goods. His health and business suffered brutally in Mobile. In November 1764 he complained that "we are all starving here" and begged his Georgia sponsors to "send some meat if at all possible." He eventually set up a profitable if illegal trade with New Orleans but ended up with debts owed him that would never be recovered. He spent much of his time trying to collect debts—either his own accounts or those of fellow merchants. Trade was filled with other risks as well. An April 1765 shipment of goods was so damaged that it had to be sent back to Savannah. Strachan envied a fellow merchant who decided to return to Georgia and despaired of conducting business in "the most disagreeable and unhealthy place in America." In 1766 he noted that "most of the people have already and the rest are preparing to quit Mobile as soon as possible so that in a short time, I expect it to be entirely deserted." Strachan decided to return to Savannah in July 1768 but was diverted home to Scotland to claim his inheritance. His escape was not complete, however, as business complications from his sad sojourn on the gulf followed him home.[53]

As the population increased and politics stabilized, conditions improved. In 1770 a soldier wrote home, "It is impossible for you to have an idea of the alterations that have taken place in this infant colony." Food was abundant, and "society is much increased, civil and military disputes seem now to be at an end."[54]

Although the garrisons of Pensacola and Mobile suffered periodic food shortages, mostly caused by reliance on outside sources for flour, rice, and beef, civilians in the towns did become self-sufficient in food. They imported wheat; exported indigo, tobacco, timber, potash, tar, and pitch; and grew a variety of vegetables. Much of the frontier economy survived because many Mobilians and other West Floridians preferred hunting and the Indian trade to agriculture.[55]

Colonial officials such as Robert Farmar, Phillip Livingstone, Jacob Blackwell, and Daniel Clark acquired sizable land grants. Elias Durnford owned Belle Fountaine, a five-thousand-acre plantation on the eastern shore near Croftown—about which were scattered several farms—and other holdings. All told he claimed to have fourteen hundred cattle and horses. His French neighbor Charles Parent made tar at his plantation.[56]

A typical planter would have a couple of dozen slaves to work his estate of between one and two thousand acres, of which he cleared less than one-tenth. He would plant corn and perhaps some rice. Some tried indigo and others tobacco, usually with disappointing results. Lumber and cattle were the most reliable endeavors. The planter kept a garden plot near his house and maintained a few fruit trees or perhaps a small orchard. He would build fences to keep cattle from trampling crops, a shed to house milk cows, and a barn for horses. Smaller animals and fowl were penned up, but hogs ran loose. His house was built with timber cut and trimmed on the site, its siding covered by weatherboard on the outside and plastered on the inside. A shingled roof extended on all sides to form a veranda. The design was simple, with few doors and windows. Floors were planking laid over the beaten dirt. There were usually two fireplaces. Furnishings were modest, perhaps some crystal or silver, and furniture was shipped from England and passed down among family members. The socially conscious planter would keep on hand port wine and Jamaican rum for entertaining.[57]

Mobile's most consistent business remained the Indian trade. In March 1764 some eight hundred skins went from Mobile to Charleston. By July 1765 that number had grown to more than four thousand. Throughout the 1770s, indigo and timber were shipped from Mobile and Pensacola, along with some fifty tons of raw deerskins and thirty-five tons of Indian-dressed deerskins each year.[58] The American Revolution disrupted the trade, cutting off Mobile and Pensacola from Charleston and Savannah.

The peltry trade remained intimately connected with Indian diplomacy. When Robert Farmar landed in Mobile in October 1763, it was just weeks before the beginning of a major Indian congress sponsored by the departing French. He found himself surrounded by Native Americans. He resented the "most disagreeable custom the French have introduced amongst the Indians . . . of giving them victuals and drink."[59] He found he had little choice but to follow suit. The British were constrained to deal with the Native Americans of the southeast in the manner to which they had become accustomed.

A proclamation of October 1763 attempted to regulate the Indian trade and to establish a uniform colonial policy. Trade regulations banned traders from the forest and allowed them to buy and sell only in designated villages. In March 1765 Mobile hosted a major Indian conference attended by twenty-seven hundred Choctaw, as well as representatives of the Cusseta, Pascagoula, and Chickasaw. One British participant, David Wedderburn, wrote a sympathetic account of the proceedings:

> For these three weeks past, there has been a congress here of the Chactaw [*sic*] and Chickasaw Indians to settle the boundarys of the province, at which I assisted. The dance of the Calumet, the peace Song, the brushing with Eagles Tails, are the finest ceremonys I ever saw. The giving an Indian name which they did to us Chiefs, is a most elegant Ceremony. The ball play is the most severe exercise I ever saw, and the most manly. . . . I believe I have got more improvement by keeping Company with the Indians, than by any Company I have kept for a great while. They have that gentle mildness of manner, which is the mark of true valor, in a higher degree, than any people I ever saw. No Indian ever interrupts another while he is Speaking. For five days in the week at least for some weeks I have dined with forty or fifty Indians in the room, without being in the least troubled.[60]

Treaties signed at Pensacola and Mobile in the spring of 1765 formalized relations between the Choctaw, Chickasaw, Creek, and the English. The southeastern Indians agreed to keep the peace, to return runaway slaves and soldiers who deserted, to cede lands for settlers along the Gulf Coast, and to conduct trade at fixed prices. The Choctaw chief, Tomatly Mingo, acknowledged his people's dependence on "Guns Cloathing and other Necessaries" provided by "white Men" but insisted the English uphold their "fatherly" responsibilities by providing plentiful trade and presents. They should maintain the post at Fort Tombecbe and act to "caution and restrain" traders who mistreated Choctaw men and women.[61]

The English found it difficult to keep their word. They abandoned Fort Toulouse almost immediately after the transfer and Fort Tombecbe by January 1768. Several traders violated the 1765 treaties by establishing farms and cowpens near Indian villages. Others began to hunt for themselves. Unlicensed traders began to wander through Choctaw, Creek, and Chickasaw villages, bartering rum for deerskins and horses, which they brought to Gulf Coast merchants. In 1772 Captain Ouma from the Choctaw village of Senecha demanded a halt to the flow of "rum that pours in upon our nation Like a great Sea from Mobile." He was particularly upset with the Mobile trader and interpreter Simon Favre.[62]

Conditions on the frontier had deteriorated, straining the viability and altering the accepted practices of frontier exchange. Protest and rebellion expressed themselves in episodes of social banditry. In response to worsening conditions, and perhaps to pressure colonial officials to keep their promises, Indians stole livestock, pillaged supplies, and terrorized settlers. Harassed merchants and farmers pleaded with colonial authorities to defend their properties.[63]

The American Revolution further complicated life for the region's European settlers and Native Americans alike. The major Indian nations of the southeast tried their best to stay out of the conflict while using it to their advantage. Most colonial inhabitants were oblivious to the disturbances to the north. No West Florida delegates attended the first or second continental congresses. Nonetheless, the American Revolution greatly affected Mobile and the rest of West Florida. American privateers disrupted shipping, and loyalist refugees swelled the population. The growing loyalist presence and the frontier population of soldiers and Indian traders predisposed the colony to support England.[64]

The war hit close to home in February 1778 when James Willing, a former resident of British West Florida, ravaged British towns along the Mississippi River, took refuge in New Orleans, and threatened to attack Mobile and Pensacola. In early March 1778 a Spanish observer reported the alarmed state of Mobile. Sixteen Mobilians implored Lieutenant Colonel Alexander Dickson to use his influence to get reinforcements sent to the town. The West Florida council recommended that "every measure that can possibly be taken should be pursued for the immediate defense of the town and fort of Mobile." No troops were available, however, and the matter was dropped. Still, strangers in Mobile and Pensacola were subjected to loyalty oaths, and Charles Stuart sent Alexander Cameron's Loyalist Refugees to Mobile. The merchant John McGillivray volunteered to raise a militia. Ultimately, Willing was captured in November 1778, terminating his efforts to spark an uprising in West Florida. Indeed, his actions probably deepened loyalist sentiments in the colony.[65]

In response to the growing danger, Governor Chester called a meeting of the West Florida Assembly in 1778. First convened in November 1766, the assembly had met only sporadically over the years. In 1778 the delegates included four members from each district of West Florida: Pensacola, Mobile, Manchac, and Natchez. The Mobile delegation was reluctant to participate because of a dispute over election writs. The proceedings were disrupted by a hurricane that hit Pensacola in mid-October. Chester was disgusted with the delegates' squabbles over prerogatives and property and soon dismissed the assembly for good. Nevertheless, to the con-

A fanciful engraving of Gálvez's attack on Fort Charlotte in March 1780 placed the fort at a commanding height above the bay. It was actually built at water level.

Museum of Mobile.

sternation of the military establishment, Chester refused to proclaim martial law.

West Florida was ill prepared for war. The Spanish officer Jacinto Panis observed in March 1778 that Mobile was "badly fortified and exposed." The fortress "threatened ruin," the artillery was "almost dismounted," and the ditches were "choked up" in some places. When General John Campbell arrived in West Florida later that year, conditions at Mobile had not improved. The fort and barracks were "almost a scene of ruin and desolation."[66]

Campbell ordered Elias Durnford to Mobile to strengthen Fort Charlotte. When civilian workers demanded two dollars a day, Durnford employed the garrison and slaves to carry out the repairs. Fort Charlotte required a garrison of three hundred men to defend it, yet Durnford reported in December 1779 that the fort had "eighty sick, or at best, convalescent men." By the time of the Spanish assault Durnford had about three hundred men under his command at Fort Charlotte, only a "small part" of whom were regulars.[67]

Spain joined the war against Great Britain in 1779. The Spanish minister of the Indies, José de Gálvez, believed that "Mobile and Pensacola [were] the keys to the Gulf of Mexico" and that the English presence must be removed. Louisiana, in his view, "should be considered the bulwark or barrier protecting the vast empire of New Spain."[68] The task of strengthening the Spanish presence on the Gulf Coast fell to Gálvez's young nephew, Bernardo Gálvez, governor of Louisiana. In September 1779 Gálvez quickly captured the British forts on the Mississippi River (Fort Bute near Baton Rouge and Fort Panmure near Natchez). He launched his Mobile campaign early in 1780.

Campbell was certain that Gálvez meant to attack Pensacola and that maneuvers around Mobile were a diversion. He was mistaken. Gálvez's Mobile expedition left New Orleans on January 11, 1780. His forces consisted of 274 regulars, 323 white militiamen, 107 free blacks and mulattoes, 24 slaves, and 26 Americans—a total of 754 men. Delayed by a fierce storm, Gálvez's fleet of twelve vessels regrouped off the bar at Mobile Bay by February 9. Five ships from Havana arrived on February 20, carrying 1,412 men, equipment, and supplies. Gálvez proceeded to Dog River, just nine miles below Mobile, as the British prepared for the assault. The Spanish crossed Dog River on February 28 and advanced to within two miles of Fort Charlotte. Meanwhile, the *Valenzuela* fired on the fort from Mobile Bay.

Gálvez dispatched Colonel Francisco Bouligny to request Durnford's surrender. Pointing out that Gálvez's two thousand men far outnumbered Durnford's one hundred soldiers and some sailors, Bouligny insisted that the Spanish hoped to avoid the "extremities of war." Durnford respectfully refused the request. Their official business done, the two officers shared dinner and drank "a cheerful glass to the health of our kings and friends." Afterward, Durnford sent Gálvez a dozen bottles of wine, several chickens and loaves of bread, a lamb, and provisions for British prisoners. Gálvez returned the favor by dispatching a variety of fruits, tea biscuits, corn cakes, and a box of Havana cigars, along with assurances of good treatment for the prisoners. With due apologies for interrupting the pleasantries, however, the Spanish commander reproached Durnford for burning parts of the town near the fort. "Fortresses" he wrote, "are constructed solely to defend towns, but you are commencing to destroy the town in favor of a fortress incapable of defense."[69]

As Campbell finally launched an ill-timed and ill-fated relief expedition from Pensacola, the Spanish pressed in on Fort Charlotte. After a day-long exchange of fire on March 12, Durnford raised the flag of truce at sunset. He proposed terms for capitulation the next day. Gálvez rejected Durnford's terms and offered his own conditions, which Durnford had little choice but to accept. The fighting cost the British one man killed and eleven wounded, two of whom later died. Spanish casualties included eight killed and twelve wounded. Durnford assured Campbell that "no man of the garrison hath stained the lustre of the British arms."[70] At 10 A.M., Tuesday, March 14, Durnford's weary force filed out of Fort Charlotte. Gálvez took possession of the fort and raised the Spanish flag.

Gálvez left the fort and town in the command of Colonel José de Ezpeleta y Galdeano. Intent on recapturing Mobile, Campbell sent land and sea forces to harass the Spaniards at Mobile that winter. In January 1781 the Spanish repulsed

British attacks on Dauphin Island and across the bay from Mobile. Taking the offensive in March 1781, Ezpeleta organized the transport of nine hundred men for Gálvez's siege of Pensacola. Pensacola fell in May 1781, and West Florida became a Spanish colony.[71]

Spanish Mobile, 1780–1813

On May 16, 1780, José de Ezpeleta ordered the inhabitants of the Mobile district to take a loyalty oath to the Spanish government. Those who refused would be allowed to take their goods and leave. A majority of the settlers did swear their fealty to the new Spanish government.[72] They faced a situation of considerable uncertainty.

The Treaty of Paris of 1783 confirmed Spanish possession of the Floridas and recognized U.S. claims to all other territory east of the Mississippi River. Despite the 1783 treaty, the boundaries between the Spanish colonies of Florida and Louisiana on the one hand and the United States on the other hand remained in doubt for the next dozen years. The failed Jay-Gardoqui Treaty of 1785 did not resolve the disputes.[73]

Spain continued the policy of its predecessors, using the southeastern Indians as a buffer against Anglo-American expansion. Trade with the Indians remained the key to diplomacy, and Mobile remained the center of the Choctaw (and sometimes the Chickasaw) trade. The Native American population of the lands disputed between the United States and Spain in the 1780s was about fifty thousand: twenty-two hundred Chickasaws, fifteen thousand Choctaws, fifteen thousand Upper and Lower Creeks, two thousand Seminoles, and fifteen thousand Cherokees. Initially, Spain conceded much of its Indian trade to the remarkable Frenchman Antoine de St. Maxent, who established a profitable, and mutually beneficial, relationship with his new rulers. He married two of his daughters to Spanish governors in Louisiana and provided some seventy-five thousand pesos to finance his son-in-law Bernardo Gálvez's expeditions against Mobile and Pensacola. He acquired almost exclusive control over the Indian trade. In 1783, however, he was arrested in Havana for smuggling, bringing the Indian trade in Spanish Louisiana and Florida to a virtual halt.[74]

In 1784 Spain negotiated alliances with the Creek, Choctaw, and Chickasaw. Spain signed the Treaty of Pensacola in May 1784 with Creek leader Alexander McGillivray. The son of a Scottish trader in Georgia and a Creek mother, McGillivray was closely aligned with the loyalist British trading firm of Panton, Leslie and Company and helped secure the Creek trade monopoly for his associates.[75]

A month later in Mobile, Spain concluded separate treaties and tariff agreements with the Choctaw, Alabama, and Chickasaw. The Choctaw trade passed to the firm of James Mather, who operated out of Mobile. Mather, however, proved incapable of meeting the needs of the Choctaw and Chickasaw. Mobile Commandant Vicente Folch (1787–1792) complained that he lacked adequate supplies of goods or gifts to entertain the large delegations of Indian leaders that came to Mobile.[76]

Concerned by the expanding trade between the Indians and U.S. merchants, the Spanish conceded the Choctaw and Chickasaw trade to Panton, Leslie and Company in February 1789. Thus a company formed by Scottish-born merchants who had fled from Georgia to East Florida during the Revolution controlled the Indian trade for all of Spanish Florida. They practically dominated Indian relations as well. They maintained stores in St. Augustine, St. Marks, Pensacola, Mobile, Nogales, and the Chickasaw Bluffs near present-day Memphis. Their trade was not restricted to Indians, however; they became primary suppliers for the garrisons and colonists as well. Trade links between West Florida and the Bahamas became routine. Panton and Leslie were soon allowed to purchase rum, sugar, and coffee in Cuba, and they also participated in the Caribbean logwood trade.[77]

Not only did Spain concede the Spanish-Indian trade to a company of British loyalists; it also encouraged Anglo-American immigration to Spanish Louisiana and Florida. The goal was to populate the hinterlands with useful immigrants, convert them into loyal Spanish subjects, and thus forestall U.S. territorial expansion. Spain expanded its military presence in the region, establishing Fort San Esteban de Tombecbe on the Tombigbee River in 1789, Fort Nogales (near Natchez) on the Mississippi River in 1791, and Fort San Fernando de las Barrancas (near Memphis) in 1795. In 1793 the Treaty of Nogales created a Creek, Choctaw, Chickasaw, and Cherokee alliance under Spanish sponsorship. Writing to the Mexican viceroy in 1796, Governor Carondelet (1792–1797) insisted that "Louisiana must be protected, lest we forget—if only to protect Texas, California, and the other provinces of New Spain."[78]

Nonetheless, Spanish troops were few, and the scattered military outposts languished in neglect. The immigration policy proved disappointing—only small groups from the United States trickled into the Spanish dominions, and they were an unruly element.[79] Spain's policy in the southeast was further complicated by the outbreak of war with France in 1793 and with Great Britain in 1796. The United States exploited Spain's European difficulties. The Treaty of San Lorenzo in 1795 acknowledged the thirty-first parallel as the boundary of West Florida, conceded U.S. navigation rights on the Mississippi, and called for mutual protection against Indian attacks along the frontier. The treaty eviscerated Spanish Indian policy and undermined Mobile's traditional role. In giving the United States jurisdiction of the entire South above the thirty-first parallel, Spain also "ceded" more than 90 percent of the southeastern Indians.[80]

After the treaty, the United States established a network of government-sponsored trade factories in the southeast. Because U.S. factors could not legally extend credit nor provide the traditional gifts, Panton and Leslie retained a competitive edge. At the end of the century, they still controlled almost all of the Choctaw and Chickasaw trade and more than one-third of the Creek trade.[81] Business became hazardous, however, with their shipping vulnerable to wartime attacks.

Spanish officials and company representatives alike seemed to recognize the inevitability of the American advance. In October 1796 the company began to settle its affairs with the Cherokee. In the spring of 1798 Spanish forces evacuated Nogales and Natchez, the last remaining Spanish strongholds in U.S. territory. Panton and Leslie closed its Chickasaw Bluffs store in 1799 and drastically curtailed its operations at St. Marks. By the turn of the century, William Panton "had become thoroughly weary of the stresses of the Indian trade" and would have preferred to sell his company to the Spaniards. Over the next decade, Panton's successors played an important role in arranging the cession of Indian lands to the United States in exchange for the redemption of Indian debts to the company of about $200,000, easing the transition from Spanish to U.S. rule.[82]

Throughout the Spanish period, Mobile remained under the command of military officials. Until 1803 it was under the general orders of the Spanish governor in New Orleans. From the Louisiana Purchase until 1813, Mobile was responsible to the governor of West Florida at Pensacola. The Mobile district was bounded by the Perdido River to the east and by the Pearl River to the west. The northern limits were much less clear, however, because of the conflicting claims of the Choctaw, Chickasaw, Creek, and the United States. Mobile's commandant ruled on military, political, and judicial matters. He appointed lesser officials to the various parts of the district. They handled routine civil and criminal cases. Mobile's commander was primarily concerned with making land grants, protecting the Indian trade, and defending settlers from Indian attack.

Although Spanish gradually replaced French as the official language, as Peter Hamilton noted a century later, "French law and customs were too deeply rooted to be easily eradicated." Yet, "Spanish rule was mild and the inhabitants well satisfied." William Dunbar, the Natchez planter-scholar, remarked in 1790 that "the major attraction of Spanish rule was that there was little or no rule at all for honest citizens."[83]

By the 1780s, the population of Spanish Louisiana and West Florida encompassed more than forty-two thousand inhabitants, not counting the Indians. This number included some sixty-four hundred persons living in the seven small settlements of West Florida. The population of the Mobile district grew throughout most of the Spanish period. Starting with 746 people in 1785, the Mobile district reached 1,725 in 1795, declining slightly to 1,537 in 1805.[84]

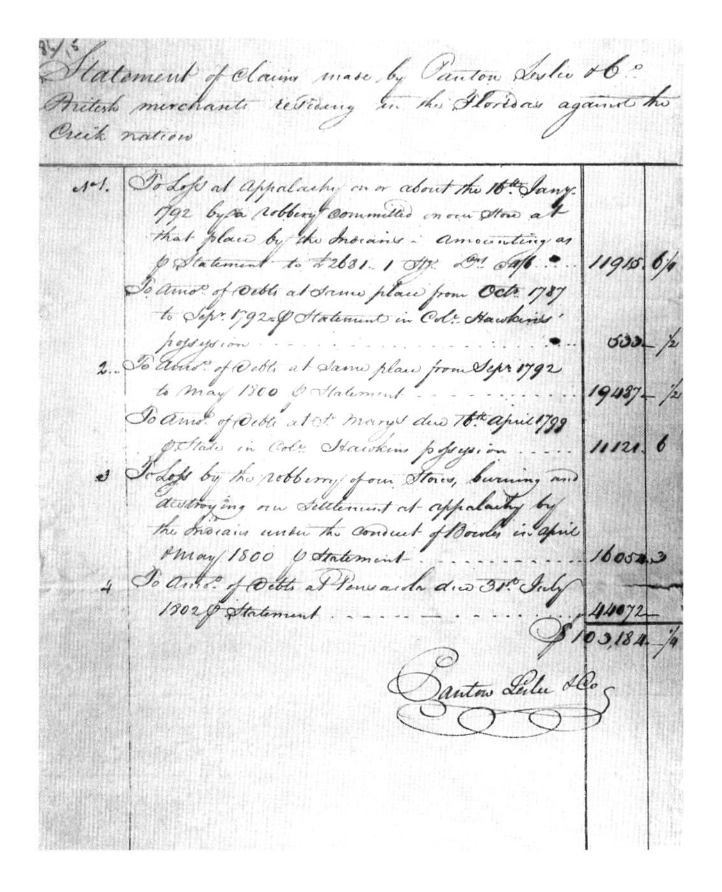

Statement of Claims made by Panton Leslie & Co. British merchants residing in the Floridas against the Creek nation

No.		
No. 1.	To Loss at Appalachy on or about the 16th Jany. 1792 by a robbery committed on our Store at that place by the Indians - amounting as p Statement to £2681.1 Stg. Drs.	11915 6/4
	To Amot. of Debts at same place from Octr. 1787 to Sepr. 1792 p Statement in Col. Hawkins' possession	633 1/2
2.	To Amot. of Debts at same place from Sepr 1792 to May 1800 p Statement	19487 1/2
	To Amot. of Debts at St. Marys due 16th April 1798 p State in Col. Hawkins possession	11121 6
3	To Loss by the robbery of our Stores, burning and destroying our Settlement at Appalachy by the Indians under the conduct of Bowles in April & May 1800 p Statement	16052 3
4	To Amot. of Debts at Pensacola due 31st July 1802 p Statement	44072
		$103,184 [illegible]

Panton Leslie & Co.

Panton, Leslie and Company statement of claims against the Creek nation, 1787–1802.

Local History Division, Mobile Public Library.

Hamilton asserted that "the Spaniards were little more than the governing class of a French community," but a later historian described the inhabitants of the Mobile district more accurately as "a polyglot, heterogenous population." At the time the town passed to U.S. hands, it extended only to Joachim Street to the west, St. Louis Street to the north, and south of the fort to the marshlands stretching down to Choctaw Point. Royal Street faced the river to the east.[85]

Hamilton provided a romanticized glimpse of life in Spanish Mobile creatively reconstructed from property records. "About the streets walked stolid Spanish officials and the vivacious French inhabitants, together with negro slaves and picturesque Choctaws, while only after the Louisiana Purchase of 1803 would be seen a wide-awake Yankee, come to make his fortune."[86] The small Spanish officer class shared power and prestige with the Indian traders and old Creoles of Mobile. Most officials were just passing through, but at least some took steps to become rooted in the colony. Commandant Enrique Grimarest married Mobile's Ana Narbonne in 1782, but she died shortly afterward, and he left in 1785. Miguel Eslava was the public storekeeper in Mobile from 1784 to 1813 and used his post to acquire considerable property. A gentleman named Irigoyen was administrator of the royal hospital and owned substantial property adjacent to it, which he sold in 1809. Rafael

Hidalgo, a surgeon at the hospital until 1811, set down roots through his marriage to Elizabeth Chastang. Still, they seem to be exceptional.

Not surprisingly, the Indian traders Panton and Forbes and their associates topped Mobile's elite. In 1799 Andrew Ellicott observed that Mobile's John Forbes lived "in an elegant stile" and was "highly esteemed for [his] great hospitality and politeness by all classes of people." Forbes and his associates, such as the Innerarity brothers, dominated much of the desirable real estate in Mobile, especially along the waterfront. They joined other such leading landholders as Spanish officials Miguel Eslava and Antonio Espejo and such prominent Creole families as the Krebs, Rochons, Chastangs, and the Andres. Benjamin Dubroca owned "almost the whole southwest quarter of the block bounded to the south by St. Michael and Joachim." Free blacks and mulattoes such as Julia Vilars and Martha Triton lived alongside eminent whites.[87]

"The creoles loved the water," Hamilton related. They held innumerable grants along Mobile's waterways. Many also held property upriver, where such names as Dubroca, Duplantier, Hobart, Rochon, Trouillet, Narbonne, Chastang, Andre, Trenier, Mottus, Durette, Demouy, and Juzan dotted the landscape.[88]

Some inhabitants dated from the British era. The Irishman Cornelius McCurtin came to West Florida around 1769 and became a Spanish militia officer in Pensacola and Mobile. In 1788 he lived with his wife, Eufosine Bosage, eleven slaves, eighty cattle, and ten horses on a plantation that produced corn and chickpeas. He also owned property on Dauphin Street in Mobile. Other British refugees included the two John Linders, father and son. The elder Linder was born in Switzerland in 1720 and lived many years in Charleston as an engineer and surveyor. He was appointed *alcalde* (administrator) of the future St. Stephens area by Pedro Favrot in September 1785. The younger Linder, before he settled in the Mobile district, had been a bandit leader during and after the American Revolution, engaging in "repeated acts of robbery and rebellion." The Linders owned considerable land in south Alabama. In 1785 they had eighty-two black slaves, twenty-seven horses, and seventy-two cattle, and they produced corn, tobacco, rice, and chickpeas. Baley Chaney was a close friend of the Linders who came to the Mobile district shortly after the American Revolution. In 1786 he lived with his wife, three children, and six slaves. He produced one hundred barrels of corn in 1785. Two years later, he produced 800 pounds of tobacco and 150 barrels of corn.[89]

Mobile and its hinterland under Spain perhaps saw some movement toward a slave-based plantation economy. According to a list drawn up in 1795, Mobile had some twenty-nine planters with 192 slaves. In all, the Mobile district included forty-nine planters owning 284 slaves. Merchant John Joyce had twenty-eight, and the widow Rochon held thirty-two. Nevertheless, most planters owned just a few slaves.[90] Furthermore, most of their production seems to have been destined for local consumption.

Not surprisingly, conditions for slaves remained harsh and legal restrictions extreme. The Spanish in Louisiana had adopted the relatively mild French Code

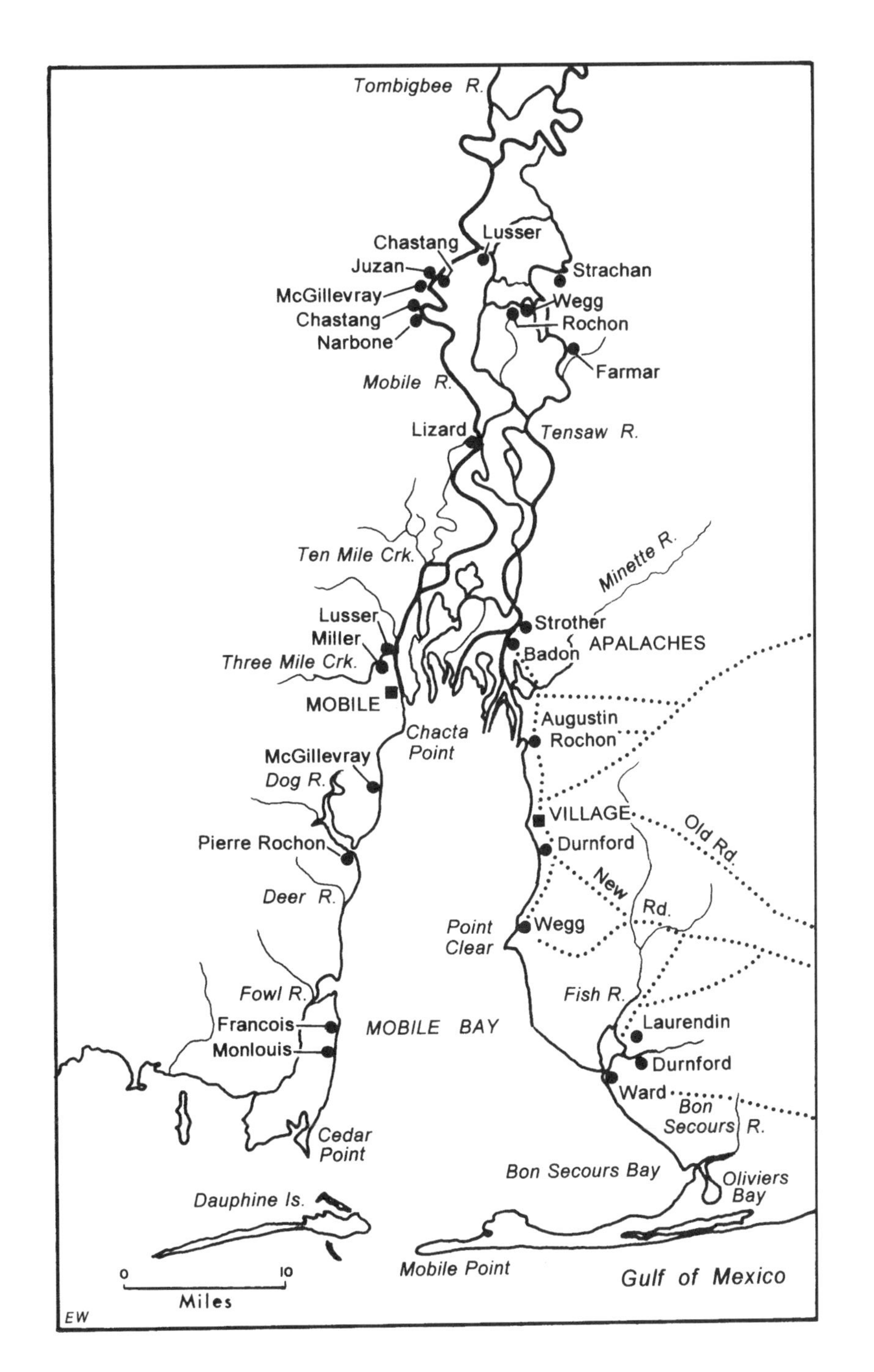

Mobile Bay and the Tombigbee-Tensaw region showing important plantations and roads.

Map by Eugene Wilson based on F. de Borja Medina Rojas, *Jose de Ezpeleta, Governador de la Mobila, 1780–1781* (1980).

Noir of 1724. Conditions probably worsened in response to the 1791 explosion at Saint Domingue (later Haiti) and the 1795 conspiracy at Point Coupee. The slave trade was temporarily halted.[91] Flight continued to be an option for recalcitrant slaves, and some fled into Indian country.

Free people of color occupied important positions in Spanish Mobile and enjoyed a perhaps surprising range of opportunities. They were able to enter contracts, buy and sell property, run businesses, sue and be sued. As of 1802, Mobile's black militia had a first sergeant and twenty-one black and mulatto militiamen. The unit was segregated from the white troops and at times was employed to track down runaway slaves.[92] In 1788 free people of color comprised 20 percent of Mobile's free population. By 1805 they were 30 percent of the free population. In 1805 there were 76 white females for every 100 white males, and there were 105 free black females for every 100 free black males. The gender imbalances, along with other factors, encouraged interracial unions. Bishop Luis Peñalver y Cárdenas visited Mobile in 1799 and wrote that the Spanish officers "live openly with their mulatto concubines as do many of the people, and they are not ashamed to name the children in the parish registers as their natural children." For example, Dr. John Chastang lived on his estate near St. Stephens where he and his concubine, Luisa, a free black from Mobile, had several children, all of whom were recognized by the father.[93]

Several free people of color worked as sailors carrying supplies between Dauphin Island and Mobile. The free mulatto Alexo was a male nurse at the royal hospital. Andrés, a free black, took charge of the care and cleaning of smaller boats in the Mobile coast guard. The free black Louison was the baking contractor for Fort San Esteban in 1791. Nicholas Mongulas was a master mason. Carlos Lalanda was perhaps the most prominent mulatto in Mobile. He had bought Belle Fontaine on Mobile Bay in 1796, and he later acquired other properties at Dog River, Grand Terre, and Tensaw. In 1811 he commanded the mulatto militia and obtained the contract to supply biscuit and hard tack for the Mobile garrison.[94]

Whatever the attractions of life in Mobile under Spanish rule, the heterogenous inhabitants must have shared a sense that change was inevitable, especially after the Treaty of San Lorenzo of 1795 and certainly after the Louisiana cession of 1803. From 1797 to 1799, Andrew Ellicott of Pennsylvania worked to determine the actual location of the thirty-first parallel dividing Spanish West Florida and the United States. When he completed his labors, Fort San Esteban was found to be north of the line and abandoned. The Americans founded Fort Stoddert on the thirty-first parallel.

In 1802 Spain returned Louisiana to France. The following year, having given up his plans to reestablish a French North American empire, Napoleon sold Louisiana

Know all men by these presents, That I, Mary Ann Widow Jacob a free Mulatto Woman of the Town of Mobile, do covenant, that I sell really and truly to Charles Lalande, also a free man of Colour; a certain tract of land to me appertaining, situated on the Western side of the Bay of Mobile at a place called Belle Fontaine

Sale of land at Belle Fontaine by Mary Ann, a widow and a free mulatto woman, to Carlos Lalanda, a free man of color, on April 23, 1796.

Translated Record Book 1, Mobile County Probate Court.

to the United States for $15 million. After the Louisiana Purchase the status of West Florida remained ambiguous. James Monroe and Robert Livingston, who helped negotiate the purchase, insisted that Mobile was part of the deal.

Jeffersonian expansion in the gulf region followed a clear pattern. With government encouragement, U.S. citizens emigrated to Spanish territory. Once an area was saturated with Americans, the United States quietly encouraged them to overthrow Spanish rule and to ask for U.S. assistance and eventually annexation. Fort Stoddert, garrisoned with regular U.S. troops, became a magnet for Anglo-Americans moving into the area. Hoping to discourage settlement, the Spanish governor of West Florida imposed a 12 percent duty on goods transported on the Mobile River. Although U.S. army supplies were usually not assessed, settlers' goods were, and the locals demanded relief. In February 1804 Congress passed the Mobile Act, which proclaimed the annexation of all navigable rivers and streams within the United States that flowed into the Gulf of Mexico and created a special customs district at Fort Stoddert.[95]

The Napoleonic invasion of Spain in 1808 and the subsequent Peninsular War (1808–1813) accelerated the collapse of Spanish authority in North America. The population of Spanish Louisiana and Florida amounted to about fifty thousand people, with only fifteen hundred troops available to garrison the entire region. In the summer of 1810 a group of American settlers seized Baton Rouge and expelled the Spanish garrison. The citizens of Baton Rouge declared themselves independent of Spain on September 26, 1810, and immediately requested admission to the United States. President Madison annexed the territory, claiming that it had been part of the Louisiana Purchase. The United States formally took possession of the Baton Rouge District on December 6, 1810.[96]

Freebooters from Baton Rouge threatened to seize all of West Florida in November 1810, but Edmund P. Gaines, the garrison commander at Fort Stoddert, and

Harry Toulmin, the federal district judge of the Mississippi Territory, intervened to restore calm. Recognizing the inevitable, however, West Florida governor Vicente Folch entered informal negotiations for the cession of West Florida to the United States.[97]

On the eve of its transfer to the new republic, Mobile in 1812, according to Josiah Blakeley, had "about 90 houses, all of wood and but one story high." It had "about 20 white families, those French, Spanish, Americans, and English," and Blakeley boasted that he was "acquainted on both sides of the river, for a hundred miles up, with all the best people." Although not Catholic, he occasionally attended the Catholic church for lack of any other. He noted the presence in Mobile of a fellow Connecticut Yankee named Judson, "a good man." Blakeley had acquired three islands in Mobile Bay and gushed, "Better land for rice and cotton perhaps the world does not afford." The dispute between Spain and the United States, however, "rendered it impossible to either sell or cultivate these lands." Still, things were looking up. "During this last winter the United States army, which had long been wholly idle in this country, have made a road and bridges from Baton Rouge on the Mississippi to Fort Stoddert, also from Fort Stoddert to the State of Georgia. I have seen many carriages which came from Savannah to Fort Stoddert."[98]

Blakeley referred to the Federal Road, whose completion in 1811 had unleashed a flood of white settlers into the Creek lands in Alabama. The Creeks became

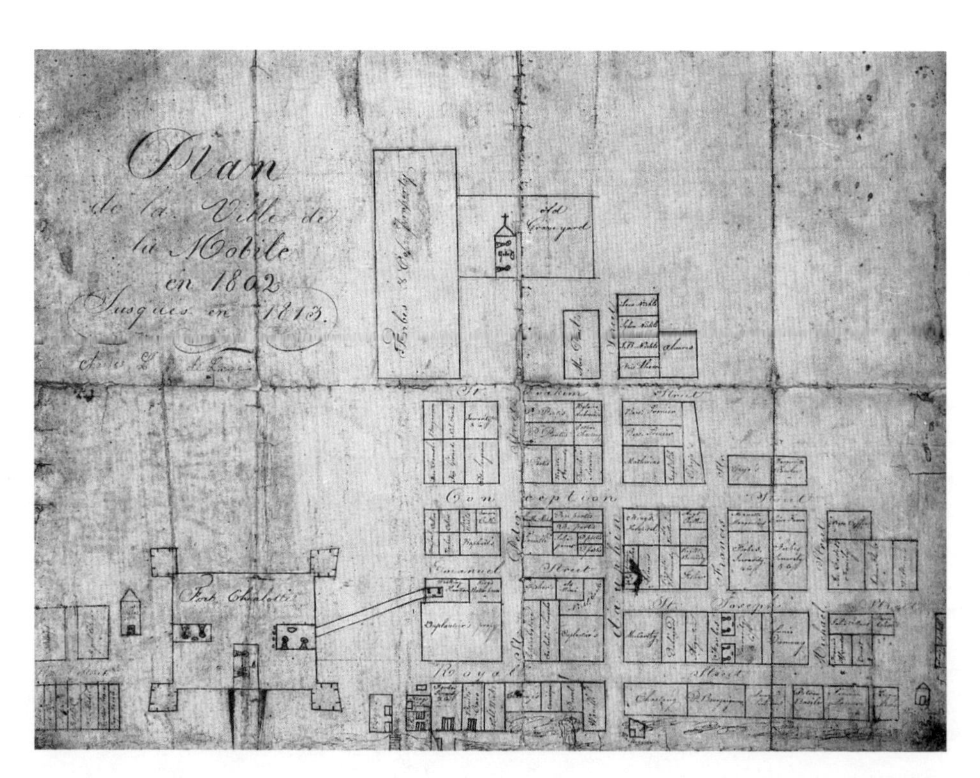

Mobile, 1802–13, drawn by Charles L. DeLage. Although none of the structures survive, most of the street names have.

Museum of Mobile.

increasingly anxious at the growing American threat. Their Spanish allies had similar cause for concern.

In April 1812, just days after Louisiana was admitted into the union, the United States formally incorporated Mobile and its surrounding area into the Mississippi Territory. David Holmes, governor of the territory, began organizing the Mobile district at once. He appointed a sheriff and other officials to control Mobile County. He divided the area into militia districts and established a municipal government for Mobile. With the United States and England at war by the summer of 1812, Holmes now courted a confrontation with Spain as well. The Spanish garrison of 130 men at Fort Carlota was not strong enough to evict the Americans from the territory, but its presence provided a source of potential trouble. The Spanish garrison and the American officials coexisted uneasily in this arrangement for the next year. In February 1813, however, U.S. secretary of war John Armstrong ordered General James Wilkinson in New Orleans to occupy Mobile and Pensacola and expel the Spanish forces.[99]

Wilkinson descended on Mobile on April 11, 1813, with eight hundred men and five gunboats. The ships sealed off contact with Pensacola from the sea while the ground troops surrounded the fort. Wilkinson's force was strengthened by four hundred additional men from nearby Fort Stoddert. With little choice, Spanish garrison commander Captain Cayetano Pérez surrendered on April 13, 1813. He and his troops were evacuated to Pensacola. The United States finally made good its claim to Mobile "without the effusion of blood." Wilkinson abandoned the idea of capturing Pensacola, but Mobile had at last become American.[100]

Epilogue

In the summer of 1813 angry Creeks, anxious over the expanding American presence and encouraged by Spain and England, attacked the American settlement at Fort Mims, destroying the place and killing the 250 people there. The massacre began the Creek War, a conflict that lasted until the following spring, when Andrew Jackson routed the Red Sticks at Horseshoe Bend. Meanwhile, the old Indian trader and Forbes Company partner, James Innerarity, conducted a brisk business with the American garrison and settlers. He was mayor of Mobile as of March 1814. He and his brother John, who lived in Pensacola, became deeply involved in the slave trade after 1818.[101] The Americans who rushed into the hinterlands with their cattle and slaves took over Indian hunting grounds and pushed aside the frontier exchange economy. Colonial Mobile, built and sustained throughout by Indian trade and the interaction of settlers, Indians, free blacks, and slaves, soon would make way for the cotton city of the Americans.

Surrender of Spanish garrison at Fort Charlotte to American forces, April 13, 1813.

Drawing by N. H. Holmes. Museum of Mobile.

Suggestions for Further Reading

Fabel, Robin F. A. *The Economy of British West Florida, 1763–1783.* Tuscaloosa: University of Alabama Press, 1988. Well-documented monograph that places Mobile within a regional context of economic and population expansion cut short by the American Revolution.

Hall, Gwendolyn Midlo. *Africans in Colonial Louisiana: The Development of Afro-Creole Culture in the Eighteenth Century.* Baton Rouge: Louisiana State University Press, 1992. An important revisionist study of African contributions to Gulf Coast history.

Hamilton, Peter J. *Colonial Mobile.* Tuscaloosa: University of Alabama Press, 1976. A classic early account of Mobile by a prominent lawyer-historian.

O'Neill, Charles Edwards. *Church and State in French Colonial Louisiana: Policy and Politics to 1732.* New Haven: Yale University Press, 1966. Solid institutional history of church-state relations in early colonial Louisiana.

Owsley, Frank Lawrence, Jr., and Gene A. Smith. *Filibusters and Expansionists: Jeffersonian Manifest Destiny, 1800–1821.* Tuscaloosa: University of Alabama Press, 1997. Provocative survey of early U.S. expansionism that places the Americanization of Mobile in historical context.

Rea, Robert R. *Major Robert Farmar of Mobile.* Tuscaloosa: University of Alabama Press

1990. Biography of the first British military governor of Mobile who became a leading planter-politician in the area.

Starr, J. Barton. *Tories, Dons, and Rebels: The American Revolution in British West Florida.* Gainesville: University of Florida Press, 1976. Well-researched and highly readable narrative. Includes an excellent account of the Spanish conquest of Mobile.

Usner, Daniel H., Jr. *Indians, Settlers and Slaves in a Frontier Exchange Economy: The Lower Mississippi Valley before 1783.* Chapel Hill: University of North Carolina Press, 1992. Important work that views eighteenth-century Gulf Coast history through the lens of cultural and economic exchange among Indians, Europeans, and Africans.

CHAPTER 3

Cotton City, 1813–1860

Harriet E. Amos Doss

"MOBILE IS BECOMING a place of great importance," reported *Niles' Register* in 1822, "and it is possible, may soon be one of the most populous of our southern cities." *Niles' Register* based this prediction on the town's growth from 300 at the time of American occupation in 1813, to 809 at the city's incorporation by the new state of Alabama in 1819, and to 2,800 in 1822. Hope of financial gain lured most newcomers to the Alabama port as the Cotton Kingdom pushed into the southwest. News of Mobile's growth as a young American city attracted the attention of "distant adventurers of every description," including attorneys, doctors, merchants, and mechanics, who, according to a local physician, "have fled hither as to an Eldorado."[1]

With its multinational population, American Mobile initially lacked community cohesion. Legacies remained of foreign colonial rule: French, 1702 to 1763; British, 1763 to 1780; and Spanish, 1780 to 1813. After 1813 a "new population" headed to Mobile "to make money."[2] These inhabitants, according to an American officer of occupation in 1817, were generally "a mixture consisting of the Creoles (principally coloured), and emigrants from England, Scotland, Ireland, and different parts of the United States who are governed entirely by personal interest; and exhibit very little of what may be termed *National feeling*." Adam Hodgson, a merchant from Liverpool, found Mobile in 1820 "an old Spanish town, with mingled traces of the manners and language of the French and Spaniards."[3]

The Spanish era finally ended during the War of 1812. Because Spain allowed British naval vessels to rendezvous in Mobile and other gulf ports in its possession, the American government decided to occupy Mobile in order to stop this indirect aid to the British. In February 1813 President Madison ordered Major General James Wilkinson, the commander at New Orleans, to take possession of Mobile.

City hall and new market.

Engraving from *Ballou's Pictorial Drawing Room Companion,* June 1857.

Wilkinson moved effectively in mid-April to cut off the land and sea communications to the Spanish garrison in Fort Charlotte (formerly Fort Condé). He informed the commander of the garrison that he was simply relieving the forces occupying a post considered within the legitimate boundaries of the United States. The Spanish forces, who were out of provisions, surrendered the fort without bloodshed. As Spanish civilians departed along with the troops, Americans moved into the town, situated in the only territory that the United States acquired as a result of the war. Thus the United States effectively annexed West Florida by military force, whereas it later obtained East Florida by diplomacy in the Adams-Onis Treaty signed in 1819 and consummated in 1821.[4]

American Mobile expanded as private developers purchased the Fort Charlotte property in 1820. Congress had authorized the sale because the fort was no longer needed for defense. A locally formed syndicate, the Mobile Lot Company, purchased the bulk of the property. City funds paid for the demolition of the fort's walls to clear new streets laid to the river through the site. Debris from the demolition was used to fill private lots as well as easily flooded Water and St. Francis Streets. Location of the former fort was not even marked on the Goodwin and Haire map drawn in 1823, which emphasized the harbor and public buildings developed by Americans.[5]

Private interests controlled the development of Mobile for commercial and residential purposes in the 1820s. Government served to facilitate that process. Expediency often influenced the actions of real-estate promoters, who, in their haste to open new development, sometimes neglected drainage problems caused by poor grading of new streets and fire hazards resulting from wooden construction of buildings. During the early part of the decade, town government hardly assumed an activist role in regulating and supervising private interests, for those interests essentially demanded noninterference from government. In the second half of the decade, however, disaster prompted government to take on such regulation and coordination.[6]

New regulation of citizens' activities truly began to develop after a fire in October 1827 consumed two-thirds of the business district bounded by Conti and St. Michael Streets. Flames destroyed numerous businesses and 169 private homes. Property losses exceeded one million dollars. Because seven-eighths of the buildings razed were wooden, Mobilians realized the necessity of rebuilding with more durable and fire-resistant materials. Soon a new city ordinance required brick construction for the fire district. By 1831, four years after the conflagration, Mobile looked like a new city. Few discernible traces of the fire remained as brick houses replaced log huts. In 1833 the *Mobile Register* boasted that the city had "risen in all the vigor and beauty of a phoenix."[7]

Disaster graphically reminded Mobilians of the destruction that could result from the pursuit of private interests without regard to community welfare. It had the immediate, direct result of promoting construction with brick instead of wood.

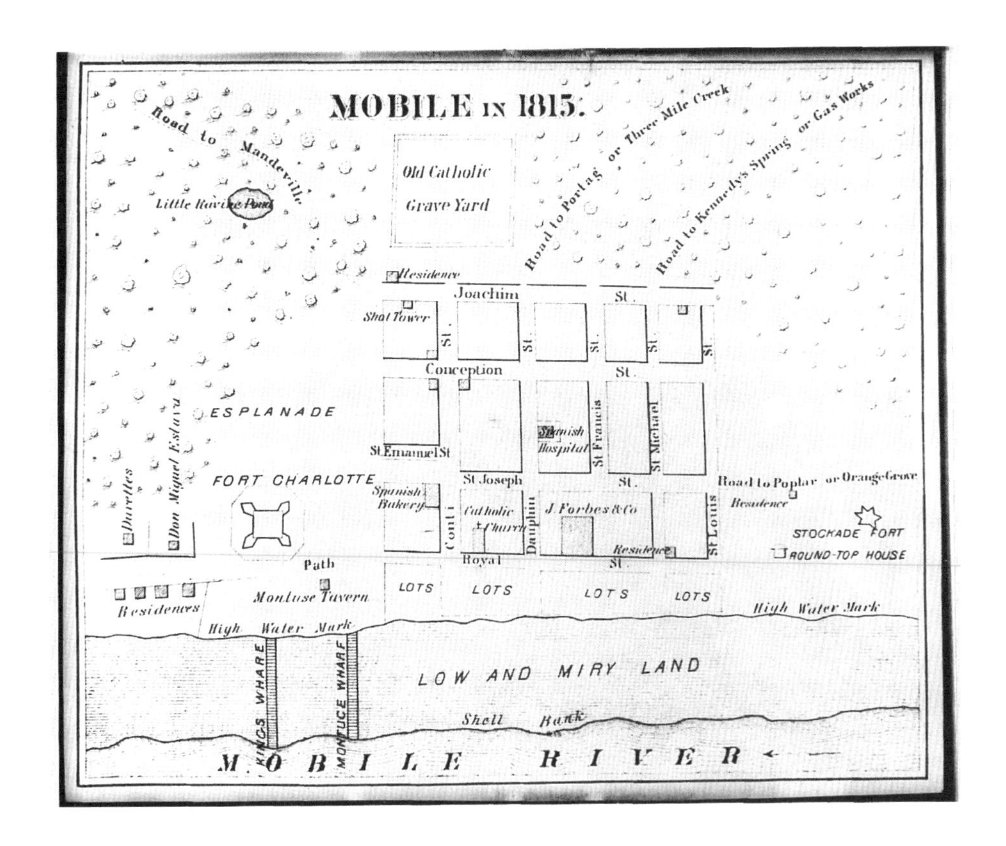

Mobile in 1815.

Frontispiece, G. M. Hopkins, *City Atlas of Mobile, Alabama* (1878).

It had the long-term, indirect result of encouraging organizations for civic purposes. In the decade after the fire Mobilians formed six fire companies to protect their property. They also supported three charitable groups that organized in 1829: the Female Benevolent Society; the Auxiliary Tract Society, an affiliate of the American Tract Society; and the Temperance Society. These groups augmented services that had been provided by the Hibernian Benevolent Society since 1822 and the Mobile Bible Society, an auxiliary to the American Bible Society, since 1825. Such voluntary associations provided more avenues for linking together the heterogeneous elements of Mobile's new American population than the one institution that had survived from the colonial era, the Roman Catholic Church. Many of the new Americans were Protestants who wanted their own churches instead of the one preferred by the Creoles. In 1822 they erected a small church, which served Protestants until various denominations formed their own congregations later in the decade.[8]

By the end of the 1820s Mobile differed markedly from the town occupied by the Americans in 1813. Some of the changes might be traced to the permanent

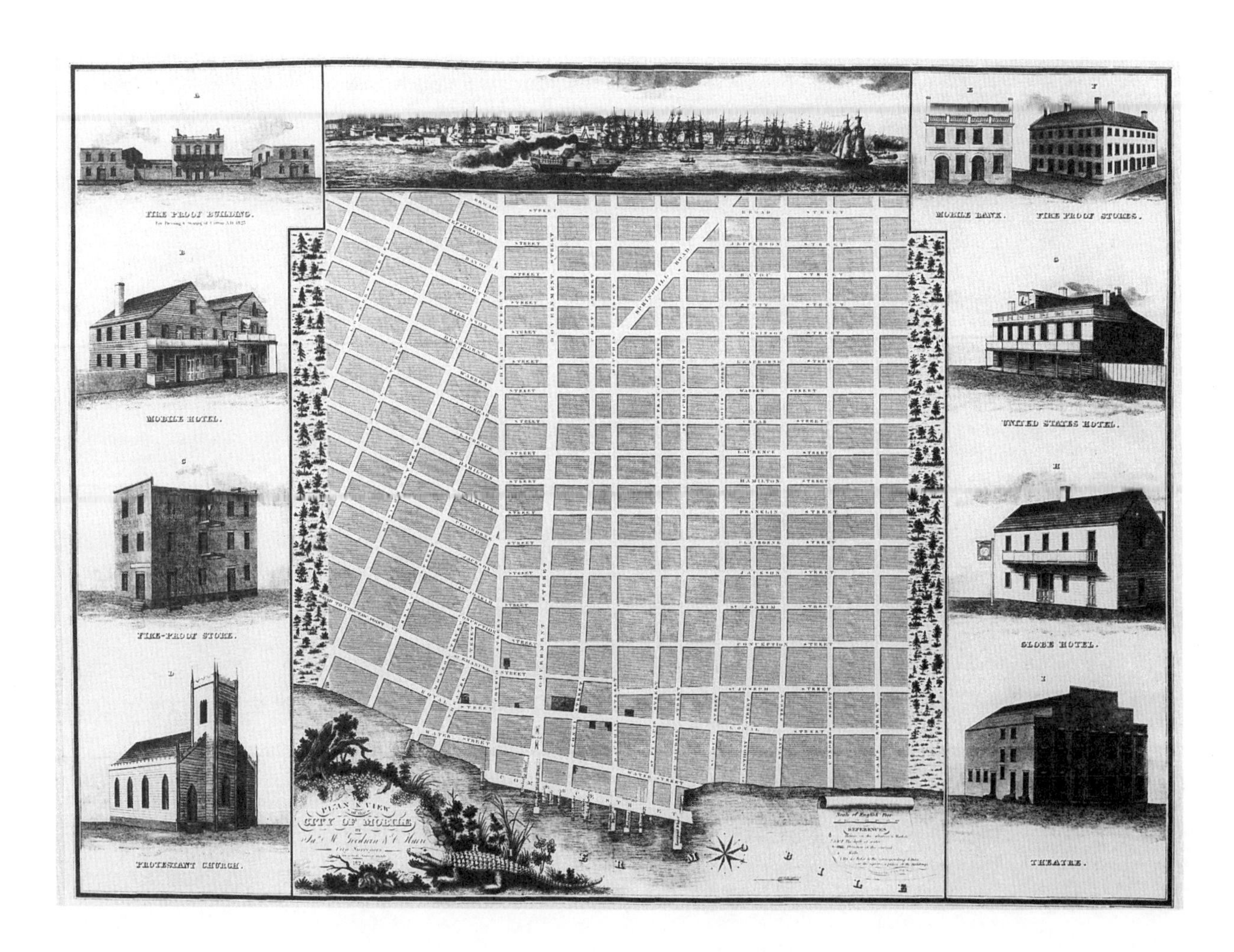

Goodwin and Haire map of Mobile, 1824.

USA Archives.

Michael Portier, vicar apostolic of Alabama and the Floridas and first bishop of Mobile (1825–59), was well respected by both the Protestant and the Catholic communities. Spring Hill College, Providence Hospital, and the Cathedral of the Immaculate Conception were all initiated under his leadership.

Archives of the Archdiocese of Mobile.

removal of the colonial government. Americans committed to private enterprise purchased the fort that had dominated the town and its commerce and used the site for new streets leading to a dozen new private wharves. They developed the waterfront property to provide the wharves and terminal facilities needed by the steamboats that had just begun to ply the Mobile River en route to the cotton districts of southern Alabama and southeastern Mississippi. The advent of steamboats provided an important stimulus to local development. Commerce in cotton would ultimately make Mobile "a place of great importance," as predicted by *Niles' Register.* Ironically, however, commerce continued in the colonial dependency pattern established with the founding of Mobile. Mercantile interests in the North simply replaced foreign imperialist governments.[9]

Export trade provided the major economic activity of antebellum Mobile, just as it had of the colonial settlement. Nonetheless, cotton, the main commodity for export, required a new superstructure of transportation and financial services. Virtually all local commercial activities, from marketing cotton to obtaining goods for planters in the interior, served the cotton trade. Local banking and insurance facilities, for instance, provided financial exchanges, credit, and security for property, respectively, rather than loans or risk capital for enterprises not directly related to the cultivation or sale of cotton. Local hotels and theaters made jaunts to the city attractive for upcountry planters and itinerant merchants who wished to combine business with pleasure. Commercial and service institutions undergirded the cotton trade, which in turn shaped the city's development.[10]

Mobile's hinterland encompassed some of the richest cotton-producing areas in Alabama and Mississippi. Alabama maintained its top rank as a cotton state throughout the 1850s. Planters in counties in both Alabama and Mississippi with access to the Alabama-Tombigbee River system that flowed into the Mobile River used Mobile as their cotton market. Navigable waterways circumscribed Mobile's hinterland, which included southern Alabama and southeastern Mississippi. Alabama river systems flowing into the Mobile River were navigable only as far north as central Alabama, so only growers in Shelby, Tuscaloosa, Fayette, and counties to the south of them could use Mobile as their seaport. Planters in northern Alabama sent their cotton via the Tennessee and Mississippi Rivers fifteen hundred miles to New Orleans.[11]

Cotton exports from Mobile grew in proportion to the production of the crop in south Alabama. Increasing cotton shipments permitted Mobile to eclipse all other southern ports but one as a cotton exporter. In the 1830s Mobile's exports surpassed those of Savannah and Charleston. As a cotton exporter, Mobile ranked second only to New Orleans after 1840.[12]

Cotton usually made up 99 percent of the total value of exports from antebellum Mobile. Lumber and lumber products, the export ranking second to cotton in value, accounted for only 1 percent of the total value of exports. Thus, during the summer when cotton was not yet ready for market, the export trade, and with it most port activity, virtually stopped.[13]

Mobile's port and harbor facilities were adequate but less than ideal for a large export trade. Vessels entered the bay on either side of Dauphin Island. The channel on the west side of the island was five feet deep; the eastern one was ten feet. In the 1840s the amount of water carried over the bar at the entrance to Mobile Bay increased from thirteen to twenty feet. While the depth of water in the lower part of the bay increased, the upper part of the bay remained at eleven feet. Vessels drawing over eleven feet of water could not proceed directly to the city; they had to pass six miles up the Spanish River, around a marshy island into the Mobile River, and down to the wharves at the city.[14]

Because it was virtually impossible for large ships to reach the wharves in Mobile, most of them anchored at Mobile Point in the lower bay. There they received and discharged cargoes. Lightering involved transferring cargoes to or from oceangoing ships with deep draughts anchored at Mobile Point to smaller vessels with shallow draughts. These lighters, as the small vessels were called, then carried cargoes thirty miles through Mobile Bay to the city wharves. In the late

The lighthouse at Choctaw Point marked one of the many sandbars that restricted access to the city's harbor to shallow-draft vessels.

Ballou's Pictorial Drawing Room Companion, June 1857.

1850s nearly one hundred local tug steamers or bay boats lightered cotton to what was called the Lower Fleet and imports from the Lower Fleet to city docks.[15]

Local businessmen gradually provided facilities sufficient for receiving, storing, and compressing cotton bales before their sale and reshipment. Having built a dozen private wharves in the early 1820s, they added four times that number by the 1850s. Even though the City of Mobile acquired title to the waterfront property by an act of Congress in 1824, the city did not take over the privately owned wharves in the antebellum period. Most of the wharves were owned by individuals, yet a number were controlled in the 1850s by the wharfinger combine of D. W. Goodman and C. P. Gage. Four dozen wharves lining the waterfront from One Mile Creek on the north to the foot of Government Street on the south were arranged so that forty-two thousand bales of cotton could be landed simultaneously without interfering with space needed for shipping and receiving other goods.[16]

The *Mobile Journal of Commerce, Letter Sheet Price Current* boasted that Mobile had better facilities for storing and compressing cotton, in proportion to the amount received, than any other American cotton port. By the 1850s Mobile had forty-two fireproof brick warehouses that could store 310,000 bales, more than half of the number exported during an entire six-month season. Operating in conjunction with the warehouses were a dozen cotton presses capable altogether of compressing seven thousand bales daily.[17]

Even more important to the cotton trade than the physical facilities for handling the staple were the agents who marketed it, the factors. Although some planters sold their own cotton, a majority employed the services of professional middlemen.

Advertisement, *Mobile City Directory,* 1859.

Technically a factor was an agent hired to sell produce for a principal (that is, a planter). A commission merchant, on the other hand, purchased various types of supplies, such as farm implements, household items, and foodstuffs, on commission for his customers. In practice the same person frequently served as factor and commission merchant.[18]

Throughout the antebellum era, itinerant factors or agents from northern or foreign firms provided marketing services for cotton. In the 1820s New York merchants began to send agents to purchase cotton directly from planters or their factors. Some cotton dealers specialized as buyers for British and French traders or manufacturers.[19]

This significant representation of northern and foreign firms in the cotton trade did not preclude southerners from opening their own factorage businesses. In Mobile southerners readily entered the cotton trade. Experienced factors from southern ports where the cotton trade was declining, such as Duke W. Goodman from Charleston, relocated to rapidly growing Mobile. A number of native southerners capitalized on their visibility in fields other than commerce within the state to open a commission house in Mobile. Robert A. Baker, a state legislator from Franklin County, and John A. Winston, a state legislator and later governor from Sumter County, each opened commission houses in Mobile in the 1840s.[20]

Transactions in cotton demanded extensive credit and additional financial services offered by banks. Close ties between banking and commerce often meant that banks suffered from the fluctuations of the cotton market as much as any other segment of the economy. The only local bank that successfully withstood all financial crises in the antebellum era was the Bank of Mobile, which had received a charter from the Alabama legislature in 1819. Nevertheless, this bank and others that served Mobile at various times during the antebellum era could not provide adequate banking capital for the export trade valued at nearly $40 million by 1860. Limited local banking facilities forced businessmen to deal directly with nonlocal banks or to use the services of local private bankers or exchange brokers who bought and sold notes drawn on foreign and domestic banks and mercantile houses.[21]

Mobile served not only as the commercial capital of antebellum Alabama but also as its leading winter resort. Residents struggled during much of the antebellum era to offer appropriate housing for the visitors who arrived for the winter business season. In the 1820s, when Mobile might still have been considered a frontier town, hotels provided plain accommodations and few services to guests. Fires repeatedly destroyed these hotels and consequently caused overcrowding of visitors. Between 1835 and 1845 when the winter population frequently was three times the number of year-round residents, hotel shortages persisted. A massive new hotel was nearly ready for opening in 1839 when arsonists burned much of the downtown area. The situation slowly improved in the 1840s. By mid-decade the city had three large hotels, two of which burned in 1850.[22]

A "decided epoch" in local development began with the opening of the Battle House in 1852. A local corporation built this truly first-class, five-story hotel on the southeast corner of Royal and St. Francis Streets, convenient to the business district. The Battle House offered many attractions for guests, with its 240 guest rooms plus dining rooms and shops. Soirees followed by suppers became regular weekly events during the winter season. City and country dwellers mingled at dances that provided "the Battle House the very cream and champagne sparkle of its excellent cheer," according to the *Mobile Register*. Planters often selected the Battle House for their honeymoons. Because few visitors came to Mobile during hot weather, the Battle House waited for the first frost to open for guests.[23]

Theaters also served to entertain the hundreds of visitors who journeyed to Mobile each winter. Newspaper columns encouraged fund-raising for the construction of theaters. After extolling the intellectual benefits theatrical amusements offered to civilization, the editor of the *Alabama Tribune* focused on meeting the demands of strangers who came to Mobile during the winter season "principally on a double errand—business and pleasure." The editor argued that visitors who found "an intense and refined gratification" in the theater would seek it elsewhere if it were unavailable locally. Or they might launch into unspecified "excesses infinitely gross, demoralizing and expensive." Thus, the *Tribune* concluded, "a pecuniary and moral evil results to the city." For these reasons a well-managed theater providing good entertainment constituted "a public benefit." Advantages that accrued to the city from the theater help to explain the repeated success of public subscription drives to build theaters.[24]

Mobilians and visitors indeed enjoyed a lively winter social season. Mystic societies that celebrated the pre-Lenten carnival may have paraded in French and Spanish colonial Mobile. American observance, however, began in 1830 when Michael Krafft, a cotton broker from Pennsylvania, and some of his friends paraded through the streets at dawn on New Year's Day. Gathering up hoes, rakes, gongs, and cowbells from a hardware store, they made their New Year's Day calls on ladies

The "original" Battle House Hotel, built in 1852. *Mobile, The New South, 1887–88.*

Local History Division, Mobile Public Library.

of their acquaintance. In later years members of the Cowbellion de Rakin Society, formed by Krafft and his friends, donned masks and staged parades on New Year's Eve before hosting a ball for invited guests. New mystic societies formed in the 1840s included the Strikers' Independent Society, Calfbellions, Rising Generation, and T.D.S. (The Determined Set or Tea Drinkers Society), Jim Oakes, and the Indescribables.[25]

Mobile also had its own salon society maintained by prominent local hostesses, with Madame Octavia Walton Levert the most famous and fashionable. Madame Levert, wife of Dr. Henry S. Levert, assembled the most fashionable gucsts for her weekly receptions. After touring Europe twice in the 1850s, Madame Levert modeled her salon after those of the French. She held open house each Monday from 11 A.M. to 11 P.M. "To be a novelty in fact or reputed, was sufficient to secure *entree* into the salon," observed Thomas C. De Leon. Madame Levert welcomed artists, actors, actresses, and writers along with politicians and filibusterers.[26]

Mobilians and visitors reiterated the same theme: the local economy depended on cotton. A clergyman described cotton as "the circulating blood that gives life to the city." As such it generated profits to merchants who in turn met payrolls, financed construction projects, and purchased consumer goods and services. Because prices set on the world market determined profits made from cotton sales, local merchants carefully monitored foreign cotton exchanges. A British visitor observed that when news arrived from Europe, merchants turned "instinctively to the Liverpool cotton report." They knew that a tiny rise or fall in cotton prices made "the difference between ease and embarrassment—between riches and poverty—between a good speculation and a bad one." As merchants' incomes depended on fluctuations in cotton prices on the world market, so did incomes for employees and suppliers of goods and services. Thus it was hardly an exaggeration for a British traveler in 1858 to call Mobile "a pleasant cotton city of some thirty thousand inhabitants—here the people live in cotton houses and ride in cotton carriages." He added, "They buy cotton, sell cotton, think cotton, eat cotton, drink cotton, and dream cotton. They marry cotton wives, and unto them are born cotton children."[27]

With cotton as the basis for its economy, Mobile, as much as any other southern port, remained essentially undiversified. Many people provided services directly related to the marketing of cotton or entertaining of planters and their factors, while few entered other economic pursuits. In plantation districts capital was tied up in land and in the slaves used to produce cotton, while in Mobile it supported business institutions that catered to the cotton trade. A substantial portion of profits from transactions in cotton undoubtedly left Mobile for northeastern American cities as well as for Liverpool and Le Havre, where international firms handled many of the transport, insurance, and market arrangements for Alabama cotton.

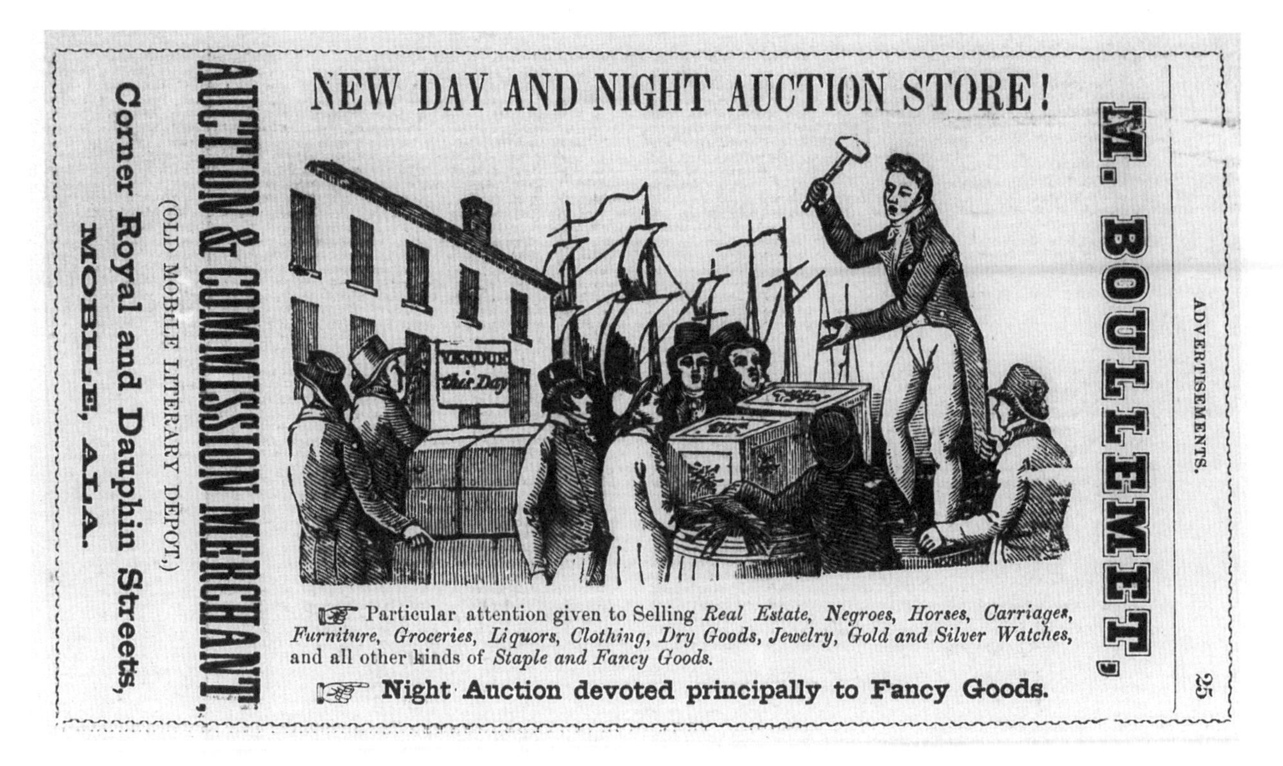

Advertisement, *Mobile City Directory,* 1856.

Representatives of those firms who made their homes in Mobile exercised much influence over local affairs. Along with other entrepreneurs, they opened the way to considerable, if narrowly focused, commercial development for Mobile. In so doing they made Mobile, more than any other southern city, dependent on New York for its economic welfare.[28]

Mobile's transformation from sleepy hamlet to busy city demanded fresh leadership, preferably from its newer residents. The creation of a city required a vision often absent in people accustomed to seeing Mobile as an obscure outpost. American newcomers, who arrived as foreign officials departed at the end of colonial rule, supplied this vision as they filled the power vacuum. Realizing that their prosperity depended on that of their town, they assumed decision-making positions in local government, business institutions, and voluntary associations from which they could supervise Mobile's growth. From these influential posts they provided the initiative needed for the city's development.[29]

Ambitious newcomers to this port city found that they could win positions of leadership soon after their arrival by taking an active part in local affairs. Within ten to fifteen years they were considered distinguished, long-time citizens of the town. Addin Lewis, the first American mayor of Mobile, was one such newcomer. A native of Connecticut, he moved south after his graduation from Yale in 1803 to serve as a tutor at the University of Georgia in Athens. Appointed as the first collector of U.S. customs for the port of Mobile, he assumed his post in 1813. Lewis worked energetically on civic improvements as collector (1813–1829), postmaster (1818–1824), president of the Bank of Mobile (1818) and mayor (1820–1822). His health eventually deteriorated so much that his annual summer vacations in Connecticut could not restore his vitality. In 1829 Lewis, then forty-nine years old, retired from civic affairs. At a public dinner in his honor, he contrasted the "forlorn" condition of Mobile on his arrival in 1813 with its improved circumstances in 1829. He observed that he had done his duty for fifteen years in Mobile with the aid of other leaders, whom he expected to continue their efforts for local improvement after his retirement to New Haven. Prominent Mobilians lauded Lewis as "one of their oldest and most respected citizens."[30]

Although they had come to Mobile from a wide variety of places, leaders shared common concerns about their new home and their roles there. More than anything else, they were preoccupied with their own individual pursuits of wealth. Their energy and enterprise made them money and developed the port of Mobile and eventually its industrial and railroad interests.[31]

As businessmen active in some aspect of the cotton trade, many leaders stayed in

Henry Hitchcock, a lawyer and businessman from New England, helped to finance the construction of many buildings in Mobile during the 1830s, including Government Street Presbyterian Church.

Engraving from La Tourette map of 1838. Library of Congress.

Mobile only during the months from fall through spring, when commerce demanded their presence. Their long summer absences had a negative effect on urban development. A visitor from the North observed in 1840, "[S]o many of the inhabitants leave there in the Summers, that their erratic life forbids them making improvements or paying much attention to these little conveniences & Comforts without which any life & especially a city one is unpleasant."[32] This description of the vacation habits of Mobilians with money remained true throughout the antebellum period. More than any other residents of Mobile, leaders had the wealth and time to spend on civic improvements, yet they were slow to do so because of their annual seasonal absences and their own sense of priorities. Once they had established themselves and guided city government through financial crises, however, they did sponsor improvements to make Mobile a more attractive place.[33]

Urban leaders of Mobile respected commerce, class, and consensus. Drawn from heterogeneous origins, they perhaps openly disagreed among themselves about politics and secretly about slavery, but they agreed on commercial priorities. Although they competed with each other in business, they collaborated on improvements to aid commerce locally. They supported government establishing an environment conducive to commerce, focusing on order rather than regulation. As men who made their own money, they revered enterprise and assumed it earned its own reward in worldly possessions and renown. They tried to shape community consensus on the value of commerce and enterprise, which they considered crucial to the city's development.[34]

Mobile's labor force was more heterogeneous, both ethnically and racially, than the city's mercantile leadership. Various subgroups of laborers competed with each other for employment in certain occupations. Slaves and free blacks filled a number of service positions in the city, thus reducing employment opportunities for whites. White skilled workers, always scarce, fared the best, yet even they encountered competition from outsiders whom employers brought in during hard times after the Panic of 1837. Competition in the labor force sharpened over the years as immigrants came to Mobile in search of jobs. This was especially true in the 1840s and 1850s. Increasing numbers of white immigrants sought jobs formerly held by slaves and free blacks. By 1860 the free male labor force of Mobile consisted of 50 percent foreign-born, 34 percent southern-born, and 16 percent northern-born workers.[35]

Shortages of skilled laborers affected industrialization in the 1850s in two ways. First, employers had to pay good wages to workers in order to attract and keep them. Second, some industrialists who were introducing operations new to the area could not recruit workers locally. Therefore, they sought both managers and operatives from the North. For example, a textile factory built just outside the city employed a manager from Rhode Island and operatives, including male and female Irish immigrants, who had worked previously in a northeastern mill.[36]

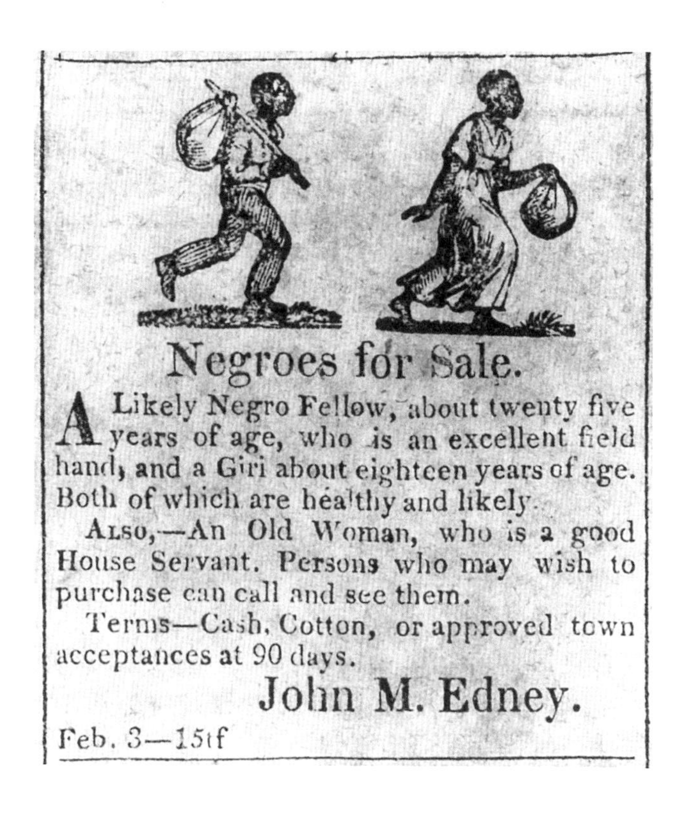

Advertisements for the sale of slaves appeared regularly in the newspaper.

Mobile Commercial Register, February 3, 1823.

The vast majority of Mobile's skilled laborers were white, and slaves supplied much of the city's semiskilled and unskilled labor. They worked as domestics and personal servants, carriage drivers and draymen, mechanics and press hands. Slaves increased in numbers each decade, particularly in the 1830s and 1840s when Mobile experienced its most rapid expansion.[37]

Until the 1850s Mobile served as the slave-trading center of the state. Dealers shipped slaves by sea from Maryland, Virginia, and the Carolinas to Mobile. Once slaves reached Mobile, local residents and planters from southwestern Alabama and southeastern Mississippi made their purchases. The planters returned home via the Alabama or Tombigbee River with their new slaves. After rail lines connected Montgomery with the Atlantic states in the 1850s, the state capital soon equaled and perhaps surpassed Mobile in the volume of its slave trade. Planters who sold cotton in Mobile, however, consistently bought and sold slaves there. For most of the antebellum period, the slave market stood on the west side of Royal Street between St. Louis and St. Anthony Streets. Nearby a three-story barracks housed slaves between auctions. In an effort to make this aspect of the slave trade less conspicuous, the city eventually banned slave depots from the downtown area.[38]

An illicit market in Mobile supported foreign slave trade despite the federal prohibition against it since 1808. Reports appeared occasionally of African natives working in the city. In 1860 the schooner *Clotilda,* owned by northern-born steamboat builder Timothy Meaher, transported what was reputedly the last cargo of contraband Africans to the United States. Slavers then transferred 116 survivors of this voyage to John Dabney's plantation on the Alabama River a few miles north of Mobile. Some slave owners in the area secretly purchased some of the Africans, and the shipowner and captain retained the rest.[39]

Slave owners were a small proportion of the free population of Mobile, less than 10 percent between 1830 and 1860. Masters and mistresses came from widely different backgrounds and occupations. In 1860 native New Englanders such as Thaddeus Sanford, a newspaper publisher turned farmer, Gustavus Horton, a cotton broker, and William Rix, a merchant, owned slaves. So did foreign-born Mobilians. Israel I. Jones and Jonathan Emanuel were English-born merchants, Ann Yuille was a Scottish baker's widow, and Albert Stein was a German-born hydraulic engineer. The largest numbers of slaves, however, belonged to two native southern businessmen, James E. Saunders and Duke W. Goodman.[40]

As costs of purchasing slaves increased, hiring slaves became an advantageous option. Employers might pay only for the services they needed rather than commit themselves to the lifetime maintenance of slaves. By hiring out their slaves, owners could generate steady income, employ surplus servants, and spare themselves from some of the responsibility for daily supervision. Income from renting out slaves helped to support a number of well-to-do widows whose husbands had willed bondspeople to them. Employers usually hired slaves for the business season in Mobile, from November through May. Some masters allowed their slaves to hire their own time and to rent their own places of residence with part of their wages.[41]

Besides slaves, free blacks filled labor positions. Their numbers remained small, however—less than 3 percent of the free labor force in 1860.[42] Free blacks in Mobile came from two backgrounds: Creole and American. Creoles were descended from early white settlers, mostly French and Spanish men who formed liaisons with slave women. Born in Alabama, they had French or Spanish surnames. A few came from Louisiana or Florida. Manumitted in the eighteenth century through liberal Spanish laws, they won protection for their freedom in the treaties by which the United States acquired Louisiana in 1803 and Florida in 1819. Some free blacks moved to Mobile in the later antebellum decades from other places in Alabama or from the upper South. They generally had English or Scottish surnames. Free blacks, Creole and American, held a variety of skilled and unskilled labor positions.[43]

Both women and children found places in the labor force. Free white women found employment in fields ranging from domestic service to teaching and shopkeeping. Children also found gainful employment in Mobile. Local orphanages facilitated child labor by providing that older children who were capable of supporting themselves be bound out to respectable persons in the community.[44]

Churches, fire companies, militia companies, occupational organizations, and ethnic benevolent societies offered foreign-born and native-born Mobilians, white and black, a variety of associations through which they might join friends for social and other purposes. These associations allowed some subgroups of laborers to separate themselves from each other. A few skilled laborers, notably printers, formed occupational associations that helped them to improve their wages and working conditions. Well-established Irish and German immigrants distinguished themselves from their destitute countrymen by forming charitable associations. Black Creoles set themselves apart from other free blacks and from slaves by affiliating with their own fire company, Creole Number 1. Churches throughout the city, especially ones in areas developed in the 1840s and 1850s, served the varied religious preferences of residents. Not only did these diverse associations formed by members of the labor force suit their needs, but they also suited urban leaders. Editorial praise for activities ranging from German Turners' May Day outings to Creole Fire Company parades indicated leaders' acceptance. As long as no laborers' group sought to take economic or political power away from their employers, they found favor with the press and municipal officials.[45] Elections for city officials invariably occurred during the cotton-marketing season. During that time, both the businessmen residing in the city only to engage in the cotton trade and the permanent residents participated in those elections and other civic affairs. On the other hand,

POLLY COLLINS,

No. 39 CHURCH,

corner of

St JOACHIM Street,

Has fitted up her house for the purpose of serving up COFFEE and CHOCOLATE, at all reasonable hours, day or night, in first rate style.

She will also keep a supply of Fruits, Cakes, Ice Cream, (in suitable season) Cigars, and Tobacco, together with a variety of Confectionaries, Cordials, Candies, and other articles usually called for in this line.

No pains will be spared to render her house a pleasant resort, and will endeavor to merit patronage.

Polly (Polite) Collins, a free woman of color, owned and operated a coffee shop in antebellum Mobile.

Mobile City Directory, 1839.

Alabama voters chose their governor and state representatives in August during the absence of many seasonal residents of the city.[46]

City officials faced especially difficult challenges when growth stalled in the wake of the Panic of 1837. Tax revenue dropped not only because of the financial exigencies of individuals but also because of the decline in property values and corresponding decline in property tax revenues that followed the panic. Because Mobile relied so heavily on property taxes for its ordinary income, it faced disaster when that source of revenue decreased substantially. The city defaulted on semiannual interest dividends due on its loans in early 1839. During this crisis of 1839, a yellow fever epidemic and a wave of arson compounded Mobile's financial problems.[47]

Negligence of officials probably contributed as much as anything else to the city's financial crisis. Absorbed with their own economic interests during the cotton boom of the 1830s, the merchants who served in city government neglected to oversee the city's finances as carefully as they supervised their own accounts. Even the legislators who examined the comptroller's books in 1840 and 1841 reported that "they could not have accomplished more without an encroachment upon their business avocations, neither to be expected or required." They did finally insist on double-entry bookkeeping, then routine for mercantile operations, after the default crisis. Profiting from experience with the pitfalls of speculative financing, they slowly guided city government to economic restraint and sound credit. Municipal investments in the 1850s, for instance, had separate accounts and sources of revenue, which made them far more secure than bonds issued in the 1830s.[48] The debt settlement of 1843 and subsequent bond issues financed major public improvement projects. New taxes generated enough revenue to support city services if officials carefully appropriated funds. No longer could city government expend funds on the speculative basis of the booming 1830s; recovery depended on fiscal responsibility. Officials weighed the benefits of services and improvements against their costs to taxpayers. Overextension of municipal finances for major public improvements had driven the city into default after the Panic of 1837 and thereafter prompted more careful use of funds in the later antebellum years. Not only did city legislators scrutinize expenditures more carefully, but they also used a clause in the city charter as amended in 1843 to justify selective allocation of tax monies.[49]

Urban leaders in America generally preferred expenditures for the downtown business district and residential neighborhoods favored by prominent merchants on the assumption that what helped these areas eventually benefited the whole city. The city fathers had followed this unwritten policy since Mobile's earliest days even though the first city charter directed officials to expend funds "for the benefit and improvement of said city, and the comfort, convenience, and safety of the inhabitants." The wording of the charter thus implied no distinction among Mobilians for the allocation of city services. The 1843 amended charter formally rationalized preferential appropriations. According to the charter, in the expenditure of tax funds "the mayor, aldermen and common councilmen shall have a proper regard to the appropriation of the same to the improvement of the different wards of the said city, in proportion to the amount of taxes paid by each ward." In other words, wards that paid the most taxes would receive the most city services. The poorest wards would receive the fewest services.[50]

City services above all accommodated the needs of commerce. Streets in the business district were paved earlier and repaired more often than those elsewhere in the city. Police concentrated their patrols in the commercial areas. They conveniently ignored gambling houses and brothels, both illegal, unless they became scenes of rowdiness that spilled over into public streets. Fire zones initially included the downtown business district and eventually expanded to include adjacent preferred residential neighborhoods. The periphery of the city received little in the way of street improvements or police and fire protection. Unless a service directly aided business interests, city fathers might ignore it until a crisis pushed them to action. Services that promoted sanitation and health in the city, for instance, often were not provided regularly until an epidemic appeared in Mobile or a nearby coastal city. The possibility of undertaking extensive sanitation projects apparently never occurred to Mobile's leaders. Municipal funds paid for lamp lighting only in the commercial district. Beautification efforts attracted municipal support late in the antebellum era and then only after civic-minded residents initiated projects and contributed substantially to them.[51]

In some ways Mobile's city officials may appear stingy, shortsighted, and narrow-minded in their attitudes toward provision of city services. Yet they also displayed vision about investing city funds in projects to boost property values and increase commerce in the city. Bond issues for these projects, which were initiated unwisely without provisions for repayment of capital, brought financial disaster to the city government. This situation checked expenditures and prompted restraint. The city's poverty and its leaders' concerns about balancing business benefits with their costs to taxpayers help explain many of the limits imposed on city services.[52]

Social services in southern cities, including Mobile, remained limited throughout the antebellum era.[53] Outpourings of benevolence came primarily from private charities. Governmental funds provided some aid, usually through established institutions, whereas private philanthropy channeled relief directly to individuals. The essential conservatism of the well-to-do providers of social services, whether they sat on municipal boards or charitable directorates, meant that symptoms of poverty such as hunger and illness received more attention than more fundamental scourges such as unemployment. Only with the public school system did leaders establish an institution that might provide long-term help to improve the lives of poor Mobilians.[54]

From the 1820s through the 1850s local newspaper columns indicated a general acceptance of the existence of poverty, even though its presence harmed the city's sought-after image of prosperity. Government officials trying to reduce the number of public charges began a strong enforcement of laws against vagrancy and begging. Vagrants, beggars, and all persons without visible means of support who remained in the city faced fines or jail terms.[55]

Municipal funds eventually financed several permanent facilities for the poor, the most significant being the general hospital. Besides the hospital, city government contributed to another facility for the poor, Widows' Row, small brick houses for needy widows. The Female Benevolent Society raised funds to maintain the houses and to care for their occupants.[56]

Yellow fever epidemics in the late 1830s prompted Mobilians to form several charitable societies to care for the afflicted and their orphans. The Samaritan Society and the Can't Get Away Club provided direct aid and medical attention to victims of yellow fever. Catholic and Protestant churchwomen founded separate orphanages to care for children left without parents by the yellow fever epidemics of 1837 and 1839. The Mobile Port Society aided sailors with funds raised by the Ladies of the Bethel Society.[57] By the late 1850s the mission to seamen included a chapel with regular worship services and Sunday school, a sailors' home with a library and reading room, and a floating bethel in Mobile Bay, all intended to show concern for men "who, by their toil, build up our cities and enrich our citizens."[58]

Mobilians also formed a host of mutual aid societies. Mutual aid in sickness and death played an integral part in the program of such groups as the Masons, volunteer fire companies, the stevedores' Baymen's Society, and the interdenominational Brotherhood of the Church. Ethnic groups also maintained their own benevolent organizations. Among immigrant aid groups, the Hibernian Benevolent Society faced the most formidable task because of the large numbers of Irish who settled in antebellum Mobile, comprising some half of the foreign-born population in 1860. Because the demands on the Hibernian Benevolent Society often overwhelmed its resources, other charitable associations, especially the Samaritan Society and the Catholic Female Charitable Society, also ministered to Irish immigrants. Other ethnic groups included the German Turners' Society, the Scottish St. Andrews Society, and the French La Socíeté Française de Bienfaisance.[59]

Charitable associations generally ministered to those whose needs isolated them from society, and institutions that benevolent societies established tended to isolate the needy even more. By contrast public schools drew rich and poor alike into the mainstream of society. Disparities between Mobile's rich and poor and between native-born and immigrant in the 1850s magnified the need for the establishment of genuine public schools. Until then indifference and inadequate finances hampered the founding of public schools. Even with the availability of numerous private and parochial schools, some tax subsidized, more than half of school-age white children attended no school in 1851. The next year Mobilians overwhelmingly voted for school commissioners, almost half of whom hailed from the North, who had campaigned for a genuine public school system.[60] The economy and efficiency in education available through the public school system definitely appealed to the business leaders who ruled the city. "The main object to be obtained by Public Schools," reported the committee that drafted the plan in 1852, "is to educate the *greatest* number, in the *best* manner, and at the *least* expense." As established in 1852, the Mobile Public School System included three levels: primary, grammar, and high school. Curriculum in the schools reflected American preferences for a "thorough English education."[61]

The public school system assumed management of the already established Creole School, thus directly providing tax-supported education for the county's black Creoles. Educational privileges for black Creoles evolved from provisions in the Louisiana Purchase Treaty in 1803 that had guaranteed to free residents of Louisiana and their descendants the rights, privileges, and immunities of citizens of the United States. The Adams-Onis Treaty by which Spain ceded West Florida (which included Mobile and Baldwin Counties) to the United States in 1819 confirmed that the free inhabitants of that territory had "all privileges, rights, and immunities

Mobile's Jewish community purchased a small plot in the "New Burying Ground," known today as Magnolia Cemetery, in 1841.

Photograph by Catt Sirten.

of the citizens of the United States." Their education at public expense placed the black Creoles of Mobile in a position that free blacks occupied in virtually no other late antebellum southern city.[62]

Public schools eventually attracted a wide cross-section of students, drawing pupils from certain free and pay schools that either closed or lost enrollment. In fact more than one-fourth of Mobile's school-age white children attended public schools by 1860. This proportion placed the city ahead of both southern and northern averages for public school attendance in 1860.[63]

Mobilians liked to believe that their city was progressive in social services. They believed that they contributed generously to charities when the needs of the poor were brought to their attention. In this belief affluent residents contented themselves that urban poverty was kept in check without major expenditures of tax revenues. When the magnitude of poverty in the 1850s belied this notion, civic leaders tended to downplay the problem. Leaders did, however, come to support a public school system that might instill community-wide values and lessons expected of

Barton Academy.

Mobile, The New South, 1887–88. Local History Division, Mobile Public Library.

potential voters and taxpayers. Recognizing that some of their fellow southern cities were also establishing public schools, civic leaders did not wish to see Mobile lag behind in an effort that might attract new people. They patterned their educational system after models developed for advanced northeastern cities on the assumption that progress demanded such imitation.[64]

In the 1850s Mobilians launched new enterprises to reinvigorate their city, which to some appeared to be stagnating. Granted, the population had doubled in the 1820s and quadrupled in the 1830s. Nevertheless, the rate of growth had slowed in the 1840s, when the population did not even double from the previous decade. To reverse this trend after the local economy had recovered from the lingering effects of the Panic of 1837, boosters promoted railroads, direct trade, and manufacturing for Mobile. These new enterprises to diversify the economy placed the city in the movement for southern commercial independence from northern domination.[65]

Railroads provided one of the several avenues to southern independence and urban growth that were suggested by a series of southern commercial conventions. Mobilians slowly began to realize that the port's historical function as a depot for the storage and transshipment of cotton offered stimulus for substantial further growth. They commented on "the ruinous fluctuations to which the city is liable [because of] her total dependence for subsistence on influences over which [Mobilians] have no control." Urban rivalry provided a major impetus for railroad building as Mobile sought to avoid becoming what the *Mobile Register* called "a mere suburb and outpost of New Orleans." Mobilians determined to connect the Alabama port with the mouth of the Ohio River, thereby tapping both the trade of the West and cotton districts of Mississippi that normally followed the Mississippi River to New Orleans. The new north-to-south line would not so much supplement or replace river trade as it would open fresh commercial connections.[66]

Despite all of the public and private investments and editorial support for railroads, only one major line, the Mobile and Ohio, resulted. Certainly it extended Mobile's hinterland, but it maintained the same function as other southern railroads: the transportation of staple crops to seaports.[67] Only a small portion of the line ran through Alabama, thus drawing local investors' attention to distant areas. Before reaching its northern terminus, it faced stiff competition from a rival railroad from New Orleans. Intrastate railroad lines projected to sustain and to enhance Mobile's prosperity by connecting the city to trade inside and outside Alabama failed to materialize before 1860. In short, railroads failed to expand Mobile's trade significantly. For its major lines of commerce the port still depended on its river system or bay.[68]

Northern shipping interests transported the bulk of imports into Mobile, a situation that advocates of southern independence wished to remedy. John Forsyth, editor of the *Mobile Register,* asked, "What is Mobile but a commercial outpost of

New York? Our merchants are the mere agents of Northern capitalists, and intent only on the calculation of how much of commissions they can obtain thence, and how long it will take to get the productions and importations of New York into their stores." To offset this problem, in the 1850s Mobilians launched companies to own and operate ships between Mobile and various gulf and Atlantic ports, thus breaking their dependence on northern shippers. Unfortunately, direct trade companies ultimately could not sustain service with New York, Liverpool, or Central America because Mobile lacked adequate exports year-round for return cargoes.[69]

In addition to direct trade, Mobilians encouraged industry to diversify the economy. They recognized that manufacturing could create a permanent industrial class to build up the city with purchases of goods and services. Editors repeatedly promoted patronage of local manufacturing enterprises for their benefits to the city. For instance, the editor of the *Alabama Planter* urged Mobilians to purchase boots and shoes from local artisans who spent most of their earnings in payments to landlords, grocers, butchers, and other retailers, "all serving to promote the general prosperity of the city and enrich our people."[70]

Home industry also promised independence from northern domination, as manufacturing promoters reminded their potential investors and customers. Local pride and economy even dictated the purchase of locally carved tombstones of Alabama marble. Jarvis Turner operated a marble yard that transformed marble from quarries near Centerville and Talladega into everything from church altars to tombstones. According to the *Mobile Advertiser,* every Alabamian should have enough state pride to direct his executors "to have the slab, intended to mark his last resting place, made from native Alabama marble." Preference for home industry, contended the *Advertiser,* "may appropriately be graven on our tombstones, as a legacy to those who may succeed us."[71]

Ironically, some industries most praised for their potential in freeing Mobile from northern domination depended on the North for managers, workers, or raw materials. The Mobile Manufacturing Company, for instance, made cotton cloth with Irish textile workers, who had previously worked in a northern mill. The owner-manager of the major local foundry, Skaats and Company, came from Pennsylvania, as did much of the iron ore used in the facility.[72]

Pursuit of progress toward diversification and in turn independence from northern domination extended to educational institutions. Economic interests, southern patriotism, and urban rivalry all sparked local support for the Alabama Medical College, which opened in 1859 to keep Alabama students and their education dollars in the state.[73]

For all of their optimism the advocates of railroads, direct trade, and manufacturing were ultimately unsuccessful. Much of their energy and money went toward a major rail line, which failed in its visionary purpose of enabling Mobile to eclipse the domestic commerce of New Orleans. Furthermore, promoters of direct trade registered no sustained success in increasing Mobile's share of the nation's import business. Industrialists launched several laudable enterprises in the 1850s, yet they could not make the city independent of the North for any manufactured items. Thus, no matter what their accomplishments, in terms of their own stated goals boosters of southern commercial independence failed in antebellum Mobile. Among their fellow citizens they found neither the interest nor the capital necessary to change the direction of Mobile's economy substantially. The city remained devoted to commerce, especially in cotton, which sold well during peaks of international demand in the 1850s.[74]

In its concentration on the cotton trade, Mobile remained essentially in a colonial relationship with the North. Acute realization of this fact in the 1850s prompted some Mobilians not only to try to alter their position within the economic system but also to hold the northern-born residents among them personally liable for their predicament.[75]

In the 1850s many Mobilians decided that their city could best pursue progress only if its political leaders were firmly committed to the South. Southern loyalty had not received such emphasis in Mobile's early American years, when citizens had chosen their governmental leaders on the basis of their contributions to urban development. By the 1850s, however, a substantial number of voters demanded from their elected officials devotion to the region. Evidence of loyalty included not only investment in and support for internal improvements projects but also birth in the South. Important political officeholders, who often had lobbied for internal improvements and other projects ostensibly to promote southern independence, suddenly attracted suspicion if they had moved to Mobile from the North.[76]

Advocates of southern independence, whatever their partisan affiliation, raised questions about the regional loyalty of any local decision maker, particularly one who was born outside the South, who supported unionist positions. What counted most for the success of a local politician in the crisis-laden 1850s was his reputation for loyalty to the South and its institutions. Not even his political record would protect him if his birth outside the South raised suspicions about his regional loyalties. Ironically, almost no one raised the issue of benefits Mobile in particular and the South in general had received from membership in the Union, especially the regional specialization within the economy. Those who maintained Unionist positions throughout the decade might exhibit true concern for Mobile and its development, yet extremists denied them even that.[77]

In the mid-1850s local politicians shifted their suspicions of nonsoutherners in their midst away from the northern born to the foreign born, especially Catholics. By this time Catholics formed a numerical majority of church members in a community where Protestants controlled major business, government, and editorial offices. The affiliation of many foreign-born Mobilians with the Catholic Church particularly troubled leaders who saw in this relationship a combination that might at some time challenge their power. After all, the foreign born made up 24 percent of the city's total population, 34 percent of whites, and 50 percent of the free labor force.[78]

Capitalizing on native-born residents' resentment of foreigners, many politicians, whose first consideration was officeholding, cooperated with the nativist American Party. The party quickly gained followers in the port city, where it made its first appearance in the state. Many Whigs flocked to the new party, apparently as a means of regaining power.[79]

In 1854 Catholic management of City Hospital provided the first test of the American Party's strength. The Sisters of Charity had administered the hospital under contract since 1852, when aldermen had praised them for their attention to care. In 1854, after receiving complaints from Protestant clergymen, some aldermen accused the nuns of a multitude of offenses, the most important being that they tried to induce Protestant patients to embrace the Catholic faith. After an investigating committee found the charges untrue, Mayor Charles C. Langdon nevertheless recommended a change in hospital administration, not because of hostility toward Catholics, he said, but because of his opposition to any sectarian management. Meanwhile, the Sisters of Charity had resigned as administrators of City Hospital. Aldermen then transferred authority over the hospital to a committee of municipal board members.[80]

After this display of strength against the Catholic nuns, the American Party gained followers rapidly. It made a clean sweep of the Mobile County elections in August, the first races entered by the new party in Alabama. As the American Party gained strength, antiforeign sentiment appeared openly and violently in 1855 before several elections. Americans elected their congressional candidate, Percy Walker, formerly a Democrat, who won with the combined support of the American Party, Southern Rights Democrats, and supporters of state aid to railroads. "Anti-Americanism *withers* in Mobile," reported the *Mobile Advertiser* after the municipal elections in December 1855, when the American Party slate for mayor, aldermen, and common councilmen won throughout the city. The new mayor, elected for a three-year term, was Jones M. Withers, a native Alabamian and a Democrat. Withers, a state legislator, resigned his seat to serve as mayor, and the outgoing mayor, Charles C. Langdon, who by this time edited the independent *Mobile News,* won election to Withers's seat in the state legislature.[81]

In 1856 Withers and a number of other prominent officeholders resigned from the American Party for various political reasons. Withers resigned as mayor when he broke with the party, but aldermen and councilmen, a majority of whom were

The Mobile City Hospital.

Annual Announcement of the Medical College of Alabama at Mobile, 1883–84. Local History Division, Mobile Public Library.

elected as Americans, nonetheless reelected Withers mayor. Withers resumed his ties with the Democrats and ran successfully in 1858 for another three-year term as mayor.[82]

The partisan agitation of nativism had subsided, but financial troubles facing Mobile in the mid-1850s, culminating in the Panic of 1857, sparked new attacks on nonsoutherners. Compared to its past rapid growth, the city indeed stagnated in the 1850s. Editors and other city boosters tried a number of measures to entice enough fresh investment capital into local projects to spur new growth. When these efforts failed, editors chided affluent residents in general for their reluctance to invest in somewhat risky ventures. Later they singled out northern-born merchants as the worst offenders. Critics of wealthy merchants who hesitated or refused to invest in internal improvements projects such as railroads implied that these merchants lacked genuine interest in local development. Critics argued that they thought this way because the profits from their trade depended largely on prices of cotton set in world, rather than local, markets.[83]

Accusations against reluctant local investors peaked in 1858 in the *Mobile Register.* According to editor John Forsyth, northern-born cotton merchants bore the blame for limited local development because of their reluctance to reinvest their profits in Mobile. "While they do not condemn, perhaps they even sympathize, with our institutions," the *Register* observed, "they do not regard them as stable, and are constantly apprehensive of change." To put it more directly, "they deem property insecure, and by fears of this sort are deterred from making investments there." These cotton traders from outside Mobile allegedly sustained interests in the city only insofar as they supported the cotton trade. During the summers they left the city and reportedly took their profits from the cotton trade with them for investment elsewhere.[84]

When the city was not booming, particularly during financial panics and sectional controversies, Mobilians tended to denigrate the civic leaders who came from outside the South as exploiters who were not doing enough to foster local growth. As one disgruntled Mobilian later remarked about the northern- and foreign-born cotton buyers: "They came like birds of passage with the earliest frost and fed fat upon wild celery and other spice berries in the season of their maturity, not greedily and voraciously . . . but always willing to leave some pickings behind for the native stay-at-home, like courteous gentlemen as they were."[85]

These accusations against nonsouthern cotton merchants involved some complicated issues. After the Panic of 1857 northerners faced accusations of not investing enough money locally and sometimes of investing too much. When some improvement venture moved along more slowly than desired, city boosters blamed financial problems on northerners in their midst.[86]

At such times critics ignored the fact that nonsouthern urban leaders had contributed materially to local progress. They had helped to establish town government and adapt it to the needs of a growing city. They had opened business links with major northeastern and foreign firms for shipping, insuring, and marketing the cotton that became the major export of Mobile. They had spearheaded both the Mobile and Ohio Railroad and the public school system as ways to strengthen the city's future prospects. They had led a variety of charitable activities to ease the suffering of the poor. They had even organized the beautification of Bienville Square. Sadly, contributions such as these were forgotten as critics focused on the stereotype of the outside capitalists who came to the South only to exploit it for their own purposes.[87]

Explanations both for the growth that propelled Mobile into national prominence and for its subsequent failure to achieve its full potential revolved around the colonial nature of Mobile's commerce. Under its French, British, and Spanish colonial rulers, Mobile had served as an export-oriented trading center, and it maintained that same function under American control. Colonial dependency, the condition that Mobile's commercially minded citizens wished so desperately to change in the war for southern independence, would continue to plague the city long after the end of that conflict. Mobile, like a number of other southern cities, was to remain economically dependent on the North for many years to come. In fact the city had achieved its greatest regional, national, and international prominence among America's cities when cotton was king.[88]

Suggestions for Further Reading

Amos [Doss], Harriet E. "'City Belles': Images and Realities of the Lives of White Women in Antebellum Mobile." *Alabama Review* 34 (1981): 3–19. A study of upper-class white women's efforts to meet what they considered familial, social, and civic obligations; it also mentions ways that less affluent white women found gainful employment.

———. "'Birds of Passage' in a Cotton Port: Northerners and Foreigners among Urban Leaders of Mobile, 1820–1860." In *Class, Conflict and Consensus: Antebellum Southern Community Studies,* edited by Orville Vernon Burton and Robert C. McMath Jr., 232–62. Westport, Conn.: Greenwood Press, 1982. A study of the impact on local affairs brought about by the northern and foreign-born entrepreneurs who marketed cotton in Mobile. These "birds of passage" frequently resided in the city only during the winter to do business.

———. *Cotton City: Urban Development in Antebellum Mobile.* Tuscaloosa: University of Alabama Press, 1985. A study of Mobile's growth as a cotton port from the War of 1812 to the eve of the Civil War, when the most prosperous merchants dominated the economic and social life of the city. It also examines North-South relationships in economic and personal terms during a period of increasing sectional tensions.

———. "Old Town, Young City: Early American Mobile." *Gulf Coast Historical Review* 1 (fall 1985): 4–23. This article traces Mobile's evolution from an old, colonial outpost consecutively controlled by three imperial rulers into a new American city, concentrating on the period from 1813 through the 1820s.

Berlin, Ira. *Slaves without Masters: The Free Negro in the Antebellum South.* New York: Pantheon Books, 1974. Berlin's analysis establishes the historical context of the significant community of free people of color in antebellum Mobile.

Craighead, Erwin. *From Mobile's Past: Sketches of Memorable People and Events.* Mobile: Powers Printing Co., 1925.

———. *Mobile: Fact and Tradition, Noteworthy People and Events.* Mobile: Powers Printing Co., 1930. Both Craighead books reprint "Dropped Stitches from Mobile's Past," columns written by the editor emeritus of the *Mobile Register.*

Delaney, Caldwell. *Remember Mobile.* 2nd ed. Mobile: Haunted Book Shop, 1969. The long-time director of the Museum of the City of Mobile engagingly tells a traditional account of Mobile's history. Chapters 11–16 deal with the antebellum era.

Hamilton, Peter Joseph. *Colonial Mobile: An Historical Study Largely from Original Sources, of the Alabama-Tombigbee Basin and the Old South West from the Discovery of the Spiritu Santo in 1519 until the Demolition of Fort Charlotte in 1821.* Rev. ed. Boston: Houghton Mifflin, 1910. Reprint, Mobile: First National Bank, 1952. First published in 1897, revised and republished in 1910, reprinted in 1952 and 1975, with an editor's introduction by Charles G. Summersell, Hamilton's work remains a basic starting point for the colonial and early American eras.

Wade, Richard C. *Slavery in the Cities: The South, 1820–1860.* New York: Oxford University Press, 1964. This scholarly work focuses on slavery in an urban setting and the life of bondspeople in southern cities. It contains many references to Mobile.

CHAPTER 4

Secession, War, and Reconstruction, 1850–1874

Henry M. McKiven Jr.

Before the Mexican War few Mobilians gave much thought to sectional issues. Politicians had little reason to raise sectional matters during a time when questions about the role of government in economic development and Indian removal were of more immediate concern to the average citizen. Efforts to place slavery at the center of American politics usually met with united resistance at the national level and failed to stir passions in states and communities across the nation, especially in the South. This period of relative sectional peace threatened to come to a crashing end, however, after the acquisition of vast new territories from Mexico. Conflict erupted immediately over whether slavery would be extended into the territories. Many southerners claimed an absolute right to carry their slaves west, whereas residents of the free states opposed slavery's expansion.

Alarmed by this revival of sectional conflict, politicians sought an acceptable compromise and thought they had found one in a collection of measures known as the Compromise of 1850. Much to the dismay of Henry Clay, Stephen Douglas, and other architects of the so-called compromise, though, many political leaders in the slave states and the free states found nothing to their liking in any of the compromise measures. In Mobile, politicians became divided between those who supported the compromise as the solution to the territorial issue and those who thought the compromise settled very little. Old partisan divisions virtually disappeared. The leading advocate for the pro-compromise position was Whig newspaper editor and soon-to-be mayor Charles Langdon.[1] Opposing Langdon were the Democrats and Whigs who organized the local Southern Rights Association (SRA). Led initially by former state representative and future United States Supreme Court justice John Archibald Campbell, the organization included Phillip Phillips, Percy

Admiral Farragut commanded his fleet in the Battle of Mobile Bay from the rigging of the USS *Hartford.*

Museum of Mobile.

Walker, Edmund Dargan, John Bragg, Burwell Boykin, Joseph W. Lesesne, and other members of Mobile's legal and political elite. These men feared that southern acceptance of the Compromise of 1850 would clear the way for the federal government to destroy the institution of slavery at some time in the future. That time would come sooner rather than later, they believed, because the South would not be able to expand and maintain the sectional balance in Congress that had always been critical to fending off attacks on southern institutions.[2]

As an organization, Mobile's SRA did not advocate secession as a means of redressing southern grievances. Its members, recognizing the devotion to the Union among the public, insisted that its goal was the preservation of the nation through resistance to radical elements. Although members thought secession might become necessary in the future, most hoped to alert southerners to the threat they faced and to protect southern influence within the Union. Indeed, the majority of the membership appeared to have shared Campbell's desire to modernize the southern economy through investment in internal improvements and public education and eventually conversion of slaves to free labor. Mobile's SRA always linked its opposition to the Compromise of 1850 with its economic agenda.[3]

Charles Langdon, editor of the *Mobile Daily Advertiser,* dismissed the SRA's repeated denials of secessionism. He warned his readers that Campbell and associates did want to destroy the Union. To support his case, he pointed to the prominence of Mobile southern rights men in the Nashville Convention, convened by some of the more radical secessionists in the region. Campbell and the others, Langdon contended, were just as radical as the men who convened the Nashville meeting and posed a more serious threat to southern slavery than the compromise did. He admitted that the compromise was not perfect but thought it settled the question of slavery in the territories without violating southern rights and would end debate over the issue. If agitation continued, Langdon feared, the Union might break apart and southern interests would suffer.[4]

Langdon, seeking for political reasons to portray the SRA as an organization of radicals, exaggerated the stated attitude of Campbell and most of the members of Mobile's SRA. Some members of the organization did, however, call for the creation of an independent South. They doubted whether slavery could be defended within the Union and viewed the U.S. Constitution as a design for the North's economic and political dominance. In a speech to the SRA in December 1850, John A. Cuthbert warned that fanatics in the North would continue their agitation, thereby encouraging slave rebellions. Another speaker assured his audience that the South could survive as an independent nation. Indeed, by escaping the economic power of the free states, the South would thrive.[5]

Langdon won over a majority of the city's voters in local elections, but barely.[6] Over the next few years Mobile politicians, intent on making southern rights the focus of political debate, reached out to new constituencies by broadening their appeals in a profoundly significant way. During the late 1840s and the debate over the Compromise of 1850, the SRA's defense of the South focused on threats to individual property rights and states' rights. It was not always clear how the issues raised affected Mobile's non-slaveholding majority. By 1850 much of the non-slaveholding population in the city consisted of wage earners who owned no property at all. Much of this laboring class, being recent emigrants from Ireland, competed with slaves for work on the docks. Few of them were likely to become pro-slavery activists under the circumstances. Southern rights Democrats decided to advance their cause by educating the non-slaveholding population about their stake in the defense of slavery. They rested their appeal on shared race, deemphasizing long-held ideas about the importance of property ownership in determining one's standing as a citizen. If a man was white, then he was a member of the superior race deserving of all the rights and privileges of any other white man. This racially based definition of citizenship clearly distinguished immigrants from all African Americans and established the premise for the most critical link in the radical southern rights case—destruction of slavery and extension of citizenship to freedmen would remove the sole distinction between the majority of whites and blacks. Thus, common interest in the advancement of the superior race would provide the shared destiny essential to building a southern nation, in the opinion of the *Mobile Daily Register.*[7]

Josiah Nott, one of Mobile's most famous citizens, provided members of the SRA with "scientific" support for the elevation of race as the primary criterion for full civil equality. His lecture to the group in December 1850 summarized his conclusions after years of skull measuring and other "research." Nott opened with his well-known argument that the "Caucasian" and African races had been created separately. He then explained the "natural" distinctions between the two. Nott told his listeners that the superior intellect of the "Caucasian races" elevated them above African peoples, allowing them to master the values of civilization and to govern themselves responsibly. Nott admitted that even Caucasians passed through a sometimes extended stage of "barbarism," but through education and experience they elevated themselves to a level higher than Africans could hope to achieve. He reminded his audience that the lower classes of whites repeatedly produced "great minds." Africans, on the other hand, rarely changed and were destined by nature to remain on the margins of "civilization." Slavery, he concluded, suited the African.[8]

Nott's ideas explicitly and implicitly threatened leading Mobilians' most fundamental beliefs about religion and the nature of the social order. Few whites were troubled by Nott's racism, but many considered his questioning of the unitary creation of humankind a direct attack on biblical truth. Nott's critics, including John Archibald Campbell, believed that all the races shared common origins. Social hierarchy, they explained, developed over time as some individuals—white men—asserted the skills of leadership with which they were naturally endowed. Distinctions between leaders and the led might be expressed through racial slavery but governed a range of human relationships. Charles Langdon once wrote of slavery as only one of many inequalities in society. Although he did not suggest that some whites might deserve enslavement, he left no doubt as to his belief that race alone did not confer equality. Campbell went ever further when, in an article he wrote for the *Southern Quarterly,* he predicted a future South in which African Americans would rise to the level of whites through education.[9]

Southern rights Democrats made every effort to convince as many white men in the city as they could that Langdon, Campbell, and those who shared their views wanted to reduce whites to the level of African Americans. They went well beyond generalities about the higher social status of all whites and exploitation of fears of race war to explain the specific interests of non-slaveholders in the peculiar institution. Slavery allowed white men to pursue opportunity in a dynamic society because it freed them from a lifetime of menial labor. Langdon and those who shared his understanding of society clearly objected to white civil equality and probably hoped to hold some whites in a perpetual state of wage slavery.[10]

Augusta Jane Evans.

Mary Forrest, *Women of the South* (1861).

Men who feared such appeals to class resentment, with its increasingly secessionist thrust, helped organize Mobile's Know-Nothing Party. The Know-Nothings had emerged in the northeast as the Whig Party disintegrated. Many Whigs joined this party, believing its program offered a vehicle for opposition to Democrats and proliferating sectional parties. The party's formation in Mobile was typical of the nation's in that Mobile's Know-Nothings feared the increasingly radical sectionalism coming from the Democrats and wanted to create a type of second-class citizenship for immigrants. Percy Walker, Charles Langdon, and other prominent men who joined the Know-Nothings understood what the southern rights Democrats were up to and hoped to deprive them of a potential source of strength by reducing the immigrant vote. They differed, to be sure, in their analysis of the dangers posed by immigrants. Some feared immigrants would join those in the United States who believed the West should be closed to slavery or, even worse, join the abolitionists.[11] Mobilian Augusta Jane Evans articulated the latter fear in her Civil War novel *Macaria* through the character of Russell Aubrey, a young lawyer who enters politics in the mid-1850s. Aubrey complains at one point that with universal suffrage the "crude foreign vote" might support the designs of northern fanatics.[12] Most Know-Nothings, however, were more concerned about the support immigrants might offer to radical secessionists, men who would destroy the nation in the name of white democracy and slavery. Although they defended the South in sectional debates, Walker, Langdon, and their allies still believed that outstanding differences could be settled short of destruction of the Union. This intense concern with the revolutionary potential of immigrant voting led Mobile's Know-Nothings to join the national party in demanding an extension of the period before naturalization to twenty-one years, reasoning that it took that long before most natural-born Americans possessed the knowledge and maturity to accept the responsibilities of citizenship.

The brief electoral success of the Know-Nothings in 1855–56 had the effect of unifying a divided Democratic Party. Democrats recognized the need for immigrant votes to win elections. The *Mobile Daily Register* denounced Know-Nothing proposals "as unjust, and contrary to the true theory of citizenship" and rejected "any discrimination between the native and adoptive citizens." Only by extending to all white men the "privilege" of voting could "a truly national character" be created and the South saved "from the evils of caste and class divisions."[13] Mobile Democrats also effectively linked hostility toward universal white male suffrage to the continuing crisis in Kansas. The *Mobile Daily Register* repeatedly charged that the men who wanted to limit white citizenship also supported limits on the extension of slavery. It attacked Know-Nothing congressman Percy Walker for voting against the Kansas-Nebraska Act, charging him with complicity in an abolitionist plan to limit black slavery while expanding white wage slavery. A reprint of a description of a free Kansas published in the *Mobile Daily Register* reminded readers of the dismal future they would face if they moved to free territory. White labor would be "far cheaper than negro slave labor. . . . [T]he hireling white man will get enough to feed and clothe his family in seed time and in harvest, and be cast off to perish in winter." The article contrasted this fate to an imaginary slave Kansas where "the white man . . . however poor" would be "a privileged and honored class like the ancient Greeks and Romans."[14]

The Democrats' strategy proved to be effective. By 1856 the Know-Nothing Party in Mobile was in decline. Mayor Jones Withers led the way when he returned to the Democratic fold and moved to elaborate more fully the distinctions between whites and blacks in his city. Ordinances designed to control blacks had the effect of elevating lower-class whites by allowing them privileges that only whites possessed. Whites and blacks might work at the same jobs, but only the slaves would wear badges and be subject to curfews. The city sought to limit competition between whites and blacks by restricting the freedom of slaves to hire themselves out. Free blacks faced curfews, and in 1859 a vagrancy ordinance provided for their arrest if they had no job. With such policies, Democrats shored up the system of slave control while practicing what they preached about the privileges of whiteness.[15]

Some Democrats in Mobile believed that by destroying the Know-Nothings they advanced the cause of the South. Others celebrated the ascendancy of sectionalism and became strident in their calls for secession if the new Republican Party won the presidency. Many former Whigs and Know-Nothings opted to try to beat the Democrats at their own game by proving that they were even more vigilant in their defense of the South than the men they had once opposed. Still, few politicians questioned the power of sectional appeals. Between 1856 and 1860 the sectional controversy colored every issue. For example, when Mobile's economy experienced a downturn in 1857–58, local leaders blamed it on the city's dependent relationship with the free states. Independence, they argued, would bring commercial growth to Mobile not possible under northern domination, especially if high-tariff Republicans controlled government.[16]

By the election of 1860 all the links in the chain that would end in secession had been forged. Deeply believing in the critical need to defend slavery and white supremacy, Mobile residents prepared to act should the Republicans win. If Abraham Lincoln were elected, many thought the South must leave the Union; others hoped less radical solutions would emerge. The election reflected this division. A plurality of Mobilians voted for moderate candidates John Bell and Stephen Douglas in the presidential election, no doubt hoping to ease the crisis by defeating Lincoln.[17]

With Lincoln's victory a climate of fear and anticipation took hold in the city. The dire predictions of the radical secessionists seemed to be accurate. Now that the Republicans were just months away from assuming power, Mobilians and other southerners expressed little confidence in the future. Urged on by the men who had built the sectional crisis throughout the 1850s, they began to debate not whether secession would take place but whether each state would act alone or all would leave the Union as a group. Those who took the latter position, the cooperationists, insisted that unified action would best demonstrate the South's resolve and, as the *Mobile Register* put it, lay "a firm foundation . . . for a new edifice ere the old one is razed to the ground." Nevertheless, these moderates could not overcome the zeal and organization of those who demanded immediate, separate state secession. By November 21, 1860, the "immediatists" had organized a Vigilance Committee to "persuade" doubters to vote for their candidates. Immediatists campaigning for election to the secession convention portrayed cooperationism as a ploy to delay an aggressive response to the Republican victory. By delaying, the immediatists contended, cooperationists hoped to prevent secession, thereby preserving a Union in which southerners would be unequal partners. Throughout the campaign, reports surfaced of Vigilance Committee intimidation of the opposition. In the election that took place on Christmas Eve, the immediatists won all seven wards of the city.[18]

When Alabama seceded, Raphael Semmes resigned from the U.S. Navy, joined its Confederate counterpart, and became its most famous naval hero as captain of the CSS *Alabama.*

Erik Overbey Collection, USA Archives.

Upon hearing the outcome of the election and news of South Carolina's act of secession, Mobilians celebrated with a parade, fireworks, and speeches. Any doubters or outright supporters of continued union wisely kept their opinions to themselves. Mobilians again took to the streets when the State of Alabama passed its ordinance of secession on January 11, 1861. They gathered at a "secession pole" near the foot of Government Street, then marched to the Customs House to the tune of "Southern Marseillaise."[19]

This use of the French national anthem is at once revealing and deceptive. Many Mobilians who marched to the music that day saw themselves as revolutionaries, as people engaged in the first act in the creation of a new order. Thus they adopted the most famous song of revolutionary France. Nonetheless, this appearance of revolutionary fervor obscured profound differences over the meaning of secession. In this regard, southerners were more like the French than they knew because just as the French Revolution was understood in different ways, so was this southern act of revolution. At Alabama's secession convention, where the process of creating a national identity began in earnest, distinctive visions emerged of what the southern nation should be. The different views were long-standing, firmly rooted in the southern past. Some representatives viewed secession as a reaction to the excessive democratization of America and called for a conservative revolution. Dargan of Mobile, for example, proposed a constitutional restriction of the rights of European immigrants. His proposal angered those who saw secession as a defense of

Kate Cumming, along with two dozen other Mobile women, went to nurse Confederate wounded in the Army of Tennessee after Shiloh.

Kate Cumming, *Gleanings from Southland* (1895).

white democracy against those who would create an elite-dominated class hierarchy. J. F. Dowdell of Chambers County spoke for thousands of Mobilians and Alabamians when he expressed his understanding of secession as a way to guarantee the subordination of Africans in slavery and thereby ensure "equality of the white race." If the convention approved Dargan's proposal, Dowdell warned, "White people will be divided into a lower and a higher class, liable to, and promotive of constant conflicts, and tending certainly to the disfranchisement of the menial or inferior class." Dowdell and others saw white unity as essential should war come. One delegate urged the convention to welcome "any white man who will enlist under our flag and march to the field to defend our independence and our homes."[20]

When war did come it was cast as a defense of white democracy against a foe determined to force white men into a status little different from African American slaves. Mobilians from all classes joined the Confederate military, urged on by their mothers, wives, and girlfriends. Those who stayed at home knew that war meant disruption in their lives, and some willingly sacrificed for the cause. Nevertheless, much of Mobile's population during the war felt a deep ambivalence, and at times open hostility, toward the war effort. The idea that citizens unified to win a victory over the demon Yankees is mostly myth. From the earliest days of the war city officials encountered considerable difficulty in securing support for the most critical tasks the war demanded. When calls went out for volunteers to work on the

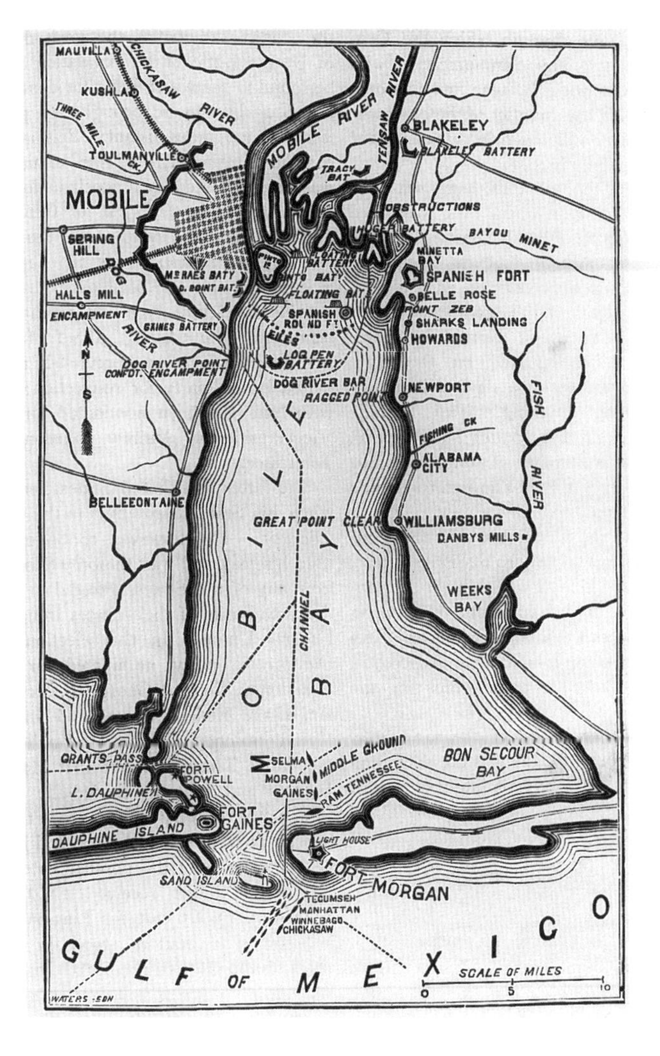

Map showing Mobile's formidable defenses against attack by land or sea.

Alexander Stephens, *History of the United States* (1882).

extensive fortifications the Confederate army wanted to build, whites responded with indifference. Few of them wanted to do work they considered suitable only for slaves and free blacks. Thus the army relied increasingly on slaves to build the city's defenses. Slave labor, however, proved to be a persistent problem. Slaves never worked as hard as army commanders wanted. Perhaps even more troublesome was the resistance of slave owners throughout the war to demands for slave labor. Those slave owners who did respond to requests for slaves complained continuously about their slaves' treatment.[21]

Mobile's white citizens reacted no more favorably when asked to pay for the building of fortifications. When city officials proposed a voluntary tax to raise $50,000 for strengthening defenses, they aroused widespread opposition. The *Mobile Advertiser and Register* urged voters to disregard "demagogues" who used the tax issue to build a political following. Failure to respond to the defensive needs of the city, the paper warned, would certainly prove in the long run to be "penny wise and pound foolish."[22]

By 1862 the average Mobilian probably could not afford to the pay the tax. Day-to-day subsistence now took the little income they earned. By the end of 1861 shortages and high prices had begun to make life in the blockaded city a trial. In late December 1861 city leaders established the Free Market, financed through contributions, to provide food to the needy. Some women in the city organized the Military Aid Society to gather and distribute food and clothing to the families of men in the army. Another women's organization, the Female Benevolent Society, provided food, clothing, and shelter to the wives and children of soldiers who died in Confederate service. One of the larger efforts to deal with problems of subsistence was the Mobile Supply Association (MSA). Organized by men of means concerned with individual exploitation of wartime conditions, the MSA tried to purchase needed goods at the lowest prices and then sell them for their cost. Some hoped that the MSA's presence would hold prices down.[23]

Nevertheless, shortages drove up prices through 1862, and demands for assistance rose with them. When W. C. Corson, an English merchant and manufacturer, visited Mobile in the fall of 1862 he found that "stocks of goods were at a low ebb. . . . [D]ry-goods, hardware, boots and shoes, crockery, and colonial-produce merchants had sold out their stocks and closed their stores." Voluntary organizations found it increasingly difficult to meet the demand for their services. More and more people simply did without. Conditions became so bad that many began to doubt whether the suffering was a natural consequence of the war. Increasingly citizens blamed shortages and inflation on unscrupulous individuals, speculators who took advantage of the war to enrich themselves. According to Corson, such charges were often accurate. He wrote of stores selling "[goods] as a favour, for cash, at enormous profits, ranging from 750 to 1,500 per cent advance." Many of these merchants, he continued, had purchased as much as they could from interior towns to sell in Mobile "at further advances." Complaints about these "extortioners" identified them with the rampant materialism believed to be characteristic of the northern foe. Southerners, many Mobilians believed, defended the institution of slavery because it was a humane economic system that promoted the "general interest of . . . social advancement everywhere." Concern with profiteering moved some citizens in March of 1862 to petition General Samuel Jones for approval of a local tax on excessive profits. Jones imposed the tax and prohibited stockpiling or hoarding of food by one individual or company. Mobilians also joined citizens across the state in demanding legislative regulation of profits and appropriations dedicated to relieving the suffering of the people, particularly soldiers' families and residents of cities.[24]

Demands for price regulations met resistance from many, including Governor

John Gill Shorter. Nevertheless, the legislature responded to popular pressure by passing two antiextortion laws.[25] With the passage of these laws, a majority in the legislature indicated they had some doubt about whether supply and demand alone set prices. Although the legislators were probably not antimarket, they certainly believed that in setting a fair price, some limit should be placed on individual profit, especially when people faced starvation. Those who called for price controls encouraged individuals to engage in profit-making activities but not at the expense of the community. Men and women who sought profits through market manipulation and "monopoly," they insisted, violated the natural law of the market, so the legislature must defend the people through regulation of profiteers.

Unfortunately, these laws proved to be useless in the absence of an extensive system of enforcement. Furthermore, even if they had been enforced, they hardly addressed the causes for shortages and inflation. Thus conditions worsened in 1863. Again a public outcry arose against "extortioners." T. A. Hamilton, secretary of the Mobile Supply Association, warned Governor Shorter that if conditions did not improve there would be a crisis of order in the city. In June Mayor Robert H. Slough responded to the problem by ordering fishermen to sell fish only to those who rented stalls in the city market at the same price they had been selling to "extortioners." He charged "extortioners" with selling fish "in the markets at enormous, exorbitant and extortionate profits, and in addition thereto, when the supply is in excess of the demand, in preference to selling at a fair and remunerative price they destroy the surplus by throwing it into the rivers or otherwise." Slough concluded his remarks by reassuring residents that the men to whom he referred were not true Confederates. They had, he wrote, "no interest in common with us . . . and are aliens by oath."[26]

It is not clear whether the fishermen were dumping surplus to drive up prices or whether Slough repeated one of many rumors that spread around the city about hoarding and other ways people inflated prices. Some of the rumors held "planters" responsible for shortages and high prices: allegedly "planters" held crops until prices rose. Others identified aliens as the culprit. Regardless of the factual basis of the mayor's charge or the origins of his information, his statement gave official sanction to the idea that scarcity and price inflation were evils rooted in individual greed rather than in impersonal market forces. This perception heightened tensions in a city already on edge.

Discontent over shortages and high prices soon produced the explosion that Hamilton had predicted. In September 1863 women took to the streets of Mobile to protest against the merchants they believed responsible for inflation. With banners calling for "Bread and Peace," they marched down Dauphin Street, breaking into stores and taking food and clothing. Reportedly, spectators stood by as the women directed their hostility at Jewish store owners. General Dabney H. Maury, commander of the District of the Gulf, ordered the Seventeenth Alabama Regiment to stop the looting, but the men refused to act. The rioters continued until Mayor Slough appeared and assured them that their needs would be met if they would return to their homes.[27] He appointed a Special Relief Association consisting of representatives from each city ward. The Special Relief Association then created the Citizens' Relief Association to assess the needs of residents. Mayor Slough also began running an appeal in the papers for donations to help the Citizens' Relief Association in its effort to aid the poor, especially the many "indigent" women in the city. To counter fears that charity might go to the undeserving, he assured potential donors that only the "worthy and industrious" would receive assistance.[28]

Available evidence does not allow precise analysis of whom the Citizens' Relief Association deemed "worthy and industrious," but by November the Special Relief Committee reported only limited progress. The Citizens' Relief Association had purchased needed clothing but could not meet demand. The committee's report concluded with a less than encouraging promise to serve as many people as its resources would permit.[29]

The association ran into the same problem everyone else confronted—rising prices. According to the *Mobile Advertiser and Register,* prices continued to go up even though the city in mid-October 1863 was well supplied with meat. The paper claimed that vegetables were "out of reach of ordinary people; none but the millionaires and Quartermasters can luxuriate on tomatoes, and Irish potatoes, pork and mutton chops, and whisky." Indeed, the high price of whiskey made its legal purchase a mark of social status. A person who could get drunk legally must have been very wealthy because that much whiskey would run several thousand Confederate dollars, the paper estimated. "A Citizen of Alabama" sent a letter to Christopher Memminger, the Confederate states' secretary of the treasury, that was critical of producers who still held commodities off the market to raise prices. The writer commented on "the phenomenon . . . of overflowing granaries with prices tending ever upwards. . . . To-day we behold the spectacle of a people in danger of perishing by famine, in a land overflowing with plenty." Such rumors of hoarding sparked more criticism of greedy merchants and farmers whom many Mobilians held responsible for the suffering of the people. One letter to the *Mobile Advertiser and Register* charged merchants in the Free Market with selling goods at inflated prices. Keepers of stalls, the writer charged, sold dear goods, such as butter, to retailers who marked the goods up even more. One woman described "extortioners" as those who took "pleasure in the comforts and luxuries procured from the hearts blood of the dying soldier, the tears of the needy widow and the dry crust that

Confederate currency printed in Mobile, 1862.

Museum of Mobile.

would hush the wail of the starving orphan." The sin of the extortioner, "Sylvia" wrote, was his deriving satisfaction "in his growing riches, which he makes from the necessities of the poor and the agonies of his suffering country."[30]

Although "Sylvia" implicitly blamed the "extortioner" for undermining the entire war effort, she did not suggest bringing charges of treason against speculators. Others were less reticent. By the end of October 1863, many in the city were explicitly linking problems at home to defeat on the battlefield. "A True Confederate" demanded that speculators be treated as traitors because they "by their acts are injuring the efficiency of every measure which demands the zealous co-operation of the people in repelling the public enemy." After arresting the "traitors," the writer suggested, Mobile and other communities must create branches of the Confederate Society. "True patriots" who joined the society would create executive committees to regulate prices and profits by holding them to a standard based on wages paid to Confederate soldiers. Recognizing the role devalued Confederate currency played in fueling inflation, "A True Confederate" wanted all members of the Confederate Society to agree to accept only Confederate money in their businesses. If the members did these things, the writer argued, they would "unmask the wolves in sheep's clothing" and foster "a strong patriotic, public sentiment, which would sweep everything before it that opposes the welfare of the country."[31]

Branches of the Confederate Society did appear across the South. The one organized in Mobile called for a more aggressive policy than "A True Confederate" proposed. Writing for his associates in the Mobile society, "Gray Hairs" denounced the government for its failure to deal with "extortioners." The Mobile County grand jury, he wrote, had issued a report acknowledging that the problem of prices could be traced to "extortioners" but proposed no remedy. The jurors, "Gray

Hairs" believed, did not understand the serious threat the Confederate war effort faced. Morale in the army suffered when soldiers "cheerfully" faced death while "those who remain at home under friendly shelter, with soft pillows and domestic comfort, proceed systematically to rob the soldier's wife and impoverish his children, and amass immense wealth and sport splendid style, by processes of *legalized swindling*—bankrupting the government and reducing the noblest of our population to prospective pauperism." Shortages and high prices, "Gray Hairs" declared, were not natural products of the market. Rather, they reflected the work of people with "no excuse nor reason for their conduct but infernal greed, a lust for gold, which would prompt many of them to barter country for 'thirty pieces of silver,' and sell their mothers for a consideration." The grand jury, the legislature, and the executive would do nothing of substance because they had "quailed before an interest so wide spread and so potential, as to set at defiance the edge of the law, and the condemnation of moral justice and the force of opinion."[32]

Not everyone shared this desire to restrict prices, especially if the government was to do the restricting. In a lengthy critique of price-fixing proposals, a correspondent to the *Mobile Register* explained the reasons for high prices and why price controls would not work. "Lorgnette" started with the reasonable argument that the primary reason for high prices was the Federal navy's successful blockade. Three years of bad cereal crops combined with crop destruction and foraging by Union forces further limited sources of supply for cities. None of these problems could be eliminated through price controls, "Lorgnette" argued. In fact, price fixing would

Blockade runner *Grey Jacket* escaping the *Kennebec* just outside Mobile Bay.

Harper's Weekly, February 13, 1864.

make the situation worse by promoting the domination of the "rich." With prices controlled, small businesses would not be able to cover the cost of purchases in the countryside. Only those with money would be able to pay agents to scour the countryside for goods. With the "rich" in control of markets, prices would go up even more.[33]

Free traders blamed the Confederate government for much of the trouble the country faced. One writer insisted that the market would function properly if the government would attack hyperinflation by taxing to absorb excess currency. As the value of money rose, producers would again sell their goods. With a competitive market restored, the writer argued, the government could end its interference with the economy. Such a strategy, the writer promised, supported the war effort by ending the misery of families, especially the families of soldiers.[34] With the home front secured, soldiers would "fight with a will for a government that legislated not only for this object but to free them from future taxes that would otherwise oppress them and their descendants for centuries to come, and make their labor subservient to the miser and the financier."[35]

The free traders' analysis of Mobile's economic woes found support among those in Mobile most involved in trying to do something about food shortages and high prices. T. A. Hamilton of the Mobile Supply Association appealed to the governor in the spring of 1863 for an exemption from antiextortion laws. He hoped removal of price restrictions would encourage food producers to sell their products. In the fall of 1863 the legislature did exclude Mobile from the 1862 restrictions on the corn trade. The MSA also petitioned the city government for an exemption from regulations requiring that meat be sold at the city market only. The *Mobile Advertiser and Register* urged the city to grant the exemption ending its monopoly on the sale of food. Prices, the paper argued, would fall because merchants would no longer have to bear the expense of a market stall.[36]

Mobile's leaders also sought relief from Confederate impressment operations. Since late 1862, Mobile authorities had been pleading with the governor to stop Confederate impressment of supplies bound for the city. Governor Shorter urged Lieutenant General John Pemberton to allow shipments from northeast Mississippi and the interior of Alabama to proceed. Corn was plentiful in those areas, the governor argued, so all that needed to be done to relieve Mobile was to distribute supplies more efficiently. Of course, Pemberton and the government, faced with problems of supplying a hungry army, could not do what the governor asked. In turn, complaints from Mobile about impressment of supplies grew more shrill as prices continued to rise. By November the complaints about speculation shared space in the city press with sharp criticisms of the Confederate government. The *Mobile Advertiser and Register* charged that the government had made the problem of extortion and would, if it did not reform itself, cause defeat. Government officials, the paper charged, "behaved in a way well adapted to break down the resources and spirit of the people, and by exhausting our means of resistance subject us to the tender mercies of our foes." The state, therefore, must stop military authorities from impressing supplies bound for Mobile.[37]

Mayor Slough's yearly address focused on the problem of prices and what might be done to ease the suffering of Mobilians. Joining those who viewed prices as a consequence of misguided Confederate policy, he blamed government interference with transportation, the blockade, and the absence of six thousand men for much of the city's trouble. He added, however, that the people themselves should bear some of the blame. Conditions were bad but were not as bad as "croakers" made them appear. The mayor urged citizens to stop "croaking" and go to work to earn a living and ease their own suffering. Those women and others unable to provide for themselves and their families received assistance from the city through its Free Market, from the state through its provisions for the wives of soldiers and the indigent, and from an array of voluntary organizations. Therefore, the city need spend no more on relief; in fact it needed to cut its expenditures in all areas. Slough's criticism of so-called croakers and call for retrenchment had little noticeable effect on city policy. The city council denied the MSA's request concerning its meat market because of its desire to ensure fair competition among butchers. The Free Market continued to be the primary source of food for many Mobilians, though it, like the regulation of butchers, violated the free trade principles the mayor espoused. Council members were more concerned with the problems of order and morale than with debates over economic philosophy.

City government should have been concerned with morale, which reached new lows as the war continued into 1864. The *Mobile Advertiser and Register* complained regularly about a growing ambivalence toward the war and, in many cases, outright hostility toward the policies of the Confederate government. It warned that the greatest threat to the nation came not from Yankee invaders but from "the apathy of the people, their weariness of the trials and privations of the tremendous struggles." Men would not volunteer for the army, fathers would not send their sons to war, and ladies would not sew for the soldiers. Lagging morale, the paper continued, caused increased desertion and malingering. Surgeons freely gave "certificates of disability," and parents and wives, whose "natural affection . . . overcomes their sense of duty to their country," pleaded with loved ones to "come back from the field." Those men who abandoned the army would be welcomed into their war-weary communities even though they deserved ostracism.[38]

The Mobile County grand jury investigated conditions in the city and heard evidence of an increase in property crimes as deprivation spread. Burglaries, receiving stolen goods, and whiskey making all increased sharply in 1863–64. The grand jury found particularly alarming the link between black burglars and the white women who sold their stolen goods. Yet, the grand jury report complained, Mobilians ignored such clear symptoms of a collapsing social order. When people charged with violations of the law came to court, they stood a very good chance of being released despite obvious guilt. The grand jury blamed this practice on jurors "picked up on the streets" who came from the same lowly world as the criminals. Citizens "most interested in the faithful administration of justice are seeking their own ease and profit" rather than serving on juries, the report concluded. Here again the selfish pursuit of personal enrichment endangered the community.[39]

Such was the context in which Augusta Jane Evans wrote one of the most popular novels of the Civil War, *Macaria, or the Altars of Sacrifice.* Writing on scraps of paper while working in a Mobile hospital, Evans, through her book, called for renewed sacrifice, especially among well-heeled women. Through her characters she laid out for readers the reasons for the war and explained why victory would save the South from a self-absorbed people, the Yankees. Irene and Electra, the main characters, dedicate themselves to serving the Confederacy, rising above the selfishness Evans and others in Mobile thought undermined the war effort.[40]

Nevertheless, in the summer of 1864 further sacrifice appeared to many to be futile. Depression deepened that summer when, on August 5, Admiral David Farragut damned the torpedoes and entered Mobile Bay with his fleet. Two days earlier the ground forces under the command of General Gordon Granger had landed on Dauphin Island. Granger's troops then placed light artillery within twelve hundred yards of Fort Gaines. As the sun rose on August 5, sentinels at Fort Morgan watched as the ships of Farragut's fleet, tied together in pairs, approached, with the more powerful vessels on the Fort Morgan side of the pass. At approximately 7 A.M. the fleet opened fire on the fort as it entered Mobile Bay, while Granger's force opened fire on Fort Gaines, effectively shielding Farragut's western flank. A Confederate navy squadron under the command of Admiral Franklin Buchanan resisted, inflicting some damage, but had no chance to stop the far superior Federal force. Having secured the southern end of Mobile Bay, Federal troops landed east of Fort Morgan and subjected the beleaguered garrison to shelling from land and sea for a little more than two weeks. Finally, on August 21 Brigadier General Richard L. Page surrendered the fort. Union forces did not follow up the operation in Mobile Bay with an attack on the city itself because Granger needed more infantry for such an attack than General William Tecumseh Sherman was willing to invest. Farragut's control of the bay did, however, end blockade running, making conditions for the residents of the city even worse.[41]

During the final months of the war, Mobilians struggled to overcome scarcity and prepared for an attack that never came. Most busied themselves with the daily challenges of living in a city lacking almost all the basic necessities of life. Others, the more well-to-do, simply thumbed their noses at the suffering around them. In

Admiral David Farragut.

Alexander Foxhall Parker, *The Battle of Mobile Bay* (1878).

the winter of 1865, one Mobile woman noted in her diary that "Mobile is gayer than ever; it seems as if people have become reckless. . . . [N]ot a night passes but some large ball or party is given." These Mobilians evidently decided to have a last fling before the world they had known passed away.[42]

On April 12, 1865, the Civil War ended for Mobile when Mayor Slough surrendered the city to Union troops approaching on Bay Shell Road. When Union soldiers entered Mobile they found most of the people sullen and hostile. Laura Roberts Pillans wrote in her diary that most residents tried to ignore Federal troops. Some women, however, expressed their feelings by walking in the middle of the street to avoid passing under American flags hanging from all public buildings.[43] Such symbolic acts of defiance, however, could not ease the deep despair and uncertainty of Mobilians in the weeks and months after Federal occupation. Ann Quigley, principal of Barton Academy, described the week the war ended as the "saddest—I have ever experienced." Four days after Mobile fell she wrote that "nothing [is] seen in the streets save the blue coated foe—nothing [is] heard but the tramp of their cavalry." Quigley expressed resentment at "Yankee ladies" who walked down Government Street showing off fine clothing while Mobile women, attired in "plain dress," watched. Few people had any money, she observed, whether rich or poor. Even northern visitors to the city found its condition disturbing. Whitelaw Reid, a newspaper reporter, described stores that were "empty and forsaken." More troubling to him, however, was the condition of the people. Mobilians, he wrote, appeared "sad and sorry." He, like Quigley, saw an equality of suffering; even the "best people" were "poor and poorly clad." Reid reported "distress" among Mobilians over the lack of money and circumstances in general. Profoundly moved by the conditions he witnessed, he left the city, hoping never again to see "such sorrow over this order of things."[44]

The people of Mobile clearly faced an immense task. Whites in the city had been told for years that social order depended on the enslavement of African Americans. They had come to define themselves as individuals in terms of the rights and privileges they enjoyed as members of the "superior race." Now African Americans were free and moving in large numbers to the city in search of work, expecting to enjoy all the rights of free men, including the right to vote. If freedmen could exercise the rights of white men, Mobilians feared, then the ideology of white supremacy would be meaningless. To less-well-off Mobilians, such a scenario was particularly frightening, for they would be cast into competition with blacks for jobs and for space, which secessionists had predicted in the 1850s. Nothing would distinguish them from a despised race; they would indeed become "white niggers."[45]

Employers of labor had other concerns. They could see the theoretical possibility of a reduced wage bill with the influx of blacks into the city. Still, their stereotypes about the African American work ethic gave them pause. Would African Americans work in the absence of the supervision and coercion that slavery afforded? Generally, Mobile's white employers answered, no. Ann Quigley expressed their attitude when she complained about the refusal of black servants to work. Former slaves, she wrote, left "their owners," forcing "ladies . . . to perform the household work." Women did not protest much because "servants . . . have become so worthless, so demoralized." All that the former slaves wanted to do was "lounge about the streets—sleep in the market—pick up a little food wherever they can." Quigley then mimicked the answer she thought one would get if he or she asked freed persons why they did not work. "'Massa Lincoln gwine take care o'dem. No more work for poor darkie—white folks take care of de selves—negros gwine rest now some.'"[46] Attitudes like Quigley's lay behind the city government's attempt to deal with the problem of labor during the summer of 1865. Mayor Slough, who remained in office along with the rest of city government until August, wanted to build a workhouse where "vagrants" would be confined for thirty days to six months while they worked for the city. The plan was never implemented, but city authorities, the police, did increase arrests of "Negro loafers, idlers, and paupers."[47]

Heightened anxiety over the behavior of free blacks and their future place in the social and economic order gave rise to interracial violence. More often than not whites initiated attacks on freedmen, though white leaders denied any responsibility. When black leaders demanded enforcement of the law, city officials usually found a freedman to hold responsible for episodes of interracial conflict. Thus the list of blacks appearing in the mayor's court grew daily.[48] Unable to testify in court, African Americans rarely escaped jail time if arrested. The Freedmen's Bureau moved to correct this glaring inequity when, in August 1865, Brigadier General Wager Swayne, the assistant commissioner of the Bureau of Refugees, Freedmen, and Abandoned Lands responsible for Alabama, ordered that civilian courts permit black testimony. Mayor Slough reacted to Swayne's order angrily and refused to do something he believed threatened white control of the black population. When Swayne insisted that his order be enforced, the mayor resigned. Swayne then replaced Slough with John Forsyth, former mayor, editor of the *Mobile Daily Register,* and at the time a relatively moderate Democrat. Forsyth promptly complied with Swayne's order. Blacks continued to be arrested, but they at least could defend themselves in court.[49]

Forsyth's service came to an end in December 1865 when Jones M. Withers won the first mayoral election under President Andrew Johnson's Reconstruction plan. Johnson's plan, though somewhat more stringent than Lincoln's, returned responsibility for governing to the state and local levels. In Mobile the Withers administration immediately moved to increase regulation of the African American population. Early in 1866 a vagrancy statute almost identical to the 1859 statute went into effect. Although the Freedmen's Bureau required references to race to be eliminated, actual enforcement of the law removed any doubts that might have existed about its purpose. In June 1866 the new vagrancy law required all those found to be violators of the statute to perform labor "for the benefit of the city that the mayor and the joint police council shall prescribe." Again the measure included no references to race, but the white police force rarely arrested whites for vagrancy.[50]

These attempts to control black labor at the local level reinforced state legislation restricting black freedom in the labor market. One state law attempted to force black children into a state of virtual slavery. The law gave the county probate judge the power to remove children from their families and place them with "masters" until age twenty-one for a male and age eighteen for a female. This "apprentice" legislation effectively denied black parents or guardians control over their dependents, which whites considered an essential and necessary component of their freedom. Probate judges could remove a child from his or her home upon their determination that the parents were not raising the child "properly." What constituted "proper" parenting was, of course, up to the judge. One provision of the law returned to slave owners their old domination of the families of freedmen

Joe Cain dressed as Chief Slackabamorinico, April 1866.

USA Archives.

by giving former owners a first claim on the children of former slaves. If an "apprentice" ran away, he or she could be arrested and returned to the master. Here again, the apprentice law was "color blind" but in practice affected only freedmen. Thus the law created a supply of bound black labor, denied the legitimacy of black families, and established a sharp distinction between the rights of whites and freedmen. The *Mobile Nationalist,* a newspaper dedicated to promoting and defending the interest of freedmen, warned readers that judges would define children as orphans regardless of the level of support and care parents provided and then bind them to "masters" in a state of "practical slavery."[51]

At the same time city and county authorities enforced laws designed to force freedmen to work, they implemented other ordinances limiting black access to relatively profitable occupations. For example, in early 1866 the common council and board of aldermen approved an ordinance requiring a bond of $1,000 for all dray owners for each dray operated. The all-black Drayman's Association sent a protest to the Freedmen's Bureau complaining that the measure would put black dray drivers out of business. Most blacks, the association claimed, did not own enough property to secure such a bond and those who did could not find an underwriter for the bond because of their race. Whites, of course, easily obtained bonds no matter what their economic condition was. Thus the government handed whites "in no respect more responsible" than black drivers a monopoly of the carrying business. Freedmen's Bureau officials persuaded the city to reduce the bond to $500, but a driver reported in March that whites still held a monopoly.[52]

Emboldened by successful restoration of economic and political control of the city, some local Mobilians moved to restore their antebellum culture. For example, Joseph Stilwell Cain revived Mardi Gras when he and six others, disguised as Chickasaw Indians, drove a charcoal wagon through the streets of the city, openly defying federal troops. "Chief Slackabamorinico," as Cain called himself, declared an end to war-born depression in 1866 because he undoubtedly thought the fundamental patterns of prewar life should and would continue. The Confederate veterans who joined him and his "Lost Cause Minstrels" had few reasons to believe otherwise, given the course of presidential Reconstruction.[53]

Freedmen and their allies had another future in mind, however, and worked mightily against the forces of reaction to realize it. Their protests against the apprentice law and the dray ordinance reflected their determination to make their own way and to enjoy the same control over their lives other Americans enjoyed. This ideal lay behind freedmen's creation of their own religious and educational institutions. Before the Civil War African Americans generally attended white-controlled churches for formal services. Nonetheless, African Americans had their own ideas about the way religion should be practiced, so many went home after the formal service and held their own. After the war they claimed as free people the right to worship in public as they wanted. As the members of the State Street African Methodist Episcopal Church wrote to the presiding bishop of the Alabama Methodist Episcopal Church Conference, "The only reason we can assign for separating from the Alabama Conference, M.E. Church South, is—that we are now freemen, and as such we desire to act for ourselves."[54] This "desire to act for ourselves" extended to schooling. African Americans recognized the importance of education and soon after the war began establishing their own schools. Black churches led the way in the effort. The State Street A.M.E. Church opened the first school for freedmen in May 1865. Soon thereafter schools opened at the Stone Street Colored Baptist Church and at St. Louis Street Colored Baptist Church. By 1868 approximately eight hundred black children attended sectarian schools. Others attended Freedmen's Bureau schools run by teachers associated with the Northwestern Aid Society. Classes were held in the Medical College and Museum, where before the war Josiah Nott had developed his theories of black intellectual inferiority.[55]

The American Missionary Society's Emerson Institute, a school for black students, opened in 1865.

Harper's Weekly, October 3, 1868.

White Mobilians understood the significance of independent black churches and schools. After all, they had denied slaves freedom of religion and access to education because they believed both encouraged rebellion against the status quo. This fear of the influence of black-run churches and schools remained after the war. Thus whites burned some churches and schools to the ground to let the freedmen know who still controlled the city. According to the *Mobile Nationalist,* one white man witnessing the burning of a church expressed a wish for the destruction of all black institutions.[56]

Virtually total white political control during the first two years of Reconstruction left many Mobile blacks with few defenses against legal and extralegal restrictions on their freedom. Recognizing the consequences of black political impotence and desiring an electoral base in the South, Republicans in the U.S. Congress effectively removed President Andrew Johnson from any role in making Reconstruction policy. They then pushed the Reconstruction Act of 1867 through Congress. The law divided the former Confederate states into five military districts, gave commanders of each district the power to use federal troops to protect lives and property, and mandated the writing of new state constitutions that would extend the right to vote to black males.[57]

Emboldened by the Reconstruction Act, a group of Mobile Republicans established a branch of the Union League as the institutional base for the mobilization of the black electorate. George F. Harrington and W. D. Turner, both white lawyers searching for a power base in the city, joined Albert Griffin of the *Mobile Nationalist,* Lawrence Berry of the African Methodist Episcopal Zion Church, and E. C. Branch, publisher of the *Mobile Nationalist,* in creating Mobile's Union League. Rapidly the league grew to between fifteen hundred and twenty-five hundred members. Although the leadership was biracial, the membership consisted almost entirely of freedmen attracted by the league's promise to "provide for security and protection of . . . political rights and privileges."[58]

White Democrats responded to the efforts of the Union League with a combination of persuasion and coercion. They stepped up their campaign to win support among the city's relatively conservative and well-off Creole population. Representatives of Creoles figured prominently in a public meeting Mayor Withers convened to discuss new political realities. The theme of the meeting was moderation. Democratic leaders joined moderate Republican judge Richard Busteed in urging all citizens to work for "harmony and accord between the races who are now brought face to face in new political relations." Of course, in the opinion of all the speakers, association with the Union League did not promote harmony. Freedmen, Mayor Withers warned, would receive little but trouble from the "radical Union League." He suggested that they accept the leadership of "conservative" whites and blacks.[59]

Reconstruction-era violence: the 1867 shooting of Judge Richard Busteed by Assistant U.S. District Attorney L. V. B. Martin.

Frank Leslie's Illustrated Newspaper, January 18, 1868.

Calls for moderation stood in sharp contrast to an ongoing campaign of intimidation directed at the freedmen. Soon after the formation of the Union League, employers in the city began to fire anyone suspected of being a member. In addition, the all-white police department continued to harass blacks on the streets and to serve as an enforcer of white domination whenever blacks challenged the authority of white employers or workers. When black dockworkers struck for higher wages in the spring of 1867 with the support and encouragement of Harrington and Turner of the Union League, employers simply dismissed the strikers and replaced them with whites. Employers in this case clearly not only exploited racial division on the waterfront for their own gain but also responded to white demands for preferential treatment. When strikers threatened to stop white replacements from working, employers called on the police for protection. The police department willingly provided the service because the men they defended shared not only their race but also, as Irishmen, their national origin. Although employers, white workers, and the police clearly had no interest in the promotion of racial harmony, the *Mobile Advertiser and Register* labeled Harrington and Turner "bad white men" responsible for "exciting feuds and perhaps open hostility between the two races with a view to their own political and official advancement."[60]

Intimidation had little noticeable impact on freedmen, who continued to assert their rights. For example, after streetcar companies refused to carry black passengers, African Americans attempted to force integration. The challenge began on a Sunday afternoon in mid-April 1867 when Roderick B. Thomas boarded a car waiting for churchgoers outside Government Street Presbyterian. The driver was under orders to abandon a car if a freedman insisted on riding. Thomas refused to move, so the driver unhitched the horses and left the car. A crowd of supportive blacks gathered on one side of the street, facing a crowd of hostile whites. When Thomas finally left the car, whites rushed to fill the seats, and the driver rehitched the horses to the car and attempted to drive away. Thomas, backed by the black crowd, rushed to reboard, sparking a brawl. Eventually whites, aided by the city police, chased the protesters away and arrested Thomas, several of his supporters, and one white man. Despite this setback, Thomas and others persisted in their efforts and made significant progress in several areas. Initially Brigadier General Wager Swayne worked out a compromise with the streetcar company to allow blacks to ride in blacks-only "Star Cars." At the same time, Swayne ordered an end to the practice of apprenticing black minors to plantations and prohibited further enforcement of vagrancy laws.[61]

Such victories, combined with continued streetcar protests, intensified white fears of racial equality. Some in the city warned that the freedmen courted disaster if they did not accept the leadership of conservative whites. Retribution from the white masses would surely come if the Union League did not stop "trading in the passions of an untutored race." Continued agitation sowed "the poisoned seeds of a bloody war of castes under the very windows of the domestic hearths that enshrine our wives and daughters."[62] Less than two weeks later, citizens of Mobile experienced what many no doubt believed to be the first battle in the *Mobile Advertiser and Register*'s feared race war. A race riot broke out on May 14, 1867, during a speech by Republican congressman William D. "Pig Iron" Kelley. Kelley's predominantly black audience listened intently as Kelley attacked "demagogues" who, he charged, were responsible for the Civil War and who still sought to deprive citizens of their rights. Throughout his remarks, the few whites in the crowd heckled Kelley, at times shouting threats. Kelley reminded the hecklers that the U.S. Army would defend his right to free speech. This remark brought even more verbal abuse. At this point police chief Stephen Charpentier attempted to arrest David Files, who Charpentier believed was responsible for the disruption. Before the arrest could be completed, however, Files allegedly fired a shot, causing a panic and more gunfire. By the time police regained control, a white man and a black man were dead, and ten people were injured.[63]

Violence erupted on the occasion of Judge "Pig Iron" Kelley's visit to Mobile.

Harper's Weekly, June 1, 1867.

Whom one blamed for the "Pig Iron Kelley riot" depended on one's political affiliation. Democrats held Radical Republicans responsible. They charged the Radicals with holding public meetings that antagonized the white community. Republicans, of course, accused Democrats of inflaming white racial fears. In the end, only the opinion of the military authorities in charge of the city mattered, and they concluded that the police, with the approval of the mayor, had failed to provide adequate security for the Kelley event. General John Pope therefore ordered the mayor, police chief, and the entire city government removed from office. He replaced the mayor with Gustavus Horton, a Unionist, and the police chief with C. A. R. Dimon. Later General Pope returned some of the fired members of the board of aldermen and common council to their offices, where they joined the new Republican members.[64]

Pope's action, although dramatic, was not intended to establish a Radical government. To the contrary, he joined Swayne in advancing the fortunes of moderate Republicans. Horton, Dimon, and other military appointees had opposed secession and endorsed universal male suffrage but did not approve of racial integration

GOING TO THE CONVENTION.

Radical Campaign Song.

O, we radicals are ruling,
Ruling and ruining the country as we know,
And the Constitution and the Union,
Straight to the devil let 'em go.

Chorus:
And its Glory, glory, hallelujah,
We'll ride the nigger, for his back is very strong,
Glory, glory, hallelujah,
And we'll go marching along.

Come let us get up a C[illegible]tion,
Where we'll tie the State so her pockets can be picked,
And let us take a pair of darkies,
Who from the back door shall be kicked.
For its glory, glory, hallelujah, &c.

What do we care for the white man?
With his starving family why let 'im go to h—ll,
Turn him off from work for the negro
To sleep and vote will do very well [illegible] charge of the
For its glory, glory, hallelujah, &c.

O, we're a jolly set of rascals,
Riding on this elephant and tramping on the right,
Mashing in the graves of the soldiers
Who once for the Union did fight.
For its glory, glory, hallelujah, &c.

O, we're a jolly set of rascals,
Poultice-eating fishers who for nigger votes do bob,
Mild-mannered [illegible] scoundrels,
[illegible] God while we rob!
Then glory, glory, hallelujah, &c.

This cartoon satirizing delegates to the 1867 Reconstruction Convention appeared in the *Mobile Tribune.* Seated on the elephant and leading the Republican delegation are Gustavus Horton and Albert Griffin.

Historic Mobile Preservation Society.

and Radical efforts to promote black social and economic equality. Military assistance allowed Horton, Dimon, Frederic Bromberg, and Albert Griffin, among others, to consolidate the domination of moderates in Republican circles. They formed the Republican Union Club and began reaching out to the white electorate, hoping to build a moderate, biracial Republican coalition.[65] This Republican strategy met with limited success because most whites in Mobile considered Horton and the rest to be as radical as Harrington. Horton's initial actions as mayor served only to intensify those fears. First he replaced white (predominantly Irish) policemen with blacks. Then he fired eighteen city laborers, seventeen of whom were Irish, and gave their jobs to freedmen. How Horton thought such decisions would advance the moderate cause is unclear. What is clear is that he handed the most rabid white supremacists among his adversaries an issue whose emotional appeal they would exploit repeatedly.[66]

Racial polarization continued during the fall of 1867 in the aftermath of the state constitutional convention. Democrats boycotted elections for the convention, so Mobile's delegation consisted solely of Republicans. Alfred E. Buck, a recent arrival in the city from Maine, John Carraway, a former slave and assistant editor of the *Mobile Nationalist,* and Ovide Gregory, a Creole and assistant chief of police, joined Horton and Griffin as Mobile's representatives. They played leading roles in writing a constitution that reaffirmed virtually every racial fear whites in Mobile had ever articulated. Carraway, for instance, successfully fought a prohibition on interracial marriage. Horton, as chair of the committee on education, pushed for integrated public schools.[67]

At the end of 1867, Democrats in the city were no more united than were Republicans. One Democratic faction urged acceptance of black civil equality and sought black votes in the state elections of 1868. In Mobile, where the military still appointed the government, these same Democrats, through a private organization called the Board of Trade, promoted publicly funded economic development schemes long linked in the popular mind with Republicans. It was Republican mayor Caleb Price who called for the spending cuts often associated with Democrats. He even closed the soup kitchens the city operated, alienating much of the GOP's black constituency. Black hostility, combined with opposition from the Board of Trade, proved to be Price's undoing.[68]

Ironically, the Board of Trade and pro-development Democrats joined Republicans in bringing back old Radical George F. Harrington. Leading Democrats, including William D. Mann, owner of the *Mobile Register,* cooperated with Harrington because he agreed with their pro-development philosophy. Freedmen accepted Harrington because he had been an advocate for them earlier and, as a racial moderate, did not interfere with their initiatives, such as a successful dockworkers strike in 1870 and the replacement of Star Cars with internally segregated streetcars.[69]

Moderate Democrats did not endear themselves to those in the party who wanted to pursue a whites-only electoral strategy. The white masses deeply resented Harrington and the Republicans for the role they had played in undermining the racial caste system. The white majority also rejected economic development schemes that seemed to benefit the few while increasing the taxes of the many. John Forsyth recognized the salience of the race and economic issues and urged Democrats to exploit white fears in the city elections of 1871. City Democrats followed Forsyth's advice and returned to power, electing Martin Horst mayor. Horst quickly moved to reward his supporters by replacing black policemen with whites soon after assuming office and by cutting government spending on social services. Horst continued, however, to fund loans to railroads and other ventures. When those projects failed, leaving the city deeply in debt, voters turned on the Democrats, narrowly electing a bipartisan "Citizens" ticket led by Republican C. F. Moulton. Moulton promised to cut spending but made very little progress.[70]

Defeat in 1872 pushed Democrats to even more extreme formulations of their twin themes of economy in government and white supremacy. By 1874 groups called the White Men's Association were being formed across the city. These organizations emerged from seething racial and class resentment widespread among the white voters. This racial and class hostility was particularly evident among white workers, as can be seen in the statement announcing the formation of the Eighth Ward's White Men's Association. The organization dedicated itself to doing battle against the "radicals" who sought the "annihilation of the prosperity of the South, the degradation of her people and the utter destruction of her distinct and independent nationality" through the manipulation of "former barbarian slaves." The men of the Eighth Ward sought more than social status; they demanded "an undisputed preference over their black competitors in the performance of the same work."[71]

Republicans did not help themselves with their attempt to pass a school integration law in 1873. In the campaign of 1874, Democrats in the city used the school integration issue to tap deeply felt class and racial resentment among whites. One editorial denounced the school integration plan as an attempt to "thrust the negro into the white school and drive out the whites" who paid for the schools with their taxes. Many of those who supported integration, it charged, were rich and sent their children to private schools. They wanted to "compel the poor man to see his children untaught or forced to associate with negroes upon the same bench in the school room." A call for a Democratic Conservative and White Man's Convention implored whites to join together in the struggle against "miscegenation, and the damning disgrace of subordination to race inferiority." Whites must "answer to the roll call of white supremacy over the black monkey mimics of civilization, who arrogate superiority over men whom God made their masters, not in chattel slavery of their persons, but to dominate them in intellect, in morals, in education, in courage and 'native worth.'"[72]

In a bitterly contested election, the Democrats won, and Reconstruction in Mobile came to a close. Like the secessionists of the 1850s, Democrats used the ideology of white supremacy to build an unstable coalition of groups with little in common other than race. This is not to suggest that white supremacy allowed elites to dominate. Throughout the era of the Civil War and Reconstruction, politicians struggled to control the most virulently racist among city whites. Nevertheless, pressure from the white masses repeatedly pushed politicians toward more radical formulations of the ideology of white supremacy than they might have desired. And here is the source of the racial mistrust, tension, and conflict that has been the most enduring legacy of the era of the Civil War and Reconstruction.

Suggestions for Further Reading

Amos [Doss], Harriet E. *Cotton City: Urban Development in Antebellum Mobile.* Tuscaloosa: University of Alabama Press, 1985. Currently the most complete academic study of Mobile's growth up to the Civil War.

Barney, William L. *The Secessionist Impulse: Alabama and Mississippi in 1860.* Princeton: Princeton University Press, 1974. Barney carefully explains the political strategy and tactics of secessionists during and after the national election of 1860.

Bergeron, Arthur W., Jr. *Confederate Mobile.* Jackson: University Press of Mississippi, 1991. Concerned primarily with the building and maintenance of Mobile's defenses. Life in the city during the war receives limited treatment.

Doyle, Don H. *New Men, New Cities, New South: Atlanta, Nashville, Charleston, Mobile, 1860–1910.* Chapel Hill: University of North Carolina Press, 1990. Addresses the problems Mobile faced in its effort to recover from the war in a changed regional context.

Fitzgerald, Michael W. *The Union League Movement in the Deep South: Politics and Agricultural Change during Reconstruction.* Baton Rouge: Louisiana State University Press, 1989. A good place to begin when trying to come to terms with the complicated politics of Reconstruction Republicans in Mobile.

Fleming, Walter Lynwood. *Civil War and Reconstruction in Alabama.* New York: Columbia University Press, 1905. Despite its interpretive bias, this is still the most thorough study of the period.

Saunders, Robert, Jr. *John Archibald Campbell: Southern Moderate, 1811–1889.* Tuscaloosa: University of Alabama Press, 1997. The only biography of a leading figure in Mobile politics who, as a U.S. Supreme Court justice in the 1850s, played a key role in the national debate over sectional issues.

Thornton, J. Mills. *Politics and Power in a Slave Society: Alabama, 1800–1860.* Baton Rouge: Louisiana State University Press, 1978. By far the best study of Alabama's journey to secession.

Globular jar from the Pine Log Creek site on the Alabama River. This site consists of protohistoric aboriginal burial mounds, circa 1560s.

University of South Alabama Center for Archaeological Studies, on loan to the Museum of Mobile. Photograph by Catt Sirten.

Indians inhabiting the southern region of Mobile Bay observe Pineda's ship as it sails along the shore.

Painting by Dean Mosher, 1992.

The French settlement, located at Twenty-seven Mile Bluff on the west side of Mobile River some fifty-five miles from the mouth of Mobile Bay, was protected by a wooden fort named in honor of the king.

Painting by Kate Phillips. Museum of Mobile.

A young Jean Baptiste Le Moyne de Bienville took charge of the struggling French colony after the death of his brother Iberville in 1706.

Mid-eighteenth-century painting, unidentified artist. The Historic New Orleans Collection (1990.49).

Henri de Tonti, an early explorer and the young colony's military leader, was a victim of Mobile's first yellow fever epidemic in 1704.

Painting attributed to Nicholas Maes. Museum of Mobile.

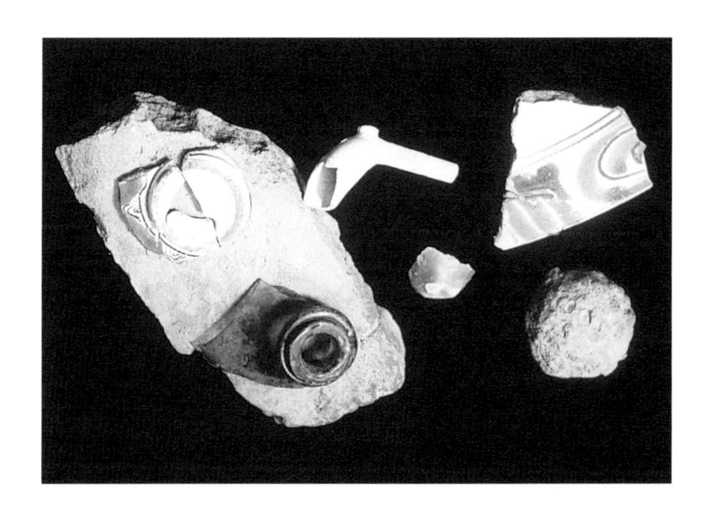

Old Mobile artifacts: brick, majolica pottery, bottle, white clay pipe, gunflint, and cannonball.

University of South Alabama Center for Archaeological Studies.

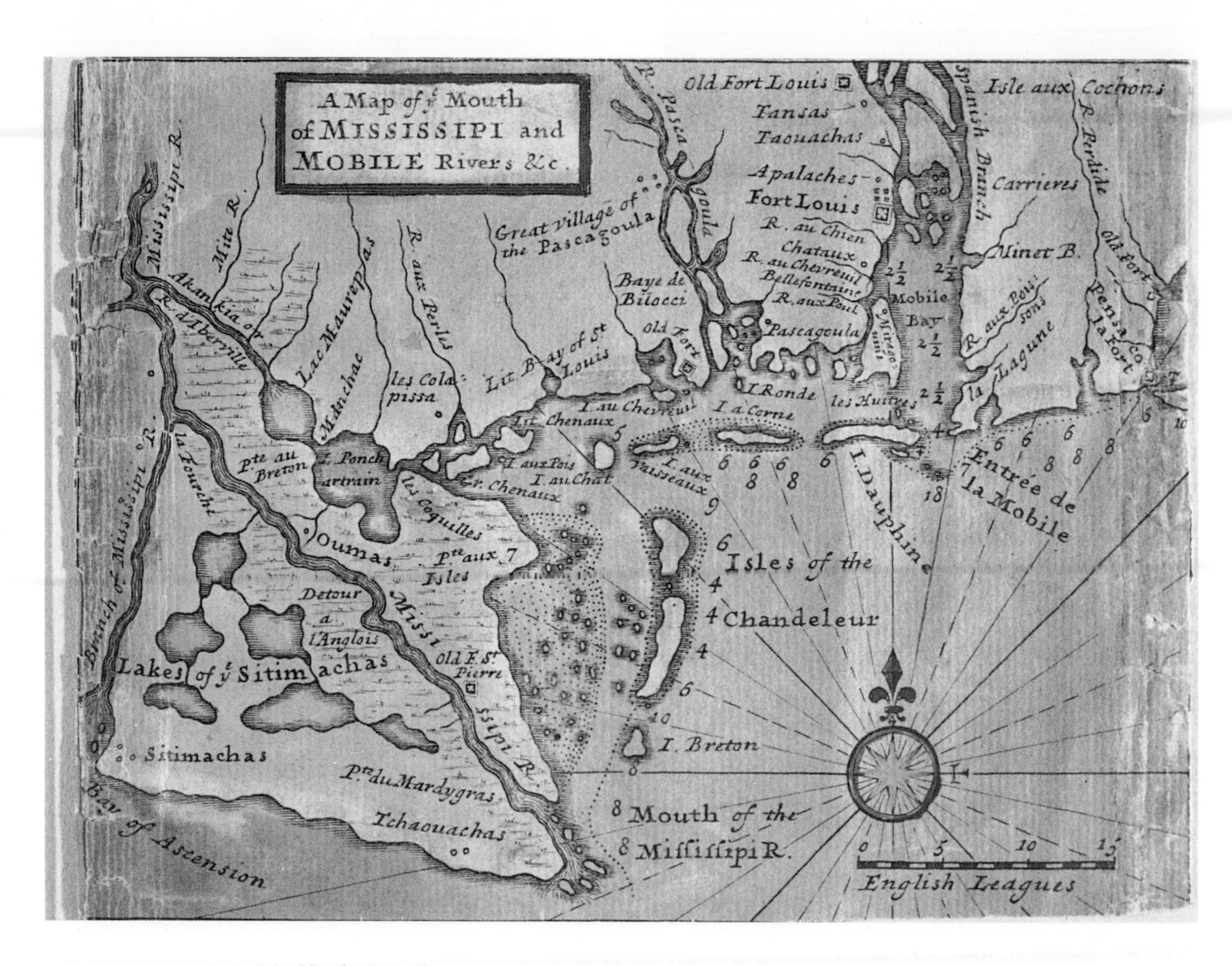

Inset of *A New Map of the North Parts of America claimed by France . . .* showing the mouth of the Mississippi and Mobile Rivers, 1720.

Drawn by Herman Moll, a Dutch cartographer living in London. Velma and Stephens Croom Collection.

Funerary tablet of a ten-year-old child, Emilie Lebec, killed by Indians on Dauphin Island in 1756.

Museum of Mobile.

Fort Condé, built by the French in the 1720s, served to defend the eastern approaches to New Orleans and protect Mobile.

Painting by Gerard Peloux. Mobile Museum of Art.

British army officer Major Robert Farmar was in charge of Mobile throughout most of the period of British rule.

Museum of Mobile.

This contemporary watercolor recorded the British attack on Fort Boyer in February of 1815. The fort stood on the site now occupied by Fort Morgan.

Mrs. Carter Smith Collection, University of South Alabama Archives.

The prosperous American Mobile viewed from the marsh opposite the city.

Painting by W. J. Bennett, 1842. Museum of Mobile.

Shallow-draft boats such as the side-wheel steamer *Swan* were used to load cotton on oceangoing ships that drew too much water to go up in the bay. The sailing ship *Isaac Bell* is anchored at Alabama Point in the lee of Dauphin Island.

Painting by J. G. Evans, circa 1850. Museum of Mobile.

This portrait of Octavia Celeste Walton Levert by Thomas Sully hangs in the Oakleigh mansion. The beautiful and witty hostess Madame Levert entertained the intellectual and social elite of Mobile at her salons during the 1850s.

Historic Mobile Preservation Society.

Oakleigh mansion was built for merchant James W. Roper circa 1833 when Mobile was fast becoming a great cotton trading port.

Photograph by Michael Thomason. USA Archives.

S. Phillip Romer's portrait titled *Choctaw Belle* is a reminder of Mobile's colonial heritage. The Bavarian-born artist worked in the Mobile area during the 1850s and 1860s.

Washington and Lee University.

Cotton fortunes built many other fine homes. The Fort Condé-Charlotte House, built circa 1845, used part of the walls of a jail constructed in 1822–24.

Photograph by Michael Thomason. USA Archives.

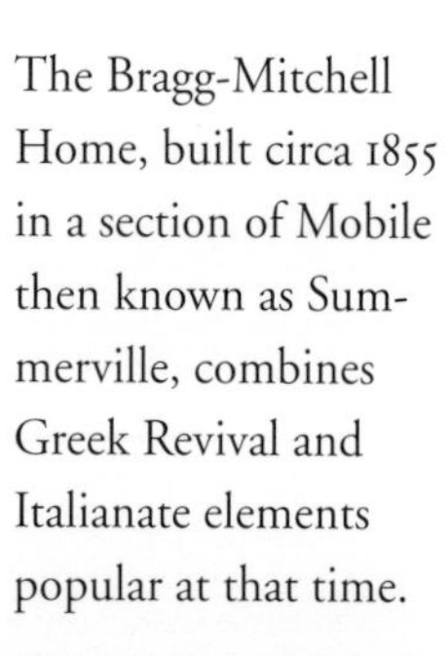

The Bragg-Mitchell Home, built circa 1855 in a section of Mobile then known as Summerville, combines Greek Revival and Italianate elements popular at that time.

Photograph by Michael Thomason. USA Archives.

Mobile's carnival began on New Year's Eve in 1830 when Michael Krafft and some friends paraded with hoes and rakes after an evening of drinking. By 1859 his Cowbellian de Rakin Society born on that night celebrated at the Battle House.

Local History Division, Mobile Public Library.

This large brick townhouse with Italianate detailing was built on Conti Street in 1867 for Martin Horst who later became mayor of Mobile.

USA Archives.

The old city prison and police station, built 1839–41, had a watch tower to look out for fires and civil disturbances.

From Ballou, *Pictorial Drawing Room Companion,* June 16, 1857.

Fire marks placed outside homes and businesses indicated that the structure was covered by fire insurance. The fire companies, all volunteer until 1888, responded more quickly to fires in buildings with these plaques.

Museum of Mobile.

Spring Hill College, the oldest Catholic college in the South and one of the first two colleges in the state, was founded in 1830. The administration building pictured here replaced the original structure, which burned in 1869. Its dome was twice destroyed by storm and fire.

Hand-colored postcard, St. John Collection, USA Archives.

City hall, now home to the Museum of Mobile, was constructed circa 1856–57. The building housed both the municipal government and the Southern Market.

Drawing by Nicholas H. Holmes III, 1982, based on plans in the Historic American Buildings Survey Collection, Library of Congress. USA Archives.

As wartime shortages grew, lack of basic food stuffs prompted a civil disturbance by hundreds of Mobile women on September 4, 1863

Illustration from *Pictorial War Record, Battles of the Late Civil War,* September 1, 1883.

Farragut's fleet in front of Fort Morgan. The Union ironclad *Tecumseh,* having hit a mine, is seen capsized and sinking.

Painting by Xanthus Smith, circa 1865–70. AmSouth Bank Collection.

View of the Battle of Mobile Bay from the water battery at Fort Morgan. The painter, Nicola Marschall, also designed the first national flag and the army uniform of the Confederacy.

Museum of Mobile.

FRANK LESLIE'S ILLUSTRATED NEWSPAPER

No. 475—Vol. XIX.] NEW YORK, NOVEMBER 5, 1864. [Price 10 Cents.

The lighthouse at Fort Morgan after the surrender, August 22, 1864.

Frank Leslie's *Illustrated Newspaper,* November 5, 1864.

Sketches by George Watters of the magazine explosion at Mobile, May 25, 1865, and the subsequent conflagration.

Harper's Weekly, June 24, 1865.

CHAPTER 5

The New South Era in Mobile, 1875–1900

George Ewert

PERHAPS NO PERIOD OF Mobile history saw the conflicting themes of continuity and change more boldly at work than the last quarter of the nineteenth century. During these years Mobile experienced dramatic changes as it adapted to postwar conditions and reacted to the technological and economic changes moving across America. While experiencing such changes, however, Mobile continued to cling to much that was traditional in origin. Institutions, habits, attitudes, practices, and ways of life and business fostered in the colonial and antebellum periods continued despite the growing pace of change. By the turn of the twentieth century, Mobile was eager for the prosperity and novelty promised by the new century but also sought to keep its historic legacy intact.

This era of contradictions is also one that witnessed what many historians describe as the bleakest series of events in the city's history. It was a time of economic depression and municipal insolvency that drove Mobile into receivership and bankruptcy and brought average citizens and civic leaders alike to the brink of despair. The long-anticipated resolution of the unstable state of political affairs appeared nowhere in sight until the last decade of the century.

The financial crisis of the first half of the period capped a long downhill slide in Mobile's finances that had begun before the war, a slide made much worse by the war and its aftermath. Yet, once bottom was reached and the problem of the city's massive indebtedness and the political and economic indiscipline that brought it on was faced and dealt with, Mobile and its citizens did finally begin a measured pace of economic development and progress.

This long decline and slow recovery during the late nineteenth century took place while Mobile and its local institutions and traditions were increasingly moving into the mainstream of national life. The period concludes with the turning

Bienville Square has been a popular place to promenade since the 1850s. The fountain was installed in 1890 in honor of Dr. George A. Ketchum, president of the Bienville Water Works.

Mobile in Photo-Gravure: From Recent Negatives (1892).

point in national history that was the Spanish-American War of 1898 and the beginning of the Progressive Era. For Mobile and its citizens the successful war with Spain opened new markets, brought new opportunities, and perhaps created a sense of closure on the city's recent harsh past.

The last quarter of the nineteenth century began in Mobile with the chaos and disorder of the election of November 1874. Commonly known as the "Redemption" election, it was an all-out war waged by the state's Democrats to take back political power from the Republicans, who had dominated politics since the advent of congressional Reconstruction in May 1867. The Democrats sought to "save" the state from the policies and practices, many of them corrupt or at least badly conceived and managed, that had come to characterize Republican Reconstruction government.

To ensure the appearance of a large mandate and to quash Republican efforts to create a two-party system in Alabama, Democrats around the state resorted to extreme measures in keeping black and suspected non-Democratic voters from the polls in November 1874. In Mobile, political terrorism became the order of the day. Fearful that an honest election would not produce the landslide victory and appearance of the mandate they sought, the local Democratic Party used drastic measures to insure success. Armed gangs roamed the streets, threatening voters at gunpoint the day of the election. Mobs gathered around polling places and allowed only Democratic sympathizers to vote. Ballot boxes were stuffed and counts altered as the Democrats tried to steal the election.[1]

Across the state the election was so massively fraudulent that a special congressional committee was formed to tour Alabama and investigate the worst trouble spots, including Mobile. Their aim was to decide whether a recommendation to void the entire election should be made to Congress. After many hours of interviews documenting abuses, the committee in 1875 published the results in a thirteen-hundred-page special report. It concluded that although widespread abuses had occurred, for the sake of national political harmony, the results should stand. The Democrats had indeed stolen the election.[2]

Even though the Democrats returned to overall control of state and local politics in 1874, this situation did nothing to settle local issues in Mobile. Local politics after the election were as chaotic and confused as they had been during Reconstruction. Grievances with and animosity between supporters of the two parties were bitter and lingered long after the election of 1874. With a large, active, and competently led urban black population and a number of whites sympathetic to the Republican Party and its liberal business agenda, the Redemption of the state's largest city was not assured. Unable to achieve a balance in city government that allowed for the harmonious participation of all interests, the political roulette that characterized this government during Reconstruction continued through Redemption and the 1880s.

The election of November 1874 brought local Democrat Alphonse Hurtel into the mayor's office, but it did not end the city's uncertain future. Hurtel was well liked in Mobile, and his ancestors were originally members of the Vine and Olive colony, which had settled near Demopolis after fleeing France. Born in Greensboro in the 1820s, Hurtel came to Mobile in 1830 with his parents and was educated at Spring Hill College. He studied law in Greensboro, took up practice in Mobile, but soon moved to San Antonio, where he was elected judge of probate. By 1860 he was back in Mobile as the city attorney. During the Civil War he served in the Gulf City Guards. In 1870 the *Mobile Daily Tribune* described a model farm he operated near Fulton and a social function that took place there. A respected Presbyterian and staunch Democrat, Hurtel was an ideal choice to end Reconstruction in Mobile. Unfortunately, he died in office in August 1877, only the second of Mobile's mayors to do so by this time, the first being Mayor John Stocking in 1834.[3]

The central issue facing the Hurtel administration was the problem of the city's indebtedness. This issue of fiscal mismanagement, created by the city's past willingness to fund private projects without regard to their soundness, had plagued Mobile's government for years. During Reconstruction the debt problem grew worse with the knowing and willful involvement of Mobile's white commercial elite and their schemes to increase economic activity in Mobile by having the city bear the risk. Now the Democrats blamed the problem of paying back the borrowed money on Reconstruction and Republican and black political abuse and corruption since the war.[4]

Like most cities, Mobile had often borrowed money to help pay for municipal services, but Mobile's track record of managing such debts was a dismal one indeed. While still officially a town early in the nineteenth century, it had begun to contract debts for purposes such as improving city streets. The first important bond issue was in 1830 for $30,000 at 8 percent. In 1834 this was increased by $200,000 at 6 percent and by the same amount again in 1836. More debt was taken on in 1839, raising the total to $513,000. Obligations for outstanding Creek War debts, the cost of a new guardhouse, and unpaid "coupons" on previous bonds brought the total up to $650,000. This debt and the lingering financial chaos brought about by the Panic of 1837 resulted in the first city bankruptcy on February 11, 1843, just twenty-nine years after Mobile became an American municipality.[5] The debt was settled through

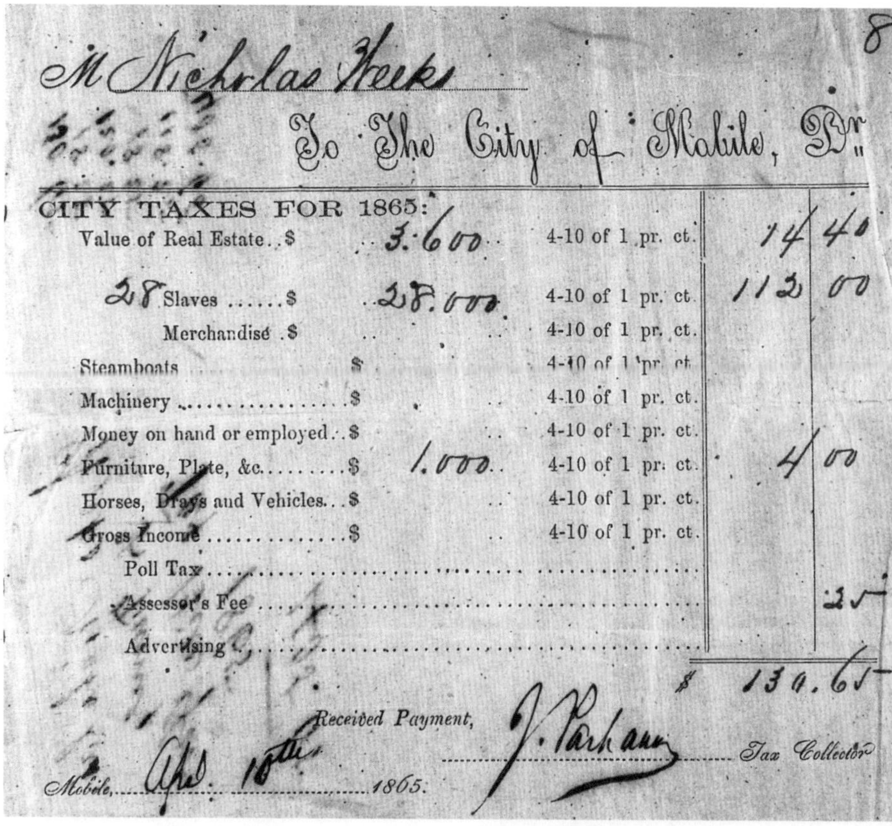
M Nicholas Weeks

To The City of Mobile, Dr.

CITY TAXES FOR 1865:

Value of Real Estate ..$	3.600	4-10 of 1 pr. ct.	14 40
28 Slaves ......$	28.000	4-10 of 1 pr. ct.	112 00
Merchandise .$		4-10 of 1 pr. ct.	
Steamboats $		4-10 of 1 pr. ct.	
Machinery ....$		4-10 of 1 pr. ct.	
Money on hand or employed ..$		4-10 of 1 pr. ct.	
Furniture, Plate, &c. ....$	1.000	4-10 of 1 pr. ct.	4 00
Horses, Drays and Vehicles ..$		4-10 of 1 pr. ct.	
Gross Income ....$		4-10 of 1 pr. ct.	
Poll Tax			
Assessor's Fee			25
Advertising			
		$	130.65

Received Payment, J. Parham Tax Collector

Mobile, April 18th 1865.

Mobile tax receipt for 1865. After the war, the city could no longer collect one of its major sources of antebellum revenue, taxes paid on slaves.

Historic Mobile Preservation Society.

the efforts of court-appointed bankruptcy commissioner S. P. Bullard, who that year arranged for its consolidation. Also included in the funding was accrued interest and the city's various floating debts. This amount, $706,191.18, was financed with new bonds of $100, $500, and $1,000 each.[6]

This embarrassing bankruptcy episode incurred a political cost. It came on January 15, 1844, when the city was forced into reorganization by legislative act. This was not the first alteration in municipal organization in the life of Mobile as an American city; there had been several previous changes. At its start the town, while still in the Mississippi territory, incorporated on January 20, 1814, and was governed by a board of commissioners who chose a president to be the town's executive officer. When Mobile became a city in the new state of Alabama on December 17, 1819, it adopted a mayor and aldermanic form of government. In 1840 this was changed to add a common council to sit beside the aldermen as a second legislative body as the city wrestled to adjust to the economic straits in which it found itself. The several acts that provided for these changes also detail other modifications in city organization and function. The 1844 reorganization of Mobile's city government was a lengthy one that consolidated all previous acts and ordinances and laid out the boundaries of seven wards, which were set out in full in the act. It would stand until after the Civil War with several modifications regarding wharves, paving, street railroads, and other such revisions.[7]

Despite the new 1844 government and the refunded city debt, there was no respite in city borrowing. In 1856 bonds were issued to fund the construction of the Mobile and Great Northern Railroad. The railroad failed, and its assets were later bought by the Mobile and Montgomery Railroad, which in turn became the Louisville and Nashville. Also, the city decided to build a new pair of public markets and to pay for their construction through a bond issue. Only one was eventually built, the Southern Market, which opened in 1858 at an estimated cost overrun of at least 100 percent. The actual cost is unknown due to a "mysterious" fire that destroyed the receipts and bills while the project was under construction. Thus, the city was still heavily in debt with the outbreak of war.[8]

Alphonse Hurtel was very aware of the financial condition of Mobile when he became mayor and had made political capital from the large increase of the debt during the recent Reconstruction years. Had not the Panic of 1873 occurred along with the resulting international depression, some of the Reconstruction railroad projects might have succeeded. By 1875, however, the city debt had reached more than $5 million. Not only was the city unable to make payments of the amount due, it could not even pay the interest.[9]

In 1875 the city mounted a major refunding effort, but only after grudging acknowledgment and admission that the city government had broken down under the weight of its debt. Some hoped that another major funding bailout could be accomplished quickly and that it would be as successful as the one in 1843 had been. Some creditors, however, refusing to compromise, had already gone into federal court and received a judgment against the city, a mandamus tax imposed by the court for partial payment of outstanding debts. Once again bankruptcy loomed. No quick settlement was possible, and the debt issue dragged on until 1879.[10]

The long delay was caused by two factors. One was the lack of unanimity on the terms of settlement or on how to proceed. Local leaders differed over how much of the debt to ask to be to scaled off, over what rate of interest the refunding should carry, and on how much the city should be asked to secure. The second factor was that the debt issue became embroiled in local politics. When Alphonse Hurtel died in office in 1877, Daniel P. Bestor Jr. was appointed to replace him. Bestor was the child of a Baptist minister from Connecticut who relocated to Alabama about 1819. His son Daniel was born in Greensboro and educated at the University of Mississippi. He studied law in the office of Robert H. Smith in Mobile and was admitted to the bar in 1867 after his war service with the Thirty-seventh Mississippi Regular Infantry. Like his father he was a Baptist and a prohibitionist.[11]

In the next city election the Democratic Party did not nominate Bestor for mayor but instead chose Palmer J. Pillans as their candidate. Pillans was defeated on December 18, 1877, in a close election by a "fusion" candidate, George Gillespie Duffee. Duffee was the nominee of the People's Party, whose composition was a blend of political interests that included support for the right of blacks to vote. He

The Mobile and Alabama Grand Trunk Rail Road Company

Number

Shares

Be it known that

Mobile

Bankruptcies became common after the Civil War. The Mobile and Alabama Grand Trunk Railroad Company went bankrupt after constructing only fifty-nine miles of track.

Historic Mobile Preservation Society.

was denounced by the city's Democratic Party organ, the *Mobile Register,* as a Communist.[12]

Duffee was the son of an Irish immigrant from Tipperary who had settled in Blount Springs. Distantly related to President James K. Polk, Duffee's grandfather had served with Andrew Jackson in Tennessee. George Duffee was born in 1835 in Tuscaloosa, where he attended private school. During the war he was a major in the Third Alabama Infantry regiment and the Mobile Rifles. Afterward he entered the cotton business and worked to found his own firm. He died in 1886 at his home on what is now Caroline Avenue, leaving a widow and nine children. His property is marked by the famed three-hundred-year-old "Duffee Oak," which still stands.[13]

Duffee ran for mayor as a reform or compromise candidate representing a blend of interests. Although not a Republican and not running as one, he nonetheless had close ties to noted local Republicans. He was married to Harriet Amanda Horton, daughter of former Republican Mobile mayor Gustavus Horton, a marriage that linked him with Mobile's first Reconstruction mayor. In his successful campaign for mayor, Duffee convinced voters that the responsibility for the city's current financial plight lay not with Reconstruction or Republican practices but with local Democrats. During the election campaign of 1874, extravagant campaign promises had been made by the Democrats. They had pledged to correct the city's financial difficulties and redress the reputed corruption and fraud of the Reconstruction Republicans. Duffee held all this up to public scrutiny in his 1877 campaign, claiming that the Democrats had failed to fulfill their promises. The period historians now call Mobile's "seven year depression," 1878 to 1885, had begun.[14]

As mayor, Duffee wanted to seek a settlement on the debt issue, but he was opposed to a "dishonest repudiation." While he argued with other local leaders who wanted to move quickly on the issue, the situation grew progressively worse. So terrible had things become that a January 1879 editorial in the *Mobile Register* bluntly stated that the city was in default of all its obligations, that the interest on these loans had not been paid, that its change bills were being sold at a terrible discount, and that its warrants were growing more worthless every day.[15]

In anticipation that drastic measures would be needed to relieve the city, a group of citizens, primarily Democrats, had been working to put together a plan. It involved two relief bills composed by distinguished Mobile lawyers including Hannis Taylor, Peter Hamilton, and John Little Smith and advanced by a number of other noted citizens. The bills were sent to the state legislature in the absence of any concrete alternative from Duffee's administration. They provided a mechanism by which the city would free itself from the real threat of a court takeover.[16]

The two bills were complementary. The first repealed the city charter, thereby abolishing the City of Mobile along with all its municipal positions and officials. It provided that the governor appoint three "Commissioners of Mobile" who would be responsible for taking charge of all city assets and the collection of all back taxes and dues assessed by the late city. These funds would then be used to pay for the settlement of the former city's debts. The commissioners, as financial agents, would also be responsible for negotiating the best possible settlement of the debt with its creditors and to send the agreement to the legislature for ratification.[17]

The second bill set up a new government for the former city of Mobile, now to be called the "Port of Mobile." The act specified details concerning the selection of officials and how they would be chosen and how the city would operate. The bill provided for the selection of eight port commissioners to be chosen by the legislature to act as municipal administrators. These eight were called the police board, and their duties were comparable to those of a city council: the board was to assume control over the city and to provide services to the citizens. The expenses for operating the new Port of Mobile were limited by law to only $100,000 annually, less than half of what the former city had expended for basic services. To pay for these expenses the police board had limited power to levy and collect taxes and under certain conditions to borrow money for current expenditures, but they were to have nothing to do with the settlement of the outstanding debts.[18]

Mayor Duffee opposed these bills on the grounds that they took away the right of the citizens to self-government and because he believed that any debt settlement that scaled off more than 60 percent, which the commissioners had a right to try to achieve, was dishonest. On January 20 the mayor spoke against the bills at an invitation-only meeting held at the courthouse to consider them. Nevertheless, at a meeting of the board of aldermen the next day that body, by a vote of seventeen to thirteen, recommended the bills be sent to the legislature. This recommendation was passed over the objection of Mayor Duffee, who then prepared and circulated a petition opposing enactment. He later sent the petition to the legislature.[19]

Despite Duffee's petition, the state passed the two bills into law on February 11, 1879, and set the calendar for the transfer of Mobile's government to the Commissioners of Mobile and the Port of Mobile. The only substantive change was in the second bill. It allowed the eight police board commissioners to be elected from the city wards rather than be appointed. Duffee had become a "lame duck" mayor.[20]

On February 18 Mayor Duffee read a letter at the board of aldermen's meeting announcing that he would comply with a notice recently served to him by the newly appointed commissioners of Mobile for the formal delivery of all city buildings and other properties and that he, as instructed, would hold the property in the name of the police board until noon March 15, the time and date the board was to take over. The aldermen expressed some bitterness at this meeting over the coming change in government and their position. Alderman James McConnell moved that a reading of the papers of the commissioners be dispensed with but was reminded that courtesy demanded they be read. He then sarcastically proposed that the annual report of the chief of police "might as well be put in the stove."[21]

On March 1 the announcement was made of the coming election of the eight police board commissioners. In addition to a Democratic/Conservative ticket, a Republican and Citizens' ticket was proposed. On election day, March 11, all candidates on the Democratic ticket were elected. Former mayor Duffee, who campaigned for a position on the police board in his district, received the fewest votes of any candidate.[22]

At its first meeting on Saturday, March 15, the new police board quickly conferred temporary appointments on the city clerk and police department officials to insure some continuity of law and order and then adjourned. On March 18 they reconvened to elect the president of the police board and the recorder, both to be held by the same person, to take the place of mayor under the Port of Mobile. After twenty-seven ballots, R. B. Owen was elected president and recorder. Fellow board members Palmer J. Pillans and Price Williams Sr. had also sought the positions.[23]

Richard Brown Owen was a local businessman and attorney who was born in Franklin, Tennessee. He had moved to Mobile at age twelve and was educated at Spring Hill College and at the University of Alabama. He read law in the office of Judge John A. Campbell, was elected to the Alabama legislature before the war, and was an official of the Mobile and Spring Hill Railroad Company. During the war he was an adjutant to Confederate general Dabney Maury. He was a Democrat and an Episcopalian. He had a very conservative business sense and was considered an excellent choice to see the city through the trials of experimental government.[24]

Meanwhile, the Commissioners of Mobile, charged to accomplish a workable debt settlement, were preparing to go about their task. The three appointed commission members, Lorenzo M. Wilson, William J. Hearin, and James A. McCaw, presented their commissions in Mobile to chancery court chancellor Hurieosco Austill on February 16 when they took their oath of office and filled their bonds. The chancellor reviewed their papers, and on March 15, 1879, the three commissioners officially took charge of the city's property and assets.[25]

Once legally in place, the commissioners attacked the debt problem. In a report issued on March 8, 1880, they summarized their progress: since taking charge a year before, the floating debt of the former city was reduced from $120,000 to less than $32,000. They publicly thanked the citizens who came forward to pay their back taxes and criticized those who had yet to do so. More than half of the interest on the funded debt of 1876 was also paid. They had made substantial progress toward payment of the total debt, but the question of the bonded debt had yet to be faced.[26]

The commissioners opened talks with Mobile's bond creditors and found that they faced immediate difficulties. On the whole the bond holders were disposed to take the entire matter to the federal courts because the state had ended the legal existence of the City of Mobile and therefore no regular process existed by which they could recover their investments. A meeting was scheduled with New York creditors for October 1878. Initially, it went badly for the commissioners because the creditors refused to discuss terms, believing that the commissioners' efforts were just another step in repudiation. The negotiations turned around, however, when William Butler Duncan interceded with the creditors on the commission's behalf. He explained that the action by the Alabama legislature revoking Mobile's charter did not mean the people of Mobile were trying to repudiate or default on the debt, that the commissioners had come to New York in the manner of insolvent merchants who were honestly trying to make a fair settlement that would stand up over time, and that they were therefore entitled to patient consideration. This intercession softened the creditors' attitude and brought the two parties into talks that resulted in an agreement that was subsequently ratified by the Alabama legislature on December 8, 1880.[27]

In this agreement the creditors liberally reduced the debt to fifty-one cents on the dollar, recognizing that for all the expenditure the city had made in bonds since the war it had received virtually nothing. This amount actually exceeded the railroad "endorsements" and removed some of the prewar or "ancestral debt" as well. Nevertheless, the creditors, being familiar with the city's history of failed attempts to refinance its debt and to handle the bond question, insisted on the creation of a separate settlement trust department. This department would be paid for out of the three-quarters of 1 percent per year the commissioners agreed to pay on the assessed value of property within the limits of the former city of Mobile toward the debt.[28]

The agreement forwarded to the governor for the state's approval provided for a twenty-five year debt repayment period. All the old bonds would be exchanged for new ones paying 3 percent per year for the first five years, 4 percent for the next fifteen, and 5 percent for the last five. The new bonds would be issued on January 1, 1881.[29] This settlement did not satisfy all the bond holders, and several filed suit against the Port of Mobile for recovery of their investments.

The port had in the interim convinced the Commissioners of Mobile and the legislature to sign over all the city's former property to it in 1881 in order to perform city services better. This action made the port the municipal equivalent to the former city of Mobile in all but name.[30]

The act that had established the Commissioners of Mobile provided that their terms would expire on February 15, 1883, and that their offices would be replaced by a single trustee to manage the outstanding debt payments. Lorenzo M. Wilson was the first trustee and served until 1886 when Zeb M. P. Inge was appointed. In

1905 Inge would brag that all suits, judgments, and other claims arising out of the old debt settlement issue were made for at least 50 percent of their value. The debt problem was finally settled in 1906 with payment of the last note, on time as scheduled.[31]

With the selection of Richard B. Owen as president and recorder and the selection of a staff of city officers, the Port of Mobile was ready to begin functioning. Whether by accident or by design, however, the legislative acts that created the Commissioners of Mobile and the police board did not allow for reelection once the initial two-year terms ended. To remedy this situation the legislature, on December 8, 1880, authorized the port officials to continue in their positions until March 1882. At that time an election of new board members, a president, and a tax collector would take place. Thereafter, elections would be held every three years. It is no surprise that in the elections of 1882 and 1885 the Democrats carried almost all offices, and Owen was reelected president each time.[32]

By 1885 the issue of the city debt had diminished; even though it was not completely resolved, it was reduced to a manageable problem. The new government was producing sufficient tax revenue to pay its obligations, but this success came at the cost of creating a municipal administration that was essentially a caretaker government holding the city together until the financial storm could be weathered.

Because the debt issue was no longer a pressing one and because the economy of Mobile was slowly recovering from the seven-year depression, the restrictions on city government voluntarily accepted in 1879 increasingly seemed a handicap and irritation. Citizens and community leaders began to look beyond mere survival and noticed that for seven years the city had stagnated with no improvements in roads and drainage, a clean water supply, or professional fire protection. Whereas other cities' basic services had improved during this period, Mobile's had languished.

Dissatisfied with the status quo, citizens moved to change the form of Mobile's government again. They wished to regain the city's fiscal autonomy, including the right to spend more than one hundred thousand dollars a year. On December 10, 1886, a bill was passed by the Alabama legislature establishing a new government for Mobile. The bill created a board of aldermen, a general council, and a mayor. The existing president and police board continued in office temporarily, but the names of their positions changed to mayor and councilmen, respectively. An election for the seven aldermen to be chosen at large was slated for the first Monday in March 1887. This term was for one year and thereafter for three years. The election of the eight councilmen, one from each ward, and the mayor was to take place the first Monday in March 1888. Each was to hold a term of three years. The mayor and general council form of government continued in Mobile until 1911, when a Progressive Era reform replaced it with a three-person city commission.[33] The transition to the new mayor and general council form of city government in 1887

Joseph Carlos Rich.

Erik Overbey Collection, USA Archives.

marked the end of the twenty-three-year period of civic instability and institutional uncertainty Mobile had experienced since the end of the Civil War.

The boundaries of the new City of Mobile were the same as the reduced boundaries of the port. When the Port of Mobile was created the western boundaries of the city were contracted to reduce the expense of services in sparsely populated areas. These boundaries would remain until 1896, when the city would reclaim its 1878 limits in an effort to give the impression of having a growing population. Throughout this era, however, the white population grew slowly in Mobile. For example, in 1860 Mobile County had 28,559 white residents. In 1890 it had only 28,369. By 1900 numbers were up to 34,306. The black population of Mobile County, in contrast, showed a marked increase. In 1860 it was 12,571. In 1890 it was 22,804, and by 1900 it was 28,409. In 1900 the population of the city of Mobile itself was approximately forty thousand.[34]

A new mayor was elected in 1888: Mobile lawyer Joseph Carlos Rich. During the campaign, Rich was considered to be a more active and progressive candidate than his opponent, the sixty-year-old Richard Owen. Owen's reputation as having been a good port president and latter-day mayor and being responsible for overseeing the city's survival during the port administration brought him respect and votes but not enough to defeat the young, energetic lawyer. Rich, born in Perry County,

Alabama, was only twenty-nine when he took office. Educated at the University of Mississippi and Vanderbilt University, he had adapted well to Mobile after establishing his law practice in the city in 1881. In 1882 he was elected to the police board, and in 1885 he married into a long-established local family when he wed Mary Toulmin.[35] Rich came into the position of mayor riding the wave of sentiment in Mobile that longed to see it move beyond the sacrifices and frugality that had dominated the city since the bankruptcy of 1879.

Armed with the new city charter, Mayor Rich and the new administration were now far freer to run the city than the old Port of Mobile had been, and they began a wave of improvements in basic services. Aware that such improvements did not come without a cost, however, the new city fathers were watchful about expenditures. One basic service improvement that had been eyed for years involved a return to a traditional source of income for the city, one that, if as lucrative as it had been before the war, would yield substantial revenue for other needs such as street paving. This initiative was a return to the municipal market monopoly on the sale of fresh foods.

Mobile had operated public markets from the earliest colonial days, as had many cities. Public markets as institutions were strongest in seaports that experienced a long period of European occupation and still had citizens who identified with their Old World roots. One of Mobile's first acts after becoming an American town was to organize a public market located at the foot of Dauphin Street on the north side. Along with the market came ordinances restricting the sale of certain fresh foods to

Leaven Watters had a butcher stall at the city-run Central Market in the 1890s.

USA Archives.

the market stall vendors. In 1823 this market was replaced by one in the middle of Government Street between Royal Street and the Mobile River. Two smaller markets were later added on Mobile's western side, one at the intersection of Dauphin Street and Springhill Avenue and the other further out at Springhill Avenue and Ann Street. By 1858 the Government Street Market was replaced by the Southern Market on the corner of Royal and Church Streets. This large complex of four buildings covered two-thirds of the block.[36]

With the expansion and renovation of the public market system, most fresh food vendors had to lease space in the markets. The stalls were auctioned off each year. This activity produced a great deal of revenue for the city and enabled it to police food quality and weights and measures. Each market was supervised by a market clerk. A fourth market, the Washington Market on the corner of Savanna and Scott Streets, was added for the south side of town in 1867 just before the advent of Radical Reconstruction in Mobile.[37]

Reconstruction mayor Gustavus Horton, believing the market system to be archaic, unenlightened, and responsible for artificially high prices, had broken the monopoly by no longer confining fresh food sales to the public markets. He instituted an ordinance creating a "green grocer" system of food sales common in the cities in the interior whereby grocers, retailers of nonperishable foods, could sell fresh meat, fish, and vegetables. Revenue from the markets rapidly declined, and so did attention to their care and maintenance. Some vendors continued to occupy stalls there because there was little competition and they were leased at a low fixed rate.[38]

Two decades later Mayor Rich and the general council viewed a return to Mobile's public market system and its monopoly as a way to raise revenue. On February 4, 1888, they repealed the green grocer ordinance. The monopoly on the sale of fresh foods at public market locations was reinstituted and even strengthened. Net revenue was earmarked for street department expenditures. The city renovated the four markets and repaired and added a fifth market, called the Orange Grove Market, on the north side of town. Although the new arrangement was popular, some grocers did not want to give up fresh food retailing at their shops. One grocer challenged the market ordinance in a lawsuit. Eventually the state supreme court upheld the city's right to form such a system.[39]

The municipal market produced a net revenue of more than $6,000 in its first year of operation despite the cost of purchasing the Orange Grove Market and renovating the other four. Although they were not producing the level of income experienced before the war, the markets continued to be an important revenue stream for the city. The market monopoly remained intact until after the turn of the century. The last public market in Mobile, the Southern Market, did not cease all food sales until September 1942.[40]

Public market reform was not particularly controversial. The opposite was the case when creating a professional fire department. Nevertheless, in September 1888 the city ended perhaps the most popular and entrenched tradition of nineteenth-century Mobile—volunteer fire companies.

Fires in cities without ample and steady running water, with predominantly wooden buildings, each with hearth fires inside for heating or cooking, were a constant and serious threat to individual and public safety. To protect against this threat Mobile, like other cities, organized formal units of volunteer citizens into fire companies to respond in the event of fire. These companies were separate legal entities chartered by the legislature. Each had a constitution and bylaws, operated its own budget, held regular meetings, recruited its own members, and elected its own officers. All joined the Fire Department Association, which, though partially funded by the city, was not under its control or jurisdiction. The self-regulated volunteer fire companies were powerful paramilitary organizations that possessed great political and social influence.

By 1888 nine active and one inactive volunteer fire companies existed. Each had a membership of from 80 to 120 and an even larger number of honorary members. Membership was by invitation only and conferred on the bearer unique status,

Although the public markets held a monopoly on the sale of fresh food after 1888, a few products such as watermelons, eggs, and cured meats were still sold in grocery stores such as Yocker's.

William E. Wilson Collection, Historic Mobile Preservation Society.

privilege, and respect, as well as enhanced social and business connections. Members were exempt from military service and certain taxes but were expected to be on call twenty-four hours a day, every day of the year. Each company had its own firehouse where it sponsored exclusive social events such as balls and cotillions as fund-raisers to supplement income from membership dues and fines.

Every year the fire companies had an annual parade on April 9, which was the highlight of the spring social season. For many years it was as popular, or more popular, than Mardi Gras. The volunteer companies had become the social backbone of

The volunteer Creole Steam Fire Company, founded in 1819, became part of the city's professional fire department in 1888. Their firehouse still stands.

Souvenir History of the Mobile Fire and Police Departments (1902).

Mobile's elite. Among the companies was the Creole Steam Fire Company Number 1. Formed in 1819, it was one of the two oldest companies in Mobile. This non-white unit had an active women's auxiliary and served as a focal point for Mobile's Creole community as it tried to protect its declining status in local society.[41]

Late in the 1880s several incidents occurred that reflected badly on the volunteer fire companies and stimulated interest in replacing them with a paid professional force. One way the volunteer companies earned income was from insurance firms who paid a bounty to the company arriving first at a fire. Several firemen, or their agents, were accused of starting fires so their company could be the first to arrive and thus get that bounty. Also, occasionally fights broke out between companies getting to a fire at about the same time as each tried to drive off the other to claim the bounty. In one instance, while the companies battled each other, the building in question continued to burn, thus causing more damage and danger than if both companies had cooperated to fight the fire instead of each other. In July 1888 Mayor Rich noted that Mobile had twice the number of firemen as any city its size and still did not have adequate fire protection. Meanwhile, the Fire Department Association asserted that the city was not making proper payment for its services and threatened to close the firehouses and go on strike.[42]

Attempts to avert this catastrophe through negotiations went nowhere. A strike deadline was set for midnight, September 1. That day Mayor Rich reassured the public he would do everything in his power to insure fire protection for Mobile. He then tried to buy whatever fire-fighting equipment he could get his hands on and succeeded in buying all the equipment of the Merchants Steam Fire Company Number 4. He also enrolled the entire Creole Steam Fire Company Number 1 (they had surrendered their affiliation with the Fire Department Association) into the new municipal force, complete with all their equipment, as the city's first paid company. Thus strengthened, Rich moved to take possession of equipment, especially hoses, that the city had previously purchased for use by the other volunteer companies and to seize the Franklin Company Number 3 hook and ladder, also paid for by the city.[43]

Former volunteer fire chief Matt Sloan was made the chief of the new paid force and went to each firehouse to inform the firemen of the city's takeover. At the Franklin Company house, violence threatened to break out. A group of volunteer firemen had plans to take the hook and ladder at midnight and conceal it. The presence of police chief Hope H. Slatter, who had accompanied Sloan, however, calmed the situation. A special citizens' committee was subsequently formed to organize formally a paid municipal fire department, which was created on September 8, 1888. In the end a number of former volunteers moved into the new paid force. The traditional April 9 parade ended, and the social and political advantage of being a volunteer fireman was over. In exchange Mobile received a fire-fighting force under city control and could move to professionalize fire protection.[44]

Another basic service that cried out for the new administration's attention was the care of city streets. They were in very bad condition after years of neglect, and street improvement was a pressing need. Early in 1889 A. C. Danner, local businessman and lumber magnate, proposed a plan to pave Dauphin Street between Royal Street and Claiborne Street, then the city's most heavily used street, with closely laid cypress blocks placed over a foundation of cypress planks and filled in with sand. Danner had already paved a section on Government Street west of Broad Street as a demonstration and hoped to get a contract from the city for further work. The cost of the Dauphin Street paving was to be paid for by the city, the Mobile Light and Railroad Company, and the property owners who fronted the area to be paved.[45]

This was not the first effort to find a solution to the problems of street improvement in a city where most streets were still sand and mud. In early Mobile, streets were said to be engineered on the model of a hog wallow, that is, with the outer edges higher than the middle, thus forming a central bog that retained water and deposited the gutter's contents into the middle of the street.

Before the war some paving was done using cobblestones, but the effort was futile because the paving was soon covered by layers of dirt, and the cobblestone paved portions became indistinguishable from the hog wallow streets. After the war another sort of pavement was laid on part of Royal Street, but it, too, was eventually covered with six to eight inches of dirt. In 1888 large and small irregular mixed block granite ballast from ships was used for paving part of Royal Street, this time opposite the Battle House. It proved to be the worst possible paving material because of its roughness; it made the street as rough "as a corduroy county road."[46]

Another variety of paving placed about 1888 on a section of Government Street was made from granite blocks broken into egg-size pieces, pressed into the earth with a roller, and covered with sand. This method was held in high regard as cheap, easily repairable, and long lasting. Another technique used was brick paving. This method cost more but created a street that was as smooth as a floor. Common building brick laid on a sand foundation was followed by a layer of vitrified brick of low porosity. This was covered with a layer of "asphaltum" and was said to produce a very desirable street surface.[47]

On December 31, 1889, Danner received the contract for his wood-paving project, but it did not result in the widespread adoption of this approach. Street improvement continued to be a slow and expensive process, and it would be after the turn of the century before Mobile was able to pave a large number of its streets.[48]

Local politics in Mobile during the 1890s had nothing of the crisis atmosphere of the two earlier decades. Issues on the local political table seemed minor compared with the problems faced then. Nor was Mobile much of a contributor to the Populist debate that was animating the rest of Alabama, other than to back the Democratic status quo when Democratic Party hegemony was threatened in the 1890s.

Mayor Rich sought the Democratic nomination for governor in 1894 but withdrew his name before the convention, which subsequently nominated William C. Oates. Mobile elected Constantine L. Lavretta to replace Rich as mayor. He served one term, and in 1897 J. C. Bush was elected mayor, dying in office in 1900. Lavretta was a noted local politician and philanthropist, and Bush was a local businessman. Both continued the agenda set by Rich and his fellow officials under the new administration, i.e., to advance city commercial and economic development and improve services.[49]

National politics did intrude onto Mobile's political stage briefly in the summer of 1895 when William Jennings Bryan, congressman from Nebraska, arrived to debate the issue of bimetallism with Mobilian Richard H. Clarke, former congressman and candidate for governor in the 1896 election. The well-attended event was sponsored by the Central Trades Council of Mobile, and its purpose, according to council president N. T. Judge, was to enlighten the working men of the city. Observers believed that Bryan was the winner because of his calm delivery and oratorical ability, although Clarke was said to have had the better and more closely reasoned argument.[50]

After Mobile came out of the seven-year depression and created a local political constitution that finally brought stability to city governance, modest but real economic development occurred that continued through the 1890s. An idea of how desperate the economy of Mobile had become during the depression can be gotten by comparing the value of exports and imports during the initial years of depression. The value of exports fell from $9 million in 1878 to a catastrophic $3 million in 1882. The $1 million in imports in 1873 fell to only $400,000 in 1882. In contrast to this dismal showing, the increase in commerce during the 1890s was dramatic. Foreign commerce in Mobile for 1890 was valued at just under $3.5 million, but in 1900 that figure had risen to more than $16 million. What occurred to bring Mobile so near to economic collapse, and what then changed to facilitate its recovery?[51]

Before the Civil War, and for many decades after, Mobile, through its port, lived or died on trade with planters and communities in the interior and their exports. The city had prospered commercially when its rivers were the only way to transport goods inland and to export cotton and when everyone used ocean-going vessels with relatively shallow draft. After the war, however, innovation in ship design produced larger vessels with deeper draft. Ports such as Mobile without deep natural

Major Andrew Damrell, head of the U.S. Army Corps of Engineers, Mobile District, directed the city's first major dredging operation since before the war.

Erik Overbey Collection, USA Archives.

harbors were unable to serve these vessels. Also, river transport via steamboat and barge was challenged by the quicker and more reliable railroads that proliferated. Railroads soon grew to compete favorably with river commerce. Mobile's port development was further hindered by the many remaining obstructions in the harbor placed there during the war to protect the port. It took years to clear the harbor.[52]

To remedy the port's difficulties and attract the larger ships coming into use, Mobilians requested federal dollars to widen and deepen the long channel to the gulf. By 1867 the channel at Choctaw Point at the mouth of the Mobile River had silted to a depth of only seven feet, but it was not until 1872 that Mobile Republican congressman F. G. Bromburg succeeded in having an appropriation passed to dredge a deeper channel. This work resulted in a thirteen-foot channel completed by 1876, but deeper water was still needed. In 1878 a seventeen-foot channel was authorized, and by 1888, after other appropriations and with the continued support of Mobile's board of trade, a twenty-three-foot channel was completed, allowing the first of the new deep-draft ocean-going steamships to dock in Mobile's harbor. Later improvements continued to increase the depth of Mobile's connection to the gulf.[53]

An example of the economic turnaround experienced by Mobile in the 1890s was the development of trade with Latin America. The growth of this commerce can best be illustrated by the example of the banana trade. An incentive of $1,500 was offered by the Mobile Chamber of Commerce to the first company to operate regular fruit ships from Central America to Mobile for one year. In 1893 the vessel *Sala* landed in Mobile carrying the first cargo of bananas consigned for the Mobile Fruit and Trading Company and began a trade that would make Mobile a major importer of fruit for the United States.[54]

The city's post–Civil War commercial and business leaders were acutely aware that the rules of commerce had changed after the war and had sought to attract railroads to Mobile with liberal bond incentives funded at public expense. These initiatives were in large measure the cause of the city's financial plight that led to the 1879 bankruptcy. Still, the expanding rail network in the interior South was responsible not only for diverting cotton from shipment downriver to Mobile but also for offering more direct delivery of goods to growing towns and communities in the interior, towns that were once dependent on river traffic from Mobile. After a wave of railroad closures, bankruptcies, and mergers, Mobile had several reliable rail lines serving it in the 1890s. The two most notable were the Mobile and Ohio and the Louisville and Nashville Railroads. Others were the Mobile, New Orleans, and Texas; the New Orleans, Mobile, and Chattanooga; the Great Northern; the

Turn-of-the-century scene at the banana docks where the modern convention center now stands.

Erik Overbey Collection, USA Archives.

Alabama Grand Trunk; and the Mobile and Northwestern Railroads. Mobile, however, did not become the rail hub some had envisioned, although the rail lines did play an important role in the gradual growth of commerce in the 1890s as they joined with the rivers in moving goods to and from the port.[55]

While Mobilians endured the political, economic, and financial chaos of the first fifteen years of the period and welcomed the more stable 1890s, they continued a social lifestyle that was deeply rooted in antebellum times. Moreover, even though some practices were changing and new social forms beginning, they were all thoroughly nineteenth century in spirit and character.

Among the new social outlets Mobilians inaugurated after Reconstruction were the militia companies. These units of state troops increasingly took on a social rather than a military role as the tension of Reconstruction subsided. Their balls, annual encampments, and interstate drill and marksmanship competitions became popular social events and yet another occasion to dress up or have a picnic. The units based in Mobile were the Mobile Cadets, the Lomax Rifles, the Washington Light Infantry, the Cleburn Guards, the Gulf City Guards, the Mobile Rifles, the Alabama State Artillery, and the Gilmer Rifles, a black company. The white units were organized into the First Regiment, Alabama State Militia, in 1875. Thomas Cooper De Leon, local impresario and promoter who seemed to have his hand in all things social in the late nineteenth century, gave up the theater in 1885 to promote Mobile's competitive drills. In that year he managed the state encampment at

A busy day at the Louisville and Nashville train station located at the foot of Government Street.

William E. Wilson Collection, Historic Mobile Preservation Society.

Arlington, south of Mobile, and in 1887 he conducted the national drill in Washington, D.C.[56]

Another development on Mobile's social scene in this period was the growth of the Garrows Bend area for outdoor recreation. Located south of Choctaw Point on a gentle curve of the western shore of Mobile Bay, it was served by the romantic Bay Shell Road that began at the foot of Conception Street and skirted the shore for miles. The popularity of Garrows Bend grew steadily during the late nineteenth century. It became even more accessible when the area was connected with the new electric streetcar line in 1893. The streetcar system also established Monroe Park and created a demand for its services on the weekends.

Garrows Bend was the site of some of the best attended recreational sites in Mobile. Huge crowds gathered at Frascati Park where the Bay Shell Road began or congregated farther south at Monroe Park and Arlington Fair Grounds. Here one could attend outdoor theater or lectures and enjoy dancing, swimming, picnicking, baseball, concerts, and amusement rides. In 1897 Frank "Buck" Taylor projected Mobile's first motion pictures in town and soon brought the screen to Monroe Park, where its outdoor theater would provide nighttime entertainment well into the twentieth century.[57]

A Mobile social tradition that took on a new character in the 1880s and 1890s was Mardi Gras. After the war Mardi Gras came into its own as the focus of Mobile's social life and grew particularly important as the commercial potential of the celebration was recognized. The Mobile Carnival Association, formed in 1871, linked the various mystic societies and put Mardi Gras on a sounder business footing. Even the Mobile Commercial Club joined in 1893 to boost attendance. The Mardi Gras court tradition, begun in 1872 when the first emperor, Felix I was crowned, was revived and expanded during the 1890s.[58]

With the increased interest and attendance in Mardi Gras the number of mystic societies grew, and business took a fresh look at the celebration. Mobile merchants had long sought to attract county residents into town each spring to make their seasonal purchases and now began to promote Mardi Gras as an additional incentive to visit and spend money. Hotels, restaurants, and retailers soon found this attraction's appeal added handsomely to their profits.[59]

African Americans experienced many of the same hardships as whites as Mobile went through its many late-nineteenth-century changes. Blacks, however, had the added difficulties of trying to establish themselves as citizens and productive members of society while overcoming the bitterness, racism, and bigotry of most of the white population. In spite of the presence of a large and accepted Creole community that could have served as a model for racial accommodation between whites and nonwhites, most white Mobilians treated as inferior the former slaves who now flocked to Mobile. Blacks were not allowed to blend into Mobile's majority political, economic, or social order. In time a separate black community would form outside of white society, with its own leaders, businessmen, institutions, churches, and culture.

In spite of the tremendous obstacles placed in their path, Mobile's black community persevered against the restrictions placed on it. Blacks became proud of those among them who were able to succeed against the odds and held up as examples to be emulated those who made it as role models and community leaders. Because many white businessmen eschewed trade with blacks, a void was created that black businessmen moved into and exploited. For example, C. First Johnson began the Union Mutual Aid Association of Mobile and owned an interest in the C. W. Peters Furniture Company, operated by general manager and partial owner Charles W. Peters. This business was said to be the largest of its kind owned by blacks in Alabama. Dr. Roger Williams, a physician, owned and operated three drug companies. Another local black doctor was A. D. Simington. Other local drug companies owned by blacks were the Gulf City Drug Store operated by C. M. Witherspoon and the South Side Drug Store owned by Dr. J. Scott.

Other successful black businessmen of the era ran a variety of enterprises. There were draymen such as Dave Patton and entrepreneur Napoleon Rivers, who owned the Standard Tea and Coffee Company. Ed Lomax owned the Bienville Vehicle Works, and D. H. Jones operated the Greater Mobile Fish and Oyster Company.

Until the motor truck replaced mule-drawn wagons, most Mobile teamsters were black. Some black businessmen, such as Dave Patton, owned large trucking firms.

William E. Wilson Collection, Historic Mobile Preservation Society.

Tailors such as T. B. Kittrell and E. A. Sumter came to be well known. A. N. Johnson published a lively black newspaper, the *Mobile Weekly Press*.[60]

However impressive such success stories were, blacks were still treated as second-class citizens. Their status became worse in the 1890s, when the class and political forces of the Populist movement created a white backlash in Alabama that resulted in the new state constitution of 1901. This document institutionalized "Jim Crow" or legal segregation of the races. It made separation of whites and blacks not just a choice but a law and denied many their civil rights. This legislation set race relations back in Mobile as blacks would continue to feel the sting of segregation for decades to come.

As Mobilians approached the twentieth century, they had a taste of what the new era promised by way of technology. The telephone, first introduced in 1876, came to Mobile in 1879 when A. C. Danner had two of the devices installed in his coal yard. The two telephones, connected by one hundred feet of wire, linked opposite ends of his yard so he could speak to employees more easily. Convinced of the practical value of the new technology, Danner and C. G. Merriweather opened Mobile's first telephone exchange in Danner's coal yard on November 13, 1879. Three days later they accepted the first thirty-two individual and business subscribers.

Early in 1880 the local grocer S. H. Solomon advertised that he had a telephone in his store and that he would take orders from any of his customers who had a telephone, thus revolutionizing home shopping in Mobile. In 1883 city government obtained its first telephones, two in the city offices of the Southern Market and one at the guardhouse at a cost of $100 per year.[61]

Beginning a telephone system was relatively simple compared to developing a reliable system of electric power. Early efforts to bring electricity to businesses and homes for lights and machines got off to a rocky start in Mobile. Throughout the 1880s a series of electric companies came and went, each promising to provide dependable and safe power and lights. It was not until the 1890s, however, that electricity arrived in practical form. With it came a radical change in transportation technology.[62]

Mobile had been planned as a "walking city." That is, if people were to get around town they depended on themselves or an animal to get them there. A distinct improvement on this system, but one still dependent on muscle power, was the street railroad system in which mules pulled cars on rails laid in the street. These operated in Mobile from 1860 until 1893. With the arrival of electricity and its powerful motors, muscle power was eliminated, and new range and speed came to mass transit. The fast, new electrified streetcars were limited only by the length of wire and rail. This innovation in transportation facilitated vast changes in Mobile's geography, creating the first true suburbs, just as it did all across America.

Electric streetcars replaced mule-drawn trolleys after 1893.

Historic Mobile Preservation Society.

Although Mobilians reflected on the period 1874 to 1900 and had hopeful expectations for the twentieth century, they did not feel the era or the new century represented a break in continuity with their past. A generation of Mobilians had grown up under the shadow of oppressive problems such as acute political uncertainty and the consequences of financial collapse and economic depression. These events reinforced the conservative tone of the city inherited from the antebellum and Civil War years.

The mood generated by the troubles of earlier lean years created a palpable spirit of government and economic caution that, in spite of the progress of the 1890s and the subsequent decades of the twentieth century, would limit Mobile for much of the next century. Not until a new wave of radical political change in local government in the 1980s, this time brought about by the consequences of the local civil rights struggle, would attitudes change. The result then would be the opening up of the city to astonishing economic and political progress and a forward-looking anticipation of the future.

Suggestions for Further Reading

Doyle, Don Harrison. *New Men, New Cities, New South: Atlanta, Nashville, Charleston, Mobile, 1860–1910.* Chapel Hill: University of North Carolina Press, 1990. An excellent nineteenth-century comparison of Mobile, Charleston, Nashville, and Atlanta.

Eichold, Samuel. *Without Malice: The One Hundredth Anniversary of the Comic Cowboys, 1884–1984.* Mobile: R. E. Publications, 1984. An introduction to Mobile's Mardi Gras via a history of one of its most interesting societies.

Gould, Elizabeth Barrett. *From Fort to Port: An Architectural History of Mobile, Alabama, 1711–1918.* Tuscaloosa: University of Alabama Press, 1988. The definitive work on Mobile architecture and its historical impact on the city.

———. *From Builders to Architects: The Hobart-Hutchisson Six.* Montgomery: Black Belt Publishers, 1997. A focus on one of Mobile's most important architectural groups.

Mathews, Charles E. *Highlights of One Hundred Years in Mobile, 1865–1965.* Mobile: First National Bank of Mobile, 1965. A brief but interesting thumbnail sketch of events in Mobile during the period discussed in this chapter.

McWilliams, Tennant S. *Hannis Taylor: The New Southerner as an American.* Tuscaloosa: University of Alabama Press, 1978. This study places the New South phenomenon into a broader American context.

St. Francis Street Methodist Episcopal Church. *Gulf City Cook Book.* Tuscaloosa: University of Alabama Press, 1990. This work gives a glimpse into nineteenth-century Mobile foodways.

Thomas, Mary Martha. *The New Woman in Alabama: Social Reforms and Suffrage, 1890–1920.* Tuscaloosa: University of Alabama Press, 1992. An overview of the women's movement in Alabama.

CHAPTER 6

Progress versus Tradition in Mobile, 1900–1920

Christopher MacGregor Scribner

In 1917, when Pat Lyons started another term as mayor, Mobile barely resembled the gulf city in which he had begun his political career in the late nineteenth century. The city underwent several significant transformations during the first two decades of the twentieth century. In 1917, for instance, Lyons served as the head of a three-man city commission, not as he had done earlier as the executive in a mayor-council form of government. Under the commission system public participation in politics declined. Beyond these political shifts, Mobile continued its long transition from a cotton port into a more diversified importing and exporting center, and railroads gained added importance. As the city's economic structure evolved, new men (with few or no attachments to old Mobile) assumed leadership positions. Social patterns changed significantly due to economic and cultural pressures. The decades-old system of racial paternalism, for instance, had hardened into legal segregation, and racial confrontation and violence ensued. Amid troubling racial developments, Mobile's leaders tried to move the city away from erstwhile patterns of regional economic isolation and join their new southern vision of progress into the American mainstream. Many elements of modern Mobile were emerging in the new century.[1]

Mobile grew considerably in the early twentieth century. The city's population rose from nearly forty thousand in 1900 to sixty thousand in 1920. The city increased at roughly the same rate as outlying Mobile County, where the number of residents jumped from sixty-two thousand to ninety-eight thousand in the period. While population in the county's urban areas grew by 23 percent from 1900 to 1910, the region's rural areas expanded by 41 percent.[2] In other words, metropolitan area growth was not confined to the city proper. Several other paradoxes related to Mobile's larger population. The city grew, but not as fast as other southern cities.

Before the Cochrane Bridge was built in the 1920s, bay boats transported people and goods across the bay.

USA Archives.

Mobile, which had been the South's eighth largest city in 1880, was the region's fifteenth by 1910.[3] Concerns about the city's retreat in the southern urban hierarchy, especially in relation to other port cities such as New Orleans and Tampa, consumed Mobile's civic leaders. Many of the actions they took during these years can be understood as reactions to this worrisome trend. Despite evidence of the city's relative economic decline, Mobile's political and economic leadership remained bullish about the community's future prospects. "Our city is attracting quite a bit of attention throughout the North and East," Lyons boasted in 1906, "and all eyes are upon her progress."[4]

As Mobile faced the new century, its residents stood ready to shed their sectionalism for nationalism. The patriotism spawned by the Spanish-American War helped to solidify feelings of national reconciliation. Mobilians embraced the New South creed, which called for an economic and philosophical reunion between the North and South. Ironically, many Mobilians initially opposed the Spanish-American War because the crisis with Cuba had hurt business at the city's port. Erwin Craighead, a Nashville native who began his journalism career in New Orleans before becoming editor of the *Mobile Register,* opposed American intervention in Cuba on the editorial page of his newspaper. Opponents of the McKinley administration's Caribbean policy compared the effects of a possible conflict to the Civil

War, an event that signaled Mobile's economic decline. In early 1898 a group of prominent businessmen sent a petition to President William McKinley with similar sentiments. The petition did not just include the signatures of the city's exporters and importers; local merchants and wholesalers signed it as well. The circular noted that "inasmuch as 80% of our entire trade with Cuba depends upon the sugar crop of the island, it is readily seen that our commerce with the Island cannot be restored at present, nor until actual peace is established." The businessmen feared war because they expected it would perpetuate the city's economic malaise. Nonetheless, a growing number of Mobilians, including local merchants not involved in international trade, believed that the economic success of the city depended on expanding that international trade. "Many small-scale businessmen, not just major industrialists of the Northeast," one historian commented, "looked to the Caribbean as a marketplace."[5]

When war erupted most Mobilians rallied to the cause, either because they hoped the conflict would end economic uncertainty or due to old-fashioned patriotism. Editor Craighead, for instance, changed his position, contending that war "means a solidifying of our people, an abandonment of sectional issues, a proving of our national power." He began to imagine how the war might pull Americans together, affecting the reunion that Reconstruction had failed to accomplish. Echo-

First Regiment of Alabama volunteers moving from Mobile Bay Camp L. V. Clark to Camp Coppinger near Crichton, 1898.

Alabama Department of Archives and History, Montgomery, Alabama.

Erwin Craighead, editor of the *Mobile Register,* 1893–1926.

Erik Overbey Collection, USA Archives.

ing the booster theme of a northern businessman who visited the gulf city, Craighead explained that residents should "let the Northern manufacturers know that we of Mobile are in earnest, and that we are ready to assist them in finding favorable location[s], and Mobile will have as good a chance as any city in the South."[6]

Unfortunately for Mobile, the Spanish-American War did not spark an economic boom in the city. Most troops and supplies, for instance, moved through other ports. Nevertheless, it did solidify the pursuit of business expansion as the cornerstone of sectional reconciliation. Many Mobilians realized that they had goals in common with business interests in other regions, such as the growth of foreign markets for American commerce.

The war also pressed the city's economic elite into a growing role in local policy making, a role that would increase throughout the Progressive Era. Mobile's civic leadership realized that they no longer needed to view the national government in Washington as an enemy because federal largesse could invigorate their city. In 1900, in one example of this newfound economic activism, various local civic groups united to form the Mobile Joint Rivers and Harbors Committee. The group in particular hoped to dredge areas of the Mobile River to improve the flow into Mobile Bay and to deepen the shipping channels in the harbor. They sought federal funds to accomplish this goal, relying heavily on the support of Congressman John H. Bankhead. Bankhead, a Confederate veteran who served in the House and the Senate during this period, delivered. Between 1890 and 1915 Mobile received $3 million in federal grants for harbor-related improvements. The port city definitely benefited from Bankhead's membership on the congressional Rivers and Harbors Committee. For example, because of the government aid, Mobile was able to more than double the depth of the shipping channel.[7]

When Mobile declined in significance as a port city for river traffic in the second half of the nineteenth century, the development of railroads ultimately helped to offset the loss. Railroads linked the gulf town to the nation's interior, particularly to Alabama's timberlands. Timber trading first boomed in the 1880s, and by 1910 timber exports accounted for $2 million. Lumber and cotton remained mainstays, but other products vied for importance, too. In the new century, Latin American trade began to predominate, even after the United Fruit Company shifted most of its banana importing from Mobile to New Orleans. Even as Mobile struggled in comparison to other southern port towns, it could boast some startling achievements. The total value of imports and exports at the port increased five times between 1894 and 1904. From 1902 to 1911 Mobile's port commerce doubled again. In that year local companies invested in extensive improvements in the city's transporta-

Timber became Mobile's largest export by 1900.

Erik Overbey Collection, USA Archives.

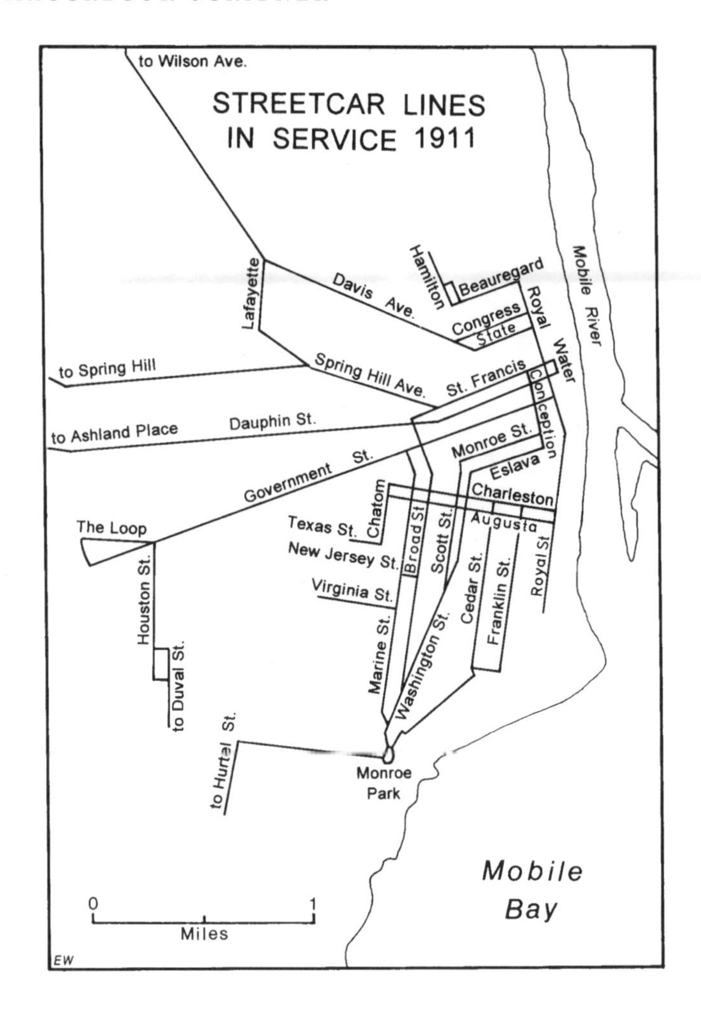

Streetcar lines.

Map by Eugene Wilson based on Asa H. Sparks, "Mobile Trolleys" in *Traction and Models* (July 1967).

tion facilities. The City Bank and Trust Company put $5 million in railroad terminals and nearby industrial plants, and the Mobile and Ohio Railroad spent $500,000 for dock improvements.[8]

To a great extent, local politicians expected area businessmen to provide the major impetus for change. Much of the development in the city, such as the white suburbs that grew to the south and west and the streetcars that both served their growth and made it possible, resulted from private initiative. The growth of middle- and working-class suburbs near Monroe Park around the turn of the century were examples of the building boom. A newspaper account explained that the urban transportation revolution helped make this growth possible. "Rapid transit has worked wonders in building up the suburbs," the newspaper noted. "Places that were unnamed a few years ago are this year's centers of population."[9]

James H. Wilson's Mobile Light and Railroad Company powerfully advanced growth. Wilson was part of a new breed of men who moved to Mobile and, thanks to an outsider's energy and desire to prove himself, helped transform aspects of city life. Such new men took advantage of the politicians' reliance on local business to set the tone of development and to expand the range of services for the city's middle-class residents. Born in Kansas in 1858, Wilson moved to Mobile in 1890 for health reasons after a successful career as a rancher in Colorado and Montana. He used his capital to form the Mobile Light and Railroad Company, and by 1892 he operated his first streetcar line. Wilson helped modernize the city by electrifying his line and that of a competing company using mule-drawn cars that he bought in 1893. Among his other activities, Wilson helped to develop Monroe Park, served by his streetcars, as a recreation center for the city. In 1901 he won a municipal franchise to lay gas mains and connections, and his company supplied electricity to residents of the city. An intensely private man, Wilson preferred to avoid the public glare, but his private actions helped to reshape Mobile.

Richard V. Taylor also exemplified Mobile's expanding social and economic order. Born in 1859 in North Carolina, Taylor moved with his family near Mobile in 1868 because his mother, sick with tuberculosis, needed a warmer climate. At age fifteen, Taylor, who had received periodic formal schooling, went to work full time in a turpentine and barrel factory. Two years later he worked as library clerk for the Mobile Bar Association. He was a diligent and driven man, full of natural intelligence. His break came when he went to work as a clerk for the Mobile and

One attraction at Monroe Park in 1904 was a "flying machine" built by local inventor John Fowler.

S. M. Coffin Collection, USA Archives.

Ohio Railroad Company. "By 1882 Taylor's quickness with numbers," one historian wrote, "had moved him up the M&O ranks to the position of head bookkeeper." Taylor continued his rise, becoming a general manager and then company vice-president of the M&O in 1910. During World War I he went to work for the Woodrow Wilson administration as a regional railroad manager. Taylor's career took interesting turns later in life, too. After his sixtieth birthday he served as a member of the federal Interstate Commerce Commission and then returned to his adopted hometown, where he won political office and attempted to develop the Mobile area's gulf-front real estate. Taylor's career emphasizes how Mobile's once-closed social and economic order had been opened to a new breed of entrepreneurial businessmen. "Dick Taylor was a man with virtually no antebellum plantation background, no family money, no social pedigree [although in 1884 he did marry into one of the city's leading families]," his biographer wrote. "Instead, he was like many other postbellum business leaders of southern cities; he maneuvered his way to the top by taking risks, working compulsively, spending the money that he made with great enjoyment, and never quitting."[10]

This Babbitt of the New South brought a new vision of leadership. Taylor, like James H. Wilson, believed that government could play an important role in supporting business and economic growth. This positive view of government, nevertheless, had clearly defined limits. The Babbitts thought that an orderly, efficient, and ultimately sympathetic government must be run as a business. This vision of a powerful centralized government was in some ways antidemocratic because these men wanted many of the day-to-day decisions to be removed from the hurly-burly of public debate. Taylor's creed, which blended many aspects of the New South thought that percolated throughout the region in the late nineteenth century, called for businessmen to take a more active role in urban affairs. "Cities are what men make them," he thundered in a 1913 speech, and "the good and evil of every town is the sum of good and evil of all of the individuals of which it is composed." As Taylor's own career showed, he expected that the federal government could be an important ally in building the local economy. Railroad development was one aspect of this regional business link, and Taylor had an "almost messianic belief that railroads were *the* vital source of business and therefore social progress." Taylor's view supported the regional rapprochement that occurred in this period.[11]

Mobile's brand of business progressivism called for investment in economic infrastructure but not for social programs designed to help the less fortunate. Many business progressives believed that a robust economy created opportunity for all. Still, they had a willful blindness toward the needy, especially when a large portion of that group included the city's black population. This creed also meant that many social services would be supplied by private charity, not state action. Mobile's City

Hospital on St. Anthony Street, for instance, operated since 1895 by the Sisters of Charity, a Catholic order, provided basic health care services for many Mobilians. The hospital ran a free dispensary, which by one estimate served about 50 percent of the city's population. Two days of any week it served whites, and two days it cared for black patients. It was not atypical for a line of forty people to snake outside the dispensary's doors.[12]

Although the city's politicians and its business leaders held similar ideas about appropriate economic and social policy, the two groups remained distinct. The business elites generally avoided the political fray, leaving municipal politics to middle-class merchants. The city's council government included a mayor and a legislative body with aldermen elected from each of the city's wards and several picked in at-large elections. Pat Lyons, for instance, won his first seat on the council from Mobile's First Ward, which was half-black. (In Lyons's winning race in 1897 about five hundred whites and three hundred blacks voted in the district.) He became mayor in 1904 and perpetuated a political system based on ward bossism and delivering services to the local community. Merchants, especially grocers, played a prominent role in local politics. "Between 1897 and 1910, Mobile's reins of government lay chiefly in the hands of middle class merchants like Lyons," one historian wrote, "together with physicians, attorneys, bookkeepers, cotton factors, manufacturers, artisans, and retailers."[13]

Born in 1850 to Irish immigrants, Lyons abandoned the shores of Mobile for a life on the state's rivers when he was thirteen. His career blossomed. He moved from deckhand to clerk to captain to part-owner of a line. Well known for operating the *Maggie Burke,* a packet ship, Lyons quit the river in 1885 at age thirty-five when he bought an interest in a local grocery store. First appointed to the council in 1894, he won his seat in 1897. In addition to politics, which consumed most of his energy thereafter, Lyons was a vice-president of the City National Bank and was active in the Knights of Columbus and various Mardi Gras societies, among other groups. People supported the genial Lyons because he acted like one of them. The popular Lyons never lost an election. As the *Mobile Register* reported in 1910, he had an "unfailing good temper, [a] generous disposition, and [a] freedom from ostentation and mannerism [that] cause him to be admired."[14]

Under Lyons's leadership the municipal government did take steps to develop the city's infrastructure. In August 1897 city voters approved plans for a municipally owned waterworks. By 1907, when the council purchased the privately held Bienville waterworks, the local government owned all of the waterworks serving Mobile residents. Although the city controlled the waterworks, it never pushed for ownership of gas or electric service.[15] The council government sought to extend additional services to local residents. In April 1902 municipal workers first paved a city street. Plans for the future were more ambitious. Projects completed between 1902 and 1908 resulted in about sixteen new miles of paved streets, at a cost of about $1 million.

Besides extending basic services, the Lyons regime concentrated on expanding the city's park system, reorganizing ward lines, and refinancing the city's debt. Although he did not build a system of city parks as he had hoped, Lyons led the restoration of Bienville Square and Washington Square, among other projects. He also sought to expand the city through annexation; however, his Greater Mobile Plan failed to pass because his opponents convinced enough voters that taxes would increase more than services. Furthermore, arguments about Prohibition confused the annexation issue. Lyons was a popular politician, but his leadership failed to bring efficient government to Mobile, at least as local businessmen defined efficiency. Critics also attacked him as being loose with the city's finances.

At times Lyons showed an allegiance to a booster ideology that overshadowed the basic needs of the city. This was seen when on September 27, 1906, after several days of heavy rains, a hurricane struck the city and outlying areas. One person estimated that 150 people died during the hurricane, most of them in Mobile County. The area suffered about $15 million in property damage. Most of the problems in the city resulted from flooding. Lyons's reaction to the damage was muted. He did not want it to appear that Mobile needed charity or the help of outsiders. He claimed that the city received little damage, an understated response that probably delayed the recovery because it did reduce outside assistance. Nevertheless, business leaders, including the city's newspapers editors, praised his handling of the crisis. His stolid leadership did help the city weather the nationwide financial Panic of 1907 without serious incident.[16]

As the new century progressed, Mobile's elite business class sought greater involvement in and control over municipal politics. They believed that the mayor-council form of government was at odds with their vision of an efficient, orderly society. First, however, they had to unify themselves. Mobile's business class had been divided into a series of organizations with competing agendas. The existence of these groups, such as the Mobile Chamber of Commerce, founded in 1841, the Mobile Board of Trade, the Mobile Cotton Exchange, and the Mobile Commercial Club, indicated a lack of unified purpose, not dynamism within the business class. In June 1910 this changed when business elites under the leadership of streetcar magnate James Wilson formed the Mobile Progressive Association. Its main goal was to attract new industry. The group's leaders proposed tax exemptions to attract manufacturing, and they compiled a series of business statistics—freight rates and cost of living, for example—and then broadcast the news via national mailings to targeted companies. The members of the Mobile Progressive Association wanted to link Mobile to the rest of the nation and boost the fortunes of their city through business investment. They considered their fortunes intertwined with those of the city at large, a belief expressed in the group's motto, "What helps the Mobile Progressive Association helps Mobile." The association had a secondary goal: to bridge the gap between business and politics. The group's vision of politics, however, ignored portions of Mobile's population, especially its black residents.[17]

Ironically, the optimistic business creed of Mobile's white civic elite was in many ways indistinguishable from the ideology of the city's black bourgeoisie. The city's black elite preached a Booker T. Washington–influenced message of self-help, racial solidarity, accommodation, and economic development. Many members of the black business class, such as A. N. Johnson, the newspaper publisher of the *Mobile Weekly Press* and undertaker, had extensive personal contacts with Washington and knew black leaders in other southern cities through Washington's National Negro Business League. This leadership class was no "talented tenth," to use W. E. B. Du Bois's phrase. It was far smaller. By one estimate, the city's black elite included less than seventy people, or less than 1 percent of the city's African American population. Besides businessmen, the black elite included preachers, teachers, and some prosperous laborers. Between 1900 and 1920 the city's total black population held relatively steady at just over 40 percent of the city's residents.[18]

The People's Drug Store on Dauphin Street, an African American business, owned by A. N. Johnson, circa 1903.

Erik Overbey Collection, USA Archives.

The fate of Mobile's blacks changed dramatically in the century's first two decades. A. N. Johnson's career offers hints at elements of the transformation from paternalism to segregation. Born in April 1865 in Marion and educated at the State Normal School there and Talladega College, Johnson became editor of the *Mobile Weekly Press* in 1894. A tireless worker with an entrepreneurial flair, he founded a funeral home in 1896. A supporter of the Washingtonian message, Johnson held an "optimistic attitude about the future of blacks in the South." Like other black leaders he was active in politics through the Alabama Republican Party. Indeed, the party selected him as delegate-at-large to the 1904 Republican convention. Yet the tide had already begun to turn against the city's blacks, no matter how optimistic or hardworking. Alabama's 1901 constitution effectively disfranchised most blacks (and many whites, too). Mobile passed its first segregation ordinance in 1902, and racial violence soon followed. Racial cooperation weakened as a result of the changes, and Johnson felt attacked both by the black bourgeoisie and by the city's white elite as he tried to continue to find the middle ground in this new order. In 1907 he abandoned Mobile (because he said he had received death threats) for Nashville, where he continued a successful business career.[19]

Other black Mobilians believed that the economic path presented the quickest route to equality. In 1901 Rev. Anderson N. McEwen, editor of the *Mobile Southern Watchman,* wrote that "the crying demand of the Negro as a race is business enterprise. [W]e must quit buying so much furniture and learn to make some, we must learn to unite in business like the white men, [and] give more employment to our people." In the early twentieth century, Mobile's black business community, centered on Davis Avenue, included thirty-three businesses. Those thirty-three establishments included ten groceries, three funeral homes, two restaurants, two drug stores, and two hardware supply stores. Joining them was a new enterprise founded by another of the city's more prominent black businessman, C. First Johnson. Johnson, born in Hayneville in 1865, had risen from a position of elevator operator at Mobile's customs house to become secretary to the collector there. In 1902 he and a partner formed the Union Mutual Aid Association, the city's first black life insurance company, and he also held a stake in a furniture business. He, too, imagined that any black resident of Mobile who was willing to work hard could follow his steps to success. Nevertheless, even during the best of times, the opportunities for the city's black businessmen were limited by both prejudice and the constricted spending power of Mobile's black population. Black businesses did best in matters of life and death (the insurance and funeral businesses, for example) in which whites did not compete. The circumscribed role of black business professionals meant that ministers continued to have a strong presence as race leaders during this period and for many years after.[20]

A. N. Johnson's decision to leave Mobile was a dramatic result of the shifting

A. N. Johnson.

G. P. Hamilton, *Beacon Lights of the Race* (1909).

racial climate. Yet it would be wrong to overemphasize the change after the turn of the century. In many ways, segregation brought legal standing to long-held customs. "Mobile's de facto Jim Crow structure was in place by the early 1870s," one historian wrote, "yet only after 1900 with the passage of municipal ordinances was de jure segregation firmly entrenched." De facto segregation separated the city's blacks and whites in schools, at hotels and restaurants, and on public transportation. Residential segregation was also a fact of city life, with blacks crowding into designated neighborhoods, especially in the Seventh Ward on the city's north side. Blacks had held local political office during Reconstruction, but an 1879 redistricting in the city put a stop to that trend. After the state's 1901 constitution, blacks virtually disappeared from the registrar's rolls as well.[21]

Alabama's 1901 constitution marked a significant turning point in state and local race relations. Alabama joined with other states in the South in hardening racial customs and eliminating the political and civil rights of its black citizens. In 1902 Mobile followed this trend when the municipal government considered segregating the city's streetcars, an idea several other Alabama cities had already adopted. Black leaders opposed the ordinance, fearing that African Americans would be forced to ride separate cars and thus more clearly be second-class citizens. Some black leaders hoped that the debate would cause the streetcar company to add more cars, especially along Davis Avenue. Despite the black leaders' pleas, the city government passed Mobile's first segregation ordinance, which went into effect on November 1, 1902. The vaguely worded law did not call for separate cars, but it required that blacks fill the cars from the rear and whites sit from front to back. The conductors of the privately owned streetcars would have to enforce the laws.

The initial response to the law was uncertainty. Black protest heightened the confusion. Few whites expected that Mobile's blacks would follow the lead of Montgomery's African American population and protest the new law through a boycott. Nevertheless, that is just what they did. The boycott lasted nearly two months, during which time Wilson's Mobile Light and Railroad Company began to feel the economic pinch because of the dramatic drop in riders. Wilson pressured city politicians to remedy the problem. The boycott, however, collapsed because no consistent form of alternate transportation could be established. Segregated transportation would stand, proving the foundation for future laws.[22]

In Mobile segregation heralded worsening racial relations. Some whites thought segregation would create more orderly contacts between the races by regulating those encounters. In truth it confused traditional relations, undermining racial harmony while deepening inequality for blacks. In 1906 for the first time in memory, a group of whites lynched a black man. He had been accused of rape. The incident, which occurred outside city limits, touched off similar incidents in the following years. As the leading historian of the Progressive Era in Mobile noted, the city's

This elaborate hearse belonged to C. W. Allen and Edgar Harney Undertakers, circa 1910.

Johnson-Allen Mortuary, USA Archives.

elites, especially the newspaper editors, "criticized mob violence while continuing to depict blacks stereotypically in their newspapers as more prone than whites to violence, drug addiction, and alcoholism." Another lynching, in which a mob took accused criminal Richard Robertson, a carpenter, from the county jail and hanged him across the street from the city's oldest church, made it clear that segregation moved hand in glove with violence. Because the Robertson lynching occurred within city limits, it led to an intensified round of hand-wringing among the city's white elite.[23]

Even as race relations worsened, there were some examples of improvements, however modest, for blacks. For instance, although they continued to lag behind whites in education, they did make gains. In 1910 only 63 percent of school-age blacks attended school compared with 81 percent of whites, with black education receiving unequal funding. Nevertheless, black illiteracy declined, although it remained far above white rates. In 1900, 44 percent of blacks in Mobile could neither read nor write, but by 1920 that percentage had fallen in half, to 21 percent. In contrast, during the period only about 1 percent of Mobile's whites were illiterate. In 1912 City Hospital, the city's charity hospital operated by Catholic nuns, built a new three-story brick addition to the hospital to serve as its new black ward, replacing the unattached wooden building that formerly had served that purpose. The building included patient wards on the second and third floors and a clinic, laboratory, and x-ray equipment on the ground floor.[24]

The deteriorating political position for the city's blacks was evident in two presidential visits to the city. In 1905, when President Theodore Roosevelt came to Mobile as part of a southern tour to build support for a lily-white GOP, A. N. Johnson proposed that the president address the city's blacks. Furthermore, he expected African Americans would participate in the civic festivities for the president because of their long-time support for his party. He was wrong and became angered when blacks were excluded from all ceremonies. Roosevelt also refused to meet privately with black leaders. The visit epitomized the interrelationship between segregation and progressivism in Mobile. When President Woodrow Wilson visited in 1913 blacks did not expect to participate significantly in ceremonies honoring the Democratic president, nor did they.

African Americans reacted to Mobile's new status quo by abandoning the city for more promising places. Between 1910 and 1920 the growth of the black population fell below the city's overall growth rate, a decline from about 44 percent of the population to about 39 percent. Out-migration likely accounted for the change. When World War I opened opportunities for southern blacks in northern factories, black Mobilians, like other black southerners, migrated to the industrial cities of the Middle West. In a 1917 letter to the *Chicago Defender,* one person observed that there are "lots of idle men in Mobile, lots have trades but they are not supplied with work and can't get anything." To many of Mobile's African Americans, trapped like their parents in dead-end menial jobs, it was apparent that they would have to escape the gulf city in order to enjoy any economic opportunity or political freedom.[25]

Despite its promised rewards segregation brought more uncertainty than order, as the lynchings indicated. The lynchings also showed cracks in the solidarity of the city's white residents. In response to the racial violence, white civic elites formed an organization that sought to promote law and order, whereas another group of white citizens supported the sheriff from whose jail the lynching victim had been taken. One member of the law-and-order group spoke of "the hoodlum crowd" that would rather take justice into their own hands. Such divisions among whites were also visible in other "reform" efforts, such as Prohibition, another major cultural battleground.[26]

At the turn of the century Mobile could be a raucous, vibrant port city where many resisted efforts at social control. Many opposed the national and state Prohibition movements that gained momentum in the early twentieth century. Like many other port cities in the South, Mobile had a more tolerant and open attitude toward alcohol consumption and other behavior, a belief no doubt furthered and expressed by its Mardi Gras traditions. The city also featured a large Catholic population, traditionally sensitive to restrictions on alcohol. Mayor Lyons, for instance, owned a share in a local brewery. "Our mayor is a Catholic," one Mobile citizen explained to the governor in 1907, "and you know what that means and the whole trend of thought along these lines in a Catholic city is one of tolerance." In addition to its moralistic elements, Prohibition also took on racial overtones. Many white Mobilians wanted to restrict blacks' access to alcohol and to close dives, known as "blind tigers," in the city's black neighborhoods. Some wets also opposed state-imposed Prohibition because the city paid for some services, such as education, through liquor taxes (after 1911) and distilling and liquor sales (after 1915). "Blind tigers" and bootlegging would continue to be widespread in Mobile even after the city began to regulate saloons.[27]

Mobile was a loose, energetic, and social city, and its residents liked to have control over their own affairs. "Pleasure seeking so largely prevails [in Mobile]," a Presbyterian minister commented at the turn of the century, "that it seems to have become a business so extensively carried on as to be an actual hindrance often to the successful prosecution of what is legitimate and substantial." Would-be movie censors, for example, failed to win their objectives. Women's groups such as the City Federation of Clubs and the Southern Association of College Women fought in vain for tighter restrictions. The municipal government resisted their overtures, claiming that self-censorship by the theater owners and existing statutes banning obscenity or the exhibition of indecent material were enough. The police, government officials explained, could enforce present laws if necessary, but the government did not want to expand these powers. Pat Lyons considered movie censorship "so subject to abuse that it was a dangerous experiment to try."[28]

Baseball was a popular public activity during this period that no one proposed to censor. Thousands of youngsters, both black and white, played separately in the city's parks, and adults competed in semiprofessional and professional leagues. Around the turn of the century, the Mobile City League featured players on teams sponsored by local businesses. In fact, by 1915 Mobile was the only city in Alabama that allowed Sunday baseball. In 1903 a Mobile professional team joined the Cotton States League. After winning the league crown in 1907, the next year the Mobile Sea Gulls joined the Southern Association, the premier professional baseball league in the South. Attendance at the Sea Gulls's games inched past the one hundred thousand mark in 1913 but then shrank, declining with the team's fortunes. By the 1917 season just 27,121 attended Monroe Park as the team remained mired in the league's second division. After that year manager Pat Flaherty changed the name in an effort to reverse the team's luck. He wanted to shed the jinx of the Sea Gulls and picked the name Bears as a more virile substitute. "Bears mean something. A bear can bite, he can claw, he can hug, and he'll fight at the drop of a hat," said Flaherty, who added, "Sea Gulls didn't mean a thing in the world: there was no pep to it." The opening day game in April 1918 against the New Orleans team drew five thousand fans, perhaps showing renewed interest in the team, but the season was soon suspended because of World War I.[29]

Although the city united in support of its baseball teams, many more serious matters divided its residents. Religious tensions and definitions of proper American citizenship were among the conflicts that helped foster a sense of deep uncertainty in early-twentieth-century Mobile. As the century turned, anti-Catholicism became stronger and more bitter.[30] For example, Mobile had a local chapter of the Junior Order of the United American Mechanics, then the nation's most virulent anti-Catholic fraternal group. The cultural divisions revealed by the debates over lynching and Prohibition convinced Mobile business elites that they must take a more active role in city government—and that they had to lessen the public's raucous participation in and influence over these debates. Beyond the moral and cultural conflict, Prohibition mixed into many of the day's political questions, such as annexation, race relations, taxation, and finance matters. Disagreements over these issues derailed proper political dialogue and impeded orderly government. Prohibition's public disagreements, like the social unrest associated with lynching, threatened local harmony by fracturing public opinion. This unruliness helped convince business elites, particularly the members of the Mobile Progressive Association, that the city needed a new kind of government. They contended that the mayor-council government was inefficient and thus blocked the city's prospects for growth. Their desire for governmental efficiency was intertwined with demands for a more controlled and orderly society and less energetic political debate.

In the summer of 1910 the Mobile Progressive Association began to push for a change in Mobile's government. Erwin Craighead, the *Mobile Register*'s editor, was a leader of the commission government movement. The commission model swept the nation's cities after Galveston, Texas, adopted the form in 1900. Proponents of a commission government, such as Craighead, believed that it allowed politicians to make more informed choices, free from the emotional and electoral pressures of the masses. Not a small amount of elitism and distrust of the people accompanied this position. As Craighead wrote in one editorial: "The trouble with office-holders is that they imagine that they are elected to do the thinking for the dear but ignorant people, whereas their true function is to carry out the will of the people as expressed in the laws." Left unstated was the belief that only the economic elite or their allies, the disinterested experts, could adequately interpret the people's will. In other words, it was better for the people to learn their will through the decisions of their leaders than to express it through the democratic process. Craighead also contended that the council had poorly managed the city's affairs and had been rife with corruption, negligence (especially on school contracts), and nepotism. The mayor and the council, he charged, had hindered the city's economic growth.[31]

By late spring of 1911 the matter was ready to go before Mobile's voters (whose ranks had been thinned by the state's 1901 disfranchising constitution). Proponents of the change seconded Craighead's arguments about the commission and added that the new government would give Mobile a more industrious image, thus attracting additional outside investment. They viewed it as a step in the city's overall business plan. Opponents attacked the proposal as undemocratic. They hoped to capitalize on a split over Prohibition in the pro-commission forces, but this failed as a wedge issue.

The proposal up for debate called for the replacement of the mayor and council with three commissioners. Each commissioner would be elected citywide, and each would control particular departments, such as police, fire, and water, with full powers of hiring and firing. The three commissioners would select a mayor (whose additional powers were largely ceremonial) from among their number.[32]

On June 5, 1911, Mobile's electorate, by a 2,227 to 1,401 margin, selected change. Voters in every one of the city's wards embraced the proposal, although the plan carried the First (Lyons's base) and Sixth Wards, both of which had heavier working-class concentrations, by narrow margins. Just 40 percent of the city's nine thousand registered voters participated. Dick Taylor and other members of the city's business elite celebrated the results, seeing the new government as part of the modernization of the city. Once again, they imagined, Mobile was perched at the brink of exploiting its vast potential.[33]

For all the hype surrounding the change in government, it had a limited effect on policy initiatives and did not root out charges of inefficiency or patronage, as its advocates had hoped. In the end, the biggest change related to the switch to the commission did not so much involve what the city government should do, but who should rule and who should participate in politics. The upper-middle class and professionals, the core of the commission's support, became the city's new political mandarins, replacing the middle-class merchants and retailers who had long provided Mobile's political leadership. Overall participation in politics dropped dramatically as a result of the switch. For example, in the 1915 municipal elections just 534 voters went to the polls. Nor did the commission government end political infighting and squabbling. One commissioner fought a recall effort that he contended had been orchestrated by the *Mobile Register*.[34]

Some old-line leaders, especially Pat Lyons, survived and indeed flourished in the new regime. Lyons, who had been appointed by the governor to the commission, overcame fierce opposition to win reelection in 1912. Three years later he outlasted another opponent, and in 1917 his colleagues named him mayor. Joining him during the first six years of commission rule were Lazarus Schwarz and Harry Pillans. Schwarz, a German Jew, was a successful haberdasher and real-estate owner who had served as a councilman earlier. Pillans, born in Texas in 1847, was a lumber agent and lawyer, another of the new breed of Mobile businessmen. His family

First city commission meeting, 1911. The commissioners were, right to left, Harry Pillans, Lazarus Schwarz, and Pat Lyons.

Museum of Mobile.

migrated to Alabama in 1852, and he served in the Confederate infantry as a teenager. The trio followed traditional policies, such as paving streets, extending water and sewer services, and seeking new lands for expansion. The commission government, nonetheless, was part of a wider movement to promote professionalism in local government. Soon after the change in government, the police moved to a civil service system, with clear regulations for duties, conduct, hiring, and advancement.

Most other actions were cosmetic. Mobile's government failed to move in new directions. A significant barrier to government activism remained the city's low municipal budget. In 1915, for instance, Pillans estimated that the city's revenues totaled about $475,000, an amount about one-thirteenth of New Orleans's revenues. The commissioners did not try to expand the government's income, which might have given them flexibility to pursue additional programs. For the most part they were content to perpetuate limited government because it matched their sense of business progressivism. Business-centered government favored economic development (investment in infrastructure or tax incentives for industry), but it had little interest in social services or cultural support.

In this period Mobile's residents witnessed greater attention to public health issues, but this circumstance was as much due to the efforts of the city's energetic health officer, Dr. Charles Mohr, as to any specific policy intention. In 1914 Mohr organized a program to catch and destroy rats. He also sought to prevent communicable disease (one way was to inspect local dairies) and to improve the sanitary conditions in the city jails. Many of the public health initiatives came as a result of local implementation of federal programs. In 1912 the United States Public Health Service organized the nation's first malarial investigation at the health services' Marine Services Hospital.[35]

The government's limited program of social reform received private assistance from the activities of Mobile's women. In the new century the city's women began to seek a more active role in civic affairs. Nonetheless, their attempts to expand the reach of their domestic affairs into the public arena were more limited than efforts in other cities across the nation. For example, few took positions on controversial matters such as suffrage. Mobile's women, especially the wives of the city's elite, had long been involved in charitable activities, and in the Progressive Era these efforts were concentrated and expanded. Their goals matched the business progressivism of their husbands. Women's groups, especially the Junior League, had an active role at City Hospital and in 1904 helped organize a Young Women's Christian Association. In 1911 women united the various charitable groups under the auspices of the Associated Charities of Mobile. Lura Craighead, born into a socially prominent Nashville family and wife of the *Mobile Register*'s editor, and Annie Waterman, wife of a young shipping entrepreneur, were leaders in the united movement. The group's charter sought to encourage "self-sustenance, self-respect and general uplift among the poor." They envisioned their work being short-term and limited. They hoped that their success would make future efforts unnecessary. Like their husbands, these women thought that the poor were responsible for their circumstances and thus bore most of the burden of their own uplift. In its first few years the Associated Charities of Mobile concentrated on providing reformatories for the young and conducting campaigns for sanitary milk and the betterment of the library.[36]

Mobile's efforts at self-improvement and economic growth suffered a blow when Europe's volatile political landscape exploded into war in 1914. The shutting of foreign ports and the slowing of international trade hurt Mobile's economy. Despite its determination to aid Mobile's business growth, the commission could not manufacture prosperity, and even as they uttered optimistic pronouncements, city leaders admitted the port's decline. The "financial conditions of business institutions and people" suffered, and unemployment increased. The city's indigent population grew, and Mobile felt the burden of "a great many worthy people [who] are now indigent who are able to care for themselves under ordinary circumstances."[37] City residents began to look elsewhere for jobs. From 1914 through the end of 1916 thousands of blacks and hundreds of whites abandoned the city. The out-migration

Below, left:
Lura Craighead.

Erik Overbey Collection, USA Archives.

Below, right:
Annie Waterman.

Erik Overbey Collection, USA Archives.

The 1919 launching of the SS *Latham,* one of two concrete ships begun in Mobile before the armistice ended the experiment.

Museum of Mobile.

actually left the city strapped for workers when it finally stood ready to benefit from war-related activity. Indeed, out-migration at the start of the European phase of the war had slowed Mobile's population growth. Mobile had grown 34 percent from 1900 to 1910 but just 17 percent from 1910 to 1920. Outlying areas, such as Whistler, with its burgeoning railroad yards, grew faster in the period. Mobile, for instance, accounted for two-thirds of the county's growth from 1900 to 1910 but less than half of its growth in the next decade. In 1918 Mobile needed five thousand to ten thousand workers to fill all the vacant jobs in the city and outlying regions. Local industry "daily call[ed] for skilled and unskilled help of most every kind" but received inadequate replies, Mayor Lyons noted.[38]

Over its course the war did, at least temporarily, reorient some of Mobile's economic prospects. Manufacturing became more important, especially those industries related to shipbuilding and steel production. Between 1898 and 1914, for instance, the manufacturing activity in the city increased marginally. The number of establishments grew from 119 to 133, but only 98 more people out of a total of 2,604 were employed, and the value added by area industry also grew slowly. By 1919, however, industry employed 9,316 Mobilians. Most of the new jobs could be attributed to the 5,729 men employed by shipbuilding and steel enterprises. Moreover, the value of the products they made jumped four and one-half times over the 1914 level.[39]

Mobilians rallied behind the war effort after the United States entered the conflict. Groups took up the banner of national patriotic organizations. The Liberty Bond campaign, the Red Cross drive, the War Saving Stamp programs, and the United War Work Campaign took center stage in the city. Local groups supplemented the official effort of the army and local police in guarding Mobile's docks, shipyards, and wharves. With a small (and declining) but still important immigrant community, some Mobilians worried about the loyalty of their foreign-born neighbors. Some immigrant organizations, such as the German Alliance, stopped meeting during the war to allay concern. Bowing to threats, the German Relief Association changed its name to the Mobile Relief Association and ceased conducting its meetings in German. The *Mobile Register* touted the patriotism of Mobile's citizens of European heritage. "They are not Germans, nor Austrians, nor Swedes, nor Italians, nor Mexicans, nor Cubans, nor Spaniards," an editorial commented, "nor anything else but good Americans." Nonetheless, the Americanization fervor may have helped fuel anti-immigration and anti-Catholic sentiments in the city. The Ku Klux Klan, in its second incarnation that included an anti-Catholic strain, established a presence in Mobile. In 1918 Klan members stopped a work slowdown by abducting a labor leader and by intimidating "idlers and draft dodgers." Three years later, the Mobile Klan boasted several thousand members. Social and cultural tensions racked Mobile as residents tried to make sense of a changing order. The perceived need to control immoral behavior during the war did lead the city commission finally to prohibit prostitution in the city, a long-time demand of moral reformers and women's groups.[40]

Thousands of people line Government Street for a parade celebrating the end of the Great War.

S. M. Coffin Collection, USA Archives.

As the war neared its close, Mobile's leaders worried whether the city could sustain its productivity and prosperity. They commented on the "crowded housing conditions, the crowded streetcars, theaters, moving pictures, [and] streets," but they continued to promote the city through a national advertising campaign because they expected that some war-related industry would vanish after the armistice.[41] The war nonetheless had significant long-term impact. The initial economic downturn at the docks convinced Mobile's leaders that some local problems required more than local solutions; they needed concerted state or national effort. In 1916 the successful formation of the State Harbors Commission, an idea first introduced in 1909, was a result of that belief. The new agency of experts and influential locals would consist of seven members appointed by the governor. These unpaid commissioners were given full jurisdiction over the area's rivers and harbors. Some Mobilians feared that the commission meant that they would lose control over their port; nonetheless, the formation of the state agency indicated that many believed the government had a role in matters of economic development. The State Harbors Commission, however, accomplished little in its first few years because of political infighting and its own minuscule budget.

City leaders wanted their efforts for the docks to be part of a wider program to improve Alabama's river system, and they knew the state could not accomplish this

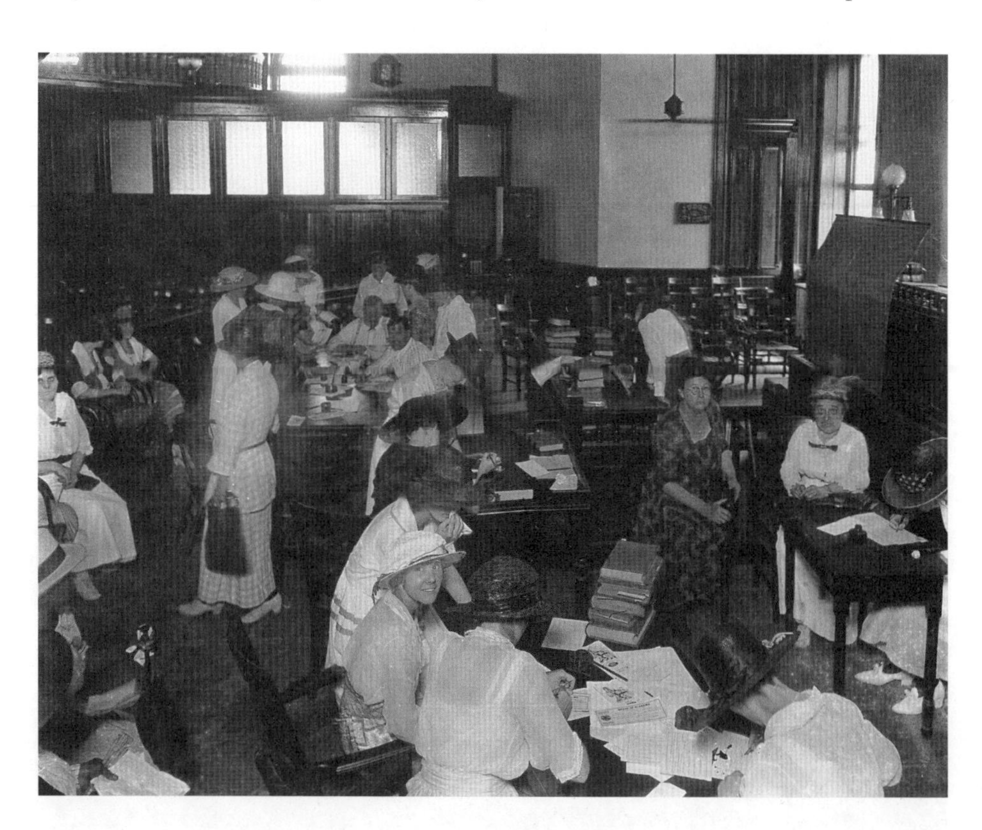

By the end of the Progressive Era, women were ready to participate in public affairs. Approximately two thousand women registered to vote in Mobile County in 1920.

Erik Overbey Collection, USA Archives.

project alone. Such dramatic public works initiatives required the federal government's assistance. Fortunately for Mobile (and Alabama) the war convinced Washington that it needed to promote port development and internal transportation nationally. The city government passed a resolution contending that "Mobile's shipping [is] the most important feature of its commercial life" and that efforts to promote its health "should be pushed most vigorously in Washington." Beginning in the next decade, Mobile would benefit from the federal interest in transportation-related matters.[42]

During the first two decades of the twentieth century Mobile took clear but tentative steps into the modern era and a fuller participation in national life. In this period the city's leaders espoused a belief in positive government, yet at the same time they limited and more strictly defined citizenship. They imagined that such a paternalistic system would work because of their faith that society's stresses and social ills could be resolved by economic development. Many of their initiatives in this regard came as a result of pressures from outside events. City leaders attempted to reverse the port's decline, with mixed results. The economy, nevertheless, became more diversified as new men pursuing new interests, such as railroads, assumed leadership positions. The government changed from a council to commission system to support their vision of business progressivism. Still, Mobile's circumscribed progressivism made few attempts to reach out to the city's poorer or less fortunate residents. Indeed, despite women's charity efforts and attempts at health reform, there was a general hardening of attitudes toward those who were different or less fortunate. Anti-Catholicism flourished, and relations between blacks and whites worsened as the city's white leaders segregated the races. All of these changes had consequences that the new Mobile would have to face in the decades to come.

Suggestions for Further Reading

Doyle, Don H. *New Men, New Cities, New South: Atlanta, Nashville, Charleston, Mobile, 1860–1910.* Chapel Hill: University of North Carolina Press, 1992. The most comprehensive study of Mobile elites in the New South era; its chapters on other cities, including Atlanta and Nashville, provide useful comparisons to the Mobile experience.

Grantham, Dewey W. *Southern Progressivism: The Reconciliation of Progress and Tradition.* Knoxville: University of Tennessee Press, 1983. Although overlapping some of the material in Woodward and Tindall, this shorter work is best in its analysis of the southern politics of the period.

Link, William. *The Paradox of Southern Progressivism, 1880–1930.* Chapel Hill: University of North Carolina Press, 1992. A detailed look at the Progressive Era in the South that underscores the tensions leaders in the region felt in trying to shape and define the new order.

McWilliams, Tennant S. *Hannis Taylor: The New Southerner as American.* Tuscaloosa: University of Alabama Press, 1978. A brief but rich study of a leader who helped to shape Mobile in the new century.

Tindall, George B. *The Emergence of the New South, 1913–1945.* Baton Rouge: Louisiana State University Press, 1967. Tindall follows Woodward's high standards by writing a sweeping study that combines first-rate archival scholarship and an excellent summary of existing literature.

Woodward, C. Vann. *Origins of the New South.* Baton Rouge: Louisiana State University Press, 1951. This work remains the best starting place for an understanding of the New South.

CHAPTER 7

Mobile during the Interwar Years

Billy Hinson

In the years between World Wars I and II Mobile experienced significant economic development. The port grew and helped to entice to the area new and expanded manufacturing establishments. Political and civic leaders aided this development with farsighted projects that also included promotion of tourism. The depression interrupted this progress, but the city had economic foundations that enabled it to survive and then continue its industrial development. Still, meaningful changes in much of the city's social life, especially in patterns of race relations, were unfortunately delayed.

Mobile entered the 1920s with expectations of continued economic progress. On the first day of the decade the *Mobile Register* recalled that 1919 was a prosperous year and predicted that 1920 would be better because many industrial projects were under way. It listed port and trade developments, construction of new plants, expansion of existing factories, and beginnings of new businesses. Contractors were anticipating a building boom, and bankers were expecting record-breaking deposits. In fact, in January 1920 the following firms were incorporated in the Mobile area: the General Brokerage Company, which chartered steam and sailing vessels; the Gulf Packing and Preserving Company, which operated a seafood packing factory at Bayou La Batre; the Neal Jones Lumber Company, with a capitalization of $32,000 and headquarters in Mobile; the Mobile Importing and Trading Company, with a stock of $25,000 and emphases on handling limes and blackstrap molasses; and the Mobile Tractor Company, with a capital stock of $1 million.[1]

World War I had promoted economic development especially related to shipping and the port. In 1914 the Tennessee Coal, Iron, and Railroad Company (TCI) started building a shipyard just north of Mobile at Chickasabogue. In 1916 the Alabama Dry Docks and Shipbuilding Company (ADDSCO) was created and in

1917 "launched the heaviest dry dock on the coast from New Orleans to Newport News." Other companies that were established in this period included the Murman Shipbuilding Corporation, the Kelly Dry Dock and Shipbuilding Company, the Mobile Shipbuilding Company, and the Fred T. Ley Company. In spite of the optimism, however, the war's end eventually slowed economic advancement. Demands for the building and repairing of ships fell drastically, several shipbuilding companies closed, and hundreds of workers in Mobile lost their jobs. Only ADDSCO and a few small shipyards remained in operation.[2]

Although financial prospects looked bleak, civic leaders started planning a proj-

Dauphin Street looking west from Joachim Street, 1938. Wagons and trucks are promoting the Mobile Gas Company's "Old Stove Roundup."

Erik Overbey Collection, USA Archives.

ect that would prove to be an important economic boost to the city—the creation of the state docks. As early as 1908, Mobile commercial interests had established a committee that investigated and reported the need for more adequate port facilities. In 1915 they appealed to the legislature to consider this project, but the lawmakers did not respond.[3] Nonetheless, Alabamians interested in this enterprise received added incentive when Congress in 1919 authorized the secretary of war to withhold funds from new harbor enterprises that he believed could not manage the expected traffic.[4] This prompted Governor Thomas E. Kilby and members of the State Harbors Commission in 1919 to arrange a campaign for an amendment to the state constitution that would allow the creation of the state docks.[5] In 1920 Alabama voters rejected the proposed amendment, but through the efforts of Mobile's leadership and with the backing of George G. Crawford of United States Steel's Birmingham subsidiary as well as the support of Governor Kilby, voters of Alabama approved the project in 1922.[6] Afterward the legislature passed an enabling act signed into law on September 18, 1923, which authorized the state to issue bonds amounting to $10 million to be used in the construction of the Alabama State Docks. The act replaced the State Harbors Commission with the State Docks Commission, whose three members were appointed by the governor to supervise the construction of port facilities.[7] Retired general William L. Seibert, one of the builders of the Panama Canal, accepted the task of building the docks. He did so on 540 acres of swampland one mile north of downtown Mobile and thirty-five miles above the gulf by way of a straight channel forty-two feet deep.[8] The Alabama State Docks opened in 1927.

With the construction of the state docks came the expansion of the port of Mobile. By 1929 the port of Mobile had more than fifty facilities for loading and unloading ships. Thirty-two piers and wharves were connected directly with the railroads, and four railroad companies owned their own piers and wharves. The Turner Terminal Company had the most important privately owned pier. The City of Mobile owned the municipal wharf, and the State of Alabama owned the state docks.[9] An additional warehouse was constructed in 1930, and in 1937 cold storage and quick-freeze facilities were added. By 1937 Mobile had fifty-five piers, wharves, and docks. Their total length was 50,200 feet.

The state docks and expanded port facilities encouraged industrial growth in Mobile by enticing to the area International Paper's Southern Kraft Division (1928), Aluminum Ore Company (1937), the Standard Oil Company (1937), the Pan American Shell Corporation (1939), and other businesses.[10] The docks also benefited farmers by more efficiently handling their crops, enabled processors of seafood and tropical fruits to quick-freeze and hold their products for later distribution, and served shippers and consumers with lower prices than competing ports. All of this meant higher employment and a stronger local economy.[11]

Five railroads served Mobile. The Louisville and Nashville ran from Cincinnati through Louisville, Nashville, Birmingham, Montgomery, Mobile, and New Orleans. Two others, which merged in 1940, were the Mobile and Ohio and the Gulf, Mobile, and Northern. They became the Gulf, Mobile, and Ohio and connected Mobile with southeastern Mississippi, St. Louis, and Jackson, Tennessee. The Southern Railway had a short line from Birmingham to Mobile. The Alabama, Tennessee, and Northern also served Mobile.[12]

One of the important companies associated with the port of Mobile was ADDSCO. It was formed by a group of men with a vision of making the port of Mobile a leading ship repair and building center. During World War I ADDSCO expanded and prospered. After the war ADDSCO officials invested in new machinery and properties and acquired some competing plants. In 1920 it shifted most of its operations to Pinto Island and completed a new ten-thousand-ton dry dock on a tract there purchased during the war. In 1936 ADDSCO acquired from a competitor additional facilities that included not only a twelve-thousand-ton and eight-thousand-ton dry dock but also outfitting wharves and other shops. It became the leader in ship repair and building on the Gulf Coast.[13]

Another contributor to the success of the port of Mobile was John B. Waterman. Born in New Orleans in 1866, he came to Mobile in 1902 as East Gulf man-

Aerial view of the new Alabama State Docks, circa 1927.

Erik Overbey Collection, USA Archives.

ager for a British steamship firm. On June 10, 1919, Waterman, Walter D. Bellingrath, and C. W. Hempstead organized the Waterman Steamship Corporation. That November they started business with one ship, the *Eastern Sun,* leased from the U.S. Shipping Board, which was trying to build a strong American merchant marine by having private companies manage ships built for the war effort.

Waterman continually expanded its business. Throughout the 1920s it acquired a growing fleet of government-owned ships; organized a subsidiary, Ryan Stevedoring Company, Inc.; and became the only government operation sanctioned at the port of Mobile. It purchased three ships from the government in 1926 and fourteen more in 1931. In the 1930s it bought stock in the Pan Atlantic Steamship Corporation; took over the Mobile, Miami, and Gulf Steamship Company; purchased the Biloxi Grit Company and seven more ships; began to manage three Canadian vessels owned by the International Paper Company; and established two subsidiaries—the Gulf Florida Terminal Company, Inc., and the Gulf Shipbuilding Corporation. By 1938 the Waterman Steamship Corporation had three steamship lines, operated three American flag vessels, managed more than a dozen chartered vessels, and sailed throughout the world. John B. Waterman became chairman of the board in 1936 and died on April 30, 1937. By the time of his death he had made a significant contribution to his goal of making Mobile a major port.[14]

Interior of International Paper Company, circa 1929.

Erik Overbey Collection, USA Archives.

Mobile's industrial growth was also aided by the establishment of Southern Kraft Division by the International Paper Company. The company began construction on September 9, 1928, and started operations a year later. International Paper considered other cities for its plant but chose Mobile because its water supply was plentiful and because its wood was suitable for paper manufacturing. In addition the Chamber of Commerce conducted a successful campaign to raise $100,000 to meet an International Paper requirement that this amount go to the company.[15] In the beginning the plant had two machines producing bag and wrapping paper, employed about five hundred people, and had an annual payroll of more than $1 million. In the worst year of the depression, 1932, the Kraft mill added a third machine.[16] By 1940 it employed more than eighteen hundred people.

Another boost to the Mobile economy came when the Aluminum Ore Company, a subsidiary of the Aluminum Company of America (Alcoa), took a ninety-nine-year lease on property of the state docks and constructed a $4 million plant on a seventy-five-acre plot of land on the Mobile River adjacent to the docks. Mobilians learned about the plans on July 9, 1937. Construction soon started, and the plant opened on July 22, 1938.[17] Alcoa had previously mined bauxite in Arkansas and shipped it to East St. Louis to be refined into bauxite oxide, called alumina, which was shipped to smelters. Demands for more ore in the 1920s led the company to ship bauxite into the port of Mobile and haul it by rail to the East St. Louis refinery. Alcoa decided to increase its refining capacity by establishing a bauxite refinery in Mobile. The city was chosen because of its port facilities, geographic location, and labor supply. The first delivery of alumina was shipped in August 1938 to Badin, North Carolina, where smelters converted it to aluminum. The company expanded and had 374 workers in 1940.[18] The news of the alumina plant brought national attention to Mobile's modern port facilities and its low-cost electric power, and other industrial plants located in the port city. Numerous firms in 1940 were making substantial additions to their Mobile facilities.[19]

The growth of Mobile businesses was aided by the construction of the Cochrane Bridge over the Mobile River. The city commission called for a conference of interested parties to be held on Wednesday, July 1, 1925. John T. Cochrane Sr., president of the Chamber of Commerce, submitted to the conference a $1.8 million plan that created a committee of seven to report in thirty days on the feasibility of a bridge across the bay.[20] Cochrane, who was also president of the Alabama, Tennessee, and Northern Railroad, was elected chairman of the committee. It proposed, and the conference approved, a plan for the organization of the Mobile Bay Bridge Company with seven directors and the issuance of mortgage bonds to finance the project. The sale of $25 million in bonds was concluded in November 1925, and contracts were let in 1926. The bridge was completed in sixteen months and named for Cochrane.[21] It formally opened on June 14, 1927, with numerous dignitaries, including Alabama governor Bibb Graves, attending. Sample rates were as follows: one dollar for each passenger automobile and its driver and ten cents for each additional occupant; two dollars each for trucks over five tons; ten cents each for foot passengers; and fifteen cents for a bicycle and its rider.[22] On that first day "550 motor vehicles representing eleven states crossed the 10½-mile structure, spanning five rivers and described as one of the longest bridges in the world."[23] Before the bridge was constructed one could not reach Baldwin County by automobile except by ferrying across on bay boats, which charged $3.10 an automobile and $0.40 for each occupant. This was very expensive for most Mobilians, and anyone who did cross by ferry often found it time-consuming and wearisome.[24] Completion of the Cochrane Bridge provided Mobile with a much faster and less expensive vehicular route to Baldwin County and beyond. Traffic increased yearly, and by 1940 approximately 1,100,000 vehicles used the bridge annually.[25]

Cochrane later led a movement to open the bridge toll free. In the gubernatorial campaign of 1934 candidate Bibb Graves endorsed the free bridge idea, and after his election he worked to fulfill his stand. Eventually the state bought the bridge for $2,146,323 and ended the toll. As expected, a free bridge brought increased traffic.[26]

The construction of the Bankhead Tunnel further aided the flow of traffic to and from the eastern shore. Some citizens had favored building a bridge with a lift span instead, but government officials were opposed to this because it would constantly interrupt vehicular and waterborne traffic. In the summer of 1938 Wayne F.

The Cochrane Bridge, spanning the headwaters of Mobile Bay, opened to traffic in 1927.

Erik Overbey Collection, USA Archives.

Sections of the Bankhead Tunnel afloat in the Mobile River, 1940.

Erik Overbey Collection, USA Archives.

Palmer Sr. of Wilberding and Palmer, Inc. proposed to the city commission a plan to build a tunnel from the foot of Government Street under the Mobile River to Blakeley Island. The city commission favored the plan and obtained the support of Alabama senators John H. Bankhead and Lister Hill, who obtained federal funding of $4 million from the Works Progress Administration (WPA). Groundbreaking took place on December 29, 1938.

An amazing technological accomplishment occurred. A trench was dredged in, not through, the river bed to house seven tubular sections that ADDSCO, pioneering marine engineering technology, built with dimensions of 298 feet x 30 feet. The steel-plated tubular sections were floated from the ADDSCO construction site and sunk in place. Their exterior hull was then filled with concrete to hold them in the desired position. Steel collars with rubber gaskets sealed the joints between each tube. The joints were welded from the inside and further sealed with rings of concrete.

The result was a single-tube tunnel 45 feet below the surface of the river and 3,109 feet long, with just under one-third of its length beneath the river. The engineers designed the tunnel to reduce entrapment of fumes by installing exhaust ducts under the roadway, locating a ventilation shaft in a building on Blakeley Island, and including in the building three large blower fans that renewed fresh air in the tunnel every two minutes. Construction of the tunnel was a boost to the local economy because it provided business to local shipyards, iron foundries, and steel-fabrication shops and created jobs for about one thousand men, who completed the project in just twenty-two months. The underwater tunnel, unique in the South at that time, was named after former U.S. senator and congressman John Hollis Bankhead, who had promoted development of American waterways and highways. Opening ceremonies occurred on February 20, 1941.[27] That day Mobile seemed to be a showcase of a southern city on the move.

Important exports from Mobile throughout the interwar years were iron, steel and fabricated products, lumber and lumber products, coal and coke, cotton, and petroleum. Imports included syrup and molasses, bananas, bauxite, and manganese ore. In the early 1920s the chief exports were lumber, iron and steel products, cotton, coal, naval stores, and staves, and the chief imports were molasses, bananas, manganese ore, sisal, nitrates, potash, and manufactured articles.[28] Cotton trade as well as lumber exports declined in the 1930s whereas export of petroleum products increased greatly. Meanwhile, the 1930s saw a tremendous growth in bauxite imports.[29] Even while the main exports of the past—cotton, lumber, and naval stores—were declining, the port's national ranking rose during 1934 to 1938 from twenty-first to fifteenth place in volume of export and import tonnage.[30] Latin America became more important for Mobile's foreign trade. The city's exports to and imports from Latin American countries doubled from 1930 to 1940. Coastwide trade with ports on the Gulf, Atlantic, and Pacific Coasts also aided Mobile's commerce.

Despite all the innovations of the 1920s, commerce, not industry, dominated Mobile's economic life. During the 1930s the retail businesses that increased in number the most were groceries, household furniture, radios, gasoline filling stations, and eating and drinking establishments. Businesses decreasing in number the most were in the automobile groups, lumber, building, hardware, and drug stores.[31] Much of this change reflected the effects of the depression.

Two of the most successful and interesting local capitalists were involved in the grocery business: Alfred F. Delchamps Sr. and his brother, Ollie. In November 1921, with a $1,000 investment they opened the first Delchamps Food Store in a 20 foot x 50 foot frame building at Canal and Lawrence Streets. Their business grew, and they established another store in a residential section of the town in 1922. Each year they opened another store. In 1928 they opened a warehouse and bought directly from the manufacturers. In 1929, at St. Louis Street and Washington Avenue, they opened their first supermarket store, which was then the largest food store in Alabama and their first self-service store, except for meats. In 1932 the Delchampses closed down their last frame store and started opening yellow brick buildings. Their first grocery outside of Mobile was in Pensacola. In 1937 they purchased the three stores of Coleman Grocery Company and, with ten stores, became the largest food retailer in Mobile.[32] It was indeed a remarkable story of entrepreneurship and innovation.

Another successful business innovation involved tourism. Sam H. Lackland, a local entrepreneur, originated the idea of the Azalea Trail because he believed that masses of azaleas in bloom would attract tourists in the spring. The Junior Chamber of Commerce encouraged Mobilians to plant more azaleas. People responded with enthusiasm, and many plants were seen in bloom during the first tour conducted on February 22, 1929. On that day, a large number of invited guests left in a motorcade from the Chamber of Commerce building on St. Francis Street at 4:00 P.M. and followed signs along the trail that stretched for fifteen miles. In subsequent years, the Junior Chamber of Commerce distributed publicity material outside of Mobile.[33] In 1930 during the Second Azalea Trail, thirty cars from New Orleans took part in the motorcade. The next year the Crescent City sent seventy. The event proved so popular that the city commissioners, in the depression year of 1933, placed 275 light pink azaleas in Lyons Park. Beginning in 1936 the Mardi Gras queen formally began the Azalea Trail by cutting the ribbon. By 1940 approximately one hundred thousand visitors came annually to see Mobile's azaleas.[34]

Another tourist attraction was the Alabama Deep Sea Fishing Rodeo, an event that was suggested by State Game and Fisheries commissioner I. T. Quinn of Montgomery. He discussed the proposal with Mobilians L. G. Adams, Sam Lackland, and others. Adams chaired a committee that planned the first rodeo for August 26 through August 28, 1929. Men and women participants from eight states stayed in barracks on Dauphin Island. Some 260 people entered the contest and later expressed interest in the rodeo being an annual event. The first rodeo had no name, but its success led to the formation of the Alabama Deep Sea Fishing

First Delchamps grocery store, Lawrence and Canal Streets. Ollie and Alfred Delchamps talk with a salesman.

Erik Overbey Collection, USA Archives.

Second Annual Alabama Deep Sea Fishing Rodeo, 1930. L. G. Adams, president, stands to the right of two lucky Fishermen.

Erik Overbey Collection, USA Archives.

Rodeo Association with Adams as president. Attendance grew each year, with people from a wide variety of backgrounds freely mingling with each other. In 1940, 520 people participated, of which 231 came from twenty-three other states and the District of Columbia.[35]

The era's greatest innovation was Bellingrath Gardens, which was not originally envisioned as the tourist attraction it became. Walter D. Bellingrath, the son of a German immigrant, had grown up in Atlanta, where he acquired the franchise to Coca-Cola, moved to Mobile in 1904, and made millions. In 1918 he purchased a site twenty miles south of Mobile on the Fowl River and established a fishing camp, Bellcamp. After he and his wife took a trip to Europe where they viewed gardens at well-known estates, they envisioned a beautiful garden at their camp. With the assistance of "Doctor Loding," a botanist who had worked in the Kew Botanic Gardens in England, and the aid of architect George B. Rogers, Bellingrath built an elaborate private garden. He opened it to the general public on February 28, 1932, and the response was overwhelming. Snarled traffic kept many from even entering the gardens. So many people came that Bellingrath decided to charge admission to help maintain the garden. In 1940 the estate included one hundred acres. In 1939 approximately fifty-eight thousand visitors came to view the garden.[36]

The attention brought to Mobile by the Azalea Trail and the Bellingrath Gardens contributed to the growing wholesale nursery business in the area. The Semmes Nurseries had begun in 1913 with cultivation of orange trees, pecans, and some ornamentals. In 1920 Tom Dodd and his brother-in-law, Fred Welch, opened the Dodd and Welch Nursery on land located fifteen miles west of Mobile. When Dodd bought the Welch interest in 1926 he changed the name to Tom Dodd Nurseries. He faced difficult times during the depression of the 1930s but survived and began to thrive.[37]

Many Mobilians suffered during the Great Depression, but the devastation was not as deep as it would have been if Mobile's economy had been dominated by industry instead of commerce. Still, the depression retarded area industrial development for several years.[38]

The stock market crash of October 1929 was the revealing barometer of conditions. The *Mobile Daily Register* described the drop in prices on October 24 ("Black Thursday") as a "terrifying stampede of selling." After the October 29 crash, however, the paper reported that the stampede was checked by powerful financial institutions. Later articles by the paper downplayed the seriousness of the stock market plunge, spoke of prosperous times ahead, and urged spending to solve economic problems.[39] Nonetheless, optimistic statements could not stem the onset of economic distress.

The repercussions of the depression are telling. Mobile's wholesale trade declined dramatically, with sales falling from $52,531,000 in 1929 to $36,740,000 in 1935. Retail sales for Mobile County fell from $39,494,000 in 1929 to $27,566,000 in 1935. Part of the decline in wholesale and retail trade was related to falling business at the port of Mobile. From 1929 to 1935 the value of exports dropped from $55,509,000 to $30,770,000, and the value of imports fell from $10,706,000 to $6,392,000. The number of vessels entering and leaving the port also dropped significantly.[40]

The bank holiday was a setback for the city. Mardi Gras had just ended, and Ash Wednesday came on March 1, 1933. On that day Governor B. M. Miller declared a bank holiday. The First National Bank, the Merchants National Bank, and the American National Bank decided to remain open. Mobilians read in the *Mobile Register* on March 3, however, that Merchants National Bank restricted withdrawals to 5 percent of deposits in certain accounts, such as savings and checking. The paper reported on March 4 that the First National Bank was also restricting withdrawals, but the American National Bank operated without the restrictions. Nonetheless, the three Mobile banks had to close their doors on March 4 because the four federal reserve banks in the district suspended operations. After President

Roosevelt declared a bank holiday on March 9 and then signed the Banking Act of 1933 on March 13, Mobile banks were reopened on March 14. On that day 111 merchants in the city announced in a full-page ad in the *Mobile Register* that they would cash checks on Mobile banks. People then showed their confidence by making deposits that far exceeded withdrawals.[41]

Economic retrenchment was widespread during the depression, especially beginning in 1933. City officials spent $11,076 less to operate in February 1933 than they did in February 1932. In March 1933 the Saenger Theater started operating only on weekends and at reduced prices. The Mobile County School Board was unable to pay teachers. The Mobile County Teachers' Association appointed committees to confer with the school board. One survey showed that more than half of the 230 teachers favored closing schools immediately until satisfaction about future pay was met. Teachers' salaries were three months behind. On March 14, with the reopening of banks after the bank holiday, the school board released checks amounting to about $21,000, which paid a quarter of one month's salary for public school employees.[42]

Business failures and mergers occurred. For example, the three principal banks survived the depression, but Mobile National Bank was taken over by Merchants National Bank. In a case involving the newspapers, the *Mobile Press* purchased the *Mobile Register* and the other daily, the *Mobile News-Item,* stating that two newspapers could not be financially successful in Mobile. The *Mobile Register* became the morning paper, and the *Mobile Press* became its afternoon edition.[43]

Telephone service was similarly affected. In 1879 Mobile had been the first Alabama city to have telephones. In that year Southern Bell established the Mobile Telephone Exchange. Long-distance service was established in 1888 with Pascagoula and Montgomery. A local company started a rival concern, and by 1902 Mobilians could choose between two, Southern Bell or Mobile Home Telephone Company. Some subscribers, especially businesses, had two telephone lines running to their establishments. Southern Bell dominated and even had to add a prefix to the telephone number in the late 1920s. During the depression, however, hundreds of subscribers dropped their phone service. Mobile Home Telephone Company sold out to Southern Bell. In 1929 there had been more than eleven thousand telephones in service, but by 1935 the number had dropped to ten thousand.[44]

Mobilians had to cope with the loss of jobs and purchasing power: industrial plants received fewer orders and laid off employees, and wholesalers and retailers lost business, reduced inventory, and let workers go. Some families moved in with other relatives, and many people cultivated small gardens to reduce their grocery bill. More housewives began to sew and make clothes. If they did not walk, people formed car pools to go to work, church, and stores. As unemployment increased so did the number of beggars. Some civic leaders condemned street begging, and the city helped the Salvation Army open up a house where the needy could receive meal tickets in return for performing work in a wood yard. Civic clubs and churches raised money to aid the unemployed. Still, in June of 1932 some three hundred unemployed people marched on city hall to demand help for their starving families.[45]

The decade of the depression was dreadful, but in time Mobile began to rebound. Contributing to the resurgence was a gradual commercial revival and the region's abundant water resources, timber, and inexpensive transportation, which attracted new industries. In addition, Europe and Japan started making preparations for war and increased their purchase of U.S. products, especially alumina, which Alcoa had started producing in Mobile in 1938.[46]

New Deal programs also aided recovery. The agency through which most of the economic assistance was provided was the WPA. It sponsored such diverse projects as improving parks and playgrounds; building a community center on Davis Avenue; hiring nurses and clerks at City Hospital; decorating public buildings and institutions, including having murals painted; hiring library assistants; and constructing the auditorium for the American Legion. It also provided for the resurfacing and paving of streets; demolishing and repairing the fairground; constructing the concrete runway and apron at the airport; propagating plants to be used on highways and in parks; enlarging the swimming pool at Spring Hill; installing a spillway; and surfacing tennis courts. The city had to contribute a small part of the funds for most of the projects, but the federal government provided the lion's share. The city paid $22,358.80 on these projects, whereas the federal funds totaled $476,700.70.[47]

Commissioner Cecil F. Bates boasted of justice for the "negro population of Mobile" regarding water sport facilities and park areas. He called attention to the outstanding community house on Davis Avenue. It had the only swimming pool in the city's public parks, except for Lyons Park, and had separate dressing rooms for males and females. In addition, with the construction of tennis courts and wading pools, Davis Avenue Park was "probably . . . the best equipped and complete negro park in the South." The WPA provided $25,935, and the city contributed $260 to build it.[48]

One specific example of a local WPA venture was in the Arts Projects program. Artists painted mural panels on the inside walls at the entrance to the old city hall. On the south wall were the murals *Bienville the Builder, 1702, The Canoe Fight, 1813,* and *Dedication of Barton Academy, 1836,* and on the east were painted *First Steamboat, 1818* and *Trunkline Completed, 1861.* Three more mural panels were painted on the north wall: *Last Importation of Slaves, 1859, Construction of the Submarine Hunley,* and *Mother of Mystics, 1867.* Under the Arts Projects program, loans of pictures were made to tax-supported institutions. Some pictures were hung in a room of the Chamber of Commerce and later became city property. In addition a bronze tablet was placed at the site of the prison in Fort Charlotte.[49]

WPA grants were diverse. They allowed the Junior Chamber of Commerce and the Federated Garden Clubs to make hundreds of azalea beds with flowers obtained from Kiyona Nursery, R. B. Davis Nursery, and Tom Dodd Nursery and to plant azaleas at such places as the Elk's Club, the Shrine home, and McGill Institute. Most of the flowers were planted at the homes of individuals, with usually one to four beds per home. The federal government provided grants for "Housekeeping Aide Projects," which employed needy people as housekeeping aides. Racial prejudice was evident when the project moved from 315 S. Ann Street to 100 N. Ann Street and people in the neighborhood of the house at the northeast corner of Ann Street and Old Shell Road objected to its use as a gathering place for whites and negroes in a residential section. WPA funds went to the Department of Public Welfare of Mobile County to set up sewing rooms and hire people to make clothes and mattresses and distribute them to needy people in public and private institutions in the city and county. At the end of January 1937 the city had a total of twenty projects employing 594 women with a payroll of $23,000 a month. WPA funds also went to projects to hire people to make toys at 955 Springhill Avenue (later relocated to 69 North Joachim Street); for the building of the federal court house; for the construction of Fort Whiting, which was completed in 1938 and named in honor of Captain Julian Wythe Whiting of the Confederate army; and even for the employment of musicians.[50]

Other agencies of the federal government provided work and funds for the city. The National Youth Administration had numerous projects for young people, such as marking of one-way streets, supervising playgrounds, and teaching in school. In 1935 the Federal Emergency Relief Administration provided the labor for building two tennis courts at the YWCA. The Civilian Conservation Corps (CCC) hired some young men from Mobile and established two camps in Mobile County, one at Camp Rendell near Chunchula and the other at Cedar Creek Park near Citronelle. Mobile also benefited because these men made trips to the city, where they spent money, and because the CCC purchased food and supplies from local stores.[51]

While Mobile experienced tremendous economic changes in the interwar years, it also underwent social changes that were not as momentous in their effects on the character of life. Prohibition was one example. The Volstead Enabling Act to enforce Prohibition took effect on January 16, 1920. The *Mobile Register* reported that John F. Kramer, general Prohibition commissioner, was ready to enforce the act. Nevertheless, liquor was abundant in Mobile during the twenties because the port made smuggling easy and the city lacked sufficient law enforcement officials. The federal government decided to make an example of Mobile, and in November

1923 agents concentrated their efforts there. They seized $100,000 worth of alcohol and claimed they had uncovered a huge rum ring. The federal grand jury indicted seventy-one leading men of the community in April 1924, and the first trials were held in May. Six men who were convicted testified against Sheriff Paul Cazales, ex-sheriff and legislator William H. Holcombe, Chief of Police Patrick J. O'Shaughnessy, and other well-known people such as Frank Boykin, George L. Donaghue, Captain Jewett Scott, Robert Holcombe, Judge J. B. Connaughton, W. J. Hamlon, and Alfred Staples. Their trial was held in February 1925 and led to convictions for Boykin, William Holcombe, O'Shaughnessy, and Donaghue, who

City commissioners Cecil F. Bates, Harry T. Hartwell, and Leon Schwarz photographed at Mobile's new airport, circa 1930.

Museum of Mobile.

were each given two-year sentences. Many of the other defendants were heavily fined.[52]

Evangelist Billy Sunday traveled throughout the nation after the passage of the National Prohibition Act. He and his evangelistic team came to Mobile on New Year's Day, 1927. They arrived at the Louisville and Nashville Station at 12:43 that afternoon and were met by Mayor Harry T. Hartwell and other dignitaries and a large tabernacle band. The evangelistic party stayed at the Cawthon Hotel. They held a revival that lasted six weeks, January 2 through February 13. Services were held in the tabernacle, which was the old Warrant warehouse between Water and Royal Streets just north of St. Anthony Street. It seated sixty-five hundred people and had a floor of sawdust or shavings in order to reduce noise when people walked around. No services were held on Mondays in order for Billy Sunday to rest after his Sabbath exertions. The city provided free light and water and five policemen for the revival. During the campaign Billy Sunday stressed the evils of alcohol.[53]

Somehow, Mardi Gras survived the era of Prohibition and the decade of depression. The festivities had been revived after being suspended in 1918 and 1919. Mardi Gras had been halted during World War I because joyous celebrations seemed inappropriate when people were suffering and because a need existed to concentrate all energy on raising funds for the war effort. The first Mardi Gras of the 1920s returned to the tradition of wearing masks because city commissioners repealed the wartime ordinance that had banned them. A new feature was added in 1929, the children's Saturday afternoon floral parade with a young boy and girl reigning over the floats. The idea was originated by Sid Simon, who was asked by Alfred Staples, a carnival king in 1916 and later president of the Mobile Carnival Association, to think of a Mardi Gras event for Saturday afternoon. It became one of the most popular daytime festivities. During the depression years the Mobile merchants were still able to provide money for bands and decorations, and the mystic societies provided the floats. The center for banquets and festivity was the Battle House. Still, the effects of the depression were noticeable in fewer floats and parades. The Mobile Carnival Association coordinated the five days of parades and chose the royal king and queen whose rule climaxed the social season. Blacks in Mobile held their first Mardi Gras parade in 1938 as a result of the efforts of A. S. May, founder and president of the Knights of May Zulu Club. In 1939 two additional black groups were organized. One of them, the Colored Carnival Association, held a parade on Davis Avenue.[54]

Mardi Gras was just one of many forms of entertainment for Mobilians. Baseball grew in popularity during the 1920s. The city had a minor league baseball team in the Southern Association from 1908 to 1931. As noted in the last chapter, the team, originally named the Mobile Sea Gulls, was renamed the Mobile Bears in March 1918. When the Bears began their 1920 season on Wednesday, April 14, the

The Mobile Bears photographed at Monroe Park in 1922 after winning the Southern Association pennant.

USA Archives.

mayor continued a tradition by proclaiming a half-day holiday. He urged citizens to attend the game and asked merchants, corporations, and associations to close their businesses for the occasion. Nearly every business agreed to close down for the opening game. The Bears won 9 to 0 against New Orleans with the largest crowd ever in attendance at a baseball game in Mobile. Their best year was 1922, when they won the Southern Association pennant and the Dixie Series. They also had winning seasons in 1923 and 1928. For the 1931 season they were known as the Mobile Marines before they were moved to Knoxville and nicknamed the "Smokies." In 1932 the Southeastern League was organized but was disbanded the same year because of the depression. The Mobile team was the only moneymaker in the league. The Southeastern League re-formed in 1937 and disbanded in 1942. In 1937 the Mobile Shippers were started and were in the Southeastern League until its demise. The Shippers played in the Little Dixie Series in 1937, 1938, and 1941 and won in 1937. Later the Mobile Bears re-formed and from 1944 to 1961 were in the Southern Association. Interest in black baseball teams in Mobile also grew after the formation of the Negro National Baseball League in Kansas City in 1920. Some of the better known black teams from Mobile were the Mobile Black Bears, the Mobile Tigers, and the Mobile Black Shippers.[55]

Many interesting baseball-related events occurred in the 1920s. One of the most famous involved Babe Ruth. On April 1, 1924, the New York Yankees played Rochester in an exhibition game at Monroe Park and beat them 8 to 2. The Babe hit a home run over the center field wall. After the game he went to Spring Hill College and gave students some pointers on how to hit home runs. In 1926 a hurricane leveled the Mobile Bears' bleachers at Monroe Park. Commissioner Hartwell was instrumental in getting the city commission to offer to the Bears a parcel of city land at Tennessee and Ann Streets. The resulting field was named after him and was officially opened in April 1927. On that day Mayor Hartwell himself announced a half-day holiday for the city schools so people could go to the game.[56]

Other baseball leagues were formed for intracity games to provide entertainment, recreation, and exercise for employees. The Commercial Twilight Baseball League was reorganized in 1923, composed of the Gulf, Mobile, and Northern Railroad; the Mobile and Ohio Railroad; Merchants Bank; and McGowin-Lyons Hardware Company teams. They played three games a week after work, and city commissioners assumed the responsibility of maintaining the playing field located across from the Louisville and Nashville Railroad shops.[57]

Movies also became a big part of entertainment life. Nevertheless, throughout the 1920s a controversy continued over closing down movie houses on Sunday and establishing a board of censors. When the state legislature entertained the idea of passing a Sunday blue law that would affect many businesses as well as the motion picture theaters, one of those objecting was H. C. Farley, manager of the Empire Theater, who asked city commissioner Hartwell to do what he could to prevent such legislation from passing. Charles W. Greer, chairman of the Civic Betterment League, even argued that Sunday motion pictures benefited young men and women by combating the evils of idleness. On the other hand Reverend C. B. Arendall, pastor of Dauphin Way Baptist Church, insisted that motion pictures on Sunday desecrated the Sabbath, were powerful weapons of the devil, and were of no economic benefit to Mobile. Interest in censorship grew after the Queen Theater at 220 Dauphin Street showed a film titled *The Western Adventurer,* which included an "indecent" barroom dance. Mayor Harry Pillans attended the movie and concluded that the film violated city ordinances. He ordered Paul Ford, owner of the Queen Theater, to cut out the objectional part. Ford wrote Savini Films of Atlanta, Georgia, to complain about the film and threatened to cancel business with them if he was not assured of better movies. He apologized to the commissioners and promised to cut the "immoral scenes." Meanwhile, the Mobile Ministerial Association passed a resolution asking the Board of City Commissioners to establish a Board of Censors for movies and theatrical performances. A committee of women also asked the commissioners to provide better regulation. The commissioners responded by authorizing the chief of police to determine whether violations of existing laws had occurred and to make arrests. Such controversy did nothing to diminish overall attendance at movies or a demand for new theaters. The new Saenger Theater opened on January 19, 1927. This magnificent showplace that cost $750,000 to build was owned by brothers Julian and A. D. Saenger of New Orleans. The first movie shown was *The Eagle and the Sea.* School children in Mobile were given a holiday to attend the opening of the Saenger, which had more than nineteen hundred seats and was one of the first air-conditioned buildings in Mobile.[58]

The port city had long supported musical performances. Men took the lead in founding musical social clubs. The origin of these clubs can be traced to the establishment of the Mobile Musical Association in 1848. In 1894 women established the Clara Schumann Club, which became the leading music association in the city through the interwar years. Others were the Polymnia Music Circle, which was founded in 1911; the Music Study Club, which was established in 1915; and the Chopin Club, which was begun in 1916. All four federated in 1916. They presented concerts in the early 1920s as did the High School Orchestra, Drago's Band, and the Little Theater Orchestra. It was not unusual for a member of a club to be a pianist or organist in a church or synagogue or perhaps even in two. For example, Frederick A. Dunster, director of the oratorio section of the Music Study Club, was the organist at Government Street Presbyterian Church and Temple Shaarai Shomayim. In the 1920s and 1930s, band concerts were held during the summer months in Bienville Square, usually for two or more hours beginning around 5:30 P.M. They were often sponsored by local civic organizations such as the Kiwanis Club. During this period the Auxiliary of the League of American Pen Women published a number of songs. This association of women professional writers, artists, and musicians was established in Mobile in 1916. Among the songs published and now forgotten were Julia Fowler's "Mobile Blues," Mrs. E. W. Francis's "Love's Way" and "Cracker Jack Roy," and Rosine Pillichody's "Alabama" and "The Song of the Warrior River," which the state adopted for use in the public schools. The Mobile Symphony Orchestra was sponsored by the Chopin Club in 1923 and from 1924 to 1929 by the Mobile Symphony Association, which promoted four Sunday afternoon concerts a year, most of them at the Lyric Theater, until the depression. From 1924 to 1942 the Tellier Concert Orchestra, known as the Pythias Orchestra before 1926, presented concerts with such numbers as Sousa's "Stars and Stripes Forever" and A. S. Bowman's "Southern Melodies." Other local ensembles in the interwar years included the fourteen-member Fire Department Band directed by William Buerger, a women's orchestra conducted by Elisabeth Dijas, and a young men's choral group called the Mastersingers.[59]

The motion picture industry (before sound) provided lucrative employment opportunities for professional musicians playing in pit orchestras at the Lyric, Bijou, Queen, Dauphine, and Saenger Theaters; however, the depression and the arrival of the sound track picture ended that. Some of the musicians found jobs when the WPA funded an orchestra. Swing music and the radio led to a change in public taste. Some critics complained about a decline in formal music training and claimed that some music teachers in public schools could not even play the piano.[60]

Another occasion deemed deserving of a holiday was the revival of horse racing in Mobile in 1921. Mayor Pillans proclaimed the opening day of the races, March 10, as a municipal holiday. The *Mobile Register* reported that many retail stores closed at noon, and most had posted signs that stated, "Gone to the Races." An enthusiastic crowd of five thousand came out early and stood and cheered with waving hats and handkerchiefs as the horses finished the races.[61]

Golf grew in popularity during the interwar years. At the end of World War I the city had one golf course, the Mobile Country Club. Originally (approximately 1899) located on the Bay Shell Road, it was moved to Springhill Avenue in 1914. By the end of the 1930s Mobile had three additional courses: Chickasaw Golf Club on Fifth Avenue and the corner of Sixth, Oak Hills Public Golf Course on St. Mary's Lane, and Spring Hill College Golf Links on Old Shell Road.[62]

Mobile certainly took its entertainment seriously. The Board of City Commissioners established a Park and Planning Board in November of 1926, and the board established a recreation department. By 1931 the department was planning activities for each month, including leagues for football, baseball, volleyball, and basketball.[63]

Many in the city were intent on promoting education and in the 1920s took important steps to achieve that goal. Among their advancements were a new library and a new high school. Mobile's "public" library initially was a subscription organization started by the Franklin Society before the Civil War. Other subscription libraries were established and were financed not only by subscribers but also by gifts and fund-raisers such as lawn parties and flower shows. The main library was run by an association of women who established an organization known as the Mobile Public Library with Mrs. James K. (Florence) Glennon as president. They appealed to the city commissioners to provide funds to continue the operation of the library and offered the city their property at the northwest corner of Conti and Hamilton Streets if it would erect a new building for a library. On April 2, 1918, the commission appropriated a subvention of twenty-five dollars a month but rejected the offer to build a new building. In June it increased the appropriation to fifty dollars a month. The organization kept asking and received support from such people as Toulmin Gaines, a prominent physician, and Leo Brown, a respected attorney. By 1925 pressure began to mount for a larger library in a new building. The *Mobile Daily Register* said that one would have great difficulty finding a city the size of Mobile with its cultural and historical background that had such a need for a library. On December 15, 1925, the city commission unanimously voted to set January 25, 1926, for a special election on a $250,000 bond issue to build a public library. The voters approved, and, with a gift of $30,000 from Eli H. Bernheim of New York City and the donation of $1,000 by Lucy R. Gardner, the new library building became a reality. The Mobile Public Library at Washington Avenue and Government Street was opened to the public on Saturday, September 15, 1928. Architect George B. Rogers designed the building in the classical Greek style, and it held twenty thousand volumes. The auditorium was named Bernheim Hall. A year later the library had twenty-six thousand volumes catalogued and in circulation as a result of donations from individuals, the YMCA's contribution of its small library, and the library's purchase of additional volumes. During the depression the city stopped appropriations, and the directors and civic groups, such as the Friends of the Library organization, kept the library going. In 1931 a branch was established at 560 Davis Avenue to serve the African American population of the city, who were barred from the main library. It was funded by a bond issue and the sale of the old library building on Conti Street.[64]

By the 1920s a sound public school system was operating in Mobile. In 1920 the city directory listed twenty-five white and seven black schools in the area; in 1939 those numbers were twenty-five and twelve, respectively. By 1939 Mobile also had twenty-three accredited private schools. Spring Hill College, the oldest institution of higher learning in the state of Alabama, was the city's only four-year college.[65]

The most spectacular event in education in the 1920s was the building of a new high school to accommodate the growing student body. The idea was first discussed in 1910 and was mentioned in the newspapers for several years after that. World War I diverted attention, but in 1920 discussion was revived. In response to renewed interest, Superintendent of Education Samuel S. Murphy stated that a successful building program would require a bond issue, which he said was the trend throughout the nation. In January 1920 the Board of School Commissioners became serious about a new high school because they had run out of space. They called a mass meeting for January 22 to discuss the bond issue. The assembly was held at the Chamber of Commerce, and John T. Cochrane was appointed to head a committee to study and report on the financial needs of the school. Six weeks later the seventeen-member committee recommended a 2 mill property tax on all city property for the operation of schools but suggested the postponement of a bond issue until an assessment of building needs was made. On March 22, 1922, the board, after hearing a committee report that a new high school building was needed, appointed another committee to locate a site for it. The school commissioners also asked the city and county commissioners to approve a bond issue for the new school, which meant calling for a vote. They agreed and set the election for January 23, 1923. The school board led the campaign for passage of the bond issue. It asked civic, fraternal, business, social, labor, and press organizations to cooperate in the

Mobile High School (now Murphy) under construction, circa 1925.

Erik Overbey Collection, USA Archives.

campaign. Frank L. Grove, the new high school principal, supervised the preparation of campaign literature. At 3:00 in the afternoon before election day fifteen hundred students marched from Barton Academy down Government Street to Royal Street to convince Mobilians that a new school was needed to accommodate their large numbers. Many organizations were active in supporting the campaign. The voters overwhelmingly approved the city and county bond issue of $700,000.[66]

Even before the bond election the Board of School Commissioners had started considering a site for the new high school. They could not seem to agree and at one time had four locations under consideration. Finally, they tentatively agreed on the Davis Avenue property as the site for the new high school, although an advisory council had recommended the Carlen Street site. The Carlen site was eventually chosen for what became Murphy High School. For a year after the purchase of the Carlen Street property the school board considered plans for the building. The architect was George B. Rogers, who consulted frequently with Frank Grove. Finally, the plans were completed. On December 14, 1924, Barton's entire student body went to the new school site for the laying of the cornerstone of the new high school.[67]

Designed in the style of Spanish Renaissance architecture, the campus was constructed on a twenty-five-acre tract on Carlen Street and was patterned on a college plan with each building named for the primary subject taught there. At noon on Friday, April 9, 1926, students were dismissed from their classes at Barton Academy, and teachers, assisted by helpers, spent two days moving furniture, supplies, and personal belongings to the new school. It was opened on April 12 with almost eighteen hundred students who had been crowded into Barton Academy. The

Mobile Register reported that excellent planning led to a smooth transition. As the students left school at 3:00 P.M., work was still being done on the auditorium. The cafeteria served fourteen hundred meals that first day, and some students brought their own sandwiches from home and sat at the cafeteria tables. In 1928, Mobile High School was renamed in honor of Superintendent Murphy, who had died on April 12, 1926.[68]

Significant developments also occurred in the Mobile County Training School. The school began in 1880 when classes for African Americans were started at the Old Baptist Church in Plateau with William Gleason as the first teacher. The school was later relocated to a building donated by Fred Green, was then moved to Booman's Union Hall, and was subsequently reestablished on three acres of land donated by two members of the community, Isaac Green and Jeff Giles. In 1910 the Mobile County Training School became a part of the Mobile County Public School System. In that year, I. J. Whitley became the principal. He subscribed to Booker T. Washington's emphasis on industrial, or vocational, education to prepare a person to learn practical things in life, such as bricklaying and carpentry, skills that were needed in one's own community. Whitley died in 1923. In 1926 the school was fortunate in getting Benjamin F. Baker as principal. He served until 1947. During his years he raised funds through school activities, built teacher living quarters on the campus, had students build a cafeteria, and succeeded in getting the school accredited in 1934 by the Southern Association of Colleges and Sec-

Principal Benjamin F. Baker provided strong leadership at Mobile County Training School for more than twenty years.

S. Blake McNeely Collection, USA Archives.

ondary Schools, the only African American school in the county with this rating.[69]

African Americans faced widespread discrimination in the interwar years. One black man in particular worked to overcome the racial barriers. John L. LeFlore was born in Mobile on May 17, 1903, and was graduated in 1920 from the Owen Academy. In 1922, employed as a postal worker, he married Teah Beck. After LeFlore quarreled with a white man about getting on a trolley, he helped reestablish a chapter of the National Association for the Advancement of Colored People (NAACP). He became its executive secretary in 1926. He worked continuously and diligently, if not always successfully, to get blacks to register and vote and to have equal accommodations on trains and street cars, equal educational and public library facilities, equal pay for teachers, and counsel for blacks accused of crimes. The numerous letters he wrote are filled with detailed examples of discrimination. For example, he pointed out specific trains where dressing rooms and bathrooms for blacks were not supplied with the same facilities provided for whites. In addition, he persuaded the NAACP national office to hold a regional conference of the Georgia, Florida, Mississippi, Louisiana, and Alabama branches to discuss common problems such as Jim Crow laws, lynching, denial of due process, employment discrimination, lack of public playgrounds and parks, lack of black voters, homicides, lack of WPA jobs, and salary differences between blacks and whites in similar jobs. LeFlore encountered opposition not only from railroad companies but also from some within the black community. He accused one Baptist preacher of trying to obtain an annual railroad pass by encouraging blacks not to complain because, the preacher was

Mobile County Training School library, circa 1940.

S. Blake McNeely Collection, USA Archives.

arguing, conditions on railroad cars were not so bad. LeFlore also wrote that "two or three selfish little Negroes" hurt a cooperative spirit by pushing for early elections of new NAACP officers. He waged an uphill battle against discrimination in the interwar years. For example, in 1939 only 224 blacks were qualified to vote. Nevertheless, between the years 1936 and 1940 he was able to secure "desegregation of Pullman and dining car service of eight major railroads."[70] He never gave up and eventually would see success in the decades after World War II.

African Americans had a town-within-a-town that centered on Davis Avenue. One attraction was Dixie Park, which had a Ferris wheel, roller coaster, merry-go-round, ball park, and place to roller skate. Patrons could attend dances at night with music provided by live bands. Walking down Armistead Street, people could smell the tobacco aroma from the Lagman cigar factory, where more than twenty-five employees produced handmade cigars. In 1931 Mobile's first branch library was located on Davis Avenue largely as a result of the efforts of citizens in the area, including dentist Edward T. Belsaw. African Americans owned drugstores with soda fountains, such as the Owl Drug Store, and barber shops, such as Abrams. Two white entrepreneurs, twin brothers John H. King and Charles B. King, owned the Pike Theater on Davis Avenue. Many gospel singing groups, such as the Dixie Spiritual Singers and the Pope Sisters, started and performed in churches in the area. Still, right before and right after World War I, many blacks emigrated from Mobile and moved north. Black businesses lost clientele, and many sold out to whites.[71]

The Gomez Auditorium and Pike Theatre on Davis Avenue, now Martin Luther King Drive, circa 1940.

Julius Marx Collection, USA Archives.

The city of Mobile expanded physically three times in the interwar years. In 1923 it annexed an area located roughly north of Old Shell Road to Pleasant Avenue, bounded on the west by Tuscaloosa Street and Stanton Road and on the east by a small amount of land east of Louiselle Street and St. Mary's Lane. In 1930 the city annexed an area between Dauphin Street and Springhill Avenue bordered on the east by Fulton and Tuscaloosa Streets and on the west by Florida Street.[72]

In early 1931 city leaders discussed the extension of city limits to include the Bon Air community, the business section of Crichton, and a part of Toulminville. In April they decided not to include Toulminville because of opposition voiced at a citizen's meeting there. They finally made the same decision about Crichton because of a voters' meeting that was attended by one hundred community residents as well as the entire Mobile county delegation of state legislators. An annexation bill was introduced in the house on July 9. The bill passed the house and senate and was signed by Governor Miller on July 22. The Bon Air section that was annexed included land from Dauphin Street just east of Kirby Street, south past Government Street to Eslava Creek, then meandering south-southeast along the creek to Halls Mill Road, and then east to Houston Street and north to Government Street. From that point the annexation went west to Glenwood Street, then north past Government to Fulton Street, and on to Dauphin Street. Another area annexed was the land from the intersection of Springhill Avenue and Florida Street north along Park Avenue to Three Mile Creek then along the creek to Stanton Road, and south to Springhill Avenue. The city was growing westward, and the annexations increased its area size from fourteen to a little more than twenty-two square miles. Population increased from 60,777 in 1920 to 68,277 in 1930 to 70,602 in 1939.[73]

In Mobile the interwar years were a time of economic prosperity, change, and progress. World War I fostered growth in shipping and expanded port facilities. Civic leaders with vision supported projects such as the Cochrane Bridge, the Bankhead Tunnel, and tourist attractions that promoted economic expansion. Economic growth was interrupted by the depression, but the city's resources, federal programs, and growing international markets stimulated by war in Asia and Europe led to recovery. Improvements to the port of Mobile attracted such industries as Alcoa, International Paper, and National Gypsum, and Mobile's economy became more integrated with and dependent on corporate America. Generally speaking, cultural activities kept pace with commercial and industrial progress. Individuals, organizations, and government leaders supported theater, the arts, music, education, and sports. Nonetheless, significant social change was deferred, and African Americans continued to face wide-ranging discrimination. World War II would affect this and many other facets of life in Mobile.

Suggestions for Further Reading

Davis-Horton, Paulette. *Avenue . . . The Place, The People, The Memories.* Mobile: Horton, Inc., 1991. Gives a well-illustrated history of the lifestyle of the African American community along the street that was the center of their activity in Mobile.

Delaney, Caldwell, and Cornelia McDuffie Turner. *Infant Mystics: The First Hundred Years.* Mobile: N.p., 1968. This work gives a mental image of successive Mardi Gras events in Mobile.

Higginbotham, Jay. *Mobile: City by the Bay.* Mobile: Azalea City Printers, 1968. A compilation of fascinating stories and events in Mobile.

King, Jean, ed. *Delchamps: 50 Golden Years, 1921–1971.* Mobile: Delchamps, 1971. An account of this grocer's business expansion and marketing techniques.

Mathews, Charles E. *Highlights of One Hundred Years in Mobile.* Mobile: First National Bank, 1965. Entertains and educates the reader with a collection of important events in Mobile's past.

McLaurin, Melton, and Michael Thomason. *Mobile: The Life and Times of a Great Southern City.* Woodland Hills, Calif.: Windsor Publications, Inc., 1981. The best survey of the city's history. Well illustrated.

South Central Bell Telephone Company. *Hello, Mobile: The History of Telephone Service in Mobile, Alabama, 1879–1979.* Mobile: South Central Bell, 1980. An informative narrative of the extension of telephone facilities in the city.

Summersell, Charles Grayson. *Mobile: A History of a Seaport Town.* Tuscaloosa: University of Alabama Press, 1949. Offers a concise history of the city with emphasis on the period before the twentieth century.

Watson, Bama Nathan. *The History of Barton Academy.* Mobile: Haunted Book Shop, 1971. Highlights the progress of public education in Mobile.

CHAPTER 8

Mobile and World War II, 1940–1945

Allen Cronenberg

World War II set into motion changes that perhaps altered the American South in more profound ways than the Civil War.[1] World War II was, in its broadest sense, a global struggle to preserve democracy and individual freedoms from the tyrannies of the Axis powers. The fight against racism and oppression abroad galvanized efforts to end racial and gender discrimination and inequality at home. World War II offered opportunities—made possible largely by the executive policies of President Franklin Roosevelt—for African Americans and women to prove that they could fly fighter planes and build ships as well as anyone. World War II accelerated the transformation of the United States into a more democratic and equitable society. There would be no unchallenged return to a Jim Crow South. The vast expansion of federal authority at the expense of the states during the depression and World War II, however, threatened established political, economic, and social relationships, producing bitter reactions across a broad spectrum of the South. In many ways, the racial and populist politics that emerged in much of the region in the decades after World War II originated in the war years.

World War II also stimulated the growth of what would later be called the Sunbelt, and no city in the American South was transformed by World War II more than Mobile. Connected for decades to the Atlantic economy through the cotton trade, Mobile had largely served the interests of its agricultural hinterland. Benefiting from the buildup to World War II, the city emerged as a major industrial and commercial center linked to world markets.

Although Mobile's economy had already begun rebounding from the depression by the late 1930s, it was the massive outlay of federal defense expenditures that ignited its rapid growth. Japan's aggression in China and Adolf Hitler's provocations in Europe awoke some American leaders, especially Franklin Roosevelt, to

America's need to restore its military defenses weakened by the legacies of isolationism and the depression. These developments converged to launch Mobile into unparalleled growth and prosperity in the early 1940s.

The city's recently improved port and competitive transportation routes to the nation's industrial heartlands, especially Birmingham's iron and steel mills, secured Mobile's prosperity and growth. Without them there would have been no ADDSCO, Waterman Steamship with its Gulf Shipbuilding subsidiary, Brookley Field, or Alcoa. Still, such things rarely happen without individual ambition and leadership. Probably no two individuals had more to do with Mobile's growth than John B. Waterman and Congressman Frank Boykin. While building a viable steamship line after World War I by taking advantage of railroad freight rates that favored Mobile over New Orleans and nimbly winning mail contracts that subsidized cargo operations, Waterman also championed the improvement of Mobile as a port. Congenial and connected congressman Boykin was Mobile's most effective cheerleader. "If you can't get to Heaven, at least visit Mobile," Boykin was fond of saying.[2] His influence produced contracts for shipbuilders and persuaded the army to choose Mobile over Tampa for what became Brookley Field.

John Waterman alone did not develop Mobile as a first-rate port. Rare, progressive, and cooperative political leadership in Mobile and Montgomery created the Alabama State Docks in the 1920s, enabling Mobile to surpass Pensacola, which had the finest natural harbor on the Gulf Coast, as a port. Lacking vision and leadership, Pensacola failed to improve its docks, especially after the hurricane of 1926

Waterfront patrol.

McNeely Collection, USA Archives.

and, in contrast to Mobile, received no Florida state government assistance to develop its port until 1943. Maintaining a channel in Mobile Bay to accommodate deep-draft, oceangoing vessels was also a prerequisite to Waterman's dreams and the success of the state docks. Although the Alabama State Docks languished throughout the depression, by the late 1930s its 550-acre site with three steel and concrete piers capable of berthing twenty-two oceangoing vessels was attracting major national companies looking for a site that had access to an ocean port and adequate docks with modern cargo-handling equipment. Summing up his four years as governor of Alabama, Chauncey Sparks said no investment "has contributed so bountifully to the progress of this state" as the Alabama State Docks.[3]

In Europe, Nazi Germany overran Austria and Czechoslovakia through intimidation and invaded Poland on September 1, 1939. After Poland's defeat, Europe settled into an illusory peace. In the spring of 1940, this "Phony War" ended when German armies attacked Denmark, Norway, the Netherlands, Belgium, and then France. The surrender of France brought all of western Europe under Hitler's heel. Great Britain struggled alone, and soon Hermann Goering's Luftwaffe began its massive bombing attack on British cities and industries. The fall of France in the summer of 1940 and the terrifying Battle of Britain in that autumn propelled President Roosevelt and his stunned congressional allies to undertake measures to shore up America's flagging defense preparedness, including a $5 billion defense appropriation bill, the establishment of a selective service system, and the activation of National Guard units for intensive training. Mobile soon felt the effects of each of these measures.

In mid-September 1940 Congress passed a conscription bill requiring males between the ages of twenty-one and thirty-five to register with local draft boards. Wednesday, October 16, was proclaimed registration day throughout the nation. County committees consisting of the sheriff, probate judge, and circuit court clerk organized the registrations, which took place at regular polling places with volunteers serving as registrars. The greater-than-anticipated numbers of draft-age men in Mobile County caught officials off guard. Two army airplanes brought extra forms and registration cards from Montgomery. By the end of the day more than twenty thousand individuals had registered with the selective services in Mobile County. After assigning draft numbers by lot, Mobile County selective service authorities named the first draftees on October 29. The county's sixty-three draft boards worked swiftly, classifying each registrant according to physical health, mental ability, and mitigating factors such as employment in vital defense industries, family responsibilities, or, in rare cases, deeply held religious and moral opposition to warfare. Without speculating on reasons, the *Mobile Register* noted a sharp increase in applications for marriage licenses just prior to national registration day.[4]

From the outset, the selective service process was to be organized and implemented by state and local officials on the principle that local officials would be in a better position to judge the "equities of the law in its application to their neighbors." One glaring deficit in this scheme was that African Americans were excluded from membership on the local boards. As a palliative, Governor Frank Dixon appointed two appeal boards consisting of African Americans with "advisory" authority. Dixon also appointed a panel of black physicians as "Additional Examining Physicians."[5]

Only days after Congress authorized the selective service system, President Roosevelt ordered National Guard troops to active duty. Mobile's three hundred National Guard officers and troops learned that they would join other units of the Thirty-first Division at newly established Camp Blanding in Florida in late November. General John Persons, a Birmingham banker, commanded this "Dixie" Division, which consisted of National Guard units from Alabama, Mississippi, Louisiana, and Florida. Three of the division's companies traced their origins to Mobile and had seen service in the Civil War. The Thirty-first Division Signal Company dated back to 1845 as the Mobile Cadets. After serving in the Spanish-American War, World War I, and the Mexican expedition as an infantry company, the unit was reorganized in the 1920s as a signal company. The division's headquarters company originated as the Mobile Rifles, and its ordnance company descended from the Bienville Blues. Many Mobile guardsmen served in the division's medical detachment, and the military police company came from Prichard. Several Mobilians, including George A. Haas, Joseph Langan, and E. B. Peebles, served on the division headquarters' staff for much of the war.[6]

Delays in preparing Camp Blanding for the arrival of thousands of troops postponed the departure of Mobile's guardsmen until December 10, 1940. Following farewell parties organized by the *Mobile Register* for local National Guard enlisted men at Fort Whiting and for officers at the newly opened Admiral Semmes Hotel, Mobilians gathered at the Louisville and Nashville train station for a rousing send-off. Chalked messages reading "See you in the spring of 194?" belied the optimistic presidential order calling the troops to active duty for only one year. Japan's attack on Pearl Harbor dashed the dreams of being home for Christmas in 1941.

Members of Alabama's naval militia, consisting of six officers and sixty-nine sailors of the naval reserve, were inducted into active duty by March 1941. Most of these reservists received additional training at Norfolk and were assigned to duty on the USS *Long Island.* A smaller contingent arrived in Mobile to serve on *YP-45,* the unit's seventy-five-foot patrol boat armed with a four-inch gun, that operated in the Gulf of Mexico.[7]

Thanks in part to the influence of Alabama's Democratic congressional delegation, the state shared generously in defense preparedness. By October 1941 defense investments in Alabama totaled $600 million, including $150 million in construction. The Office of Production Management calculated that Alabama ranked seventeenth among all states in defense projects and contracts. Mobile's success in obtaining lucrative defense investments resulted in large measure from the persuasiveness and arm-twisting of portly, jovial millionaire Democratic congressman Frank Boykin.

Born in Choctaw County in 1885, Boykin went to work at age eight as a water boy for a railroad gang. He got rich in the 1920s, proudly boasting in later years that he "got bowlegged totin' my money" from land deals on Florida's west coast. When FDR appointed Congressman John McDuffie to a judgeship, south Alabama elected Frank Boykin in 1935 to the first of fourteen terms in the House of Representatives. As a politician Boykin was a pragmatist. Unlike more prominent Alabama politicians—such as Henry Steagall, Lister Hill, and John Sparkman—Boykin was not a New Dealer, but he remained loyal to the Democratic Party. He outspokenly supported FDR after efforts to get native son Will Bankhead, Speaker of the U.S. House of Representatives, on the 1940 presidential ticket failed. Gratefully, FDR sent his wife, Eleanor, to Alabama. Mobile rolled out the red carpet for this first visit ever by a First Lady. After speaking at Murphy High School on the subject of a day in the life of the president, Eleanor Roosevelt toured Bellingrath Gardens, which was at the height of the azalea season.[8]

Boykin's knowledge of Gulf Coast maritime matters, acquired during his employment in the shipbuilding industry in World War I, landed him on the House Merchant Marine and Fisheries Committee. His clout with the Maritime Commission secured substantial contracts for Mobile's shipyards in the early 1940s. Moreover, Boykin's timely intervention with army air chief "Hap" Arnold led to the selection of Mobile over Tampa as the site of a $26,500,000 supply depot and aircraft modification facility. In 1940 the army took possession of a one-thousand-acre site on Mobile Bay and began construction of Brookley Field, the only one of the army's nine air depots with an ocean terminal that served the southeast and the Caribbean. The depot reached a peak employment of sixteen thousand workers in 1942.[9]

The $5 billion defense appropriation bill that was signed into law in early September 1940 brought a $32 million contract for Gulf Shipbuilding to build four destroyers. Originally owned by TCI, the ninety-acre Chickasaw shipyard, consisting of eight ways on which ships were constructed, had been purchased by the flourishing Waterman Steamship two years earlier. In order to provide comfortable and convenient housing for some of its shipyard workers, the company purchased more than four hundred housing units from lumberman Ben May's Chickasaw Development Company. The first vessel built by Gulf Shipbuilding since 1921 was the ten thousand ton freighter called the SS *Fairport,* which slid from the ways on November 16, 1941.[10] Gulf Shipbuilding eventually completed seven 2,100-ton

World War II Brookley Air Force Base.

USA AF photograph, USA Archives.

Fletcher class destroyers, the first warships constructed in Alabama since the CSS *Tennessee* was built in Selma during the Civil War. Thirteen 220-foot minesweepers, sixteen 180-foot minesweepers, and one landing ship dock also slid down the ways of the Chickasaw yard during the war years. In addition to naval construction, Gulf Shipbuilding turned out thirty C-2 cargo ships. A repair facility located at the state docks converted, altered, and repaired dozens of other vessels.

On his death in 1937, John Waterman was succeeded by able executives who guided the wartime growth of the company—Ed A. Roberts and, later, Captain Norman Nicolson, who rose through the company's ranks and was much loved by those who served under him. When World War II broke out, Waterman Steamship, headquartered in the Merchant's National Bank building, owned thirty-eight American and eight foreign flag ships and chartered twelve vessels.[11] After the entry of the United States into the war, Waterman served as agent for 125 vessels of the War Shipping Administration. Other subsidiaries included Ryan Stevedoring Company, which handled cargo in most East Coast, West Coast, and Gulf Coast ports; Pan-Atlantic Steamship Corporation; Gulf Florida Terminal Company; and Waterman Dock Company in Puerto Rico.

ADDSCO, like Gulf Shipbuilding, dated back to World War I, but its two yards—the upper yard located on Pinto Island and the lower yard on the west bank of the Mobile River and just south of downtown—languished in the interwar era. ADDSCO's renaissance began with the launching of *Pan-Pennsylvania* on October

18, 1940. This 15,400-ton tanker—the biggest ship ADDSCO had ever built—employed a cheaper, faster all-welded process that supplanted riveting. ADDSCO's first Liberty ship, *J. L. M. Curry,* slid from the ways in late January 1942. (Liberty ships were mass-produced cargo vessels designed for wartime use by the Allies.) Although ADDSCO could not match the construction schedules of Henry Kaiser's shipyards on the West Coast, it made significant strides. In 1942 it took ADDSCO nearly 250 days to build a Liberty ship, compared with Kaiser's 110. By the spring of 1944, however, it took an ADDSCO crew less than seventy days. By the end of the war, ADDSCO had built 20 Liberty ships and 102 T-2 tankers and repaired or converted almost 3,000 other ships for the army, navy, War Shipping Administration, and private corporations.[12]

The rapid expansion of defense-related jobs fueled a stunning growth in population. By early 1941, metropolitan Mobile's population reached 112,000, an increase of 30,000, or 36 percent, since 1920. Surpassing Montgomery, Mobile once again became Alabama's second most populous city. Between 1940 and 1943 eighty-nine thousand people—mostly poor whites and blacks—descended on Mobile. By March 1944 Mobile County's population was 233,000, having risen 64 percent in four years. This population led to unprecedented investments to expand public services and utilities. Modern buses replaced clanging streetcars in 1940, and bus service to rapidly growing suburbs was added. As noted in the previous chapter, the $4 million Bankhead Tunnel under the Mobile River, providing easier access to

Launching of the destroyer *Capps* by Gulf Shipbuilding in 1942. The ship received seven battle stars for World War II service.

Waterman Collection, USA Archives.

Wartime trailer housing project in Prichard, 1945.

ADDSCO Collection, USA Archives.

Pinto Island and saving seven miles to the eastern shore, opened on February 20, 1941. More than one hundred thousand pedestrians thronged through the tunnel, composed of seven huge steel tubes fabricated at ADDSCO, before the first motorists were permitted to enter at 10:00 P.M. In just slightly more than a year, one million vehicles had driven through it, exceeding even the rosiest of projections.[13]

Mayor Cecil Bates and Mobile's city council struggled to meet the educational and housing needs of the city's swelling population. Murphy High School, built in 1926 for eighteen hundred students, had thirty-four hundred students clogging the hallways by the spring of 1941. Despite this explosive growth, George Kenan, a 1943 graduate of Murphy High School, remembers that the quality of education was quite good, especially in the sciences. Because of housing shortages rents doubled as workers flocked into Mobile. As early as the spring of 1942 Gulf Shipbuilding informed government officials that the shortage of housing in the Mobile area resulted in excessively high turnover of its workers. In one twelve-week period forty-five hundred workers, or half its work force, quit the shipyard mainly because they could not find housing. Prodded by Congressman Boykin, federal housing officials provided financing for eleven thousand housing units in sixteen projects scattered across metropolitan Mobile, only two of which were for African Americans. Nonetheless, housing remained scarce and expensive. In his 1943 book *State of the Nation,* John Dos Passos wrote that Mobile looked "trampled and battered like a city that's been taken by storm." He described the crowded, littered streets and the people who lived in tents and chicken houses in backyards and on park benches. Some men slept in "hot beds." After all, he quipped, men work in three shifts, so why shouldn't they sleep in three shifts? Advertisements in the *Mobile Register* encouraged homeowners with spare rooms to take in boarders.[14]

Business was booming by the summer of 1941. According to national business data, Mobile, whose sales surged by 40 percent in the previous year, was second in retail growth only to San Diego, which registered a 46 percent increase in business sales in the same period. Cotton commodity prices reached twenty cents a pound for the first time since 1929. Utility companies struggled to keep pace with demand for their services. By late 1940, when nearly twice as many Mobile families and businesses—nearly fifteen thousand—had telephone service as in 1925, the phone company announced plans for a major expansion and the introduction of a modern dial system. Similarly, Alabama Power Company took steps to meet the rapidly growing demand for electricity. The original steam plant built in 1912 on the site of the old slave market at the corner of Royal and St. Louis Streets had been supplemented by a steam plant at Chickasaw, which Alabama Power Company leased in 1921 and purchased eighteen years later. On the eve of World War II, most of the city's electrical power came from the Jordan Dam on the Coosa River about 180 miles away. Responding to a 48 percent surge in electric power consumption in the Mobile area between 1940 and 1942, Alabama Power Company expanded the Chickasaw plant to meet the needs of residential customers and industrial users, especially the shipyards, Brookley Field, and Alcoa's power-hungry bauxite refining plant at the state docks. In January 1941 National Airlines, which joined Eastern in offering connections to the East Coast, Florida, and New Orleans, opened a reservations office at the Admiral Semmes Hotel. After World War II, Waterman Steamship Company would begin offering air service to the Caribbean.[15]

Boom times, however, brought sharp increases in the cost of living. Mobile, in fact, led the nation in percentage increase in living costs in the early war years. Shortages and eventually rationing of many goods caused some hardships on the home front, but, for the most part, Mobilians willingly cooperated with this wartime necessity. Scarcity of women's stockings at department store counters—resulting from sharply curtailed imports of silk from Japan-threatened Asia and increased production of parachutes—caused a frenzied buying spree in the summer of 1941. The *Mobile Register* editorialized that for many women this development was "more cataclysmic" than the fall of France.[16]

Rationing of many consumer products, including sugar, tires, coffee, shoes, hosiery, and gasoline for vehicles, began in 1942. Ration books were issued at elementary schools throughout the country in May. Gas rationing—somewhat less than four gallons per week for each automobile owner—was caused not so much by petroleum shortages or refining bottlenecks but by a critical scarcity of raw rubber resulting from Japan's conquest of rubber-rich areas in Asia. The rubber shortage meant few new tires. Mobile's automobile tire quota for the month of February 1942, for example, was slashed from 200 to 106. To conserve vehicle tires and gasoline, a nationwide maximum speed limit of thirty-five miles per hour was imposed. Rationing of some goods was repealed quickly. A flurry of criticism forced the War Production Board to reverse itself and make more rubber available for girdles and other foundation garments. Coffee rationing—one pound every five weeks for each individual over fourteen years of age—was necessitated by German U-boat operations in the Caribbean Sea, which disrupted imports from Central and South America. By late July 1943 coffee rationing ended as the German U-boat menace in the Caribbean subsided.[17] New automobile sales virtually stopped after January 1942 as car manufacturers converted production lines to the manufacture of military vehicles.

Shortly after going on daylight savings time—a measure to save electricity—in the summer of 1941, Mobile launched its first aluminum scrap drive, one of many during the war years. In this program, sponsored by a women's home defense committee, children received a free ticket to a movie for every aluminum pot they brought in. A year later, metal scrap drives among black and white citizens netted four tons, or twice the city's quota. The *Mobile Register* heaped special praise on the success of seven hundred black youths organized into "commando units" for the scrap drive in Mobile County.[18]

Mobilians—whites and blacks—loved their carnival, and the 1941 Mardi Gras had been the grandest ever. Although some mystic societies had already begun construction of their floats before Japan's attack on Pearl Harbor, a sober mood descended quickly on the city as the nation prepared for a long war and many sacrifices. The 1942 Mardi Gras was canceled, and although some smaller parties were held, the city endured the absence of the exuberant and festive parades and carnival balls for the duration of the war.[19]

The booming wartime shipyards enabled hardworking blacks and poor whites to earn decent wages. When Herbert and Estella Aaron, parents of a future baseball slugger, moved from Camden to Mobile during the early days of the depression, they were so poor they had to live in the Texas Hill area, where Hank Aaron was born in 1934. Working as a boilermaker's assistant at the busy ADDSCO shipyard on Pinto Island, Herbert Aaron and family moved in 1942 into the more pleasant Toulminville neighborhood, where Hank played sandlot ball.[20]

Another legendary Alabamian, Hank Williams, also worked intermittently at ADDSCO during World War II. Williams, a Montgomery high school dropout and founder of the Drifting Cowboys, moved to Mobile after back problems prevented him from enlisting in the army. Living with relatives, Hank worked off and on as a welder's assistant in the shipyard until his mother, according to most sources, arranged several performances and went down to Mobile to fetch her son. He had become by that time infatuated with pretty, blond Audrey Sheppard, who had a young daughter from a failing marriage.

Mobile's black population grew from twenty-nine thousand in 1940 to forty-six thousand a decade later. Many were attracted by high-paying defense jobs, whereas for others the rapid growth in population offered unparalleled entrepreneurial opportunities. Joseph Williams, an African American from Birmingham, hoboed to Mobile to work in the shipyards but soon discovered more money could be made in the restaurant business. His Williams's Electric Barbecue at 962 Davis Avenue was grossing seventy thousand dollars annually in 1945, selling pork sandwiches for twenty-five cents and rib plates for forty cents.[21]

The surging demand for skilled labor in the shipyards led to strife between workers and management. Strikes at ADDSCO in 1941 and 1942 were largely concerned with wages and benefits, and disturbances in 1943 erupted when ADDSCO attempted to integrate black and white workers on the ways. A year later, in the late spring of 1944, persistent antagonism between black and white workers again aroused fears of violence.

In early 1941 news came that the Maritime Commission planned to add four new ways at the ADDSCO's Pinto Island facility at which twelve to sixteen ships would be built over the next few months. This announcement was followed by a walkout on the night of January 23. On behalf of thirty-four hundred striking workers, the Industrial Union of Marine and Shipbuilding Workers of America demanded higher wages. Prompt mediation by a federal labor conciliator led to a wage settlement and a return to work on February 3, 1941. ADDSCO agreed to raise the minimum hourly wage, which had been established at thirty-five cents an hour in 1938, to fifty cents an hour. Workers earning more than fifty cents an hour would receive a four-cent raise. Under the new scale, the top wage at ADDSCO, earned by machinists, was ninety-seven cents an hour. Workers would receive one and one-half time for normal overtime and double pay for more than eight hours overtime on Saturdays or for any work on Sundays or holidays. Although boasting that Mobile's shipyard workers were the highest paid south of Baltimore, the union made important concessions of its own, dropping demands for a sixty-nine cents per hour minimum wage and for a closed shop.[22]

Another serious labor dispute erupted at the ADDSCO shipyard in September 1942 when workers balked at the introduction of a municipal-owned ferry service to Pinto Island that would cost them five cents each way. The city was already in turmoil over public transportation. Only two weeks earlier, black Mobilians threatened to boycott the local bus system—the National City Lines—after a white driver shot to death a black soldier from Brookley Field as the young man was getting off the bus following a heated exchange of words. John LeFlore, the postal carrier and energetic secretary of the local chapter of the NAACP that he cofounded in 1925, promised that Mobile's black population would resort to a "walk to work, walk to church, walk to shop" campaign if NAACP demands—including the disarming of bus drivers—were not met. Tempers cooled, averting a boycott, after the bus company promised to treat black passengers courteously and agreed to disarm its drivers.[23]

The ferry strike, however, proved more flammable. Previously the shipyard had operated free ferry service across the river, but at the prompting of the Maritime Commission, the city of Mobile purchased two ferries from New Orleans to replace the company-run ferry. Exactly what precipitated confrontation and violence at the ferry landing at the foot of Canal Street in the early morning hours of Thursday, September 17, 1942, remains unclear. The introduction of a ten-cent round-trip ferry fare was relatively trivial. Despite earlier pledges to submit grievances to arbitration, local Industrial Union of Marine and Shipbuilding Workers president Asa B. Kendrick urged workers at ADDSCO's Pinto Island yard to boycott the ferry and to strike a demonstrative pose.

After a gathering of workers at the union's Royal Street office, police arrested Asa Kendrick for inciting to riot and charged more than twenty-five other individuals with disorderly conduct. Wild West justice was meted out the next day when the defendants were hastily tried, convicted, and sentenced by Judge Norvelle R. Leigh III. Asa Kendrick's plea for a jury trial and for representation by counsel was summarily rejected by the judge, who remarked at Kendrick's sentencing that his only regret was that he could not, under the law, give Kendrick more than six months hard labor. Fearing violence, Governor Frank Dixon ordered several Alabama Guard companies to assist local authorities in maintaining order.[24]

An angry mass meeting of ADDSCO workers assembled at Bienville Square that evening and shouted down several conciliatory speakers, including union officials who disavowed the ferry disturbance, referring to it as a work stoppage, not a strike. The crowd's mood turned, however, as Labor Department conciliator Walter F. Schaffer addressed them. Schaffer proposed letting the War Labor Board decide the ferry matter.[25] Workers voiced approval of the plan, but most vowed they would still not use the city-owned ferries.

Over the weekend, work resumed at the Pinto Island shipyard, and the angry mood of previous days subsided. On Sunday night at a packed meeting at the Congress of Industrial Organizations hall, workers voted to use city ferries pending a visit by a committee from Washington in early October to investigate. The crowd applauded Walter Pollard, an official with the War Production Board, who blamed not the ferry issue but the miserable living conditions in Mobile for the disturbances. Pollard cited the findings of the Tolan Migration Committee, which had found Mobile to be among the most congested areas in the country, suffering from severe housing shortages and inadequate utilities, recreation facilities, and medical care.[26] Pollard promised that the committee coming from Washington in early October to investigate the ferry issue would also examine these broader concerns. Work at the ADDSCO yards returned to normal despite continued grumbling. Asa Kendrick, released from jail on an appeal bond, urged cooperation and vowed that he would begin riding the ferry.

Officials from the Industrial Union of Marine and Shipbuilding Workers, War Production Board, Maritime Commission, and War Manpower Commission assembled at the Admiral Semmes Hotel for two days of hearings on the ferry strike and related matters. Emphasis of the meeting quickly shifted from the ten-cent round-trip ferry toll to more substantial problems, such as housing, transportation, and water supply. In a city where employers were estimating that their turnover rate for employees was running about 4 percent a week, it is not surprising that one of the committee's most important recommendations was for the city to impose an immediate moratorium on evictions, a problem caused, in part, by unscrupulous landlords who were evicting tenants on sometimes flimsy grounds in order to gouge new tenants with ever higher rents.[27]

Only a month after the ferry strike, the Maritime Commission honored ADDSCO and its workers with its highly prized "M" pennant and workers' merit badges for outstanding production performances.[28] ADDSCO and Houston Shipbuilding became the first two shipyards on the Gulf Coast to earn these coveted awards. The ceremony on Pinto Island on Saturday, October 24, 1942, was unique in another way as well. Joining L. M. Garrison, a company foreman, in raising the "M" pennant was Mrs. M. M. Hill, the wife of a sailor and mother of two children. Before World War II Mrs. Hill had never worked outside the home for wages. Now she was a slacks-wearing welder at ADDSCO. Following the award ceremony, *Arickaree*—the first tanker built at the Pinto shipyard and the largest vessel yet launched on the Gulf Coast—slid down the ways.

The appearance of a woman worker on the award ceremony stage at the ADDSCO shipyard coincided with a major effort by the War Manpower Commission, the Federal Employment Service, and Mobile business leaders to convince women that they could "take on a man-sized job" at the shipyards, Brookley Field, or other local industries. Nationwide, this campaign foresaw 75 percent of all women working outside the home within the next few years. Articles in the *Mobile Register* featured women who had found employment in the work force as well as those who had joined one of the auxiliary military forces or performed important defense-related volunteer work. Rising wages were a strong incentive for housewives who had never worked outside the home as well as for women in lower-paying jobs, such as teachers, retail clerks, and waitresses, to enter the defense industry work force. Increasingly, women sought training and employment in the shipyards, at Brookley Field, and in other defense-related industries. Teachers, for example, whose annual salaries ranged between $670–$1,150 for whites and $340–$660 for blacks could earn $1,400 as typists or $1,800–$3,000 as welders or electricians in defense industries.[29] Many Mobilians would later claim they never had as much money in their pockets as they had during World War II.

Brookley Field also pioneered in the hiring of people with disabilities for wartime work. Eileen Sutton, a Mobile native, blind since birth and an employee of the Tennessee Valley Authority, returned home in 1941 to take a job as typist at the navy signal station at Brookley Field. Two years later, with labor in tight supply, Brookley Field began recruiting individuals with physical disabilities or conditions that normally would preclude them from gainful employment—hearing and vision impairments, artificial limbs, and even pregnancy. In 1944 the *Birmingham News* reported that Brookley Field had become "the nation's proving ground for vocational rehabilitation" and a place where, for the first time, "the door of economic independence was opened" to persons with disabilities.[30]

Women held about one-fourth of all defense-related jobs in Alabama during World War II. At ADDSCO nearly twenty-five hundred women were in the company's work force of thirty thousand. Although about half of these women performed work traditionally held by females, many also held jobs as welders. The *Mobile Register,* in a story about women pioneers in the welding trade, wrote that, except for one woman who insisted on wearing her red oxfords, it was difficult to distinguish men from women in their welding outfits.[31]

These three women were selected to become wartime welding instructors at the Alabama Dry Dock and Shipbuilding Company.

ADDSCO Collection, USA Archives.

Many of these female welders, including housewife Gladyce Ghoesling and twenty-three-year-old Ottis Patterson, had never held jobs outside the home. Lucille Waite had worked as a waitress in a dinner club before arriving at ADDSCO. Nearly all of the friends of petite, eighteen-year-old Josephine Abad were surprised when she took up welding. "Little Willie"—as her coworkers nicknamed her—declared in the interview that her real ambition was to be "a crane operator" in the shipyard.[32]

By 1944 about 10 percent of Gulf Shipbuilding's twelve thousand workers were women. A considerably larger percentage of the work force at the Mobile Air Service Command at Brookley Field—almost seventy-five hundred, or nearly 50 percent—was female.[33] By 1945, as victory in Europe and the Pacific looked more certain, defense contractors began laying off workers, especially women. By the postwar era, the percentage of women in industry had returned to prewar norms.

Defense work also offered unparalleled opportunities for African Americans, especially men. At the height of wartime ship construction in 1944, ADDSCO employed nearly seven thousand African Americans—20 percent of its employees. Prior to the spring of 1943, however, not one was employed in a skilled position. Most performed menial tasks, although some worked as helpers alongside skilled white workers. The fact that white women were being employed in semiskilled jobs such as welding rankled many seasoned black workers, who resented the failures of the shipyards and educational institutions to provide them with the training they needed to be upgraded into the more skilled positions.

Responding to critical shortages of skilled and semiskilled labor and prodded by the Fair Employment Practices Committee to conform to a presidential order requiring defense contractors to engage in nondiscriminatory employment practices and to upgrade the skills and positions of black workers, ADDSCO attempted to integrate African Americans into crews on the ways. During the night shift on May 24, 1943, ADDSCO assigned twelve black welders to a white crew. As news of an integrated crew spread during the morning shift, disgruntled whites—women as well as men—began assaulting black workers in the shipyard. Contemporary news accounts that reported that eight black workers had been injured in the melee seem to have greatly underestimated the number.[34] Virtually all black workers fled in terror from Pinto Island. The subsequent arrival of troops from Brookley Field restored a semblance of order.

Coinciding with far more violent racial disturbances in Los Angeles, Detroit, Harlem, and Beaumont, Texas, conditions remained tense at ADDSCO for several weeks. Turmoil in the ADDSCO shipyard led to the closing of liquor stores in the city and forced civil defense officials to cancel what would have been Mobile's biggest and most authentic blackout of the war. Fearing further violence on Pinto Island, black workers remained at home until several prominent African American ministers and civil rights leaders, including John LeFlore of the NAACP and Franklin O. Nichols of the Urban League, convinced them that ADDSCO officials were capable of providing adequate security.

In deference to what was called "the Southern practices in labor relations between the races," an agreement among ADDSCO, maritime union officials, and federal labor and war production authorities created four separate, segregated (Jim Crow) all-black crews overseen by white supervisors.[35] These crews, however, built only hulls. The remaining work—machine work, installation of electrical systems, pipe fitting—was completed by white crews. On the other ways, black workers continued to perform menial labor. Reassured by the presence of troops at the shipyard and guarantees of their personal safety, African American workers returned to their jobs, and normal production schedules resumed.

Many Mobilians blamed outsiders, especially "rednecks from Mississippi" for inciting the violence at ADDSCO. Mobile sheriff W. H. Holcombe, in a letter to Governor Chauncey Sparks, attributed the "somewhat explosive situation" in Mobile to the overwhelming influx of humanity into the city.[36] Fearing subsequent outbreaks of racial violence, Sheriff Holcombe, federal officials including the Federal Bureau of Investigation and various defense intelligence units, and ADDSCO recruited informants to provide forewarning of impending trouble at the shipyard.

In a bizarre footnote to the racial melee at the ADDSCO shipyard, Inferior Court judge Tisdale J. Touart cited the publisher of the *Mobile Register,* R. B.

Black welders at the Alabama Dry Dock and Shipbuilding Company.

ADDSCO Collection, USA Archives.

Chandler, for contempt of court because of an editorial criticizing the court's leniency in dealing with the four white defendants accused of assaulting black shipyard workers.[37] The newspaper had found it curious that Judge Touart had released one of the defendants under a "peace bond" rather than ruling on his guilt according to the evidence. Piqued by the criticism, Judge Touart dispatched Sheriff Holcombe to the newspaper office with a contempt order compelling Chandler to appear in court. Chandler, normally a staunch defender of the status quo, wrapped himself in the First Amendment, vowing that he would never let threats of jail sentences influence his paper's editorial policies.

At Chandler's trial on June 11, 1943, Judge Touart found the publisher guilty, sentencing him to a ten dollar fine and six hours in jail. Remanded to Sheriff Holcombe's custody, Chandler was taken to the county jail. Within twenty minutes the newspaper's legal counsel appeared with a writ of habeas corpus obtained from probate judge Leigh, and, after posting a five thousand dollar bond, Chandler was set free. Chandler pledged a fight to the Supreme Court, if necessary, to ensure freedom of the press in Mobile. Some days later, however, after tempers had cooled, the case was dismissed.[38]

Almost exactly one year later, on May 25, 1944, racial tensions in Mobile flared again when black troops at Brookley Field opened fire on white military policemen who entered their segregated housing area to investigate a robbery complaint. A few days later rumors flew in the ADDSCO shipyard that white workers intended to attack black employees on the occasion of the launching of *Tule Canyon* on May 31, 1944. It seems that white workers resented the fact that an all-black crew had built this ship in seventy-nine days (a record for Gulf Coast shipyards) and that at the launching praise would be heaped on them for this accomplishment. Informants reported that whites would attempt to "clear the yard of all Negroes and prevent them from witnessing or participating in the launching."[39]

ADDSCO officials promptly responded to rumors of violence by stationing one hundred armed civilian guards at strategic spots and planting among the crowd more than one hundred employee-informants to "talk down any adverse comment or act as a dead weight on the crowd should a riot begin." With management's blessings many black workers in the first shift left the shipyard. Unofficial estimates indicate, however, that approximately 80 of the 450 African Americans on the first shift remained at the ways to participate in the ceremony. The navy also responded with a show of force, dispatching an armed guard to protect its repair facilities at the shipyard and to "provide protective custody for Negroes in the event of a race riot." Unfounded rumors that the Coast Guard had small craft offshore to rescue workers and that state militia troops were massed at Royal and Theater Streets, poised to rush through Bankhead Tunnel to quell rioting on Pinto Island, perhaps also served as deterrents to violence. Although *Tule Canyon* slid into the water at

12:20 P.M., about an hour behind schedule and without incident, the episode illustrates the seriousness of continuing racial tensions at the shipyard. Although local and state authorities responded in desultory fashion, ADDSCO and federal officials moved swiftly and resolutely to avoid a repetition of the violence that had scarred the shipyard a year earlier.[40]

Ingalls Shipbuilding in nearby Pascagoula, which employed about one thousand African Americans in a work force of about nine thousand, also experienced some minor racial violence. Gulf Shipbuilding, which depended on Navy Department contracts more than any other shipbuilder in the Mobile area, employed the fewest African American workers and experienced no racial conflict.[41]

The rapid growth of population put nearly impossible demands on education, public safety, housing, and public services. Nationally known commentator Agnes E. Meyer, whose husband owned and published the *Washington Post,* visited Mobile in 1942. There, she wrote a decade after her visit, "I found a situation that was completely out of hand." She estimated that two thousand children roamed city streets because schools were overcrowded. Crimes among the young, including arson, rape, and theft, were common. She was especially shocked by sexual immorality even among young girls. Meyer quoted Thomas J. Toolen, bishop of Mobile, as fearing that "a future race of gangsters" was being created.[42] Although the city's neglect of public education, she wrote in contemporary articles, was largely to blame, the solution to such overwhelming problems in what would later be called "impacted areas" could come only from massive federal aid to education. The Eighty-first Congress responded to these needs with the Lanham Act, which provided federal education funds to hard-pressed cities such as Mobile.

Child care for working mothers was another critical issue. The lack of day-care facilities made it difficult to recruit mothers with young children into defense work. In the summer of 1943, Mobile, with federal assistance, opened five centers, which operated between 6:30 A.M. and 6:00 P.M. These centers, which charged only a small fee for food, took care of children between the ages of six and eleven.[43] Mobile became the first city in Alabama to establish a child care program to assist mothers in defense work.

Opportunities to make fast money through bootlegging, gambling, and prostitution abounded as thousands of people eager for easy money poured into Mobile. Some members of Mobile's police force succumbed to temptation. In early October 1940 a federal grand jury indicted 40 of Mobile's 115 policemen for accepting bribes from bootleggers. These indicted policemen were immediately suspended without pay. American Legion volunteers agreed to assist with police functions during the crisis. In an effort to root out corruption in the Mobile force, the city council hired Arthur Thalacker, head of the Burlington, Vermont, police force, to serve in the newly created post of inspector of police. Thalacker, ridiculed as a carpetbagger, was never popular with the Mobile Police Department and police chief Emory Warren. A year after Thalacker's appointment, critics spread rumors that he was often intoxicated on duty. Many leading preachers in Mobile, however, defended Thalacker and praised his crackdown on corruption. Hounded by malicious rumors, Thalacker, as well as Chief Warren, resigned from the police force. The subsequent appointment of Dudley E. McFadyen as police chief, a law enforcement veteran with a good reputation, smoothed over most of the internal problems of the police department.[44]

For years Mobilians demonstrated their support for the war effort in many ways. Even before the United States entered the war, many women participated in a "Knittin' for Britain" campaign. Laverne Taylor remembers knitting watch caps for the Red Cross to distribute in Great Britain. Churches and civic groups initiated clothes drives for war refugees and the suffering people of Russia, China, and other hard-pressed Allied countries. Clarke Holloway, a classmate of Taylor, has never completely forgiven his mother for having tossed his favorite Chippewa hunting boots into a clothes drive for Russian peasants. The Country Club of Mobile hosted a performance by famous opera singer Mary McCormic, who stayed with the parents of Emily and Jack Friend, to raise money for the canteen corps of the Mobile chapter of the American Red Cross. The exclusive Athelston Club provided lunches for Red Cross workers and other wartime volunteers. Junior Leaguers founded the Women's Committee for Home Defense with Frances Taylor Peck as chairwoman. In the spring of 1941, six charitable and religious groups established a

One of Mobile's few wartime day nurseries, 1521 Washington Avenue, 1943.

ADDSCO Collection, USA Archives.

chapter of the United Services Organization (USO), chaired by Mobile businessman Alfred Delchamps, who also headed up a Red Cross campaign to raise forty-five thousand dollars for war relief. By the end of the year, a USO servicemen's club, directed by Ellis Ollinger, opened at the corner of Government and Warren Streets. At about the same time, the first industrial women's USO club in the Deep South was established in the historic Bishop Portier House on Conti Street. A refurbished Seamen's Bethel on Government Street provided temporary shelter and recreation for transient white merchant seamen. In February 1942 the Downtown Servicemen's Center opened at the St. Francis Street Methodist Church. Headed by Kathryn DeCelle and supported by more than two dozen churches and civic organizations, it afforded military men and merchant sailors a "home away from home" throughout the war years. The Dorie Miller Club, managed by Marshall Robinson, provided shelter and entertainment for black sailors.[45]

Mobile women served in many auxiliary branches of the military. Twenty-six-year-old Virginia Unruh and her sister Margaret—both nursing graduates of City Hospital—were the first two Mobilians to volunteer for the army's nurses' corps. By September 1942 the Unruh sisters were stationed at Fort Bragg but expected to be stationed overseas in the near future.[46]

Already months before Japan's attack on American forces at Pearl Harbor, the United States was deeply involved in the struggle against the Axis powers. The Roosevelt administration found loopholes in existing neutrality laws to enable the United States to aid Great Britain by such means as the Lend-Lease Act, the

Hostess Kathryn de Celle with soldiers at the Downtown Servicemen's Center, St. Francis Street Methodist Church, 1942.

USA Archives.

Above left: Virginia Unruh. USA Archives.

Above right: Margaret Unruh. USA Archives.

"Destroyers for Bases" deal, and, eventually, naval escorts for Allied convoys. Mobile became an important port through which military supplies and equipment were sent to lend-lease partners. In 1941, for the first time in its history, the Alabama State Docks at Mobile handled more than two million tons of cargo.[47]

In late March 1941 the United States and several of its Western Hemisphere allies seized Axis property and interned foreign nationals in what were innocently called "concentration camps." Fearing sabotage of enemy and neutral vessels in U.S. ports, and acting on the basis of an obscure law enacted during World War I, Coast Guard sailors seized sixty-nine Axis and Danish ships in several U.S. ports. Crews on twenty Italian and two German ships—875 officers and seamen—were arrested on charges of sabotaging their own vessels or violating visa regulations. The result was a bizarre legal tangle involving complex issues of constitutional and international law.[48]

One of the seized Italian ships, the 4,953-ton *Ida Z.O.,* had taken refuge in the port of Mobile in June 1940, just days before Italy entered the war against France. The thirty officers and crew lived aboard the vessel and were rarely seen in Mobile except when members of the Apostleship of the Sea, a Catholic mission for mariners, took the Italian seamen to Sunday mass at either St. Patrick's Church or the Cathedral of the Immaculate Conception. When Raymond I. Smith arrived at the dock early on Sunday, March 30, 1941, to transport the Italians to mass, he was surprised to find men from the Coast Guard escorting them off the ship. Accused of using acetylene torches and sledgehammers to destroy the vessel's boilers, crankshaft, fuel pumps, and generators, and thus immobilizing the ship, the sailors were taken to the Mobile County jail.[49]

The jury trial of Batista Martini, captain of *Ida Z.O.,* and sixteen crewmen charged with sabotage opened in federal district court in Selma in July. United States district attorney Francis H. Inge of Mobile argued the government's case against the defendants. The men were found guilty of the charges, and prison sentences—ranging from two years for Captain Martini to six months for ordinary seamen—were imposed by the court. The Italians were to be deported after having served their sentences, if wartime conditions permitted. Although an appeal by the Italian sailors succeeded in vacating their convictions and obtaining a new trial, the entry of the United States into the war precluded their release from custody. Instead, the Italian seamen joined nearly sixteen hundred other Italians at an internment camp at Fort Missoula, Montana, where they remained until Italy's withdrawal from the war in 1944.[50]

Events on the high seas also drew the United States closer to war in the months prior to Pearl Harbor. The sinking of the neutral American merchant ship *Robin Moor* off the west coast of Africa prompted a *Mobile Register* editorial to demand "adequate naval protection" for U.S. merchant ships and to "meet force with force."[51] In early September 1941 a German U-boat fired a torpedo at *Greer,* an American destroyer stationed off the coast of Iceland. No harm was done, but Roosevelt issued orders to the navy to "shoot first" if threatened by Axis forces.

Six weeks later, during the night of October 17, 1941, *U-568* torpedoed *Kearney,* which was escorting a slow Allied convoy across the north Atlantic. Of the approximately 190 sailors on the American destroyer, 18 were Alabamians. One of those was eighteen-year-old Buford Perry, born in Atmore and the son of a lumberman whose family had moved to Mobile in 1932. Buford Perry volunteered for the navy in 1940 and joined his older brother, Novie Lee, on *Kearney.* On the night of the attack Buford Perry was standing watch in the engine room. He escaped death when the general alarm sounded, and he dashed to the flying bridge to man one of the .50-caliber machine guns. A short while later, the U-boat launched a spread of three torpedoes, one of which slammed into the engine room of the destroyer, killing eleven men, including Russell Burdick Wade of Winston County. *Kearney* limped to Iceland for repairs and later returned to combat.[52] Among the nine Allied merchant ships sunk in the convoy defended by *Kearney* was *Bold Venture,* a former Danish vessel that was now operated by Waterman Steamship Company. An alarmed Congress voted to install deck guns manned by navy gun crews on American merchant ships.

Attacks on merchant vessels also came from the air. In early September 1941 German aircraft sank *Steel Seafarer,* a merchant vessel operated by Isthmian Steamship of New York and Mobile in the Gulf of Suez. In late October, an air attack on Waterman's *Iberville* in the Suez Canal did little damage but demonstrated the perils facing American vessels and sailors.[53]

Americans who read newspapers or listened to news on the radio could have anticipated war with the Axis powers. Nonetheless, Japan's audacious attack on Pearl Harbor early on Sunday morning, December 7, 1941, caught almost everyone by surprise. Seventeen-year-old Mobile native Quinton Pollard, whose marine battalion was temporarily camping near Hickham Field, witnessed the attack. He recounted that he was so green that when the call to arms sounded, he grabbed his mess tin thinking it was chow time, but when he realized the pilots of the low-flying aircraft bombing the airfield were Japanese, fear quickly replaced hunger. Confusion reigned at Pearl Harbor for hours. For three days the battleship *Arizona,* whose forward magazine had exploded, killing one thousand sailors, burned in the harbor.[54]

Hours earlier when Mobilians had arisen, the temperature was hovering around freezing. Restrictions on electrical power usage, including restraints on burning Christmas lights, had been lifted because of recent heavy rains. Window-shoppers had thronged downtown on the previous day. After the bleak depression days, economic conditions were rosy: jobs were plentiful, wages were rising, and cash registers were jingling. Wartime demands were expected to lead to a doubling of industrial employment in Mobile over the next six months, from sixteen thousand to more than thirty-two thousand jobs.

If they were not going visiting after church and lunch, some Mobilians headed off to a movie or eagerly awaited one of their popular Sunday afternoon radio programs. One of the era's most popular movies, *Sergeant York,* starring young box-office sensation Gary Cooper, was playing at the Saenger Theater. Fred MacMurray and Madeleine Carroll starred in *One Night in Lisbon,* a "36-hour loveblitz" at the Roxy. Elsewhere in town, the East Side Kids romped in *Bowery Blitzkrieg* at the Century, and audiences at the Azalea swooned over sultry Merle Oberon and dashing Melvyn Douglas. Mobile's movie houses charged adults forty cents for matinees and fifty cents for evening movies, and children got in for half price.

On that Sunday many Mobilians were looking forward to their favorite radio programs. Two of the top big bands—Sammy Kaye and Jimmy Dorsey—attracted large listening audiences to their afternoon programs. Jack Benny, the Great Gildersleeve, and Charlie McCarthy left radio audiences slapping their thighs. Other listeners hung on the edge of their seats while Bulldog Drummond solved the latest crime. As night fell that Sunday, however, Mobilians gathered somberly around their radio sets to hear what popular newscasters Edward R. Murrow and Walter Winchell had to say about the carnage at Pearl Harbor.

Like most Americans, many Mobilians remember exactly what they were doing when they first learned of the disastrous events at Pearl Harbor. Nell Burks, whom R. B. Chandler had recently hired as a "girl reporter" for the *Mobile Register,* remembers that her husband, Bill, was off fishing when she heard the news at their Summerville apartment. Clarke Holloway, a student at Murphy High School, was resting under a pecan tree at his father's veterinary clinic when his mother came out to tell him the country was at war. A classmate, Laverne Taylor, and her family were visiting friends for the weekend in Fairhope when they heard the news. William Frank McCall Jr., later a major in the Sixth Army, learned about the attack when he turned on his radio after returning from church.[55]

Immediately following Pearl Harbor, the Federal Bureau of Investigation placed

The Bob Hope Show entertained Alabama Dry Dock and Shipbuilding Company workers on March 1, 1944.

ADDSCO Collection, USA Archives.

alien residents from Axis nations under surveillance, and in February 1942, agents raided the homes of eighteen resident alien families in Mobile. The children of Japanese-born Kosaku Sawada, however, recall suffering no slights or indignities during World War II. The elder Sawada, a native of Osaka, had immigrated to the United States in 1906. Failed ventures raising rice in Texas and citrus crops in south Alabama had brought the Sawadas to Mobile, where they founded Overlook Nursery. Mobilians remember the family as unquestionably loyal and outstanding members of the community. Mona Yarbrough of Montrose remembers that many prominent Mobile families vied for the services of Kosaku Sawada, who achieved fame as one of the nation's foremost hybridizers of camellias. One Mobilian recalls that she was very fond of the Sawadas because they "had beautiful manners and were not nosy."[56]

Daughter Lurie Sawada, a 1943 graduate of Murphy High School, recalls vividly how she learned the shocking news of Japan's attack on Pearl Harbor. After singing in an ecumenical production of Handel's *Messiah* at the Dauphin Way Methodist Church, she caught a ride home with friends. As they drove through the red gate archway to the nursery, she saw many cars parked at their house. Fearing something was wrong with her father, she ran into the house, which was filled with customers and friends who had come to offer to defend the loyalty of the Sawadas in this crisis. Lurie found her father uncharacteristically sobbing at this outpouring of friendship.[57]

Like his sister, Ben Sawada, now a retired Methodist minister who was a student at Murphy High School in the mid-1940s, recalls no prejudice against their family during the war. He points out that fellow students elected him to a number of offices in high school. His only election defeat was to a very popular and capable girl who edged him out in a race for student body president. After being drafted into the army in 1941, older brother Tom Sawada served in the Quartermaster Corps in the Pacific during World War II.[58] Mobile's acceptance of its few Asian Americans in the 1940s stood in sharp contrast to their treatment on the West Coast. After World War II the museum at the Statue of Liberty in New York harbor commemorated Kosaku Sawada as one of five exemplary Japanese immigrants who had made extraordinary contributions to American society.

Although the danger of an Axis invasion was greatly exaggerated, indeed nonexistent, the United States undertook a massive effort to reactivate and expand coastal defenses and prepare the civilian population for wartime disasters. Only Japan possessed carrier-based aircraft capable of posing even the most remote threat to American coasts. Although lacking carriers and land bases from which air attacks could be launched against the continental United States, Germany had submarines, or U-boats, in sufficient quantity to threaten Allied shipping in the western Atlantic Ocean and even in the Gulf of Mexico.

Operation Drumbeat, Germany's first U-boat offensive in American waters in World War II, ranged southward from New England to Florida in early 1942 and heightened tensions. In a second wave of German U-boats that arrived in American coastal waters between April and June 1942, German commanders concentrated on tankers and bauxite carriers.

In May 1942 war came much closer to Mobile when German U-boats began sinking ships in the Gulf of Mexico with impunity. The sizable crowd of well-wishers gathered on Pinto Island on May 3, 1942, for the launching of ADDSCO's fourth Liberty ship, *Arthur Middleton,* was unaware that two German U-boats—

Mobile's Sawada family, 1947.

Erik Overbey Collection, USA Archives.

having sailed from their base at Lorient, France, weeks earlier—were slicing through the Florida Straits into the Gulf of Mexico.

The first U-boat to draw blood in the Gulf of Mexico was *U-507*, commanded by career officer Harro Schacht. At 9:40 A.M. on May 4, 1942, about eighty miles northwest of Dry Tortugas Island, Schacht fired a torpedo at *Norlindo*. An explosion between number three and four holds sank the freighter within twelve minutes. Five crewmen working in the after hold could not escape and went down with the ship. Twenty-eight crewmen, including ten from Mobile, jumped into the water and were subsequently rescued by a United Fruit Company ship.[59] The next day, and in the same vicinity, *U-507* sank the tanker *Munger T. Ball*. Only four of its crew of thirty-four survived the attack. Less than three hours later, Schacht overtook and torpedoed another tanker, *Joseph M. Cudahy*, as it frantically and vainly sought shelter in Tampa. Navy PBY-Catalina patrol aircraft rescued the master and nine of the ship's thirty-seven crewmen. During the next two weeks, Schacht sank four more freighters and another tanker. In the meantime Erich Würdemann and his *U-506* launched its own reign of terror in the Gulf of Mexico, sinking five and damaging two tankers and sinking one freighter. Both commanders won Knight's Crosses for their successes.

Two Alcoa ships in the bauxite trade between Mobile and South America had been torpedoed and sunk in April with the loss of sixteen lives. At midday on May 6, 1942, *Alcoa Puritan*, steaming from Trinidad with a load of bauxite bound for Mobile, was attacked by *U-507* about fifty miles southeast of the mouth of the Mississippi River. The first torpedo barely missed the ship's stern. Spotting the torpedo, Captain Y. A. Krantz tried to outrun the U-boat. During an ensuing forty-five-minute chase, German sailors fired approximately seventy-five shells from the deck gun, of which nearly fifty hit their target, tearing holes in the ship's superstructure. With a damaged steering mechanism *Alcoa Puritan* began turning in circles, enabling the U-boat to overtake the stricken vessel. Krantz ordered all hands to abandon ship. After observing *Alcoa Puritan*'s crew going overboard in a lifeboat and two life rafts, *U-507* launched a second torpedo, which exploded with such terrific force in the engine room that the vessel sank within a minute. The forty-one crewmen and seven passengers, now crowded into one lifeboat, were rescued three hours later by the Mobile-based Coast Guard cutter *Boutwell* and taken to Venice, Louisiana.[60] Miraculously, only two crew members were wounded badly enough to warrant hospitalization. Three weeks later a German U-boat sank *Alcoa Pilgrim* in the Caribbean Sea south of the Mona Passage. By the late spring and into the summer of 1942, the area designated by the navy as the Gulf Sea Frontier—stretching from Jacksonville, Florida, to Galveston, Texas—was the most dangerous place in the world for shipping.[61]

Sinkings in the Gulf of Mexico had immediate economic impact. Within four days of the first loss of merchant shipping in the gulf, and even before the general public learned of these attacks, marine insurance underwriters sharply increased war-risk rates for merchant ships sailing in the gulf and Caribbean and immediately halted publication of insurance rates for tankers. Cargo rates for the gulf jumped from $0.75 per hundred dollars to $2.50 per hundred.[62]

By the end of the summer of 1942 the worst of the U-boat offensive in the Gulf of Mexico had passed. Naval authorities had instituted convoying for Allied shipping. Navy destroyers, smaller Coast Guard subchasers, Coast Guard patrol planes, and army bombers swarmed over the gulf. Three U-boats were sunk in the gulf and Florida Straits—one by the U.S. Navy, one by the Cuban navy, and another by a Coast Guard patrol plane out of Houma, Louisiana. Afterward U-boats occasionally ventured into the gulf generally on their way to or from the Caribbean. The last U-boat attack on shipping in the Gulf of Mexico came on December 3, 1943, when Hans Pauckstadt in *U-193* torpedoed *Touchet.* This vessel, a C-2 type tanker launched at ADDSCO only a few weeks earlier, carried a cargo of 120,000 barrels of heating oil. Fatally damaged by two torpedoes, the tanker sank stern first with a loss of ten armed guards. Altogether, some two dozen German submarines operated in the Gulf of Mexico, sinking nearly sixty ships between May 1942 and December 1943.[63]

Although Operation Drumbeat led to a dimout along the East Coast, including south Florida waters, in May 1942, it was not until nearly mid-June—after the U-boat campaign was well under way in the Gulf of Mexico—that the dimout was extended to the gulf states from the Florida panhandle to Mississippi and, later, to Texas. Regulations prohibited municipal lighting and illumination of commercial buildings in all towns within ten miles of the coast and in towns with populations of more than five thousand within twenty-five miles of the gulf. For the duration of the war, nighttime football and baseball games in coastal towns, as well as bonfires and automobiles on beaches at night, came to an end. Operators of automobiles within five hundred yards of the sea could use only parking lights or headlights whose tops had been painted black. Seaward lights in beachfront homes had to be extinguished or concealed by heavy curtains. Supplemental regulations forbade flounder gigging and soft-shell crabbing between Cedar Point and Dog River, temporarily ending two "ancient summer sports."[64] Coast Guard units patrolled beaches on foot and horseback to search for saboteurs or spies and to report violations of dimout restrictions. Because Mobile lies thirty-two miles inland from the Gulf of Mexico it was not immediately clear how dimout regulations would affect the city.

The first statewide blackout drill was conducted on Saint Patrick's Day in 1942. Beginning in Mobile and moving northward, every community of more than five thousand inhabitants extinguished its lights. Although local civilian defense officials, headed by Fred Arn, voiced satisfaction with the success of later dimouts, military officials complained as late as August 1943 that Mobile's shipyards were not in full compliance with regulations and that the city's glow—useful to German submarines aiming at silhouettes of targets—was visible at sea.[65]

With federal and state aid local governments organized civilian defense programs to conduct air-raid drills. In the summer of 1942 the state defense council began distributing sirens and other equipment to local civilian defense organizations. Ground observer corps units scanned the skies for enemy aircraft, and Civil Air Patrol units patrolled coastal waters for enemy naval craft. Local civilian defense officials made plans for medical treatment and evacuation of the wounded in the event hostilities reached Mobile County. White casualties were to be treated at one of Mobile's four hospitals—Providence, Mobile Infirmary, Mobile City, and United States Marine Hospital—that together had 550 beds. If strain on local medical facilities proved to be too great, white casualties were to be taken to one of Selma's three hospitals. African American casualties in Mobile requiring more than simple first aid on the scene were to be evacuated to John A. Andrew Memorial Hospital in Tuskegee nearly two hundred miles to the northeast.[66]

The U.S. Army reactivated Fort Morgan during World War II to serve both as a temporary harbor defense position to guard the entrance to Mobile Bay and as a recreation facility for African American troops. Two 155mm guns on Panama mounts atop the bastion of the old fort faced the southeast. Two sixty-inch portable searchlights and several smaller searchlights stood ready to illuminate the entrance to Mobile Bay. With threats to the U.S. coast virtually nonexistent and with no U-boat attack on gulf shipping after December 1943, Fort Morgan was deactivated in July 1944.[67]

During World War II several vessels regularly frequented nearby waters and were a welcome sight to ships bound for Mobile. One was the auxiliary schooner *Alabama,* which lay at anchor near Fort Morgan where it served as a pilot station for vessels entering or departing the port. Mobile was home port for the Coast Guard cutter *Boutwell,* which searched for U-boats in the Gulf of Mexico, escorted convoys, and rescued seamen in distress. *Magnolia,* a buoy tender, met an inglorious end near Sand Island Lighthouse in late August 1945 when a recently completed cargo ship, *Marguerita LeHand,* struck the vessel a glancing, but fatal, blow. One crewman—knocked off the stern of the tender—was lost at sea, but the other crew members safely took to lifeboats and landed at Choctaw Point.[68]

Shipbuilding and shipping were the twin pillars of Mobile's wartime economy. Shipbuilding, which represented one-fourth of all defense contracts in Alabama, consumed 20 percent of all steel produced in the United States during World War II. At first rolling mills could not make enough thick steel plates to meet the demand for warships and merchant vessels, but companies such as the Birmingham district's TCI—the largest steel producer in the South—expanded and modified existing mills. By 1942 TCI produced 75 percent more steel than two years earlier, much of which was used in ADDSCO and Gulf Shipbuilding yards in Mobile and elsewhere on the gulf.[69]

Mobile also played an essential, but largely unheralded, role in procuring and processing bauxite. This mineral had many important industrial and military applications, including abrasives, petroleum refining, and insulation. Most important, bauxite was processed into alumina, which, in turn, was further processed to manufacture aluminum for military aircraft. During World War II American aircraft plants produced 304,000 planes, consuming 3.5 billion pounds of aluminum. Two of the country's five bauxite reduction plants were located in Alabama—a Reynolds plant near the Tennessee River at Listerhill and the much larger Alcoa operation in Mobile. In 1937 Alcoa had announced plans to build a $4 million bauxite plant on a seventy-eight-acre site at the Alabama State Docks, the first major industrial recruit to the state docks since the facility opened on the eve of the Great Depression. With its deep water port on the Gulf of Mexico and its excellent rail and river transport systems connecting the city to America's industrial centers, Mobile was ideally situated for the bauxite trade. The plant that opened a year later reached maximum output in 1943 when it produced 1.3 million pounds of alumina, or 34 percent of the industry's entire output. Alumina was then shipped by rail to one of Alcoa's plants located in New York or on the West Coast to produce aluminum ingots that were later rolled into sheet aluminum or cast into engine parts for airplanes. At the height of the war, the aircraft industry alone consumed 85 percent of Alcoa's aluminum production.[70]

Although low-grade bauxite was mined in abundance in Arkansas, the best quality came from British and Dutch Guyana on South America's northeastern coast. To transport bauxite, Alcoa operated its own seagoing fleet homeported in Mobile. Anticipating rapidly growing demand for aluminum as war spread in Europe in 1940, Alcoa announced plans to launch seven new ships in California at a cost of $17 million to augment its existing fleet of fourteen bauxite carriers.[71]

Alcoa ships in the bauxite trade sailed from Mobile with general cargo bound for Latin American ports and, by 1941, with military supplies for the Caribbean bases the United States had acquired from Britain in a swap for fifty aged, four-stack destroyers. Returning ships were laden with bauxite. A modest passenger service on suitable ships supplemented the cargo trade. Because the War Shipping Administration also appointed Alcoa as the general agent for the bauxite trade with South America, Alcoa's Mobile office had far-flung maritime administrative and logistical responsibilities.

Alcoa coordinated no fewer than nine hundred southbound and northbound sailings by bauxite carriers during World War II. The final destination on the southbound leg was either Georgetown, British Guyana, or Paramaribo, which lies about thirteen miles upriver from the Atlantic Ocean in Dutch Guyana. After off-loading general cargo at Paramaribo, smaller, shallow-draft vessels navigated up the Suriname River through dense overhanging jungle vegetation to Paranam, where bauxite was loaded. Larger vessels that could not cross the sandy bars in the river anchored at Trinidad to await Alcoa's small lighters that shuttled bauxite from the Guyanas' mines. Alcoa-owned or -operated vessels carried 3.5 million tons of bauxite for processing in the United States and Canada. Because many of these bulk carriers rarely made even ten knots per hour, they were often ripe targets for German U-boat attacks in the Caribbean and Gulf of Mexico. Of the fifty-seven bauxite carriers sunk by German submarines in the western Atlantic Ocean during the war, eight were Alcoa vessels, and another thirteen were chartered and operated by Alcoa.[72] Sixty-seven Alcoa seamen on twelve Alcoa-owned ships lost their lives to German U-boat attacks or mines, and many others took to lifeboats and faced the perils of thirst, heavy weather, and tumultuous seas before being rescued.

In addition to the Alcoa plant, several other major corporations located facilities near the Alabama State Docks. One was International Paper's Southern Kraft division mill, the second largest of its kind in the world. Employing twenty-five hundred workers, it operated four shifts a day, seven days a week. Half of its production—twenty-five million paper bags daily—was for defense purposes.[73] National Gypsum, Meyercord Compound, and American Cyanamid and Chemical operated other plants at the state docks.

Hollingsworth and Whitney was another Mobile company that contributed to the war effort. Its three hundred workers turned out protective containers for artillery shells made from paperboard rather than metal. The company earned the army and navy's "E" award for excellence, making it the only paper company in the South to be distinguished in this way. Altogether, by the end of World War II, American corporations had invested $32 million in facilities in Mobile, and the port had advanced from the twenty-fifth to thirteenth busiest in the United States.[74]

Mobilians displayed pride and more than a casual interest in warships with Alabama names, especially *Mobile,* a modern cruiser christened by Louise Hartwell, wife of Mobile mayor and city councilman Harry T. Hartwell, in Newport News in May 1942. *Mobile* joined naval operations in the Pacific in late 1943. In the following months the ship provided fire support for amphibious landings on Japanese-held islands, escorted carriers, and pounded Japanese bases with merciless fire from its six-inch guns. Earning eleven battle stars for operations in the Pacific, *Mobile* played an especially important role in the destruction of Truk, Japan's major anchorage and center of communications in the Carolines. It also fought in the

Leyte Gulf and other crucial battles to retake the Philippine Islands. Following the war, the *Mobile Register* organized a collection of general interest books and pictures of Mobile and Bellingrath Gardens to send to the ship's library.[75]

Mobilians flocked to their churches to offer prayers of thanks and safekeeping to the men and women in uniform at crucial junctures of the war. As D-Day unfolded on the French coast in early June 1944, churches flung open their doors to welcome the prayers of the faithful for the success of the invasion. A holiday spirit enveloped the city except at the shipyards, where workers buckled down to produce the ships needed for victory in Europe and in the Pacific.[76]

By the spring of 1945, Allied victory in Europe appeared certain. German resistance crumbled as American and British Commonwealth troops drove into the Rhineland from the west and as millions of Russian troops in the east swept aside the Wehrmacht as they poured through Poland, Czechoslovakia, and Hungary into eastern Germany and Austria. On April 12, 1945—a Thursday—news that President Franklin Roosevelt had died suddenly at his retreat at Warm Springs, Georgia, shocked America. Many Mobile businesses closed or paused for a moment of reflection during his funeral on Saturday, and special memorial services were conducted in many churches and in the chapel at Brookley Field on the following day. Vice-President Harry Truman, strongly supported by Mobile congressman Frank Boykin, took the oath of office as the nation's thirty-third chief executive.

On May 7, at General Dwight Eisenhower's headquarters in a red schoolhouse

Workers at the Alabama Dry Dock and Shipbuilding Company gather for announcement of V-E Day.

ADDSCO Collection, USA Archives.

near Reims, France, General Alfred Jodl accepted the terms for an unconditional, general surrender by the German government. On the following day—a Tuesday—stores and schools in Mobile closed after Truman officially announced Germany's surrender. Compared with the wild celebrations accompanying the end of World War I, this V-E Day was subdued and peaceful. Again, many Mobilians visited their churches and synagogues to give thanks, but they also prayed for the safety of loved ones still fighting in the Pacific, where the war was far from over. At ADDSCO, about fifteen thousand workers gathered for a ceremony of thanksgiving and then returned to work.[77]

Two weeks later, on May 22, Mobile welcomed Admiral Emory Land, chairman of the U.S. Maritime Commission, and navy dignitaries to celebrate Maritime Day. The festivities included launchings of a minesweeper, landing ship dock, and a tanker at the two shipyards. Admiral Land presented medals to families of five Mobile area merchant seamen who lost their lives on ships torpedoed by German U-boats. Following a Propeller Club dinner at the Admiral Semmes Hotel, white and black seamen danced the night away on dance floors at separate locations.

In the Pacific theater American marine and army divisions leapfrogged from island to island toward Japan while Japanese resistance grew more desperate and determined as Allied forces drew nearer to the home islands. One of the Pacific war's bloodiest battles took place at tiny Peleliu Island in the Palaus. Two Mobil-

Celebration at the Admiral Semmes Hotel on Maritime Day, 1945. Left to right: Rear Admiral C. L. Brand, U.S. Navy; Captain Norman Nicholson, president, Waterman Steamship Company; Congressman Frank Boykin (standing); Admiral E. S. Land; Captain Holmes, president of the Propellor Club.

ADDSCO Collection, USA Archives.

ians, John Dury New and Eugene Bondurant Sledge, achieved unsought distinction in that crucible of fire.

The invasion of Peleliu by the First Marine Division, an attack regarded at the time by some military planners as an essential stepping stone to the liberation of the Philippines but now generally seen as an unnecessary waste of American lives, was expected to succeed in three days. Instead, it took American forces a grim month of bitter combat to secure the island. Unexpectedly, the Japanese had drastically altered tactics for defending their Pacific islands. Rather than making a stand on shore, they moved into the island's interior to build strongholds in coral, hillside caves, and bunkers. After a three-day naval bombardment of the island that did little to soften Japanese resistance, marines went ashore under murderous gunfire. Unable to dig positions on the island's coral beaches, they advanced toward withering machine gun fire, deadly mortar barrages, and grenades lobbed by an unseen enemy. Once having established a perimeter just inland, the marines were subjected to terrifying nighttime bonzai attacks by the fanatical Japanese.

John Dury New was among those marines struggling to establish a foothold on Peleliu. Having concealed that he was only sixteen years old, John New had enlisted in the marines immediately after Japan attacked Pearl Harbor. Following training at Parris Island and duty at Quantico, Private New was attached to a marine replacement battalion that shipped out for the Pacific from San Diego in the autumn of 1942. In the next months he saw combat at Guadalcanal and in the campaign to take Cape Gloucester on New Britain. In mid-September 1944 Private First Class New, now in the First Marine Division, took part in the invasion of Peleliu, a battle that Eugene Sledge later described as the "assault into Hell."[78]

New's duty was to protect a forward observation post directing mortar fire against Japanese emplacements. Suddenly, from a cave below, a Japanese soldier hurled a grenade into the observation post. With complete disregard for his own safety, New flung himself onto the grenade, saving the lives of his two comrades. In recognition of this sacrificial act to save the lives of fellow marines, the Congressional Medal of Honor was posthumously awarded to New's father on June 23, 1945, in a ceremony at the Pensacola Naval Air Station. John New became the only Mobilian to receive the Congressional Medal of Honor in World War II.[79]

Eugene Sledge, known to his marine buddies as "Sledgehammer," survived the hellish combat at Peleliu and, later, at Okinawa. Aided by a forbidden combat diary, he later described those gruesome campaigns in an autobiographical account. *With the Old Breed at Peleliu and Okinawa* rings with such unmatched authenticity that Paul Fussell, himself a combat platoon leader in France during World War II and an authority on the literature of war, has described it as "one of the finest memoirs to emerge from any war."[80] Sledge, whose mother was a founding member of the Historic Mobile Preservation Society, was born in Mobile in 1923. He suffered from malaria and rheumatic fever as a child, but his physician father taught him how to hunt, fish, and observe nature with a keen eye. Sledge attributes his survival in the Pacific theater to a measure of good luck and to the predator's skills and instincts developed in his youth.

After a stint at Marion Institute, Sledge joined the marines and was sent to the Pacific. At Guadalcanal he boarded an LST for a three-week journey to Peleliu. Although there were many First Marine Division veterans on his LST landing craft with whom to share war stories about the tough Guadalcanal and Cape Gloucester campaigns, Sledgehammer went into combat unprepared for the horrors awaiting him at Peleliu and Okinawa. Indeed, in the fighting at Okinawa, only 26 of the company's original 235 soldiers and 24 of the 254 replacement troops came through alive and unwounded. One of the few members of Company K not to be wounded in combat, Sledge refers to himself as "a fugitive from the law of averages."[81]

By the early summer of 1945 Japan's home islands were subjected to merciless bombing. Newly developed napalm, much of it manufactured in Huntsville arsenals, turned Japanese cities and industrial centers into vortexes of searing flames. Still the Japanese refused to surrender. Fearing an invasion of the home islands would result in unacceptable casualty rates, President Harry Truman decided to drop a secretly developed atomic bomb on Japan.

The *Mobile Register*'s headline of August 8, 1945, read "Atomic Bomb Dissolves Jap City." The blast that leveled Hiroshima two days earlier, readers learned, was equal to the bomb loads of two thousand B-29 Superfortresses. On August 9 yet another atomic bomb was released on Nagasaki. Finally realizing that further resistance was suicidal, Emperor Hirohito agreed to surrender. Mobilians celebrated VJ-Day quietly and soberly.

More than 15,000 men from Mobile, of whom 2,300 were enlisted and 13,150 were inducted, donned military uniforms in World War II. Of this number, three hundred lost their lives in combat or in a service-related death, were missing and declared dead, or perished as prisoners of war. Among the dead were 249 Mobilians in the army or army air force, twenty-one in the Marine Corps, twenty-six in the navy, and one in the Coast Guard.[82]

Of all World War II legends along the Gulf Coast, one of the most enduring has been the often-repeated story that German submarines sailed into Mobile Bay, up the Mississippi River, or close enough to Galveston to spot cars on streets through the periscope. Many Mobilians today claim to have known someone who had spotted German sailors wandering the streets of Mobile or towns in Baldwin County, attending movies, having clothes cleaned, or purchasing fresh foods from local merchants.[83] Rumors abounded of Axis agents or sympathizers—almost always local citizens with German surnames—on the Gulf Coast who purportedly provided offshore German U-boats with shipping intelligence and with fuel or other supplies. Although the landing, capture, and execution of two small bands of German saboteurs in Florida and Long Island in 1942 gave some credence to these stories, German naval records do not substantiate such needless and reckless adventures.

The only two World War II German submarines known to have entered Mobile Bay came during peacetime. Just after Christmas 1945, *U-505,* which had been captured in dramatic fashion by a U.S. Navy task force led by the escort carrier *Guadalcanal* off West Africa in June 1944, tied up to a pier at the foot of Government Street. John F. Palmer of Mobile, a gunner on the USS *Pillsbury,* had taken part in the capture of *U-505,* which was the first enemy vessel taken prize by the U.S. Navy on the high seas since 1815. After being towed across the Atlantic, *U-505*—now with an American crew—set sail on a cruise to twenty-four Atlantic and Gulf Coast ports to breathe life into a flagging Victory Loan Drive. Mobile, the last stop of the cruise, responded to the call as ninety-one residents purchased $1,000 war bonds on the first day of the visit. Another German submarine, the former *U-2513,* which was a modern type-XXI electrical boat that surrendered to Allied forces at the end of World War II, also visited Mobile on Navy Day in October 1946.[84]

As the war wound down, it became evident that the vast wartime merchant fleet would no longer be needed. Lobbying by Congressman Frank Boykin convinced the War Shipping Administration and the U.S. Maritime Commission to select a site four miles up the Mobile River to serve as an anchorage for excess ships. The first vessel, *Elwood,* arrived in late August 1945. A two-mile channel led from the Mobile River to the Tensaw River where nearly three hundred ships, mostly Liberty ships and T-2 tankers, were eventually anchored in this mothballed "ghost fleet."[85]

By the spring of 1945 the number of industrial employees in Mobile was well below peak levels reached in 1943. At war's end Mobile shipyards employed only eighty-five hundred, and the area's total economy saw the work force shrink by forty thousand. As defense-related production slumped, many workers had been laid off or headed home, perhaps to regain or claim jobs there before veterans returned.[86] Ironically, jobs went begging, and defense industries in Mobile advertised for workers to fill four thousand critical jobs.

In the following months discharged servicemen began returning home. ADDSCO reported that seven hundred former workers applied for reemployment after being discharged from military service. Some veterans whose military service had brought them to Mobile—such as Sergeant Jasper Llewellyn, the first soldier to be discharged from Brookley Field under the new discharge point system—settled in Mobile after the war.

Living standards soon improved as peace returned. The tight housing situation eased as defense workers departed. Rationing ended or eased in the summer of 1945. Owners of automobiles were delighted to learn that they would be entitled to six gallons of gasoline a week instead of four.[87] Shoe rationing, however, did not end until early 1946. Consumer items would soon become more plentiful, and many people had money to spend. Rationing and the scarcity of many consumer items during the war—especially automobiles and appliances—had forced people to save. The successful war bond campaign had been a patriotic way for civilians to save for a better postwar world and to satisfy pent-up consumer expectations.

Probably nothing changed postwar American society more than the GI Bill of Rights, which, in Alabama, was supplemented by state programs for military veterans. The GI Bill created unparalleled opportunities for job training, higher education, and home ownership. Prior to World War II less than 7 percent of Alabama's population had any education beyond high school. By 1950 the number of Alabamians with some college education had increased by 43 percent, and the number of African Americans with at least one year of college almost doubled.[88]

No southeastern state benefited economically from the war more than Alabama, and no city was more affected by government investments in facilities for defense production and government purchases through defense contracts during World War II than Mobile. Forecasts for the postwar future of Alabama and Mobile were rosy. As early as the summer of 1943, when Allied victory was by no means a sure thing, Mobilians began pondering the city's future after the war. A *Mobile Register* editorial commented on optimistic stories in recent issues of *Fortune* and the *Christian Science Monitor* predicting that the South was poised for continued industrial growth after war's end.[89] Prominent businessmen and community leaders reiterated

The "ghost fleet" anchored in the Tensaw River after the war.

McNeely Collection, USA Archives.

this theme many times in succeeding months. Some business leaders, including executives at Waterman Steamship, who established an airline to serve the Caribbean, also dreamed that Mobile could become the nation's gateway to Latin America.

There were many social issues, especially race relations and gender roles, whose challenges had been accelerated by the war and that would shape Alabama for decades to come. Mobile's civic leaders, aware that the city's well-being hinged on their ability to deal with local problems fostered by tumultuous wartime conditions, moved quickly to plan for the city's future. In 1945 farsighted civic leaders advocated massive investments to improve the city's infrastructure and municipal services. Despite the loss of jobs in the defense sector the Census Bureau confidently predicted that Mobile would be among the top seventeen cities in the country to retain its wartime surge in population. A citizens' committee recommended municipal spending to expand and improve the Alabama State Docks; transform City Hospital into the finest hospital in the state; make improvements in water, sewer, and garbage services; pave more streets and install adequate storm drains; and construct a new five-thousand-seat auditorium as well as a new stadium.[90] This bold plan propelled Mobile into the second half of the twentieth century.

Suggestions for Further Reading

Cronenberg, Allen. *Forth to the Mighty Conflict: Alabama and World War II.* Tuscaloosa: University of Alabama Press, 1995. This survey examines the military and home front roles of Alabamians and suggests that World War II may have had a more profound impact on Alabama society than the Civil War.

McMillen, Neil R., ed. *Remaking Dixie: The Impact of World War II on the American South.* Jackson: University of Mississippi Press, 1997. These essays look at World War II's impact on the American South and on the emergence of a postwar Sunbelt.

Sledge, Eugene B. *With the Old Breed at Peleliu and Okinawa.* New York: Oxford University Press, 1991. Written by a Mobile native, this is one of the most important combat accounts to come out of World War II.

Thomas, Mary Martha. *Riveting and Rationing in Dixie: Alabama Women and the Second World War.* Tuscaloosa: University of Alabama Press, 1987. This pioneering work examines the important roles Alabama women played in the defense industry, in war-related volunteer activities, and in coping with war-related scarcities.

Honored guests received elaborate invitations for balls held by the mystic societies. The Order of Myths' theme was "Odd Craft" in 1884.

Local History Division, Mobile Public Library.

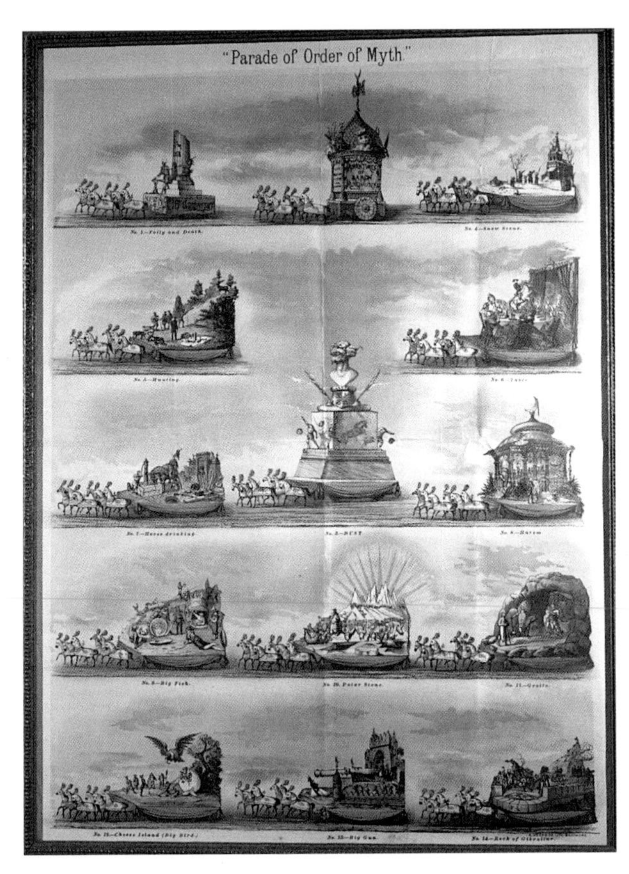

The Order of Myths, organized in 1867, was the first mystic society to parade on Fat Tuesday. In 1883 the Order of Myths' theme was "The Adventures of Baron Munchausen."

Museum of Mobile.

The city's militia companies were almost as important to late-nineteenth-century Mobile as its mystic societies. The city also hosted an important interstate drill competition in 1885 near Frascatti Park on the bay front.

Frank Leslie's Illustrated Newspaper, May 2, 1885.

After a hurricane destroyed Frascatti in 1893, Monroe Park became Mobile's most popular recreation area. Developed by the electric trolley company to generate business, it was easily reached by street cars. Its attractions included a baseball field, penny arcade, roller coaster, outdoor movie theater, and carousel.

Eichold Collection, University of South Alabama Archives.

Mobile looking south from Conti Street between Royal and St. Emanuel Streets.

Harper's Weekly, February 2, 1884.

Bird's-eye view map of Mobile in 1891.

USA Archives.

A New Orleans ship captain, William L. Challoner, painted this view of Mobile's waterfront, circa 1895.

Historic Mobile Preservation Society.

Riverboats still brought cargo to the cotton docks at Mobile although railroads carried more and more of this commodity after the Civil War.

Eichold Collection, USA Archives.

The antebellum Battle House Hotel was destroyed by fire in 1905, but the "new" Battle House continued to offer first-class service to those who could afford it.

Eichold Collection, USA Archives.

A Queen Ann cottage, circa 1895, with shingled turret and finely carved "gingerbread" at 112 S. Georgia and a home at 1752 Dauphin Street with an elegant blend of late Victorian stylistic elements, circa 1897, grace Old Dauphin Way, one of Mobile's seven historic districts.

Mobile Historic Development Commission.

Mobile's state docks, opened in 1928, made Mobile competitive with the major southern Atlantic and Gulf Coast ports.

Painting by Roderick MacKenzie, circa 1930s. Mobile Museum of Art.

Walter and Bessie Bellingrath opened their private gardens on the Fowl River to the public during the Great Depression. The gardens quickly became a popular year-round tourist attraction, and so it has remained.

Bellingrath Gardens and Home.

The design for a 1936 Infant Mystics Mardi Gras float, "Home of Tarzan," by J. Augustus Walker.

Museum of Mobile.

Black Mobilians held their first documented Mardi Gras parade in 1938. During the early years of the Mobile Area Mardi Gras Association, individuals known as "Mollies" participated unofficially in the parades.

Drawing by Louis Colston III. Museum of Mobile.

Launching a section of the Bankhead Tunnel at the Alabama Dry Dock and Shipbuilding Company, 1939.

Pastel by Roderick MacKenzie. Mobile Municipal Archives.

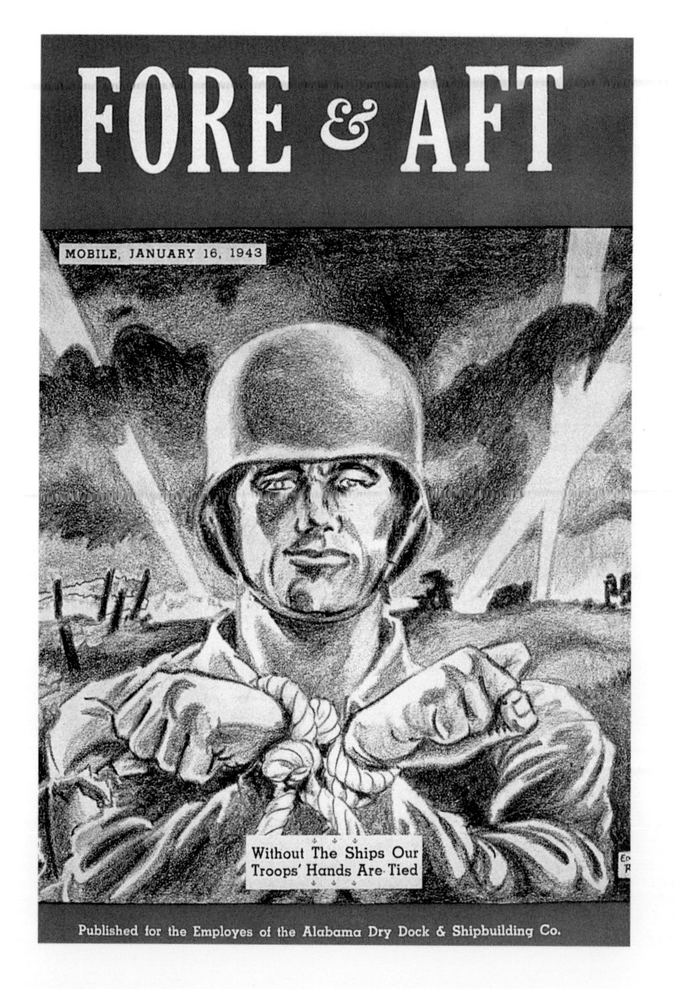

Edward Ryan's illustration on the front cover of the Alabama Dry Dock and Shipbuilding Company's employee publication shows a soldier's hands tied when home front production slows down.

Fore and Aft, January 16, 1943. ADDSCO Collection, USA Archives.

The Waterman Globe is pictured here in its original location, the lobby of the Waterman Building, circa 1950. The globe is now on display in the Mitchell Center on the campus of the University of South Alabama.

USA Archives.

The First National Bank building under construction in 1965 dwarfs Mobile's earlier skyscrapers, the Waterman building (1948), Merchants National Bank (1929), and the Van Antwerp building (1908).

Photograph by James Hastie. USA Archives.

After an intensive fund-raising drive, the battleship USS *Alabama* was towed to Mobile and anchored permanently along the causeway in September 1964.

Photograph by James Hastie. USA Archives.

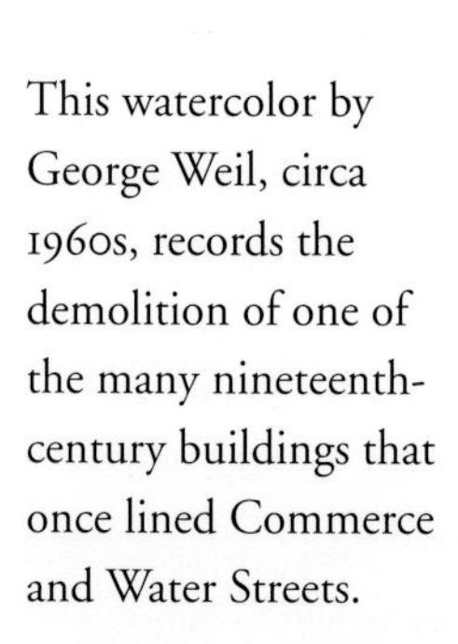

This watercolor by George Weil, circa 1960s, records the demolition of one of the many nineteenth-century buildings that once lined Commerce and Water Streets.

Mobile Museum of Art.

President Nixon addressed a large crowd on the waterfront for the beginning of construction of the Tennessee-Tombigbee Waterway in 1971. The completed Tenn-Tom opened to traffic fourteen years later.

Photograph by C. T. Mayer. USA Archives.

The University of South Alabama, founded in 1964, included a medical school by the early 1970s. The university's founding president, Frederick P. Whiddon, with Governor George Wallace seated behind him, is at the podium for the dedication of the College of Medicine building in 1973.

Photograph by Andy Dees. USA Archives.

The Order of Athena, one of the many new mystic societies formed after World War II, first paraded in 1955. Onlookers scramble for flying moonpies during this 1987 parade.

Photograph by Michael Thomason, USA Archives.

The Pincus Building on the corner of Dauphin and Royal Streets, built in 1890, is one of the many nineteenth-century structures that have been restored in the city's historic commercial district.

Mobile Historic Development Commission.

On December 31, 1991, Mobile celebrated the arts with a new festival called First Night. Indoor and outdoor entertainment attract many visitors to the downtown area each year.

Photograph by Catt Sirten, 1998.

Visitation Convent's Chapel of the Sacred Heart, built in 1894, underwent extensive restoration in 1999.

Photograph by Catt Sirten, 1999.

The statue of Ervin Cooper is an attraction in the recently completed waterfront park named for the late chairman of Cooper Stevedoring. The park is located next to the Arthur R. Outlaw Convention Center.

Photograph by Catt Sirten, 1999.

CHAPTER 9

Politics and Civil Rights in Post–World War II Mobile

Keith Nicholls

THE POLITICAL HISTORY OF Mobile in the post–World War II era is dominated by the issue of race. As politics generally is a struggle over the distribution of societal values, politics in Mobile during this period is characterized by the black community's struggle to gain and keep their most basic constitutional rights and to use those rights to garner a more equitable share of the economic resources and social opportunities that bring security and prosperity. This struggle pitted Mobile's African American community against a conservative white establishment unwilling to share political authority or modify its cultural values. The most enduring legacy of this period, one that will most likely prevail well into the twenty-first century, is the inclination of politicians, the media, and the public to define many political issues as racial issues, a tendency that promotes racial polarization and exacerbates racial tensions.

Because the roots of this conflict can be traced to slavery and the failure of post–Civil War Reconstruction, the renewal of the conflict in the post–World War II period is often referred to as the Second Reconstruction. Nationally, historians point to the 1954 Supreme Court decision in *Brown v. Board of Education* as the first major accomplishment of the Second Reconstruction. On the regional level, however, the picture is more complicated. Mobile's black leaders, chief among them John LeFlore, who, as noted in previous chapters, was a postal clerk and head of the Mobile chapter of the NAACP, had been working for decades to improve living conditions and economic opportunities for African Americans. In most instances, they did not demand political rights, nor did they challenge the institutionalized segregation that was the law of the land. Rather, they pushed for concessions within the segregated framework: increased availability of basic facilities and services, such as rest rooms and restaurants; vocational training for blacks and employment opportunities; and official attention to allegations of police brutality and other issues of public safety.[1]

By the end of World War II, however, Mobile's civil rights leaders became impatient with the slow pace of change and turned their attention to political rights and the evils of segregation. From their perspective the *Brown* decision was not the beginning of the Second Reconstruction. Rather, it was a welcome affirmation of the federal government's willingness to support them in their renewed struggle to remove the legal and institutional barriers to black progress.

The impetus for renewing the struggle in Mobile, as in much of the South, can be found in the wartime experiences of its citizens. One primary factor involved the needs and demands of a nation at war. As seen in the last chapter, with the presence of Brookley Field, plus ADDSCO and the Alabama State Docks, the war brought major economic opportunities to Mobile. These opportunities were sufficiently extensive to allow Mobile's black community to share significantly in the economic boom. In addition, federal government control of civilian employment at military installations and regulation of the shipbuilding industry helped to insure that blacks were not as harshly discriminated against in the distribution of these benefits as would otherwise have been the case. This situation improved the socioeconomic status of many of Mobile's blacks and resulted in rising expectations for the future. It also helped to politicize issues of racial discrimination.[2]

A second factor can be found in the wartime military service of many Mobile citizens. As noted by historian Melton A. McLaurin, the ideological clash between

March after the assassination of Dr. Martin Luther King Jr., 1968.

Palmer Studio Collection, USA Archives.

the Allies and the totalitarian powers, emphasized by the Nazi treatment of Jews, awakened hope that the United States would finally subdue the forces of prejudice and discrimination within its own borders. This perspective was manifest in the attitudes of many soldiers, both black and white, who had fought in the war. First-hand knowledge that African American soldiers were fighting and dying for a democratic country in which they were denied their most basic rights of citizenship had a consequential effect on soldiers of both races. The undeniable injustice of that situation motivated many black veterans to take up the cause of civil rights; it likewise motivated many whites to join them.[3]

Toward the end of the war came a Texas court case that had an important impact on the progress of the civil rights movement in Mobile. In 1944 the Supreme Court, in *Smith v. Allwright,* outlawed the white primary, declaring that it was unconstitutional for the Texas Democratic Party to prohibit blacks from voting in the party's primaries. This civil rights victory provided a catalyst for shifting the focus of the Mobile chapter of the NAACP under the leadership of LeFlore from issues of discrimination in job opportunities and accommodations to issues of voting, representation, and political power. As a result, the black community undertook to challenge Alabama's own version of the white primary. On May 3, 1944, twelve qualified and registered black Mobilians presented themselves at the polls in an attempt to vote in the Democratic primary. They were turned away while photographers from *Time* and *Life* took pictures.[4]

After a period of legal and political wrangling, including the threat of legal action by the U.S. attorney general, Alabama's Democratic Party gave in and allowed qualified blacks to vote in their primaries. The first opportunity black Mobilians had to use this newly won right was in the Democratic primary held on May 7, 1946. The *Mobile Register* noted that few blacks voted and that no incidents occurred.[5] It may seem somewhat surprising that both the Democratic Party leadership and the rank-and-file membership came to accept black participation in party primaries without major conflict. Without doubt, the stand of the federal courts in the Texas case and the negative national media attention in Mobile both contributed to the willingness of Alabama's Democratic Party to end white-only primaries. Nonetheless, another important reason the party gave in without a major fight was that with so few qualified black voters during this period, black participation was not seen as a threat. That situation, however, was destined to change.

The very fact that blacks would be afforded additional opportunities to participate in politics encouraged efforts to increase registration. For example, in January 1946, 19,000 whites were registered to vote in Mobile County, but only 275 blacks. Thus, although the county's population was approximately one-third black, blacks comprised less than 2 percent of the electorate. In anticipation of black participation in the May 1946 Democratic primary, black voter registration activity increased dramatically; by the time of the actual election, the number of blacks registered in Mobile County had more than doubled to 691.[6]

Increased opportunities to participate were not the only encouragement to black voter registration. During this period large numbers of black veterans were returning to Mobile after being mustered out of the armed forces. As noted earlier, their wartime experiences had heightened their sense of injustice at being treated as second-class citizens in the democracy they had fought to defend. As a result they became more politically active, forming such organizations as the Negro Voters and Veterans League and pursuing the opportunity to register and vote. As the number of returning soldiers grew, registration continued to increase, so that by end of 1946 the number of black voters had almost doubled again to thirteen hundred.[7]

Even though the actual number of black voters was still very small, the percentage increases that occurred during this period were significant. As a result, Mobile's white segregationist establishment came to view these changes as a serious threat. Predictably, the result was white backlash. On the local front, efforts to hold down black registration took several forms. A strict quota system existed in which only a specified number of blacks would be allowed to register on any given day. Also, maneuvering made it possible to keep lines of black registrants very long and slow moving, whereas whites experienced no such delays. Furthermore, blacks were required to have a sponsor to testify to their good character. The difficulty of arranging and coordinating these activities further discouraged black registration.[8]

Despite these efforts it was becoming more and more difficult for the forces of reaction to keep qualified blacks from registering and voting. The focus shifted to the state level, where attempts were made to insure that very few blacks were officially qualified. After much wringing of hands and gnashing of teeth over what was to be done, Alabama's conservative white establishment settled on an approach involving a state constitutional amendment. The proposed amendment would restrict voting registration to only those persons who could "understand and explain any article of the constitution of the United States in the English language."[9] Voter registrars would be responsible for determining which articles would be interpreted by prospective registrants and deciding whether their explanations were acceptable. Because of the variability and ambiguity of constitutional interpretations, this law would give county registrars the discretionary power to deny virtually anyone the right to register to vote. In the ensuing battle over the adoption of this constitutional amendment, two native Mobilians, Gessner McCorvey and Joseph Langan, came to play important roles.

The idea of going beyond a literacy test and requiring a "constitution interpretation" test was actually the brainchild of McCorvey, a prominent lawyer from Mobile who had served as president of the Alabama Bar Association and as a trustee of the University of Alabama. He also served as chairman of the State

Gessner McCorvey.

Erik Overbey Collection, USA Archives.

Democratic Executive Committee, the ruling body of the Alabama Democratic Party. It was from that position that he rallied conservative support for his idea of a "constitution interpretation" test. One of his primary allies, and the sponsor of the proposed amendment in the Alabama legislature, was E. C. (Bud) Boswell. Because of his legislative sponsorship the proposal came to be known as the Boswell amendment.

On the other side of this conflict another Mobilian, Joseph N. Langan, came to the forefront of state politics. Like so many others during the period, Langan had recently returned to Mobile after military service in World War II. Also like many others, Langan, because of his experiences, had changed his attitudes about race. Coming of age in the South during the depression, he had accepted the legitimacy of racial segregation. During the war, however, he had firsthand experience with black soldiers fighting and dying for a democracy in which they were not allowed to vote. Also, serving side by side with many highly capable and professional black soldiers heightened his perception of the injustice of racial discrimination. In an interview conducted in October 1972, Langan claimed that wartime service had forced him to really look at some basic principles of life and "the fact that we are all creatures of God. . . . I could not consider any person to be less entitled to anything in life than I was."[10] These perspectives disposed Langan to take a progressive approach to issues of race in the postwar South.

Joseph Langan.
Mobile Register.

As an ambitious young attorney with prewar political experience and an impressive war record, Langan was in a prime position to enter politics on his return to Mobile. Accordingly, he ran for the Alabama senate and was elected in 1946. The battle over the Boswell amendment was one of the first major controversies the new senator faced. Langan came out strongly against the amendment, but as a fairly liberal freshman senator in a conservative legislature, it was unrealistic to believe that he could prevent its adoption. In fact, when the issue was put to a vote in October 1946, Langan was one of only two legislators who voted against it.[11]

Before the amendment could take effect, however, it had to be submitted to and approved by Alabama voters. It was scheduled to appear on the ballot in the general election of November 1946. Although the legislative vote had been overwhelmingly in favor of the amendment, there was considerable opposition in the general population. Liberals and progressives were against it on principle; both blacks and poor whites were justifiably anxious that it would be used to disfranchise them. As chairman of the State Democratic Executive Committee, McCorvey organized and financed a campaign to overcome this opposition and insure that the amendment was ratified by the voters. A letter from McCorvey, which subsequently became part of the public record, revealed the true intentions of the amendment's proponents. It was written to members of the State Democratic Executive Committee to justify the expenditure of $3,500 in committee funds in support of the ratification of the Boswell amendment. McCorvey explicitly stated his commitment "to fight for white supremacy in our state and to make the Democratic Party of Alabama the 'White Man's Party.'"[12]

The forces of reaction were successful. The amendment was ratified on November 7, 1946, by a vote of 54 percent to 46 percent. It went into effect immediately and was indeed effective in accomplishing its primary purpose of restricting black registration. In the first two years after passage of the Boswell amendment, 2,800 whites were registered in Mobile County, compared with only 104 blacks, most of whom were schoolteachers. Whereas less than 4 percent of the new registrants were black, Mobile County's population of 230,000 was estimated to be 36 percent black.[13]

Believing that the key to continued progress for African Americans was political participation and that the Boswell amendment was an all-too-effective obstacle to black registration and voting, Mobile's civil rights leadership turned its attention to challenging the "constitution interpretation" tests. On March 1, 1948, Hunter Davis, along with nine other black Mobilians, filed suit in federal district court against the Mobile County Board of Election Registrars, claiming that the Boswell amendment was unconstitutional. The lead defendant was board registrar Milton Schnell, and the case became known as *Davis v. Schnell*.[14]

It was in this case that Joseph Langan's efforts had significant impact. He had convinced Governor Jim Folsom to appoint one of his political allies, E. J. Gonzales, to the Mobile County Board of Election Registrars. Subsequently, Gonzales became a key witness for the black plaintiffs in *Davis v. Schnell*. He refused to join his fellow registrars in denying the discriminatory application of the Boswell amendment. Rather, his testimony supported the black plaintiffs.[15]

After additional corroborative testimony from the plaintiffs, the district court concluded that the requirement to understand and explain the constitution was tantamount to interpreting the constitution. They noted that even learned Supreme Court justices disagreed on the validity of each other's constitutional interpretations. Consequently, the court determined, the Boswell amendment gave Alabama voter registrars naked and arbitrary power to decide who could vote and who could not and therefore constituted a denial of equal protection of the law.[16] Thus, the "constitution interpretation" tests were declared unconstitutional. Their use was discontinued, and dramatic increases in black registration resumed. Along with these increases, however, came another white backlash in the form of a new amendment that might avoid the blatant unconstitutionality of the previous effort while accomplishing the same goals. This new amendment was, like its predecessor, proposed by Gessner McCorvey and sponsored in the Alabama legislature by E. C. Boswell. Known as Boswell Jr., it was introduced in the legislature's annual session of 1949.

In the battle over Boswell Jr., Joe Langan again took the other side. He and his allies were determined not to lose the ground so recently won when the Supreme Court struck down the original amendment. Facing a large and hostile majority of conservative white supremacists in the legislature, the anti-Boswell forces knew they would lose if the amendment was put to a vote. Their only hope was to use the filibuster. On September 9, 1949, Joe Langan and three other senators were successful in filibustering Boswell Jr. to its death.[17]

For Langan, however, these successes were not without consequences. Having become known as a liberal, a Folsom ally, and soft on the race issue, he was defeated in his 1951 attempt to win reelection to the senate.[18] Although some might view this loss as a setback, it actually freed Langan to pursue a position from which he could have a more direct and powerful role in politics and civil rights in Mobile: a seat on the Mobile city commission.

Langan's entry into municipal politics was facilitated, in part, by an alliance he had formed early in his senate term with the key leader of Mobile's civil rights movement, John L. LeFlore. Whereas Langan was a relative newcomer to civil rights issues, LeFlore had been actively involved in the struggle for most of his life. As noted earlier, he began his civil rights activism as a young man when a streetcar conductor demanded that LeFlore give up his seat to a white man, LeFlore refused, a scuffle ensued, and LeFlore was arrested.[19] LeFlore's heightened awareness of the injustice of segregation motivated him to devote much of his life to pursuing justice for blacks, a struggle in which he was joined by Langan in the late 1940s. The alliance would last until LeFlore's death in 1976.

It was in the summer of 1947 when LeFlore, as head of the Mobile chapter of the NAACP, met with the local legislative delegation over problems in the area of public school education. As the senator from Mobile, Langan served as the head of that delegation. At the time, the Mobile School Board was pushing for a beer tax increase to be used for improvements in the public schools. LeFlore proposed that a portion of that increase be used to rectify the great disparities between black and white teachers in terms both of workloads and of pay. Langan shocked the school board and his colleagues in the local delegation by threatening to withhold his support for the tax increase unless the school board accepted LeFlore's proposal. Because it was a firmly entrenched tradition for the full legislature to defer to the wishes of a local delegation on local legislation only if the delegation was unified, the school board had no choice but to agree. Unfortunately for black teachers in Mobile County, the school board later reneged on its agreement. Still, the issue did not go away. In April 1949 the school board proposed an additional tax increase on cigarettes. This gave Langan the leverage he needed. He withheld his support for the new increase until after the original agreement for parity between black and white teachers was implemented.[20]

One might anticipate that Langan's involvement in this controversy would hurt him with Mobile's whites as much as it helped him with blacks. Actually, however, the picture was more complicated. Since 1911 Mobile had been governed by a three-member commission elected from the city at large. The Progressive Era establishment of this commission form of government can be viewed primarily as a victory for Mobile's civic and commercial elite. In the guise of reform, this elite used the at-large provision for commission elections to block various factions of working-class whites from participating directly in municipal decision making.[21] Because each candidate for a commission seat was required to win a majority of votes from throughout the city at large, no minority could single-handedly control the outcome of any race. In order to be successful, commission candidates had to build coalitions of voters. In the early days, these coalitions were made up of various groups of whites; the participation of blacks was not a major issue because so few blacks were eligible to participate. By the time Langan first ran for the city commission in 1953, however, that was not the case.

With increasing numbers of blacks registering in the post–World War II period, there was a clear potential for them to become a sizeable minority, with the result that black participation would no longer be irrelevant. Because at-large elections and racially polarized voting virtually insured that blacks could not elect a black candidate, the only opportunity for the black community to play a meaningful role in elections was for black voters to become sufficiently numerous and cohesive to serve as a swing vote. If two white candidates received equal shares of the white vote, even a small number of black voters could determine the outcome of an election. Indeed, as early as 1953 that was the case.

Another factor that favored Langan was that the 1953 election occurred before the *Brown v. Board of Education* decision was announced by the U.S. Supreme Court. The Court's decisions in favor of black civil rights had not yet created the intense white backlash that was to come after the 1954 decision to desegregate public schools. Thus, the more progressive middle- and upper-class white elements of Mobile's electorate were capable of forming coalitions with the small but growing minority of black voters to have major impact on the outcome of commission elections.

In the 1953 election for city commission, all three conservative incumbent commissioners faced challenges from a new generation of political leaders. Langan defeated the twenty-year incumbent, Charles Baumhauer, by running on a platform of economic development and municipal improvements. The other two incumbents were also defeated by their more progressive challengers, Henry Luscher and Charles Hackmeyer. It is interesting to note that all three winning candidates were endorsed by the civil rights organization that was acting as the political arm of the NAACP at that time, the Citizens Committee for Good Government.[22] The election of 1953 can be viewed as a watershed for Mobile civil rights when blacks helped to usher in a new generation of progressive political leaders who took the reins of government and began to move the city forward.

The following year brought the Supreme Court decision in *Brown v. Board of Education* of Topeka, Kansas. The Court declared that separate but equal was intrinsically unequal and that children in public education facilities could not be segregated by race. Although this decision did not have any impact on education in Mobile's public schools for more than a decade, it was not without major consequences. It further encouraged blacks in their pursuit of civil rights and resulted in a flurry of activity. It also caused a severe white backlash that fundamentally altered the political landscape of Mobile.

The primary backlash occurred at the state level when on June 1, 1956, Alabama attorney general John Patterson sued the NAACP in Montgomery County Circuit Court for failure to register as a foreign (out-of-state) corporation.[23] Patterson's goal was to have the NAACP permanently outlawed in the state of Alabama. In subsequent legal proceedings, court orders were issued prohibiting the NAACP from operating in Alabama and forbidding it to register as required by law. The NAACP was further ordered to produce extensive records and documents, including membership lists. Fearing retaliation against its membership, the organization refused; a contempt citation was issued along with a heavy fine. Unless and until the NAACP was cleared of contempt by paying the fine and turning over the membership rolls, its case could not be heard, and it could not resume operations.

After losing an appeal to the Alabama Supreme Court, the NAACP turned to the U.S. Supreme Court, where it received a much more sympathetic hearing. The federal court rejected all of the procedural delaying tactics of the Alabama courts and ordered the state to give the NAACP a hearing on the merits of the case. After five months of stalling, the Alabama Supreme Court refused to direct the circuit court to give the NAACP its hearing on the merits, claiming that in ordering Alabama to do so the U.S. Supreme Court was "mistaken."[24] It took a total of eight years and six appeals to the federal courts before the NAACP finally won the right to resume its operations in Alabama.

It would certainly seem that the primary motivation of state authorities in this case was to halt the progress in civil rights that had been achieved by the NAACP. Nevertheless, although they were amazingly successful in halting the NAACP, the authorities did not succeed in halting the progress in civil rights, especially in the Mobile area. Wiley Bolden, a longtime civil rights leader and a colleague of LeFlore, testifying in a subsequent civil rights case, explained the reaction of Mobile's civil rights leadership to the outlawing of the NAACP: "So, we went, what you might call underground, and organized the Non-Partisan Voters League and we kept the work of civil rights going just the same."[25] In fact, the Non-Partisan Voters League became the premier civil rights organization in the greater Mobile area.

Although there is some confusion regarding the founding date of the Non-Partisan Voters League, it did exist prior to the 1956 outlawing of the NAACP. In the early 1950s various civil rights organizations operated in the Mobile area. These included, among others, the NAACP, the Non-Partisan Voters League, the Negro Voters and Veterans League, and the Citizens' Committee.[26] It seems that leadership and membership in these organizations were very fluid, with the same individuals involved in different organizations at the same time.

In the early 1950s, as black registration in Mobile increased sufficiently so that a relatively small group of black voters might swing a close election, it became more and more important to have effective organizations to insure cohesion, provide guidance to voters, and encourage political activity. Before the NAACP ceased operations in Mobile, several of these other civil rights organizations competed in fulfilling these political functions. Once the NAACP was gone, much of its leadership and membership was effectively transferred to the Non-Partisan Voters League. Because the league could operate without restriction, it moved to take over the full range of civil rights functions and thus became the dominant civil rights organization not just in Mobile but throughout the Gulf Coast region.

One of the primary methods by which the league attained this dominance was through its control of the black vote. As black voting increased sufficiently so that it had potential impact on the outcome of elections, white candidates came to count on the league to deliver the black vote as a bloc. This was accomplished through the use of a sample ballot called the pink sheet (or pink ballot), so named because of the color of paper on which it was printed. This sample ballot clearly specified the endorsements of the league. It was distributed widely throughout the black community typically on the day before the election with the expectation that black voters would use it in the polling booth to guide them in casting their official ballot. That expectation was regularly realized.[27]

In addition to the political success of the league's pink sheet operation, the organization earned a prominent place in the civil rights history of Mobile because of its successful efforts on behalf of the black community at large. Many of its accomplishments resulted from direct and determined pressure on the white establishment to end racial discrimination. Where such efforts did not accomplish the desired results, the league initiated legal action on behalf of Mobile's black community. From the mid 1950s until the early 1980s, their efforts resulted in drastically increased opportunities in the areas of jobs, education, and accommodations. According to league records, "Hundreds of cases aimed at protecting the rights of black people to equal dignity in our land, particularly in Mobile and Alabama, have been handled by the Non-Partisan Voters League since 1959."[28]

A large proportion of the league's actions dealt with job discrimination. Although the details are far too extensive to describe in full here, it is important to note the wide-ranging nature of the cases. League efforts resulted in the integration of Mobile's police and fire departments and helped open job opportunities for blacks throughout city and county government. The league acted formally as third-party intervenors in job discrimination complaints against local branches of the U.S. Postal Service. Even the Alabama National Guard was integrated as a result of league efforts. The league also initiated successful job discrimination actions against ADDSCO, the telephone company, two major paper manufacturers, and several local retail outlets.

In addition the league regularly conducted "travel surveys" of the air, bus, and train transportation systems of the South to determine the extent to which services and facilities were available to blacks. Some fourteen formal complaints brought before the Interstate Commerce Commission resulted in the integration of waiting rooms, rest rooms, and restaurants in travel terminals from New Orleans to Montgomery to Pensacola. After the 1964 Civil Rights Act provided the necessary legal

Police chief Dudley McFadyen with black policemen, 1960.

LeFlore Papers, USA Archives.

African American firemen at the new Henry J. Reid Station on Stimrad Road in the Happy Hills area, circa 1961.

LeFlore Papers, USA Archives.

foundation, the league directed "desegregation tests" at some 225 Mobile-area food service establishments. Those efforts resulted in seventy-five Justice Department complaints, seven successful lawsuits, and broadly expanded access for blacks.[29] Such efforts continued into the late 1970s when the league successfully challenged the proliferation of "private clubs" that were designed and established to perpetuate segregation.

The Non-Partisan Voters League was also involved in the legal defense of blacks wrongly accused of crimes. An early example of major judicial significance was the case of Willie Seals, a black Mobilian who in 1958 was convicted of rape and sentenced to death by an all-white jury. The league fought the conviction on the grounds that blacks had been systematically excluded from the grand jury that indicted Seals and the trial jury that convicted him. In 1963 the U.S. Supreme Court let stand an appeals court ruling that overturned the conviction on those grounds.[30] The case had a sweeping impact on the segregated judicial systems then in existence throughout the South. It took much additional legal maneuvering, but the persistence of the league also paid off for Willie Seals, who was finally released from prison in 1970.

One of the league's greatest and longest legal battles was the Mobile County public school desegregation suit, commonly known as the *Birdie Mae Davis* case. The original complaint was filed on March 27, 1963, in U.S. district court. Plaintiffs in the case were Birdie Mae Davis, Dorothy Davis, and Henry Hobdy, three black students who had been refused admission to all-white Murphy High School. They sued on the grounds that the refusal was a result of racial discrimination and thereby violated their Fourteenth Amendment rights as established in the U.S. Supreme Court's decision in the *Brown* case. As a result of the suit, the three students were admitted to Murphy for the 1964 school year. Nonetheless, the issue was far from settled. White students fought desegregation with several violent confrontations in area schools in the late 1960s and throughout the 1970s. School officials maintained an obstructionist and intransigent stance, moving extremely slowly and only when forced by explicit court action.

In a 1970 opinion that set the stage for the first major consent decree, circuit judge Goldberg wrote, "We do not tarry now to count the many appeals to this court in furtherance of this hope, for we are concerned today with only a single recent episode in this almost Homeric odyssey. We wonder when the epilogue will be written." These words were penned after slightly less than eight years of litigation. It was obviously difficult then to imagine that the epilogue would not be written for another twenty-seven years. Some of the delay was caused by the expansion of the action to include teachers and administrators, but most of it was the result of purposeful procrastination by school officials and the elites who guided them. While the *Birdie Mae Davis* case, especially in the latter stages, seemed to take on a

Woolworth's segregated lunch counter, 1950.

Erik Overbey Collection, USA Archives.

life of its own, it served as a severe test of the Non-Partisan Voters League's willingness to persevere in the cause of civil rights.[31]

The league also fought segregation in education outside the Mobile area. When George Wallace "stood in the schoolhouse door" at the University of Alabama in Tuscaloosa, one of the students he tried to block was Vivian Malone, a Mobile public high school graduate who had been recruited and financed by the Non-Partisan Voters League.[32]

Another major success of the league resulted from its efforts to force an end to the one-hundred-year exclusion of blacks from the representative institutions of Mobile city and county governments. This goal was accomplished through two federal court suits contesting the use of at-large elections on the grounds that they unconstitutionally diluted black voting strength: *Brown v. Moore* dealt with both the county commission and the county school board, and *Bolden v. City of Mobile* was directed at the city. Both actions were originally filed by league lawyers in 1975, both involved long and arduous court proceedings, and both were ultimately successful. The final action in *Brown v. Moore* occurred in 1984 when the U.S. court of appeals affirmed the first black school board member's right to vote on school board business pertaining to integration. That right had been denied by the school board president on the grounds that, being black, the black board member had a conflict of interest when it came to integrating the public schools.[33] The final out-

Plaintiffs in the *Birdie Mae Davis* school desegregation case with Wiley Bolden, John LeFlore, and NAACP attorney Derrick Bell, 1964.

LeFlore Papers, USA Archives.

come of the *Bolden* case came with the 1985 election of three black Mobile city council members, the first such occurrence since Reconstruction.

The impact of *Bolden v. City of Mobile* was extensive and far-reaching. The case also constituted the last major accomplishment of the Non-Partisan Voters League and the most recent significant civil rights advancement for black Mobilians. Accordingly, it will be discussed more fully later; first it is important to return to a general review of Mobile politics in the period in which the Non-Partisan Voters League operated.

The three commissioners elected in 1953—Langan, Luscher, and Hackmeyer—worked well together through the mid-1950s, especially in formulating and implementing plans for capital improvements and economic development. One of the few issues that polarized the commissioners involved the establishment of a race relations committee.

After the 1954 Supreme Court decision to integrate public schools and after the Montgomery bus boycott of 1955, race relations in Alabama and across the South became more and more strained. While black expectations and demands were on the rise, many whites were drawing a line in the sand. In an effort to ease tensions and insure effective interracial communication, several southern cities had established biracial committees. Joseph Langan supported such a move for Mobile, but his fellow commissioners came out publicly against it. Despite their opposition, Langan called a town meeting to discuss the concept. The reaction among those attending was very positive, and the proposal moved forward. On April 3, 1956, the Biracial Committee, composed of seventeen whites and thirteen blacks, met for the first time.[34]

Whereas the effort was supported and praised by blacks and liberal whites as a positive step in race relations, others, including Langan's fellow commissioners and the editorial voice of the *Mobile Press Register,* expressed serious doubts. They believed that such a committee might be used to encourage and facilitate blacks' demands for equality, integration, and political power, thereby heightening tensions rather than alleviating them. As it turned out, however, such fears were unfounded. The committee actually became a conservative force in race relations, co-opting black leadership and promoting what might be referred to in today's parlance as a "kinder, gentler" segregation.[35] This outcome was not lost on the rising generation of black civil rights leaders, who came to view such efforts with suspicion and mistrust. At the time, however, the committee had a calming and stabilizing effect on race relations and contributed to the development of Mobile's reputation as an exception when compared with other southern cities torn by racial strife and tension.

As the 1957 city elections approached, Mobile's three incumbent commissioners were justifiably optimistic about their futures. The city had grown significantly through annexation, a variety of much-needed capital improvements was under way, and economic prosperity generally reigned. There were no major incidents or problems in the black community; race relations, if not ideal, were stable and predictable. It was no surprise that all three incumbent commissioners were reelected. Nevertheless, this appearance of prosperity and calm did hide some significant shifts.

A closer examination of the 1957 election reveals that the coalitions of support for these commissioners had changed. Rather than relying on the broad-based support that had characterized the 1953 election, both Luscher and Langan came to depend more on a combination of lower- to middle-income blacks and upper-income whites. Hackmeyer's was a populist coalition of lower-income whites and blacks. Thus, in all three cases, blacks provided a bloc of swing votes that had significant impact on the outcome of the election.[36] At the time these changes appeared to be rather subtle, but the following election would demonstrate their import.

In 1961 all three incumbent commissioners—Langan, Luscher, and Hackmeyer—ran for reelection. Although Langan had no serious opposition, both of his colleagues faced challenges from the right. During the general election both Luscher and Hackmeyer had received considerable black support, a fact their opponents publicized to the white community in the runoff election. Luscher and Hackmeyer were effectively portrayed as the candidates of blacks, and both went down to defeat. Thus, by the time of the 1961 election, race was politicized to the point that blacks were considered a highly visible and controversial bloc, thereby lessening the desirability of their support.[37] The black vote, at least in certain circumstances, could become the kiss of death for white candidates. As a result, race baiting came to play a regular and recognizable part in Mobile municipal politics. Indeed, the black vote was referred to as the "bloc vote," and conservative white candidates would regularly refer to support in "bloc wards" as a good reason to vote against their opponents.

The result for the black community was unfortunately ironic. As black participation in politics increased, so did the perceived threat to the white community, resulting in increased racial polarization characterized by white bloc voting for conservative and reactionary candidates. Because whites constituted approximately two-thirds of the population, racially polarized voting in at-large elections denied blacks the opportunity to cast the swing vote. Thus, as black participation increased, their ability to affect the outcomes of elections actually decreased.

This development was evident in the 1965 election, where even the previously popular incumbent Joe Langan was in trouble. In that election he failed to win a majority in any of Mobile's predominantly white wards. Consequently, he was forced into a runoff with his primary conservative challenger, Joe Bailey. Langan barely managed to win the runoff with minimal support in the white community and almost unanimous support among blacks, or, as it was put by the *Mobile Press Register,* Langan's tremendous margin in bloc wards carried him nearly over the top despite a 40 percent showing in the rest of the city's polling places. At the same time both of the other successful candidates, Lambert Mims and Arthur Outlaw, won with majority support among whites and minimal support from blacks.[38]

Another development in Mobile politics at this time involved polarization within the black community. A younger generation of more militant African Americans began to challenge John LeFlore and the Non-Partisan Voters League for control of

Pickets protesting a 1964 Freedom Rally. NAACP lawyer Jack Greenberg of New York was the featured speaker.

Non-Partisan Voters League Records, USA Archives.

Mobile's civil rights movement. A new organization, Neighborhood Organized Workers (NOW), developed under the leadership of Noble Beasley. The group, which had been growing steadily throughout the decade, represented members of the black community who were dissatisfied with the progress of civil rights. In an extensive study of Mobile voting patterns, political scientist James Voyles claimed that Beasley represented the lower-income blacks and stood in direct opposition to the policy of the Non-Partisan Voters League of supporting white candidates with views acceptable to the league. NOW attempted to displace the league through the use of militant tactics, including demonstrations, picketing, and the threat of violence.[39] Although NOW denied involvement, Mobile was rocked by violence that included a rash of fires and the firebombing of John LeFlore's home. Based in part on its notoriety, NOW had become a significant political force in Mobile politics by the late 1960s.

The conflict between NOW and the league came to a head in the 1969 city commission election. As long as the league could successfully deliver the black vote, it could continue to win concessions from the white establishment politicians. Furthermore, as long as it continued to win concessions, it could maintain some degree of loyalty in the black community. From the perspective of Noble Beasley, these concessions were too little, too late. He claimed that the alliance between the league and Joe Langan actually worked to slow the progress of civil rights. In the 1969 election, at the height of NOW's power, Beasley hit on a strategy. Partly

John LeFlore's home after firebombing, June 28, 1967.

Photograph by Ulysses A. Miller.

A 1969 campaign ad. Non-Partisan Voters League Records, USA Archives.

because he wanted to destroy the influence of the pink sheet and partly because he did not believe any black should vote for any white candidate, Beasley instituted a black voters' boycott.[40]

In that election Mims's and Outlaw's handpicked successor, Robert Doyle, received large majorities in the white wards, winning easily with minimal black support. Joe Langan was again challenged by Joe Bailey. In his campaign Bailey pushed race baiting to the limit. He ran ads in the Mobile newspaper with vote totals from the 1965 election showing that Langan had received 3,840 votes to Bailey's 243 votes in predominantly black wards. He also ran ads that carried photographs of Langan and LeFlore with the caption, "Will you let this pair run your city for another four years?"[41] As in previous recent elections, Langan received less than majority support in the white wards. Furthermore, although he still received considerable majorities in the black wards, turnout was so low that the black vote was not sufficient to swing the election. Thus, the longtime friend of the black political establishment went down to defeat. Still, although it is clear that NOW's boycott did have an impact, it should also be noted that Hurricane Camille, having ravaged the Mobile area just two days prior to the election, also contributed to the low voter turnout.

By the early 1970s the militant movement in the black community had begun to fade, in part because of the legal troubles of its leaders. Noble Beasley was absent from the scene for several months while he was in police custody for the daylight shotgunning of a rival black leader. Although cleared of the charge, he was unable to influence the 1973 election because both he and one of his major allies in NOW, Doc Finley, were jailed in early 1973 on charges of extortion, income tax evasion, and distribution of heroin. Although NOW still existed, its members were fearful that the prosecution of Beasley and Finley constituted reprisals from the white establishment that might also be forthcoming against any replacement leadership. As a result, according to its last president, Frederick Douglas Richardson, NOW's followers went into hiding, and the organization folded.[42]

Even though NOW was no longer a factor, the Non-Partisan Voters League could not return to its previous role as broker of the black vote because white politicians were no longer courting the black vote. In the 1973 election the primary issues as indicated in newspaper accounts of the campaign involved community development with a focus on public works such as storm drainage and street paving. The only issues with any mention of race involved black candidates' platforms that called for increased public works and community development in black areas of the city.[43] Two of the incumbents, Lambert Mims and Robert Doyle, were reelected with minimal African American support. As a result of his implication in a scandal involving management of the city auditorium, Joe Bailey, the other incumbent and Langan's successor, fell short of a majority in the general election and was upset in the runoff by Gary Greenough, the principal planner for the South Alabama Regional Planning Commission. Once again, all the successful candidates won on the basis of their support among whites; none sought or needed support from the black community.

The trend of diminishing black political influence had bottomed out. In 1953 all three city commission winners did well in black wards, often receiving as much as 60–70 percent of the vote. By 1969 none of the winners received a majority vote in any of the black wards. As Voyles concluded, although the numbers of blacks voting in Mobile had increased sharply since 1960, the power of blacks to influence elections in a positive fashion had decreased.[44] Blacks had once again been cut out of the system. After the 1973 election blacks were forced to confront the fact that their primary difficulty was the majority vote requirement of the at-large procedure of the electoral scheme. Blacks could never elect one of their own as long as the overwhelming majority of whites refused to vote for an African American candidate. Because sympathetic white candidates were damaged by significant black support, blacks could no longer expect to wield influence as a swing vote. Thus, the only reasonable alternative was to challenge the form of city government, particularly the at-large election provision, as discriminatory.

On October 9, 1975, Wiley Bolden, along with a number of other prominent black citizens of the city, filed suit in federal district court challenging the constitutionality of Mobile's municipal government. The *Bolden* plaintiffs contended that the use of at-large elections "discriminates against black residents of Mobile in that their concentrated voting strength is diluted and canceled out by the white majority in the city as a whole."[45]

Before the case went to trial an incident occurred that was to color the racial climate in Mobile for years to come. On March 28, 1976, Mobile police received a call regarding suspicious activity by two black males at the McDonald's restaurant on Government Street. Police officers responding to the call apprehended one of the suspects at the scene, but the other, twenty-seven-year-old Glenn Diamond, managed to flee. Eight white officers later found him hiding under a house. They handcuffed Diamond, placed a rope tied into a hangman's noose around his neck, looped the rope over a branch in a nearby tree, and threatened to lynch him.

The ostensible purpose of this mock lynching was to obtain a confession from Diamond regarding his involvement in the robbery of a restaurant three nights earlier. As described in a subsequent newspaper account, the results were far-reaching. By the time it was over, eight policemen had been suspended. The NAACP called for justice, the Ku Klux Klan rallied in support of the police, and the Mobile Police Department was thrown into a turmoil that took years to settle.[46] Without doubt this situation contributed to the racially charged atmosphere in which the *Bolden* case was heard.

As luck would have it, the *Bolden* case was first assigned to Judge Brevard Hand. It would not be inappropriate to consider Judge Hand the "hanging judge" for civil rights plaintiffs. When first appointed to the federal bench in 1971, he draped his

CAPABLE AND KNOWLEDGEABLE REPRESENTATION
IMPORTANT FACTORS IN THE ALABAMA LEGISLATURE
VOTE
JOHN LeFLORE
A SERVANT OF ALL THE PEOPLE
99TH DISTRICT
ALABAMA HOUSE OF REPRESENTATIVES
TUESDAY, MAY 7, 1974

LeFlore was one of the first African Americans elected to the Alabama state legislature since Reconstruction.

LeFlore Papers, USA Archives.

office wall with a huge Confederate battle flag. Under intense criticism he was forced to strike the colors, but his judicial decisions continued to reflect his ultra-conservative philosophy.[47] Fortunately for the *Bolden* plaintiffs, the city hired the local firm of Hand, Arendall, Bedsole, Greaves, and Johnston to handle its defense. Because that firm was founded by Judge Hand's father, the plaintiffs were automatically afforded the opportunity to have their case reassigned, and they immediately exercised that option. Fortune smiled again on the plaintiffs when the case was given to Judge Virgil Pittman, whose judicial reputation was as liberal as Hand's was conservative.

The case went to trial on July 12, 1976. Extensive evidence offered by the plaintiffs supported their contentions that the black vote was diluted, that black candidates were denied access to the nominations process, that white commissioners were unresponsive to minority interests, and that Mobile had a long history of racial prejudice and discrimination. In summarizing the findings, Pittman declared that the mock lynching of Glenn Diamond and the white establishment's reaction to it exemplified many of these issues: "The sad history of lynch mobs, racial discrimination and violence . . . raises specters and fears of legal and social injustice in the minds . . . of black people. . . . [The white establishment's] sluggish and timid response is another manifestation of the low priority given to the needs of black citizens and of the political fear of a white backlash when black citizens' needs are at stake."[48]

On October 21, 1976, Judge Pittman found for the plaintiffs: "The court concludes that in the aggregate, the at-large election structure as it operates in the city of Mobile substantially dilutes black vote in the city."[49] Still, what would be the appropriate judicial remedy? Judge Pittman rejected any piecemeal effort. He ruled that the commission system of government would be replaced by a mayor-council structure with nine single-member council districts and that the regular city election scheduled for August 1977 would be the appropriate time to make the switch.

The reaction among whites was predictable. The *Mobile Register* regularly began to bemoan the Pittman problem in its editorials, going so far as to refer to Mobile as Pittmanville. On November 8, 1976, the banner headline from a newspaper advertisement read, "Impeach! Appeal! Arrest!"[50] The half-page ad was sponsored by the Constitutional Crisis Committee (CCC) and claimed a tripartite approach to the Pittman problem. First, the organization would gather 250,000 petition signatures to present to Congress to initiate impeachment proceedings against U.S. district judge Virgil Pittman. Second, the organization would demand that the city appeal the decision all the way to the Supreme Court if necessary. Finally, if the first two approaches failed, the committee vowed to have Pittman arrested on charges of violating the civil rights of Mobile voters.

The white backlash was in evidence all the way to the top of Mobile government. Mayor Lambert Mims promised the CCC chairman to give the petition drive a boost by signing the impeachment petition at a highly publicized commission meeting called for that purpose. The city attorney advised against it, however, and the mayor reluctantly withdrew the offer. The impeachment effort fizzled, but the CCC's demand for an appeal was already in the works.

On March 3, 1977, before Judge Pittman's remedy could be effected, the City of Mobile's appeal was formally filed with the Fifth Circuit Court of Appeals in New Orleans. The fact that 1977 was an election year complicated the issue. Given the uncertainty of the appeals outcome and the possibility that council candidates might spend time, effort, and money campaigning for an office that might not exist, Pittman chose to postpone the election pending a resolution of the appeal. Because the appeals process continued past the August election date, those commissioners elected in 1973—Mims, Greenough, and Doyle—simply continued to serve.

On June 2, 1978, the appeals court affirmed Pittman's decision.[51] Predictably, the city appealed that decision to the Supreme Court. On Monday, October 2, 1978, the Supreme Court announced that it would hear the case. Because establishing a new government only to have it overturned by the Supreme Court would cause an undue hardship on all concerned, Judge Pittman felt compelled to postpone any implementation of his original decision until after the Supreme Court issued its ruling.

City of Mobile v. Bolden was argued before the Supreme Court on March 19, 1979. It was reargued on October 29, 1979. On April 22, 1980, the Court rendered its decision to reverse the appeals court ruling.[52] It was, however, a very close call; indeed, there was no majority opinion. The primary issue, from the perspective of the controlling plurality on the Court, was not whether discrimination and racial polarization diluted the voting rights of Mobile's black community. Rather, it was whether the at-large commission form of municipal government was established and operated with the "intent" to discriminate against blacks. According to the Supreme Court's decision, the black Mobilians could prevail only if they could show "intent," and according to the controlling plurality, they had not done so in the trial.

The judgment was reversed, Pittman's decision was vacated, and the case was remanded for further proceedings consistent with the Supreme Court's decision. Nevertheless, despite an immediate motion by the city's attorneys for dismissal, the case was not over. Judge Pittman was to take the "further proceedings" stipulation very seriously. He felt obligated to "to take additional evidence and evaluate that evidence and the record and make such additional findings as necessary to decide the issue of discriminatory purpose (intent) under the proper standard."[53]

During the second hearing of the case, which began in May 1981, city elections rolled around again. The case was still unresolved, but because the three incumbent commissioners had served without reelection since 1973, officials decided that it would be inappropriate to postpone the elections pending final resolution of the case. In the 1981 municipal election all three incumbents ran. During the campaign there was little reference to race in newspaper coverage except that both Lambert Mims and Gary Greenough promised not to appeal the second *Bolden* decision if the city lost, and Robert Doyle avoided the issue.[54] As it turned out, Robert Doyle beat his opponents handily in the general election, whereas Mims and Greenough were forced into runoffs, which they did manage to win.

The atmosphere in which the second trial took place was somewhat different from that of the first. Approximately two months prior to the start of the second trial, the body of a nineteen-year-old black male was found hanging from a tree on Herndon Avenue in Mobile. Michael Donald had been beaten and strangled, and his throat had been slashed three times. He was in the wrong place at the wrong time when the Ku Klux Klan came looking for a victim. Four Klan members were subsequently convicted for their roles in the crime, and Donald's mother won a $7 million settlement that effectively put the Klan out of business in Alabama. The senseless and shocking brutality of the murder outraged the general population. It worked to delegitimize the reactionary forces and subdue the potential for additional white backlash to the continued fight of blacks for representation in the councils of Mobile government.

During the second *Bolden* trial, the plaintiffs' attorneys produced the "smoking gun." In 1909 U.S. congressman Bromberg from Mobile, an ardent supporter of the at-large commission form of city government, had written an open letter to the Alabama legislature reminding them of their intentions: "We have always, as you know, falsely pretended that our main purpose was to exclude the ignorant vote, when, in fact, we were trying to exclude, not the ignorant vote, but the Negro vote."[55] On the basis of this and other evidence, on April 15, 1982, Judge Pittman once again found on behalf of the African American plaintiffs. Still, the ultimate outcome of the case was not settled; that would have to await action by the Alabama legislature and the voters of the city of Mobile.

The possibility still existed that the city might again appeal, but the Mobile defendants had apparently come to terms with what, by then, appeared inevitable. Thus, they began negotiations with the black plaintiffs on a compromise settlement. On January 31, 1983, all parties concerned agreed to a compromise, the most relevant provision of which called for some form of elections based on districts to be used in the next regular city election scheduled for 1985.[56] The specific provisions of the new government were to be determined by the Alabama legislature.

Representative Mary Zoghby of Mobile sponsored enabling legislation that would allow the voters of Mobile to choose between a mayor-council plan and a districted commission plan that had been developed under the auspices of the district court. The mayor-council alternative called for a seven-member council, with all members elected from districts, and a mayor elected at large. All candidates were to be elected by majority vote, with runoffs between the top two candidates being held if necessary. Although the legislation did not address the issue explicitly, benign gerrymandering would be utilized to insure that blacks constituted a significant majority in three of the seven districts.

On May 15, 1985, the city held a referendum on the form of government. The result was 25,412 (72 percent) supporting the mayor-council form and 9,940 (28 percent) voting for the districted commission. Regular elections for the new mayor-council government were held on July 9, 1985. In the July 30 runoff, the first three blacks since Reconstruction were elected to the city council: Irmatean Watson, a pharmacist, and Charles A. Tunstall and Clinton Johnson, both of whom were clergymen. Thus, after ten years of struggle and $2.2 million in legal fees (all of which were paid by the city as part of the compromise agreement), the black plaintiffs had finally prevailed. In October of that year, just prior to swearing-in ceremonies for the new city council, Irmatean Watson, the first African American woman elected to the council, was approached at city hall by black cleaning women wanting to know if she was "the one." She acknowledged that indeed she was, "and with that they began to shake her hand and hug her and weep."[57]

Although the 1985 election marked the end of the legal struggle of blacks to achieve representation in municipal government, unfortunately it did not mark the end of racial strife in the city. In fact, one of the provisions of the newly established city council virtually guaranteed the continued impact of race on city politics. When the law to establish the districted mayor-council government was drafted, the U.S. Justice Department reviewed its provisions to insure that the new government would meet the requirements of the 1965 Voting Rights Act and its various amendments. In the review process federal authorities determined that in the racially charged atmosphere of Mobile politics, three black votes on the council would not necessarily give the black community real political power. If racial bloc voting carried over from the electorate to the council, then the four white members of the council could outvote the three black members on every issue. For this reason, the Justice Department negotiated an agreement whereby "the affirmative vote of at least five members of the council shall be sufficient for the passage of any resolution, by-law, ordinance, or the transaction of any business of any sort by the said council or the exercise of any of the powers conferred upon it by the terms of this Act or by-law or which may hereafter be conferred upon it."[58]

Thus, a super majority of five votes was required for the council to conduct business. The four white members would need one black vote to pass any measure. In essence this provision was designed to give the black members effective power on the council with which to insure that black interests were accommodated. It would insure that black representation was not token representation. Although it did accomplish its worthy goal, it also carried negative consequences that continue to haunt the city. The power for the African American members is the power to withhold their support from the white majority. It constitutes a veto power—the power to keep things from happening, not the power to make things happen. From the perspective of fulfilling a positive agenda blacks are actually disadvantaged. Whereas the four white members need only one black vote to conduct business, the three blacks need two white votes to do likewise. Not only does this situation make it more difficult for the council to act quickly and effectively to resolve the numerous problems that continue to plague Mobile but also it tends to encourage the government, the media, and the public to define issues in racial terms, thus promoting and prolonging racial tension and polarization. An example of this tendency can be seen in the politics surrounding the resurrection of a race relations commission.

In 1992 the fatal shooting of a black man by police sparked a wave of violence and racial unrest in Mobile's black community. In response, Mobile's mayor Mike Dow proposed the creation of a committee to address issues of race relations, unemployment, and poverty. The mayor pointed proudly to the biracial committee of the civil rights era, claiming that it contributed greatly to Mobile's ability during the troubled 1960s to hold down civil unrest and to meet some serious economic and social problems head-on. In response, the black vice-president of the city council, Clinton Johnson, said, "I don't approve of someone putting something together and shoving it down our throats. I could not support anything similar to what we

Mobile City Council meeting, August 15, 1985.

Photograph by J. P. Schaffner, *Mobile Register.*

United States Labor Secretary Alexis Herman returned to her hometown to give the commencement speech for graduation ceremonies at Spring Hill College in 1998.

Mobile Register.

had in the 1960s, when the purpose was to hush the mouths of the black people of this community."[59]

It took some time, but the committee, called the Human Relations Commission, was ultimately established in 1994. After a year of ineffective existence with a volunteer staff and no executive leadership, the city increased commission funding from $5,000 to $24,000 for the 1995–96 fiscal year so that a part time executive director could be hired. Yet when commission funding came up for a vote just two years later, the council, voting strictly along racial lines, failed to renew the funding, leaving the operation and even the very existence of the Human Relations Commission in question.[60]

These fundamentally different perspectives of blacks and whites on both past efforts and current needs in the area of race relations exemplify a major problem in Mobile. Many in the white community and some blacks, mostly of the older generation, congratulate Mobile on its civil rights history. They point with pride to the advancements and improvements afforded blacks that were accomplished legally and incrementally and without the serious racial violence that had accompanied such changes in many other American cities in the South and elsewhere. At the

Circuit court judge Herman Thomas with his twin daughters after his investiture ceremonies at Mobile Government Plaza, June 21, 1999. *Mobile Register.*

same time the present generation of black politicians, and many of their constituents, view the same civil rights history very differently. They believe that progress for black Mobilians has been painfully slow, that it has been only grudgingly accepted by whites, and that it is fundamentally incomplete. Understandably, these varying perspectives result in misperceptions, misunderstanding, and mistrust. In such an atmosphere, race relations continue to be viewed as one of the most serious and vexing issues facing Mobile as it reaches the tricentennial anniversary of its founding.

Suggestions for Further Reading

Bass, Jack. *Taming the Storm: The Life and Times of Judge Frank M. Johnson, Jr., and the South's Fight over Civil Rights.* New York: Doubleday Books, 1993. A biography of U.S. district court judge Frank M. Johnson Jr., whose trailblazing decisions on civil rights led the charge to end segregation and racial discrimination in Alabama.

Bernard, William D. *Dixiecrats and Democrats: Alabama Politics from 1942–1950.* Tuscaloosa: University of Alabama Press, 1974. An in-depth political history of Alabama with a focus on the conservative challenge to populist control of state politics and its impact on civil rights.

Eagles, Charles W. *Outside Agitator: Jon Daniels and the Civil Rights Movement in Alabama.* Chapel Hill: University of North Carolina Press, 1993. A biography of Jon Daniels, a northern college student who was murdered while working for civil rights in Alabama in 1965. The book provides insights into the motivation of civil rights workers and their antagonists.

Gray, Fred D. *Bus Ride to Justice: Changing the System by the System.* Montgomery: Black Belt Press, 1995. An autobiography of the preacher, politician, and civil rights attorney who was involved in the Montgomery bus boycott, Selma march, Tuskegee syphilis study, and school desegregation.

Richardson, Frederick Douglas. *The Genesis and Exodus of NOW.* 2d ed. Boynton Beach, Fla.: Futura Press, 1996. A subjective history of a Mobile civil rights organization, Neighborhood Organized Workers (NOW), written from the perspective of one of its members.

CHAPTER 10

Mobile since 1945

Harvey H. Jackson III

THE WAR WAS OVER, and some Mobilians thought it was time that workers who had come "flocking in from the backwoods" for jobs to head home. This "riffraff," as some called them, had stretched city resources and frayed natives' nerves long enough. A teacher in the overcrowded school system spoke for many when she described the intruders as "the lowest type of poor whites" and wondered whether they would ever amount to anything. To her way of thinking they were the sort of folks who "prefer to live in shacks and go barefoot." "Give them a good home," she complained, "and they wouldn't know what to do with it. They . . . let their kids run wild on the streets. I only hope we can get rid of them."[1]

At first it seemed that the teacher's wish would come true. Peace brought an end to wartime prosperity. The layoffs came quickly, and by early 1946, around forty thousand jobs had disappeared. Nevertheless, city hall seemed unconcerned. "We have our port and we propose to make the most of it" was the way *Fortune* magazine reported the attitude. Local leaders believed they could build Mobile's postwar economy on the prewar model. Waterborne commerce would keep the state docks busy, provide jobs for returning veterans, and keep the most skilled and productive of the recent arrivals employed. As for the rest, the answer was simple—"surplus workers must go home."[2]

This complacency explains why postwar business boosters did not aggressively recruit companies that would turn Mobile into an industrial city. Instead, they devoted time and energy to lobbying upstate interests to assure continued support for the state docks. The effort produced results, though never to the degree or consistency lobbyists hoped, so in the future local legislators would be challenged again and again to bring home funds for the port's upkeep and expansion. Still, for the time being the docks were not the city's primary concern. As long as a benevolent federal government continued to pump money into the economy, hire local residents, and fill municipal coffers, Mobile did very well. While other bases were closing, Brookley Field not only stayed open but also expanded, and by the end of the decade its payroll of more than $45 million a year made it far and away the city's largest employer. In the years that followed, even as many Mobilians became increasingly critical of the role Washington played in their lives, citizens of the City by the Bay continued to seek and accept federal subsidies without any apparent uneasiness at the contradiction.[3]

The expected postwar downturn came and went, and by 1947 employment was back on the rise, though it would be well into the 1950s before it was again at wartime levels. Meanwhile the city leaders quietly accepted the fact that many of those employed at Brookley, at the docks, and in a revived construction industry were the very "riffraff" that so many of the old guard had wished would go home. Finding they liked the city and its style of living, the immigrants purchased homes in new developments, spent their money in the downtown's regional shopping complex, and sent their children to the new schools that seemed to be opening every year. As far as Mobile's traditional elites were concerned, these folks were and always would be outsiders; in time, however, the outsiders would think of themselves as Mobilians, and their children would never think of themselves as anything else.[4]

The turnaround was so rapid and so successful that at the end of 1947, a national "Report on Industrial, Civic, [and] Cultural Progress" identified Mobile as one of the fastest growing cities in the South and praised its leaders for having "taken

Mobile looking southwest from above Blakeley Island with state docks construction in the foreground, circa 1950.

William Lavendar photo, USA Archives.

great strides in the consolidation of its position as one of the nation's leading seaports, manufacturing centers and distribution points." Commenting on the honor, the *Mobile Press Register,* as big a local booster as any metropolitan daily in the region, went out of its way to thank the "thousands of fine people who came to live with us" and who "elected to remain permanent citizens." Old Mobile might look askance at these folks from the "backwoods," but new Mobile saw each as employees, consumers, and taxpayers. There was no going back, and, as the years went by, there were fewer and fewer who wanted to.[5]

Although most of the new residents wished to become part of the city's traditional culture as quickly as possible, those who were part of the expanding middle class seemed to seek assimilation more aggressively than their working-class counterparts. Nowhere was this effort seen more clearly than in the yearly celebration of Mardi Gras, where local elites reinforced their status by entertaining the masses. What better way for nouveau Mobilians to announce their arrival than from a float looking down on their fellow citizens? And when the older carnival associations refused to open their membership to the newcomers, the newcomers organized associations of their own. Years later one of the city's older maskers recalled how at first "his mystic society met in a pool hall, charged $35 a year in dues, and 'never heard of waiting lists'" to ride in the parade. In the decades that followed, Mobile's Mardi Gras grew with the city, and though it remained the celebration of a closed society, it would never again be as closed as before.[6]

Through the 1940s and into the 1950s, one could hear the symphony of a growing city in the sound of ships moving up and down the river, in the traffic that crowded downtown streets, and in the clang and clatter of manufacturing and commerce. Yet of all of the sounds, the one that best reflected the changes taking place were the sounds of children. The "baby boomers" had arrived, and to accommodate them Mobile built parks, playgrounds, and new schools—public and parochial—paid for by taxes and tuition raised by and collected from citizens who were not yet "overburdened" or in rebellion. Although white institutions received the greater proportion of this largess, black schools were not entirely neglected, and in 1949, thanks to state senator Joe Langan's efforts, teacher salaries were equalized regardless of race. With the metropolitan population approaching two hundred thousand, growing pains seemed the biggest problem on the horizon, and with the city committed to meeting the needs of its children, Mobile appeared ready to make the most of the second half of the twentieth century.[7]

Presenting a better image of itself became more of a concern to city leaders as Mobile entered the 1950s. Tourism had always been a high priority, with Mardi Gras, the Azalea Trail, the Bellingrath Gardens, and the Alabama Deep Sea Fishing Rodeo being among the top events and attractions. Sports were also popular, especially with working-class Mobilians, and when the AA League Bears won the

Southern Association crown in 1947, team members became local heroes. That same year construction began on Ladd Memorial Stadium, and there was talk of major college football coming to town in the future. All of this translated into publicity for the area, and local boosters were quick to note how "newspapers, wire services, magazines, radio, and word of mouth spread the fame of the Alabama port city." Even television, then in its infancy, selected Mobile as the site to film one of the episodes in the popular "Big Story" series. The City by the Bay had much to recommend it, and its advocates were hard at work spreading the word.[8]

War had been good for Mobile's economy before, and it would be good for it again. In the early 1950s, as the Korean War heated up, activity increased at Brookley Field and at the state docks. Existing industries grew, and the newspaper noted with pride that the city was becoming one the country's top pulp and paper producers. Expanded rail service established a direct link between Mobile and the Great Lakes ports, giving the city access to markets throughout the Midwest. New faces were seen down at city hall and in corporate boardrooms, and these folks began more aggressively to attract industries. Their efforts quickly produced results. Up the Mobile River at McIntosh, chemical plants were going into operation, and Alabama Power began building a giant new steam facility to provide electricity to meet the increased demand. Elsewhere, other utilities took steps to accommodate private, commercial, and industrial growth. Even Mardi Gras felt the

Miss America, Yolande Betbeze, visited her hometown to be the Azalea Trail queen in 1951.

Museum of Mobile Collection, USA Archives.

impact of the war. Although some expected the crisis to dampen spirits, and some even suggested that the mystic societies forego their parades and balls, young men in the organizations argued that because they would soon be drafted and had no idea if or when they would be able to take part again, it was unfair to cancel the events. Older members agreed, and the festivities went on as scheduled.[9]

Mobile kept right on booming when the war ended. The port handled a record tonnage in 1953, then bettered that mark in 1954. Although the docks cleared less foreign freight than in 1946, Mobile was still one of the top ten facilities in the nation—ahead of Los Angeles and San Francisco. Reporting at the end of the year, Chamber of Commerce president O. H. Delchamps told his audience that "industrially, port-wise, from the tourist angle, culturally, and in new housing did Mobile carve an enviable position of progress during 1954." Looking at the record, it is difficult to question his conclusions or fault his optimism for the future. The population was growing; industries were expanding; the city was the recognized supply and service center for merchants and manufacturers along the northern Gulf Coast; Brookley continued to pump millions into the local economy; and in the northwest corner of the county near Citronelle oil wells were coming in. The U.S. Commerce Department's mid-decade survey underscored Mobile's economic achievements and gave business leaders every reason to predict that the rest of the 1950s would be more of the same.[10]

Nevertheless, problems existed. The rapid growth of the region highlighted the need for city-county planning and for closer cooperation between local governing bodies. John Will, a columnist for the *Press Register,* recommended that the city expand its limits and take in suburban sections outside its current boundaries to accomplish these goals. With this expansion would come the need to expand services, however, and that cost money. Already the school system was caught between its growing enrollment and a lack of funds, and restrictions on local taxation imposed by the antiquated state constitution made it difficult to raise the money needed to build and maintain facilities. Hospitals were also straining from the overload, recreational facilities were far from adequate, and potholes existed in streets crowded with traffic. City leaders hoped that the federal government would help in most of these areas, including the growing shortage of low-cost housing for the poorer population. Meanwhile these leaders talked of attracting light industry into areas near downtown to provide jobs for residents of older neighborhoods, but it was a difficult chore. Will summed up the growing dilemma: "Industry favors a city where living conditions are satisfactory, [and] you can't have satisfactory living conditions without public service." Mobile, he suggested, had a long way to go.[11]

Cultural attractions are considered by many to be critical to the quality of life in any city. By most measures Mobile in the 1950s came up lacking in this area as well. During the decade the number of plays, concerts, and other performances

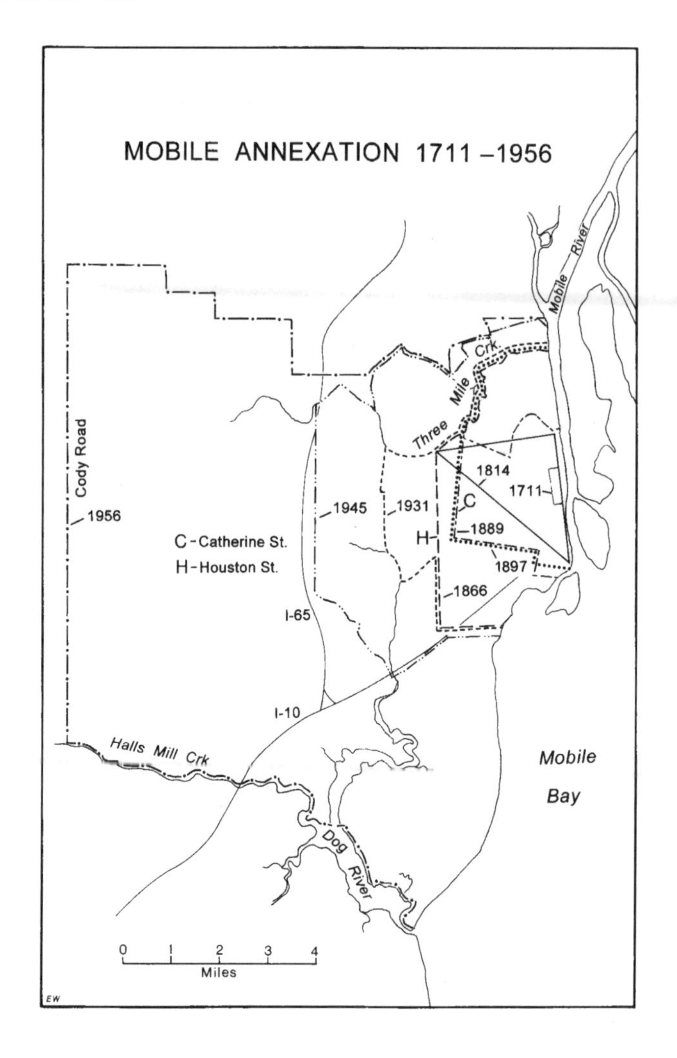

Mobile annexations.

Map by Eugene Wilson.

increased steadily, but never to the degree supporters hoped. The Joe Jefferson Players and the Mobile Theater Guild put on praised local productions, the Mobile Opera Guild and the Mobile Symphony contributed to cultural life, and subscribers to the Greater Gulf States Concert Series were entertained by touring groups such as the Ballet Russe. Nevertheless, by 1958 the series was operating only occasionally, and other groups were having difficulty getting a respectable number of patrons. Mobile had no city art gallery, no city play house for small productions, and no city auditorium for the larger shows. In 1947 an article in the local press boasted that though the city's artistic efforts "stack up poorly against NYC, Chicago or Pittsburgh," Mobile was not a cultural wasteland. Certainly, a decade later many would argue the point.[12]

Observers did credit patrons of the arts for "maintain[ing] . . . standards out of all proportion to what might reasonably be expected" when there was such a "lack of continuing, stimulating leadership" for their cause. Indeed, most believed that if it had not been for the "notable zeal" of "a minute proportion of the city's population" things would have been much worse. Many factors contributed to the situation. There was the feeling among middle and working-class Mobilians that the arts were a luxury of the elite, and consequently they refused to lend their support. On the other hand, there were fiscal conservatives in city hall who believed it was not government's place to support the arts and voted against funding. And then there was Mardi Gras. There were those who believed that because of the carnival, "philanthropies to music and other arts [were] seriously curtailed." They argued that, despite the number of people who came to see the spectacle, the event cost the city funds that would have been better spent elsewhere. Moreover, it was rumored that "Mobile's most prominent citizens," the ones who could afford to support the arts, "borrow[ed] heavily before each Mardi Gras and thereafter struggle[d] to repay in time for the next one." According to a "well-qualified observer," in the 1950s, "Mobile's lack of an art gallery, a municipal auditorium, and a history of continuity in any musical series or organization, may be traced directly to the two-week period before Lent."[13]

Nonetheless, if one looks at the arts broadly and considers popular culture as an important component of community entertainment, Mobile seemed to be more in the mainstream than these critics suggested. Granting that high culture was a minority preoccupation, other forms of recreation grew and flourished both with

WKAB announcer Larry Keith interviewed orchestra leader Erskine Hawkins at Buster's department store on Davis Avenue in 1951, and a crowd gathered for autographs.

Museum of Mobile Collection, USA Archives.

and without municipal guidance. Nightclubs and hotel bars brought in big-name entertainment, and on the north side, black establishments such as the Harlem Duke, owned by Tom Couch, played host to rhythm and blues stars and even attracted white patrons occasionally. The city may not have built an art gallery in the 1950s, but in 1957 it opened Langan Park, named for Commissioner Joe Langan, the man responsible for its existence. With lakes, gardens, tennis courts, a Little League baseball field, the Pixie Playhouse for children's theater, and an eighteen-hole municipal golf course, the park complex probably made more voters happy than paying subsidies to a symphony. The fact that so much of the new municipal park was devoted to young people reveals that something bigger than Mardi Gras was absorbing city resources. By the late 1950s public schools were so overcrowded that students were on double sessions. Segregation made the problem even more difficult to solve; with schools to build for both races, money raised from a $3 million bond issue in 1957 did not go far enough. Cultural events were certainly important, but, in the grand scheme of things, music, drama, and art were way down on Mobile's list of priorities.[14]

Still, area youngsters did more than cost money—they spent it. During the 1950s the members of the baby-boom generation made their impact as consumers, and soon adults began to cater to their tastes. John Dixon, a radio DJ who made the successful switch to television early in the decade, put together a teenage dance show, "Dixon on Disc," which quickly became one of the most popular local productions in the viewing area. Of note, Dixon never shied from playing music by black artists and even had them on his show, something that would not have happened in other Alabama cities at the time. In many ways Mobile was more attuned to the youth culture of the era than were other cities, and business leaders were especially conscious of the purchasing power of these kids and their parents. This was an important factor in the 1958 decision by the Mobile Junior Chamber of Commerce to organize America's Junior Miss pageant. Major companies, equally aware of the market, lined up to sponsor the event, and Mobile reaped a publicity windfall when the contest was televised nationally in the 1960s.[15]

Mobile closed out the decade with a mixed record of successes, failures, and problems left unsolved. Five million dollars in school construction in 1958 brought an end to double sessions, but classrooms were still crowded. Although integration was widely discussed, efforts to end segregation on city buses and a suit to "force the City Commission to throw open the new golf course . . . to Negroes" were the principal civil rights issues at the end of the decade. The buses were also the focus of attention in the fall of 1957 when drivers and mechanics went on a forty-four day strike that deprived Mobile, Prichard, and Chickasaw of mass transportation. World War II had left Mobile one of Alabama's most unionized towns, and business leaders were quick to blame their lack of success in recruiting new industries on the higher wages and benefits union members received. This tension between workers' expectations and management's desires would lead to problems in the future, but, for decades to come, organized labor would remain a powerful force in the life of the city.[16]

One topic that seemed at the center of most decade-end discussions of Mobile's future was *traffic*. Down at the docks, folks wanted more of it on the water. To accomplish this goal, local businesspersons and legislators forged an alliance with their counterparts from interior river towns and convinced the state to create an inland port system that would transform Mobile into Alabama's window to the world. Thus, docking facilities at Jackson, Demopolis, Tuscaloosa-Northport, and Montgomery were scheduled to be upgraded, and when it was announced in 1959 that the Corps of Engineers would begin work on the Jackson Lock and Dam near Coffeeville, expectations increased even more. All of this activity contributed in no small way to the revival of a dream long held by Mobilians, a dream of a waterway that would connect their city to the Tennessee River and the Ohio River valley beyond. As the 1960s approached, the vision began to appear more realistic.[17]

The other type of traffic was not welcomed. In the first decade after the war the number of motor vehicles in Mobile doubled, and with the increase came congestion usually associated with a larger metropolis. Eagerly sought federal funds helped finance a new Beltline Highway, consisting of I-10 and I-65, to alleviate some of the problem, which in turn accelerated the city's expansion to the west. Where Airport Boulevard crossed the Beltline, developers began to build Mobile's first shopping mall, Springdale, and shortly downtown merchants, discouraged by

Junior Miss rehearsal, circa 1985.

Azalea City News Collection, USA Archives.

the lack of off-street parking, began to move out. This gave residents of the growing western suburbs a downtown of their own and marked the beginning of the decline of the city's center. The process was rapid, and by the time I-10 and I-65 were completed, Springdale Mall had been joined by Bel Air Mall to create a new regional shopping hub. From the mid-1960s on, the revitalization of downtown would be a perennial issue and one that, despite progress in the 1990s, is still far from being solved.[18]

At the moment all this construction was taking place, few seemed particularly concerned with what it might do to downtown. The late 1950s and early 1960s were flush times for Mobile and Mobilians. Bricks, mortar, and asphalt meant jobs, and not all of the activity was the result of federal largess. City revenues were up, and from the surplus, commissioners financed what the *Mobile Press Register* described as "unprecedented spending on capital improvements." Meanwhile Brookley, the bellwether of the local economy, saw its civilian work force expand to nearly sixteen thousand as personnel from base closings in Ohio, Kansas, Tennessee, and Gadsden, Alabama, were transferred south. "All over Mobile," a year-end review noted, there were "new cars, washing machines, hi-fi and TV sets." Obviously the prosperity was not spread evenly, but it was spread, and citizens seemed to revel in it. Mardi Gras was as big as ever; the Senior Bowl, which city leaders "stole" from Jacksonville, Florida, in 1951 and set up in Ladd Stadium, was on its way to becoming a major national sporting event; Junior Miss and the Azalea Trail highlighted the accomplishments and charms of young ladies; and finally

Half-time at a Senior Bowl game, 1950s.

Mobile Register.

money had been set aside to build a city art gallery. As Mobile entered the 1960s, the future appeared bright indeed.[19]

Considering this optimistic outlook, many were shocked when in 1960 the results of an "Area Audit" conducted by the Southern Institute of Management were released and the city fared poorly in almost every category. The report revealed that while New Orleans and Atlanta had moved forward to become regional manufacturing and distribution centers, Mobile lagged behind. With only three medium-size department stores and one major suburban shopping mall, the city's retail potential remained "untapped," and despite all the highway construction, transportation was hampered by poor airport facilities. Tourism was growing, but city leaders were doing little to make visitors a significant source of revenue. Finally, though the employment picture might seem rosy to those with jobs, little new industry was relocating in the area, and employment in older industries was stagnant. Noting that Brookley Field employed as many civilians as all of the area's manufacturers combined, the audit observed that it would be more accurate to classify Mobile as a "government service center" than as an industrial city.[20]

Economic development was hardly the only area in which the report found shortcomings. Although an art gallery and a municipal auditorium were in the planning stages, other towns the size and age of Mobile were already enjoying such facilities. The recent creation of a United Arts Council to promote cultural activities was a hopeful sign, but it had its work cut out for it. Meanwhile citizens, confused by financial problems in the school system, were not happy with public education, an interesting observation because there are those today who connect this dissatisfaction to the advent of integration, which was still some years away. Indeed, the flight from the public schools began well before black and white students began attending together there, and parochial and private schools, which were always popular in the city, were noted in the report as being "among the community's greatest assets." Actually, "stabilized" race relations were highlighted as one of Mobile's few strong suits, with credit given to the "moderating influences of local Negro leadership and the placating policies of the City administration." John LeFlore, the leader of the Non-Partisan Voters League (the state, as noted in the last chapter, had outlawed the NAACP), and Commissioner Langan were primarily responsible for the state of affairs the report described. Although bias was known to exist, there was little evidence of "blatant or calculated [acts] to create hostility." In public matters, members of both races were said to be treated with dignity and given the opportunity to work, which helped everyone get along. Nevertheless, there were those in the white community who resented the changes in the traditional relationship between the races, changes they blamed on the federal government. It was one thing for Washington to provide jobs and services for area citizens but quite another for it to demand what was seen as social concessions in return.[21]

Much of the blame for the city's lack of progress was placed squarely at the feet of the citizenry. Noting the rapid decline of downtown, the report pointed out how parking lot owners had blocked city efforts to provide adequate off-street parking for shoppers who, not surprisingly, gave up trying to negotiate the narrow, congested streets and flocked to the "splendor" of the suburban shopping mall. It followed then that citizens lacked the "fiscal willingness" to underwrite the restoration of the many dilapidated areas at the city's core. To compound the problem, local banks refused loans to restore old homes, and as a result Mobile's architectural glory was falling rapidly into decay. What it came down to, the audit concluded, was that "Mobilians are law-abiding and religious-minded to a far greater extent than they are civic-minded." On the whole they cared little about political matters, and though they might be "vocal in their civic criticism," their "agreeable way of life has reduced their aggressiveness to follow up criticism with action." Residents, the study noted, seldom organized groups to change things or better the community, but instead remained passive and therefore ineffectual in dealing with civic issues. In addition, though this attitude seemed pervasive in all parts of society, the study found it most apparent, and most powerful, in what it termed the "old 'aristocracy' which has been long characterized by its status quo philosophy on community affairs." About the only good thing the audit had to say, apart from its comments on race relations, parochial and private schools, and the work of the United Arts Council, was that there had been "little laxness or corruption concerning government expenditures." The city commission had handled financial affairs frugally, and in the light of the fiscal restrictions placed on it and all Alabama cities by the state constitution, local government had done a good job. Many may have considered this faint praise, but at least it was something of which to be proud. A generation later Mobilians would look back on this time as a golden era of civic integrity. In the 1980s two of three men who served on the last city commission would serve time in federal prison for crimes committed while in office.[22]

Some would argue later that the Mobile Area Audit was far too negative, especially in its criticism of the role that local elites played in civic affairs, and that some of the conditions it noted were already being addressed when the report was issued. Nonetheless, the institute's conclusion that "Mobile is being left behind in the modern sweep of the dynamic, progressive times" struck a nerve and moved some citizens to action. In the decade that followed, Mobile's business and political leaders set out to build an economy based on industry, commerce, government employment, tourism, and services, and in so doing they addressed most of the matters called to their attention in the survey. They fought for and supported a new public university and set the city on a new course.[23]

The chemical industry, which was already established upriver, was the focus of special recruiting efforts, and in the next few years old plants were expanded and new ones were added. During this same period a $6 million bond issue was approved for the long-awaited municipal auditorium; construction on what would become the University of Mobile was begun by the Baptist church; the municipal airport was enlarged and improved; spurred on by a young Frederick Whiddon the new University of Alabama Mobile Center (soon to be the University of South Alabama) was planned as a four-year school; and highway construction continued to bring in federal dollars. So did Brookley Field, which observers considered "vital" to the economic health of the city. Unfortunately, southwest Alabama and Mobile's political clout was greatly diminished the year that Frank Boykin, the district's fourteen-term congressman, lost his seat when the state lost a representative following the 1960 census. Boykin had been a controversial and colorful figure, but he had kept far more tax money coming into Mobile than going out. Without him in Washington looking out for things, there was concern that the city might not get its share of the "pork" when the pie was divided up. Still, for the moment at least, Mobilians took all of this in stride. In 1961, as the city began to mark its 250th anniversary the following year, "a rabid wave of civic pride broke loose." Men in the town grew beards, women dressed in hoop skirts and farthingales, and celebratory picnics were held in Bienville Square. From all accounts, a good time was had by all.[24]

It was during these same early years of the decade that white Mobilians finally awoke to the realization that black Mobilians were not nearly as content with their lot as many believed them to be. When compared with other Alabama cities, Mobile seemed the soul of racial accommodation and toleration. Although the city remained segregated in most activities, the first black policeman had been hired in 1953, and there were twenty-six African Americans on the force a decade later. Spring Hill College had admitted black students the year of the *Brown* decision. Segregated seating on city buses ended in 1963, and soon afterward black drivers were hired. Sit-ins in other cities moved local leaders to agree quietly to desegregate lunch counters, and white fears of a drop in business proved unfounded. So different was the Mobile experience from that of its sister cities in the South that in July of 1963 the *Wall Street Journal* praised it in an article headlined "An Alabama City Builds Racial Peace as Strife Increases Elsewhere." That fall Mobile's race relations began to be put to the test. Under a court order, Murphy High became the first Alabama public school to integrate, and over the next decade the gradual ending of the city's dual school system served as the backdrop for a political realignment that today is still going on in the City by the Bay.[25]

Meanwhile, with the economy expanding, the population growing, and racial relations not yet overshadowing the city's other concerns, Mobile seemed well on its way to reversing the Area Audit assessment. Then it happened. On November 19, 1964, the Department of Defense issued an order calling for the "progressive reduction in employment" and the eventual closure of Brookley Field. No one seemed to have anticipated it. While work at other bases declined in the early 1960s, Brookley kept expanding. Personnel transferred from other posts and local residents hired at the base had pushed civilian employment to a peacetime record employment of more than sixteen thousand in 1962. With a total payroll of $95 million, army spokesmen proudly noted that Brookley Field accounted for "an estimated one-third of Mobile's gross product." The loss of a few jobs in 1963 caused "anxiety" in some circles, but at the end of that year the *Press Register* confidently observed that it was "extremely unlikely that the federal government would eliminate a base as large as Brookley." "Looking at the situation objectively," the newspaper assured the public, "we believe it is a sound conclusion that the air base will be a big employer for a long time to come." The next year proved the paper wrong.[26]

At that time Brookley was the largest base closure in U.S. history, and those laid off represented 20 percent of all the civilian jobs ever lost in U.S. base shutdowns. Yet city business and political leaders were not interested in such comparisons. They knew they were facing a crisis, and they had no choice but to deal with it. In response the Chamber of Commerce set up Task Force 200 and vowed to attract $200 million in industrial investment over the next five years. Making the most of the area's natural advantages—the port, inland waterways, fresh water, timberlands, salt deposits, and a friendly business climate—recruiters sought out businesses that complemented each other, such as paper and chemicals. Meanwhile ongoing highway construction was ringing the city with four lanes of interstate highway and funneling shoppers into the Springdale Plaza–Bel Air Mall complex, which by the mid-1960s had replaced downtown as the region's retail hub. As Brookley let its workers go, new industries opened to absorb some of them. It was not always a fair exchange, and many highly paid government employees were not able to find comparable work in the public sector; however, because of what has been described as the "frantic industrial recruiting" of Task Force 200, the group's $200 million goal was reached eighteen months ahead of schedule.[27]

Some in Mobile believed Brookley's closing was more than an economic or a military decision. It was, they hinted, Lyndon Johnson's way of getting back at the city for voting for the GOP presidential candidate in 1964 and for its role in electing Republican Jack Edwards to Congress from the district. Still, whether this was the reason or not, that election marked the emergence of the Republican Party as a major player in Mobile politics. It had not happened overnight. Since World War II a growing number of conservative white businessmen, upset with the federal government over taxes, regulations, government spending, and racial policies, became disillusioned with Democratic policies that they considered to be the root of the problem. At first reluctant to desert the party of their forefathers, in the early

1950s some of them formed the Mobile Committee of States' Rights Democrats, which in reality became what one historian has called "a sort of halfway house on their journey to the Republican party." By the 1960s the local GOP had attracted some young dynamic candidates, and the old Democratic power structure was threatened by the challenge. Although for a while George Wallace's popularity in the state kept the Democrats strong and robbed the Republicans of many of their more potent issues, the GOP had breached Mobile's political walls. By the end of the century the majority of white Mobilians counted themselves in the Republican ranks, whereas the Democrats became home for most of the city's black voters. Other issues divided the parties, but race was, and is, the most visible.[28]

There is a certain irony in what happened next. Although criticism of Washington's spending habits was a mainstay of Republican rhetoric, no sooner had Congressman Edwards arrived in the capital than he began working to get the federal government to commit funds to what would become one of the biggest (and most controversial) public works projects to be undertaken in the southeast since the days of the New Deal: the Tennessee-Tombigbee Waterway. For Mobilians, however, this was an appropriate course of action for their congressman to take. Long accustomed to federal largess and feeling betrayed by Brookley's closing, people thought it seemed only fitting that Washington should do something to compensate the city for the damage it had done. A waterway linking Mobile to the Mid-

Civilians doing precision work at Brookley Air Force Base during the cold war era.

Mobile Register.

west was a centuries-old dream, and to the new congressman the time seemed right to make the dream a reality.[29]

Business leaders did not wait for the Tenn-Tom to make up what was lost with Brookley. Highway construction continued to tie up traffic, but because Mobile had until recently enjoyed the "unenviable distinction of being among the most dangerous areas in the nation in which to drive an automobile," most citizens realized that the inconvenience was a small price to pay. Besides, construction meant jobs, so the work on Interstate 10, a new tunnel under the Mobile River, and the Mobile Bay Causeway were welcomed by Mobilians. Industrial expansion continued at a record-setting pace, earnings at the docks were up, and residential construction held steady. Money also went into the construction of the new University of South Alabama (USA), the first state-supported institution of higher learning to be established in Alabama in nearly seventy years. Created by the Alabama legislature in 1963 under the leadership of Frederick Whiddon, it opened its doors in June of the following year to 928 students and 43 faculty. In a little more than a year both figures had doubled. USA, when combined with the recently opened Baptist Mobile College and the Catholic Spring Hill College, set the city on the road to becoming a center for higher education on the Gulf Coast.[30]

Better roads held out the promise of more visitors, so following the audit's recommendation, the Chamber of Commerce set out to provide tourists with sights

Founding president Frederick P. Whiddon at the University of South Alabama's dedication ceremony, October 18, 1964.

USA Archives.

and experiences that would make them come back. As a result of lobbying led by local business leaders Stephens Croom, Henry Aldridge, Jimmy Morris, and others, the legislature loaned the state docks the money to finance a fund-raising campaign to bring the battleship USS *Alabama* to Mobile. The money was raised, the vessel was towed fifty-six hundred miles from Seattle, and on January 9, 1965, Battleship Memorial Park opened just off the causeway. Meanwhile the long-awaited Municipal Auditorium debuted on July 9th, 1964, with the popular production "Holiday on Ice." During the year that followed, the new facility was booked 325 out of 365 days as Mobilians flocked to see the likes of the Ringling Brothers Circus and the Harlem Globe Trotters in the 10,000-seat main auditorium and smaller productions in the 1,950-seat theater. The facility also contained meeting rooms for conventions, and though this feature of the complex was underutilized at first, city leaders had high hopes for the future. Battleship Park quickly became one of the region's most popular tourist attractions. The auditorium was used heavily as well but mainly for single events. The convention trade, which businesspersons hoped would bring people back downtown, developed more slowly.[31]

The problem was simple to see but difficult to solve. As Mobile's population moved west and the Springdale Plaza–Bel Air Mall complex became the major shopping center between Baldwin County and Bay St. Louis, downtown began to follow the pattern seen in cities throughout the nation. Stores closed, buildings were allowed to deteriorate, and public spaces became places to avoid. Lovely Bienville Square took on a seedy look, and the city assigned a permanent police patrol there "to keep out undesirables." Crime was on the increase throughout the city, as it was nationally, but somehow it seemed worst downtown. A former resident of Toulminville recalled how, as a teenager in the 1950s, she would ride the city bus into town, meet her friends, and then go shopping and to a movie. By the 1960s fewer and fewer Mobilians, especially white Mobilians, made that trip. Suburban malls and shopping centers were more attractive and seemed safer. Downtown was dirty and more than a little dangerous. Back in 1956, the *Press Register* reported with pride of how a busload of tourists came through the Bankhead Tunnel, and, as they proceeded along Government Street, one of them looked about and said, "Here is a city with real character." A decade later no one seemed to be saying that anymore.[32]

Put simply, so many of the things that gave Mobile its character, such as its lovely homes and its period public buildings, had either fallen to the wrecking ball or were in danger of being lost through destruction or neglect. The Historic Mobile Preservation Society had been around since the 1930s, and although some citizens took pride in what the society wanted to save, city hall seemed indifferent to its goals. Although cities such as Charleston and New Orleans, those ever-present points of comparison, had already begun to preserve and restore the buildings that defined them, Mobile did little throughout the mid-1950s. In the late 1940s the city had purchased the Richards House from Ideal Cement and leased it to the Daughters of the American Revolution. It followed that precedent in the next decade by obtaining Oakleigh for the Historic Mobile Preservation Society. Both groups devoted themselves to the care and preservation of the old homes. Still, preserving the past was not high on the list of civic goals, as revealed in the "battle of the bricks," which occurred in 1957 when the old courthouse was torn down. Having failed to save the structure, the society pressed to at least have the new courthouse built out of bricks from the old. Opponents protested, claiming that the old bricks "looked like the pigeons have been roosting on them," which they probably had. The courthouse was built with new bricks.[33]

Things began to look up in the early 1960s when the Mobile Historic Development Commission was set up and the Church Street East and DeTonti Square Historic Districts were created. It seemed that local leaders had realized, as the *Press Register* noted, that "civic and official alertness to the value of historic resources is essential" if the city was to prosper. Still, financial institutions were not entirely

Demolition of the antebellum U.S. Customs House on Royal Street, 1963.

Palmer Studio Collection, USA Archives.

behind the idea, and the practice of redlining older sections and denying owners loans would continue until federal loans became available. Meanwhile progress and preservation clashed time and again in downtown Mobile, and more often than not progress won. In 1963 the antebellum Customs House on Royal Street was demolished to make way for a high-rise office building, and in 1965, despite public protest, the famous Levert House went down. Yet these isolated tragedies were nothing compared with the damage wrought when the Mobile Housing Board went to work with $30 million in federal urban renewal money. Focusing its attention on the city's historic waterfront and older downtown residential neighborhoods, the board began clearing the land. The project soon spread into the area where the new Municipal Auditorium with its sea of parking lots was being built, and then into the Davis Avenue section, the heart of Mobile's black community, and south toward Oakdale. Advocates of progress claimed the effort was a success. Downtown traffic problems were lessened, land was secured for what were described as "productive uses"—the auditorium and eventually the massive waterfront convention center. Much of the city's substandard housing was demolished, and some serious slums were cleared and replaced by modern housing. Preservationists saw another story, however. Back in the 1930s the Historic American Buildings Survey had identified 177 historically significant structures in the city. When the era of urban renewal was finished, more than two-thirds of those buildings were gone. Few cities could match that dubious record, and preservationists, as one of them later observed, "could only cry for a city sacked." Still, in an ironic way, the demolition seemed to expose the blight that had taken over downtown and may have actually forced reluctant politicians and businesspersons to make the restoration of the city center a major priority later in the century.[34]

For many in the city, "character" was more than the preservation of historic buildings. With the opening of the Municipal Auditorium and the Fine Arts Museum of the South, the cultural life of the city began to expand, though not always in ways the devotees of "high culture" might have hoped. Although the smaller theater-concert hall was jam-packed for the Van Cliburn Symphony concert, folk singers Peter, Paul, and Mary were able to sell out the larger auditorium. In the 1960s the arts in Mobile made what the *Press Register* described as "steady, plugging progress," but many still asked themselves just "how much more cultural growth will Mobile support?" The answer would not come easily. As college and university music, art, and drama departments began to take a more active role in community affairs, more entertainment options became available to citizens. Still, to the dismay of the city's cultural elite, Ringling Brothers, TV's "All-Star Bowling," the Roller Derby, and "monster" truck contests packed the auditorium, whereas the symphony continued to limp along on a bare-bones budget.[35]

By the end of the decade the arts and entertainment in Mobile were feeling pres-

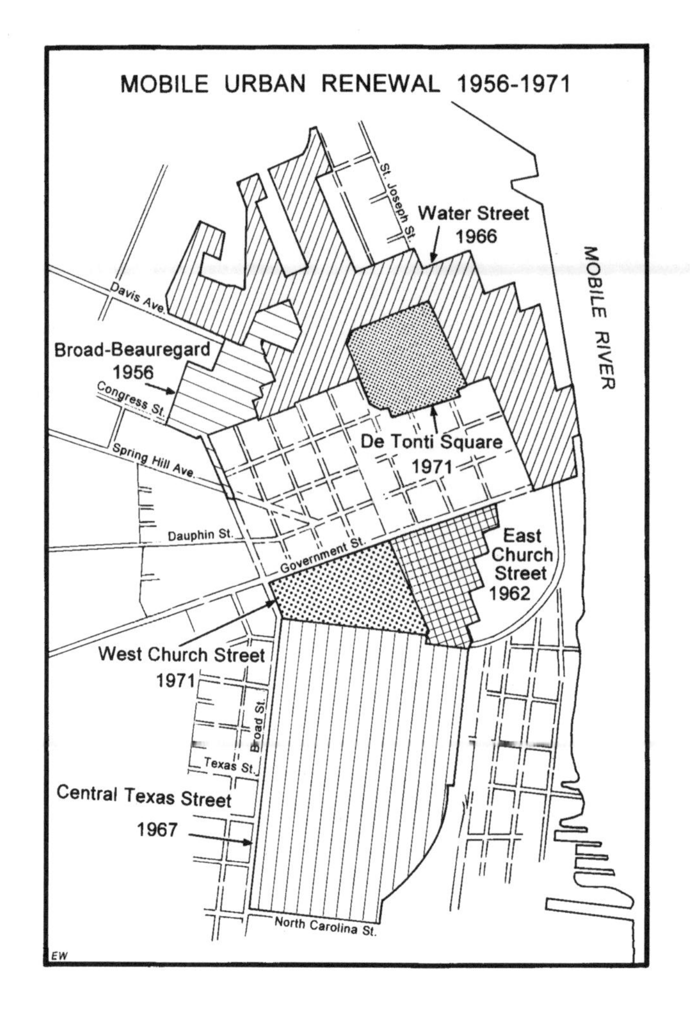

Urban renewal.

Map by Eugene Wilson.

sure from another quarter. During those years evangelical Protestant churches had grown in numbers and influence in the city even as elements of the artistic community, especially on the college campuses, were pushing the boundaries of what conservatives defined as "decency." Add to this the small but highly visible counterculture movement in the city—the hippies—and sooner or later there was bound to be a confrontation. It came in 1968 when the city commission, in its fight against what it considered "obscenity, pornography and other undesirable characteristics on the stage, screen and newsstand," pressured the University of South Alabama not to produce the controversial play *America, Hurrah*. That same year "objectionable" magazines were removed from newsstands, and civic censors tried unsuccessfully to keep the movie *The Fox* (based on the D. H. Lawrence novel) from being shown locally. Things really became nasty when church and city leaders learned that the Spring Hill College Student Government Association had invited LSD guru and "mind-altering drug advocate" Dr. Timothy Leary to speak on campus. Faced with a rising protest, the school administration canceled the appearance, but Leary vowed to come anyway. To the relief of those in authority, he did not show.[36]

Compounding concerns over the moral direction society was taking, the old racial order that had been so carefully nurtured by white society finally came apart. At the center of the turmoil were the public schools, which were not only desegregating but also trying to deal with the impact of revenue lost as Brookley closed. Some on the school board believed the deficit could be recovered through federal grants available under programs such as Head Start, but others opposed that approach because "federal restrictions and red tape [might] prove too much." The schools were not the only place the city's once-accommodating citizens clashed. Riots followed news of the assassination of Dr. Martin Luther King Jr. in April 1968, and tensions were higher than at any time since the racial incidents at the docks and Brookley during World War II. Meanwhile, when efforts to increase job opportunities for minorities seemed stalled, militant blacks in Noble Beasley's Neighborhood Organized Workers (NOW) called for a boycott of white-owned stores that lasted sixteen months before an agreement to hire black sales clerks was reached. Pressure was also put on the city to appoint more blacks to positions of responsibility, and before 1969 was out, the Municipal Auditorium had a black assistant manager and three African Americans on its board. Mobile was being desegregated, but it was a slow, sometimes painful, process for those involved. As noted in the last chapter, NOW's intervention in the city election of that year when it called for blacks to abstain from voting resulted in the defeat of long-time commissioner and racial moderate Joe Langan.[37]

Yet despite all that had taken place, in December 1969 the *Press Register* was able to announce that the past decade had been "the best 10 years in the economic history of Mobile." Task Force 200 had done its work well. Since 1960 more than $500 million had been invested in new and expanded plants in the area, convention visitors had increased from thirty-five hundred to more than forty-five thousand, and tourism had become a $40 million-a-year industry. Phasing out Brookley had hurt, no doubt about it, but as the date for the closing approached, efforts by the city and the Mobile Area Chamber of Commerce to attract civilian businesses to the base had proved successful. By July 1969, according to the local press, "most of the buildings suitable for industry had been leased on a long-term basis to manufacturers." Although only two thousand industrial workers had relocated to the base, the chamber predicted (erroneously as it turned out) that between seven thousand and ten thousand would be there by 1973. Even this number was still well below the nearly thirteen thousand civilian jobs that were lost with the closing, but with the economy expanding in other quarters, figures showed that almost as many jobs were created elsewhere in the city. Mobile still had a way to go to recover fully from what had taken place.[38]

Mobile's successful efforts to attract industries had produced a number of undesirable side effects, and in the late 1960s, as Congress, through the Environmental Protection Agency (EPA), began efforts to stop pollution and punish polluters, Mobilians learned the price they had paid for industrial growth. Of course, many citizens had long been aware that industries were fouling the air and water. For years Theodore residents had complained about the "bright orange smoke" that plants in their industrial complex "belched forth," and folks who lived near paper mills seemed to understand that there was more than a foul smell in the air they breathed. They also knew that the city itself was one of the area's biggest polluters and that raw sewage was pumped daily into the river. Nevertheless, citizens understood that these industries provided jobs and that it would take higher taxes to improve the city's sewage system. Good jobs and low taxes were higher priorities than clean air and water. In 1970 the city's biggest paper producer, International Paper, was also the area's largest private employer with thirty-five hundred workers and a payroll of more than $28 million. Alone this company pumped about $1 million a week into the local economy. Environmentalists looking for allies, such as the Mobile Bay Audubon Society, found few Mobilians willing to put such an enterprise in jeopardy.[39]

Then new industries began to threaten old, and environmentalists found they had friends after all. In 1967 and 1968 conservation officers reported massive fish kills in area rivers, and shortly thereafter oyster reefs in the bay were closed by the state. Concerned representatives from the Federal Water Pollution Control Administration held public hearings in November 1968, and though no consensus was reached, the lines between the two sides became clearer. Meanwhile the EPA was testing fish taken from the water around the city, and in June 1970 it announced that local seafood was "contaminated with mercury poison." The news, according to the local press, "hit the state . . . with the impact of a sledge hammer between the eyes." The Alabama Department of Conservation moved quickly to halt commercial fishing in the most polluted areas and to ban sports fishing as well. Facing economic ruin, fishermen and fishing camp operators filed suit against the accused industries, and, as is so often the case in Alabama, the issue was left for the courts to decide.[40]

Moved by public pressure, threats of government action, and the fear that there would be large legal judgments against them if they did not act, polluting industries began to clean up. Actually, some had made efforts to do so even before the discovery of mercury in nearby streams, but now the process took on a sense of urgency. Soon industries were proudly announcing what they were doing and how much it was costing. Much of the cost was financed by industrial development bonds, a widespread, controversial form of government intervention on behalf of industrial development. Before long some industries were boasting that they were "pollution free," but EPA officials and local environmentalists were skeptical. The tension between advocates of industrial development and supporters of environmental sensitivity remained, and in the years to come the debate between these two sides would play an important role in determining the sort of city, and county, Mobile would be.[41]

Despite warnings from business leaders that strict environmental regulations would hurt the local prosperity, in the early 1970s Mobile's economy continued to grow. Having reached and exceeded its goals of attracting new industries, Task Force 200 began "shooting for new horizons," and before mid-decade the old record was shattered as roughly $500 million was spent on new and expanded plants. Whether south of the city at the new Theodore Industrial Park or north along the Mobile River, the new industries were similar to those already in the area: paper or chemical. Improved state dock facilities enabled the port to set all-time records in cargo tonnage and profits in 1975, and work on the new tunnel construction project had kept federal money coming into the city. Complaints that wages and benefits were not keeping pace with inflation or with corporate profits led to strikes in both the public and private sectors, but even these actions did not stop the economic expansion. By the end of 1975 national publications were citing the "phenomenon of Mobile, a city which has experienced healthy economic growth despite a slumping national economy." Fueled by the region's natural assets, its "excellent business climate," and the discovery of oil and gas in the northern part of the county, investments were coming in, wages and profits were high, unemployment was low, and the area was on the verge of a housing shortage.

Built in 1967, the Marion gasoline refinery closed in the late 1980s when it became unprofitable. Reopening the facility would involve environmental issues.

Mobile Register.

Although Brookley Air Force Base and its payroll were recalled "with fond memory," Mobile business leaders believed they had weathered the crisis and weathered it well.[42]

The optimistic outlook shared by most of Mobile's commercial community was also based on the area's growing political power in the state and in the nation. Reapportionment gave the city and county its largest legislative delegation in history, and these representatives made it clear that south Alabama was going to play an important role in state affairs. Meanwhile Congressman Edwards, with a Republican administration in the White House, was able to put together a regional coalition and get federal approval for the Tennessee-Tombigbee Waterway. On May 25, 1971, President Richard Nixon came to Mobile to mark the beginning of construction and to cement ties that were essential to the "southern strategy" that would eventually make the GOP the majority party in Dixie.[43]

In the latter half of the 1970s the thoughts of city hall and Mobile businesspersons turned once again to the condition and the future of downtown. Reading the local press, one would never know the historic destruction and social dislocation brought on by urban renewal in the 1960s. Articles on slums being cleared, "unhealthy sections" being leveled, and traffic problems being solved were the standard fare, along with the occasional mention of the city's "futuristic plan designed to modernize, beautify, and reconstruct Mobile's central business [district] by 1985." Little was actually done, however. A new federal building was begun in 1972, and in 1975 construction of a hotel and of a high-rise apartment project for

The first section of the I-10 tunnel was launched at the Alabama Dry Dock and Shipbuilding Company on July 29, 1970.

ADDSCO Collection, USA Archives.

the elderly promised to bring more people to the area. Nonetheless, most of the downtown construction was on highways to carry people around and beyond the city center. Still, there were those who would not give up, who kept pushing for some way to make the urban core come alive. Because of the actions of Downtown Mobile Unlimited and the help of other interested organizations, work began in the Cathedral Square area and at the University of South Alabama–owned Saenger Theater to turn that part of the city into a haven for antique dealers, artists, and performers. The long-awaited opening of a city museum in the restored Bernstein-Bush House on Government Street in February 1976 called attention to Mobile's fascinating past. The recently organized Waterfront Arts Festival spread from the new "floating arts center" out into the nearby streets. Municipal Auditorium continued to pack in crowds, and Mardi Gras was as big a draw as ever. Then, in December 1979, city officials announced that a $30 million, four-hundred-room convention hotel with a office tower and retail mall would be built near the river. Thus, the *Press Register* observed, the decade of the 1970s was closing "with the renewed hope that the revitalization of downtown will soon take place."[44]

Even as the newspaper was reporting its hopes for the future, downtown Mobile and the rest of the city were recovering from one of the worst natural disasters to hit south Alabama in the century. On the night of September 12, 1979, Hurricane Frederic slammed into the Gulf Coast with 145-mile-an-hour winds that had diminished only slightly prior to landfall. Before Frederic had run its course it caused more than $2 billion in damage and entered history as the most expensive storm then on record. Citizens woke to look out on what one of them described as "a war zone," and when the final evaluation was completed, it showed that "at least three out of every four buildings in Mobile County received significant damage." The bridge to Dauphin Island was so battered that it had to be demolished and a new one built; trees were down everywhere, and it would be years before the pecan and the general wood product industries recovered; and city hall was wrecked to the point that government offices had to be relocated to an office complex on the beltline. Fortunately, the storm did not strike without warning, and the devastation caused along the Mississippi coast by Hurricane Camille ten years earlier had convinced residents of the folly of trying to ride it out at home. More than 100,000 people were evacuated from low-lying areas, and as a result only one life was lost. Insurance payments and federal government assistance soon arrived, providing relief for those who lost property and giving the economy "a welcome stimulus." Nevertheless, not everyone had insurance or qualified for federal aid, and for them Frederic was a disaster from which it would take years to recover.[45]

The 1970s ended with one natural disaster, and the 1980s began with another. Three times in 1980 and 1981 Mobile was hit with record floods, the last of which completely overwhelmed the city drainage system, forced hundreds to evacuate

Mobilians wait in line for ice under the watchful eye of the National Guard after Hurricane Frederic.

Photograph by Alan Whitman, USA Archives.

their homes, and caused more than $36 million in damages. Angry citizens converged on city hall, which responded with a $10.5 million relief program. Federal funds also became available, and before long Mobile had a new plan that promised to prevent future flooding. Residents, who claimed that they "panic[ked] every time the skies darkened," were skeptical.[46]

Mobilians had reason for their skepticism because even before the floods confidence in the city's political leadership had already dropped dramatically. Back in 1960 one of the few things the Mobile Area Audit had praised was the honest, forthright way in which municipal finances were handled. That situation had changed, however. During the 1970s and 1980s citizens saw twenty-five of their leaders—members of the city commission, the county commission, and the school board, and even judges and mayors—convicted for crimes. Citizens were outraged, but as has been so often the case in Mobile, it was the business community that moved to act. In 1985 the Mobile Area Chamber of Commerce sponsored a "Goals for Mobile" conference to discuss a chamber-sponsored survey that had identified a lack of leadership, business and political, as the principal problem facing the city.

Reviewing the report, the chamber chairman likened Mobile to "a drunk who has hit bottom and has no where to go but up." Few in the city would disagree.[47]

What had happened to turn Mobile's optimism to pessimism in such a short time? Certainly, government corruption played a part, but that alone could not have caused such a reversal. This downturn in public confidence can be blamed on a host of factors, many of them beyond the ability of any local leader to control—a national recession, double-digit inflation, and double-digit unemployment. Still, strikes by city workers, the ongoing debate over crosstown busing to achieve integration, and changes in the form of city government giving black voters a representative role in policy making might have been better handled if leadership had been stronger. New political interest groups, blacks and evangelical Protestants in particular, were rising in the city, splintering old coalitions and injecting issues of their own into campaigns. Although education continued to show up in polls as a top priority among Mobilians, the "taxpayers' revolt" had reached the city. Despite support from business and civic leaders, efforts to increase the millage rate for schools went down to defeat. So it was that by the end of the 1980s, Mobile's local tax support for public schools was the lowest in the state—$550 per year as compared with the highest at $1782. Moreover, though opponents of the tax increases argued otherwise, the fact that the antitax forces were overwhelmingly white whereas the city schools were becoming increasingly black suggested that race was not an insignificant factor.[48]

Although support for the public schools was waning, support for the city's colleges and university never seemed stronger. The church-related schools, rapidly expanding Mobile College and the older, more settled Spring Hill College, continued to reap high praise for their programs. Meanwhile Bishop State Junior College, which before 1965 was the all-black Mobile State Junior College and eventually became Bishop State Community College, began offering vocational, occupational, and technical programs to serve the city. In time Bishop State would become the most thoroughly integrated of Mobile's institutions of higher education. The crown jewel of the city's educational institutions, however, was the University of South Alabama. In 1989 ten thousand students, twenty-two hundred employees, and scores of alumni celebrated the university's twenty-fifth anniversary. Mobile paid tribute to an educational and cultural resource that, by then, was scattered across four campuses and pumping more than $250 million annually into the local economy. The university had replaced Brookley as the county's most potent economic force, and, unlike the former air force base, the university was locally, or at least regionally, controlled. Noted for its strong liberal arts and business programs, its music and drama productions, and its first-class medical school, it was still being led by its founder, Dr. Whiddon. USA had become as important to Mobile's progressive image as the city's much-heralded "business climate," and it was pointed to with pride in the promotional brochures sent out to anyone seeking information on the city.[49]

Indeed, it was the image of Mobile to which local leaders turned in their efforts to set the city back on the right course. Despite all the problems faced in the first half of the decade, Mobile remained one of America's most beautiful, most festive, and in many regards most tolerant cities. This open-mindedness was revealed in 1972 when, despite opposition from many local churches, voters approved legalized dog racing and two years later flocked to the new Mobile Greyhound Park to put down their bets. The track, Alabama's first legalized gambling venture in modern times, paid off royally, and the city added some $22 million to its coffers during the first six seasons. Dog racing also added another enticement for tourists, whose needs and appetites remained a high priority among city leaders. That same year the local legislative delegation persuaded the state to legalize the sale of draft beer in the city, no small matter to visitors (and locals) for whom a fried seafood platter and a frosted mug was about as close to heaven as one could get on earth. These changes did not mean that Mobile was about to go the way of New Orleans, though the fear of that happening became a staple sermon in many Pentecostal churches. Perhaps to prove that point, in 1980 city and county authorities used a local "red-light abatement ordinance" to close down suburban massage parlors that they feared would corrupt public morals. Tolerance would only go so far.[50]

During the 1970s and 1980s local police had more than their share of crimes that needed attention. Gone were the days when most arrests were for public drunkenness or disorderly conduct and when cases could be settled with the choice of "ten dollars or ten days." Gone, too, was the time when the most dangerous "controlled substance" was "poison shinny" run off in whiskey stills in nearby swamps. By the 1970s drugs, hard and soft, had come to town, and the rapid rise in robberies (twice the national average) was no coincidence. In 1972 the national crime rate was up 1 percent, whereas in Mobile it rose 6 percent, and despite efforts to reduce these figures, the trend continued. It was almost as if the corruption in city hall had spilled out into the streets, and though statistics revealed that most citizens lived safely in their homes and could walk their neighborhoods with nothing to fear, a nagging uncertainty grew with each new incident. Moreover, because so much of the crime seemed concentrated in the central city, Mobilians had yet another reason not to go downtown.[51]

Although these were rough times for the city, by 1982 the economy was beginning to turn around, and the *Press Register* could predict with more than the usual justification a year "full of promise." Construction on the I-10 and I-65 links across Mobile Bay and the Mobile-Tensaw Delta were finally completed and hailed as "an economic boom for southwest Alabama." Contributing to this confidence was news that several major oil companies had offered the state nearly $500 million just to explore potential oil fields in lower Mobile Bay, and forecasters predicted that what they discovered would erase all memories of recession. Furthermore, if news from the south was good, news from upriver was even better. Despite opposition from environmentalists and from budget cutters, the Tennessee-Tombigbee project was still under construction, and though supporters knew they would have to fight a yearly battle until it was completed, hopes were high that the Republican administration in Washington would support their efforts. Not content with just the Tenn-Tom, civic and business leaders pressed for federal money to deepen the ship channel to fifty-five feet and lobbied the navy to designate Mobile as a home port for a surface action fleet. Conservative economics and fiscal restraints notwithstanding, when there was pork being passed out, the City by the Bay wanted its share and more.[52]

The oil drilling, in which local businesspersons put so much hope, had been a long time in coming. Back in 1969 Mobil Oil had sought permission to begin operations, but local environmentalists filed suit to block exploration in the shallow, ecologically vulnerable waters of the south bay. For nine years the issue was tied up in court. Finally, in 1978 the company put up a $55 million bond and was given permission to sink one exploratory well. Natural gas was discovered, but permits for more drilling came slowly, so it was not until 1981–82 that work began again. Now the protests shifted from drilling to the question of the discharge of drilling and dredging wastes into the coastal waters. Environmentalists received little support from state or local officials because recession-battered Alabama badly needed the nearly $500 million in offshore oil leases that would come from the companies involved. Furthermore, area businesspersons were looking forward to $50 million from the leases that was promised to help deepen the Mobile ship channel. Thus, despite new lawsuits, the drilling and dumping continued.[53]

Still, state and local officials were not united on all matters pertaining to drilling in Mobile Bay. Back in 1839 the Alabama legislature had deeded some fifteen thousand acres of bottom lands between the mainland and Dauphin Island to one John Grant. He then excavated a ship channel connecting Mobile Bay with the Mississippi Sound. The property, known thereafter as Grant's Pass, was transferred from one owner to another until 1974, when more than seven thousand acres of it was given as an endowment to the University of South Alabama. Then gas and oil were discovered, and Mobilians rejoiced that their university would reap the windfall. Nonetheless, it was not to be. In 1983 Governor George Wallace's office announced that tidelands such as Grant's Pass belonged to Alabama and ordered the USA trustees to deed the property over to the state. Because most of the board had been appointed by Wallace, most observers expected them to cave in, but President Whiddon and the trustees refused. Stymied, Wallace called a special session and

A drilling platform one-half mile south of Dauphin Island, 1986.

Mobile Register.

insisted that the legislature reclaim the land. Mobilians rallied to USA's defense. The Chamber of Commerce protested, radio talk shows denounced the action, "busloads of angry south Alabamians" traveled to the capital, and local legislators tried to block the bill with a filibuster. All the actions were of no use, however. Although what the *Press Register* described as a "spiteful" attempt to give the governor the power to fire the trustees failed, Wallace's lieutenants "ramrodded" legislation through to take the land from the university.[54]

Still the university would not surrender and took the issue to court. The initial ruling went against USA, and while some officials prepared to appeal, others sought a compromise with the state. Negotiations went forward, and finally, in the fall of 1985, an agreement was reached. Under the plan the University of South Alabama Foundation would receive 28.5 percent of the lease and royalty money, which was estimated at more than $12 million from leases alone. The state would receive the remainder. The legislature approved the agreement, Wallace signed it, and the case was dropped. In the final analysis the impact the drilling had was much less than hoped. The state got all of the money from severance taxes and most of the income from royalties, so apart from a gas treatment facility near Bayou La Batre and plants near the Theodore industrial complex, the local economy received few benefits from the Mobile Bay and offshore oil fields. This was largely due to the fall in worldwide petroleum prices.[55]

The Grant's Pass compromise was not the only case in which Mobile had to accept less than what it expected. Soon after the announcement that Brookley was closing, efforts began to replace it with another military facility. The small Coast Guard presence helped, but through the 1970s the military in Mobile was conspicuous by its absence. Then in the early 1980s the Chamber of Commerce announced that it would begin an "aggressive" campaign to have Mobile designated as the home port for a carrier battle group or a surface action group. Other coastal cities were also in the running, and in 1987 the navy decided to divide the spoils among six gulf ports. Mobile received five of the group's twenty-seven ships, which translated into a total labor force of more than three thousand civilian and navy personnel and an annual payroll of $70.5 million. In 1988 ground was broken for the facility, and the folks in the Theodore area began looking forward to as many as five thousand new residents and to retail sales that would exceed $50 million. It was not Brookley Field, but it was an accomplishment to which the chamber could point with pride.[56]

The home port was not the only project about which bay area boosters could brag. In December 1984 an earthen barrier near Amory, Mississippi, was removed, and the Tennessee-Tombigbee Waterway was opened at last. It had not been an easy victory. Almost from the project's inception, environmentalists, fearing the impact on the land through which the waterway passed, sought to block the effort. Joined by railroad interests that feared competition from barge traffic, the opponents took their case all the way to the Supreme Court, where the Tenn-Tom project was upheld. Still, environmentalists and railroads were probably less of a danger to the undertaking than the congressional budget cutters who seemed to come out of the woodwork during the Reagan administration. Mobile's business community, true to the principle that federal money spent to promote the local economy was never pork, joined forces with state and local leaders from Mississippi and Tennessee and lobbied hard to keep the project afloat. It was nip and tuck at the end, but at last they won. On June 1, 1985, some sixty thousand people attended the formal dedication of the waterway, a celebration that included fireworks, festivities on the river, and, in good Mobile fashion, a Mardi Gras parade.[57]

Looking around, the sixty thousand who crowded into Mobile that June of 1985 could see evidence that the "downtown renaissance" promised so long ago was at last approaching. The hotel-office tower-mall complex announced in 1979 was now open as the Riverview Plaza, and a new municipal parking deck had been built to serve tourists who came in to see historic homes and gardens, conventioneers in town to meet and to be entertained, and locals who either worked downtown or were slowly coming back to see what visitors were seeing. New restaurants were opening; the historic Admiral Semmes Hotel had undergone an $18 million renovation and was charming guests once again; and other landmarks were being purchased, restored, and recycled as offices. So impressive was the turnaround that the *Press Register* boasted that "downtown Mobile [has been] rescued from decline." Preservationists, "savvy and seasoned" from their early bouts with developers and with city hall, now discovered allies where none existed before. Although the preservationists still had to fight to keep a proposed interstate spur along the waterfront from destroying significant historical buildings, by the end of the decade the victories were outnumbering defeats. Advocates of a revitalized downtown had finally realized that history attracts tourists, and local citizens were coming to realize the importance of preserving the city's architectural heritage and material culture. People began to move back into old neighborhoods around DeTonti Square, Oakleigh, and other historic districts. Historic homes ranging from stately mansions to simple "shotgun" houses became residences once again, and the central city slowly came back to life.[58]

After a weak and fitful start, the 1980s had proved very good for the city, and as citizens entered the century's last decade, observers declared that the "economic health of Mobile was at an all time high." Retail and real-estate sales were up, the seafood industry seemed to be making a comeback after years of near-depression conditions, construction at the home port was moving along well, and, most important of all, plans had been made, under the leadership of Mayor Arthur Outlaw, for a new $52 million, municipally owned, waterfront convention center. In Montgomery the governor praised the city for being "number 1 in the state for economic development." In 1990 Outlaw was defeated by Mike Dow in the mayoral election, and though soon after taking office Dow came into conflict with the city council over the financing of the convention complex, that project continued to move toward completion. It was a good thing, too, because during the national recession of 1991–92, Mobile's economy was, according to one account, "sustained by public works." Still, many in the city did not benefit from this activity. Poverty continued to plague Mobile's African American population, and the white (and some black) flight to the suburbs and across the bay to Baldwin County continued to drain the city of its middle class. Although some "urban pioneers" were returning to the city center and buying old houses and restoring them, everyone agreed more people were needed before the downtown district would become a community once again.[59]

The nascent downtown renaissance notwithstanding, soft spots in the city's economy still existed. The navy's $72 million home port, opened with such fanfare in 1992, closed two years later when the end of the cold war and congressional budget cutting made it expendable. Even more disappointing was the Tennessee-Tombigbee Waterway. The Tenn-Tom, which was supposed to make Mobile a

The Barnes double house at 305–307 N. Joachim in DeTonti Square is typical of southern antebellum urban dwellings. Restoration of the 1852 structure was completed in 1994.

Mobile Historic Development Commission.

A large crowd in Bienville Square enjoys a concert at Bayfest 1997.

Photograph by Catt Sirten.

major port in the trade between the heartland of America and the growing markets of Latin America, simply did not live up to expectations. In 1985, when the route opened, the U.S. Corps of Engineers projected that twenty-eight million tons of cargo would travel the waterway the next year and that by 1990 that figure would be more than thirty-two million tons. Nevertheless, in 1986 only 1.7 million tons made the trip, and by 1990 the tonnage was still under 5 million, all of which contributed to the port's declining national ranking. In 1946 Mobile's docks were rated sixth in the nation in handling of foreign freight tonnage. By 1950 it had dropped to ninth but still ranked ahead of Los Angeles and San Francisco. By 1994 tonnage at both of those ports had moved ahead of the City by the Bay. As a result the port of Mobile, which was considered "under-utilized" by the 1960 Area Audit, seemed destined to remain so. About the only bright spot in the picture was that the Tenn-Tom had unexpectedly provided recreation—fishing, waterskiing, yachting, camping, and other leisure activities—for some seven million people annually. Mobile benefited some from this, but not much.[60]

Yet, despite the problems facing them, Mobilians seem determined to keep the spirit of the city alive, to build on its festivals and events, and to add more each year. The Junior Miss Pageant and the Senior Bowl continue to draw national attention, and other celebrations, such as First Night Mobile, attract a mostly local or regional audience. Of them all, however, Mardi Gras still defines the city as nothing else did or could. Since World War II the carnival and its parades have expanded to take in the growing population of the city and the varied interests of its people. The celebration has weathered racial tensions that canceled black-sponsored events in the late 1960s, survived pressures from the hippie movement to turn some of the parades into counterculture "be-ins," accepted the ever-irreverent satire of the Comic Cowboys and groups such as the Order of the Mystic Moonpies, and yet managed to keep Mobile's festivities firmly its own and not a pale reflection of the more raunchy, riotous, goings-on over in New Orleans.

From the perspective of some of those involved in the planning and execution of the events, Mardi Gras continues to celebrate the closed society to which only the city's elites have access. From the standpoint of city leaders, the pre-Lenten festivities are a multimillion dollar bonanza for the local economy. From the perspective of the spectators, however, Mardi Gras provides a great show. Crowds drive into downtown on the interstate from the suburbs and farther, many (maybe most) in pick-ups. They park along Water Street and in lots near the parade routes, pull out the grills and ice chests, and have tailgate parties. Then they watch the parades, catch beads and moonpies thrown from the floats, have a good time, and go home. It is not New Orleans, where ladies routinely show their breasts to get maskers to throw them trinkets, and residents and visitors alike seem to prefer it that way.

Runners line up for the start of the twenty-first annual Azalea Trail Run in 1998. This event now attracts nearly nine thousand participants from around the globe.

Mobile Register.

Change might be in the wind, however. During the 1997 celebration a local correspondent reported how "one young woman . . . bared her charms last week while perched on her boy-friend's shoulders at Government and Joachim streets." No one knew if her tactic worked, but there was speculation that a policeman might be needed to control the crowd at that corner in the future.[61]

The goal, of course, is to attract Mardi Gras–size crowds to events during the rest of the year. To accomplish this the city and the Mobile Convention and Visitors Center have begun to sponsor a wide range of festivals. In 1990, First Night Mobile was organized to bring people downtown to celebrate New Year's Eve in an "alcohol free, family-oriented . . . atmosphere with safety for all." Evangelical Protestants seem to be one of this event's greatest supporters, and because this group has been one of the hardest to bring back to the central city, promoters hope that this effort will start a trend that will spread to others who have shied away from downtown. By the middle of the 1990s Mobile and the Mobile area could offer tourists some thirty festivals; nearly nine hundred amusement and recreational sites; ten theater companies; art and history museums; bookstores; and more than six hundred eating establishments. With so much to see and do, promoters, believing that the city's charms should not be limited just to visitors, instituted a "Be a Hometown Tourist" program designed to get local folks to discover once again the wonders of their city.[62]

As the century drew to an end all the work seemed to be paying off. In 1995

Hank Aaron Stadium, completed in 1997, is home to the Mobile Bay Bears. Mobilians have shown strong support for this Southern League double A team.

Mobile Register.

Mayor Mike Dow and Mobile County Commission president Sam Jones speak to the media about efforts to find funding for the ailing school system after a referendum to increase property taxes for school construction failed in 1999.

Mobile Register.

Mobile was named an "All America City" by the National Civic League for the way it had redirected its future after the economic problems, racial tensions, inner-city decline, and political scandals of the 1970s and 1980s. Although everyone admits that much work still needs to be accomplished before the city will be what its people want it to be, Mobilians seem to recognize that the redevelopment of downtown, especially the lower Dauphin Street entertainment district, and the preservation of historic homes and buildings across the city enrich the lives of all in the community, not just conventioneers and tourists. They also have a growing understanding that good schools, clean neighborhoods, and safe streets are a civic responsibility. Slowly, Mobile and Mobilians seem to be putting behind them some of the divisions of past decades. Disagreements still exist, and everyone knows they always will, but the spirit of cooperation that was once the city's hallmark is apparent again.[63]

Suggestions for Further Reading

Note: Unfortunately, the social and cultural development of modern Mobile has not received the scholarly attention that has been given to other periods in the city's history. As a result, there are few books and articles to which an interested reader may be directed. Of these, the following are recommended.

Cherney, Paul R. *Civic Index Review: Milestones in Community Development, Mobile, Alabama, 1960–1994.* Mobile: Mobile United, 1995. Although prepared as a document for community development purposes, it contains considerable information on events and activities in the city.

Dean, Wayne. *Mardi Gras: Mobile's Illogical Whoop-de-do.* Chicago: Adams Printing Company, 1971. Carnival activities as seen from the perspective of a man who has taken part.

Eichold, Samuel. *Without Malice: The One Hundredth Anniversary of the Comic Cowboys, 1884–1984.* Mobile: R. E. Publications, 1984. An inside look at a part of the carnival devoted to political issues.

Hearin, Emily Staples. *Let the Good Times Roll! Mobile, Mother of Mystics.* Mobile: E. S. Hearin and W. B. Taylor, 1996. Mardi Gras lovingly explained by an author with the social connections that give authority to her observations.

Kinser, Samuel. *Carnival, American Style: Mardi Gras at New Orleans and Mobile.* Chicago: University of Chicago Press, 1990. A comparative study of the celebration in the two cities that offers a good account of Mardi Gras as part of Mobile's social and cultural scene.

McLaurin, Melton, and Michael Thomason. *Mobile: The Life and Times of a Great Southern City.* Woodland Hills, Calif.: Windsor Publications, 1981. Although a general history of the city, it offers the best account of postwar Mobile available.

Epilogue

THE LONG HISTORY OF MOBILE, stretching three hundred years since permanent European settlement, has woven a fascinating, if occasionally enigmatic, tapestry for us. The "lessons" that this history teaches vary from person to person and from time to time, but we all can profit from its study. Certainly the contributors to this volume have reflected on the legacy of each respective era. Although some have emphasized one thing and others something else entirely, some strands exist, stretching from Bienville's time to our own, that bind our story together.

From its beginning the community we know as Mobile included and depended on people from a variety of racial and ethnic backgrounds. Bienville wanted to forge alliances with the Indians, or Native Americans, not just for reasons of French imperial policy but also because the small settlement needed all the help it could get just to survive. African slaves did not come here in great numbers at first, but they were an important part of the racial mix; over time, because there never were enough white women, racially mixed unions between Europeans, Indians, and Africans flourished and produced offspring. Some in authority spoke out against this practice, but it made no real difference. The struggling community did not have the luxury to exclude the intermixing, and it simply did not try. Perhaps of significance, no city walls have ever protected Mobile physically from the outside world except during the years of the American Civil War.

Throughout the eighteenth century, Mobile remained a small village on the fringes of European imperial ambition, often ignored or forgotten by the great powers that claimed her. The people here made their living off trade with the Indians. As the city's first century ended, settlers were beginning to challenge Native American control of the interior lands above the bay. Some of these newcomers made their way to Mobile and joined the mixture of people already here.

When Americans took Mobile from the weary Spanish in 1813 a revolution was already under way. Americans fought Indians for the land of Alabama, and by war's end the Native Americans were utterly vanquished. The newcomers flooded onto

Young man with snapper, circa 1895.

T. E. Armitstead Collection, USA Archives.

Indian lands and into Mobile. Many of the older Creole residents of the city fled to New Orleans, and though some eventually came back, the city's population rapidly became American dominated. The Americans were very interested in commerce—but with each other, not with Indians. Soon the little village of Mobile boomed as cotton began coming down the rivers. The colonial era seemed little more than a distant memory, but memories did remain, reinforced by the presence of families here before the Americans came.

Whether by Indian trade or cotton, Mobile lived off its port; that window on the world kept the community tied to the outside. Yankees, slaves at auction, famine Irish, Jewish merchants, sailors from the world over, and southerners as well were to be found here in the years before the Civil War. Some fine new buildings were built; many more—humble and grand—burned in periodic fires. Yellow fever epidemics darkened the doors of even the finest houses. Mobile was a place where just about everything could be found, a boom town of saloons and salons. It was a polyglot community, certainly by southern standards. By 1860 Mobile had nearly forty thousand residents of whom fifteen hundred or so were free people of color. The city held more free people of color on the eve of the Civil War than the total population of the eighteenth-century village.

Mobile was a tolerant town by standards of the day, but when a local bookseller tried to stock the newly published *Uncle Tom's Cabin* he was given twenty-four hours to leave, and he did. The diversity of antebellum Mobile, as great as it was, had not had enough time to coalesce into a community. There were several "Mobiles" divided by economics and ethnicity, and they would persist in the hard, lean years after the war.

Mobile was devastated by the war not physically, like Charleston, but economically. Its hopes of preeminence in the region, its challenge to New Orleans, were forever lost. The cotton trade never fully recovered, and the town limped toward century's end with little to show for the years after the war except bitterness over Reconstruction and civic bankruptcy.

As Mobile's second century drew to a close, prospects seemed to brighten. Hopes for an isthmian canal in central America and then a "splendid little war" with Spain (to quote John Hay, the U.S. secretary of state at the time) were largely responsible. A commercial community, Mobile looked for trade where it could find it and took pleasure in its developing Mardi Gras celebration and its network of ethnic and religious organizations. Dominated by a benign, if somewhat lethargic, elite, the city endeavored to replicate its climate in its approach to life. A languor that some associated with the distant Creole past seemed appropriate as the old city watched johnny-come-lately Birmingham surpass it on the eve of the celebration of its second century.

In honor of that event, Peter Joseph Hamilton, an ambitious and well-connected young attorney, undertook to tell the story of the city's first century. The result was his monumental *Colonial Mobile,* based on research in the primary sources to be found in archives in Quebec and metropolitan France. Brushing aside legend and myth, Hamilton looked at the reality of life in the days of Bienville and his immediate descendants. His fresh approach to history has caught the attention of many ever since, but none more than at the time he wrote. Among other things, he proved that Mobile's first years were spent at Twenty-Seven Mile Bluff, not along Dog River as many had long believed. *Colonial Mobile,* a fitting birthday present for the city, ushered in the new century with an air of scholarly optimism.

The search to diversify the economic foundations of Mobile, which began after the collapse of the city's cotton glory days, proceeded in earnest in the new century. If Mobile were to be a port town, then let it be a modern one, deep enough for any ship; if it were to be a shipbuilding town, then let it be one with first-rate yards. Mobile endeavored to improve the docks, modernize the streets, and build new suburbs served by fast electric street cars. Four- and five-story buildings were joined by twelve-story edifices. Even when World War I came Mobile pursued prosperity and commercial progress and did so successfully. The twenties proved to be the most prosperous peacetime decade in the city's history since the Civil War. With all the economic developments, including the new state docks, the Cochrane Bridge, the Waterman Steamship Company, and International Paper, Mobile's diverse population remained just that: diverse. Although conservative in many ways, Mobile rejected the Ku Klux Klan even as that organization virtually took over the state from 1917 to 1927. Alabama was dry, Mobile was wet; Prohibition found few supporters in the city, and toleration extended to saloons all over town.

The twenties ended with the city's tallest building, Merchants National Bank, under construction. Before the structure was finished the Great Depression struck, and years of hard times followed. As businesses closed and unemployment rose, the port city weathered the storm better than most of Alabama, but times were still hard. The promise of the twenties was gone, and despite all the New Deal programs, prosperity remained elusive until America began to rearm on the eve of World War II. That war would test Mobile's sense of tolerance more than any event in the city's long history. Lured by wartime jobs, people poured into the city and its suburbs, straining every institution to the breaking point. Schools, housing, medical care, and all public services barely managed to avoid collapse under the wartime burden. Many people were anxious for the war workers to leave once victory was achieved, but half of the "in-migrant army of industry" (to quote the 1943 film *War Town*) who came stayed when the conflict ended. Black and white, these new Mobilians were from the rural counties of south Alabama and Mississippi and the Florida panhandle. They were Protestants who sprang from stock far removed from Old Mobile. Yet, lured by economic opportunity, they stayed and in a generation became part of the fabric of the community. With the decision of many war workers to stay and with the expanding reliance on automobiles, Mobile grew geographically after the war. People no longer had to live a short walk or trolley or bus ride away from work, and suburbs sprang up around the old city. Responding to public sentiment, politicians built even more roads, and by the sixties Mobile was an automotive city sprawling across central Mobile County, surrounded by interstates and looking even to Baldwin County for suburban expansion.

While the Mobile metropolitan area grew, people began settling outside the city itself. Some moved west, and others went to the eastern shore of Mobile Bay. Towns such as Daphne, Fairhope, and Spanish Fort, which had once been distant summer resorts for Mobilians, now became suburbs. The chemical industry north of the city and the chemical/petroleum facilities to the south further dispersed the population. Urban renewal destroyed much of the old city's center, and many feared there would be no Mobile left to celebrate its tricentennial—only a sprawling mid-American suburban mass with the name but not the character of the old city.

In the 1960s and 1970s political scandals, racial tensions, and the loss of Brookley Air Force Base all seemed to exacerbate the old city's problems. The establishment of the University of South Alabama, which opened its medical school soon after the university's inception, was a bright spot, intellectually and economically. Still, situated on the city's western edge, miles from the old center of town, it seemed yet another example of a city fleeing its roots, physically and spiritually.

Perhaps paradoxically it was a controversy over yet another massive road project that highlighted the issues involved. Proponents of an interstate connector wanted to build a raised expressway from I-65 across Prichard, down to the state docks, and along the waterfront to connect with I-10 at the George C. Wallace Tunnel. Opponents fought the project, predicting irrevocable damage to many of the city's historical structures and charging that the highway would cut the center of town off from its port. Also, a proposal for a waterfront convention center was at issue. In a battle that pitted political powerhouses such as Mayor Arthur Outlaw against *Mobile Press Register* publisher William Hearin, preservation was pitted against progress.

The Cochrane-Africatown Bridge.

Photograph by Catt Sirten, 1999.

Many Mobilians had begun to revive older neighborhoods in the 1960s, and after two decades the historic preservation movement had reached into the old commercial district. Having rediscovered their historical roots, many Mobilians, new and old, fought against the raised expressway and for a downtown revitalization with a strong historic flavor.

The expressway project was modified, the convention center was built, and a series of downtown renovation projects, large and small, blossomed. The convention center, which Arthur Outlaw fought so successfully for, would subsequently be named in his honor. Most projects, with the notable exception of the City/County Government Plaza, had a strong sense of history about them. As the city moved toward its three hundredth birthday, the sprawling twin-county metropolitan area once again had a center, or at least the prospects of one. Appreciation of the port city's long history had led to a revival—and not just in bricks and mortar but in human terms as well.

After nine years of litigation in the *Bolden v. City of Mobile* case, the municipal government was changed from three commissioners to a mayor-council form in which at least three of the seven council seats would be elected by black majority districts. Inaugurated by Mayor Outlaw, the new system proved to work with little of the racial antagonism some had predicted. Drawing on the colonial heritage of tolerance, the earlier examples of men such as Mayor Joe Langan and John LeFlore, the new form of government worked well and harmoniously for the most part.

The twentieth century's last decade proved a time of growing prosperity for Mobile. Elected in 1989, Mayor Mike Dow initiated or approved a variety of civic projects, eventually known as the "String of Pearls," designed to advance further the revitalization of the city center. A founder of Quality Micro Systems (QMS), Dow was a charismatic, effective salesman for the city who saw its future in terms of broad-based citizen participation. Working with the council he supported a waterfront park; a maritime museum; the Exploreum; and relocation of the Museum of Mobile to the historic city hall. Many of these projects, and others besides, were fueled by a regard for the culture and history of the community seen in the broadest sense. Energetic and optimistic, Dow seemed to epitomize the renaissance spirit abroad in the old town on the eve of its three hundredth birthday.

Of course, serious problems remained. The city had an intolerably high rate of child poverty and of poverty in general. Many black Mobilians made great personal progress in the last years of the old century, but they also had the furthest to go. Despite the plea of the city's leadership to increase local funding, the countywide public school system was far below what even its most ardent supporters wanted it to be. Some of the migration to Baldwin County, which reached flood-tide proportions in the nineties, was fueled by a search for better schools. White flight from the city to suburbs had racial overtones, even if no one was ready to admit it in so many words. Nevertheless, no white neighborhood could be secure against an African American, Asian, or Latino moving in. It was after all, America. Still, reflecting the passage of time and the legacy of tolerance, new neighbors, regardless of race, were welcomed far more often than not. Prosperous, stable, integrated neighborhoods were no longer a novelty in Mobile.

For a community so passionately fond of its unique physical environment, Mobile's attention to the health of that environment has been one of its greatest failings. Industrial pollution, defended because it produced jobs, had gone unchecked until federal action late in the century. Paper mills, an alumina factory, and chemical and petrochemical plants fouled the air and water until gradually controls began to reverse the awful trend. Also the bay, as well as the gulf beyond, was suffering from additional agricultural and human waste pollution generated north of the city and carried to it by the state's vast river system.

Although improvements in some environmental areas have been marked, automotive exhaust gases, exacerbated by the uncontrolled sprawl of the metropolitan area, have increased. Clearly, Mobilians in the new century will have to make sacrifices and take steps to protect the environment that by and large they have refused to do before. When fishermen dare not eat what they catch, when the bay's fabled oysters are lethal, and when the mild gulf air is no longer breathable, it will be too late. Sadly, Mobilians have allowed that day to approach ominously close.

Mobile's long history shows the community's ability to weather the various storms that have swept over it, survive, and go forward. Since colonial times the transfer of Louisiana's capital to New Orleans, the loss of the antebellum cotton economy, wars, depressions, the closure of Brookley Field, and political scandals all have challenged the city. Mobile has persevered and grown despite these setbacks and emerged a stronger community in the process.

One final question everyone asks about Mobile, the city now on both sides of the bay, is, how much is unique and how much is a product of the larger American culture? No community lives in isolation from others, and certainly Mobile is no exception. Although many prefer to stress the uniqueness of the Mother of Mystics, the pervasiveness of the American way of life is evident everywhere. Perhaps one can say that Mobile is an American city with some distinctive accents, which are themselves a product of local history and experience. If one such accent is a love of Mardi Gras and another is a strong sense of social and political conservatism, then surely the long legacy of toleration is also present. Whether tolerant of religious belief, racial origin, or simple personal eccentricity, Mobilians in good times and bad have managed to build a resilient and humane legacy over three hundred years. On balance one can ask for no more.

Notes

Abbreviations

ADAH	Alabama Department of Archives and History, Montgomery, Alabama
BA	Barton Academy, Mobile, Alabama
CDC UM	Caldwell Delaney Collection, University of Mobile
GCHR	*Gulf Coast Historical Review*
GPO	Government Printing Office
MMA	Mobile Municipal Archives, Mobile, Alabama
MPL	Local History and Genealogy, Mobile Public Library, Mobile, Alabama
SHC UNC	Southern Historical Collection, University of North Carolina, Chapel Hill, North Carolina
USA	University of South Alabama Archives, Mobile, Alabama

1. Discovery, Exploration, and Colonization of Mobile Bay to 1711

1. Jerald T. Milanich, "Original Inhabitants," in *The New History of Florida,* ed. Michael Gannon (Gainesville: University Press of Florida, 1996), 1–14.

2. Ibid., 2–3.

3. Jerald T. Milanich, *Archaeology of Precolumbian Florida* (Gainesville: University Press of Florida, 1994).

4. Roman P. Chan, *The Olmec: Mother Culture of Mesoamerica* (New York: Rizzoli International Publications, 1989).

5. Tim S. Mistovich and Vernon James Knight Jr., *Cultural Resources Survey of Mobile Harbor, Alabama* (Moundville, Ala.: OSM Archaeological Consultants, 1983), 9–13.

6. Gunnar Thompson, "Counter Point: Egypt's Role in Ancient America," *Ancient American* 2, no. 8 (February 1995): 32–34; Lionel Casson, *Ships and Seafaring in Ancient Times* (Austin: University of Texas Press, 1994).

7. David Powel, *The Historie of Cambria* (London, 1584); Richard Hakluyt, *Principall Navigations* (London, 1589); Thomas Herbert, *A Relation of Some Yeares Travaile* (London, 1634).

8. Thomas Stephens, *Madoc: An Essay on the Discovery of America by Madoc ap Owen Gwynedd in the Twelvth Century* (London: Longmans, Green, 1893); David Williams, *Cymru ac America: Wales and America* (Cardiff: University of Wales Press, 1946).

9. William P. Cumming, *The Southeast in Early Maps* (Princeton: Princeton University Press, 1958), 1–3; Gonzalo Fernández de Oviedo y Valdés, *Historia General y Naturel de las Indias, Islas y Tierra-firme del Mar Océano* (Madrid, 1852), 2: 143.

10. Jean Delanglez, *El Rio del Espíritu Santo: An Essay on the Cartography of the Gulf Coast and the Adjacent Territory during the Sixteenth and Seventeenth Centuries* (New York: U.S. Catholic Historical Society, 1945), xi–xiii.

11. Robert S. Weddle, *Spanish Sea: The Gulf of Mexico in North American Discovery, 1500–1685* (College Station: Texas A and M University Press, 1985), 46–47, 187.

12. Martín Fernández de Navarette, *Colección de los Viajes . . . III* (Madrid, 1825–27), 148–49.

13. Frederick Peypus, *Praeclara Ferdiñandi Cortesü de Noua Maris Oceani Hyspanica Narratio* (Nuremberg, 1542).

14. *Relación que dio Alvar, nuñez cabeça de vaca . . .* (Zamora, 1542), 36–97; Martin A. Favata and José B. Fernández, eds., *La "Relación" o "Naufragios" de Álvar Nuñez Cabeza de Vaca* (Potomac: Scripta Humanistica, 1986).

15. Lawrence A. Clayton, Vernon James Knight Jr., and Edward C. Moore, eds., *The De Soto Chronicles,* 2 vols. (Tuscaloosa: University of Alabama Press, 1993).

16. Jay Higginbotham, "The Battle of Mauvila: Causes and Consequences," *Gulf Coast Historical Review* (hereafter *GCHR*) 6 (spring 1991): 19–33.

17. Ibid., 29, 33; Caleb Curren, *Archeology in the Mauvila Chiefdom: Native and Spanish Contacts during the Soto and Luna Expeditions* (Mobile: Mobile Historic Development Commission, 1992), 115–72.

18. Clayton, Knight, and Moore, *De Soto Chronicles,* 1: 28–31, 99–105; 2: 337–55, 546.

19. Mémoire de François Le Maire, Jan. 15, 1714, Archives Nationales, Colonies, C13C, 2, 109.

20. Relación que hizieron Guido de las Bazares y los pilotos . . . 1559, Archivo general de Indias, *Gobierno,* L. 12; Herbert Ingram Priestley, trans. and ed., *The Luna Papers: Documents Relating to the Expedition of Don Tristán de Luna y Arellano for the Conquest of La Florida in 1559–1561,* 2 vols. (De Land: Florida State Historical Society, 1928).

21. Ibid., 1: 178–84, 201–11; 2: 191–215, 308–17.

22. Ibid., 2: 296–318; Weddle, *Spanish Sea,* 265–83.

23. Robert S. Weddle, *Wilderness Manhunt: The Spanish Search for La Salle* (Austin: University of Texas Press, 1973).

24. Rivas and Iriarte to Aranda y Avellanda, May 27, 1687, Archivo general de Indias, *México,* L. 616.

25. Irving A. Leonard, *Documentos inéditos de Don Carlos Sigüenza y Góngora* (Mexico City: Biblioteca Mexicana, 1963); Irving A. Leonard, ed., *The Spanish Approach to Pensacola, 1689–1693* (Albuquerque: Quivira Society, 1939).

26. Robert S. Weddle, *The French Thorn: Rival Explorers in the Spanish Sea* (College Station: Texas A and M University Press, 1991), 3–9.

27. Marcel Giraud, *Histoire de La Louisiane Française: Le Règne de Louis XIV, 1698–1715* (Paris: Press Universitaires de France, 1953), 13–22 (both quotations).

28. Ibid., 23; Weddle, *French Thorn,* 119, 148–49; Arriola al virrey, Feb. 20, 1699, Archivo general de Indias, *México,* L. 618.

29. Richebourg G. McWilliams, trans. and ed., *Iberville's Gulf Journals* (Tuscaloosa: University of Alabama Press, 1981), 33–39, 92–105.

30. Ibid., 106–56; Journal de Levasseur-Russouelle *[sic]* du fort des Billochies, 1700, Bibliothèque Nationale, FF, 21690, f. 310–21v.

31. Giraud, *Histoire de La Louisiane,* 41–42; Gregory A. Waselkov, *Archaeology at the French Colonial Site of Old Mobile* (Mobile: University of South Alabama, 1991).

32. Patricia K. Galloway, ed., *La Salle and His Legacy: Frenchmen and Indians in the Lower Mississippi Valley* (Jackson: University Press of Mississippi, 1982), 146–75.

33. Charles Edwards O'Neill, *Church and State in French Colonial Louisiana: Policy and Politics to 1732* (New Haven: Yale University Press, 1966), 47–77.

34. Ibid., 48–49.

35. Jay Higginbotham, *Old Mobile: Fort Louis de la Louisiane, 1702–1711* (Tuscaloosa: University of Alabama Press, 1991), 132–42.

36. Ibid., 163–77.

37. Ibid., 173–74, 195–97.

38. Rueben Gold Thwaites, ed., *The Jesuit Relations and Allied Documents: Travels and Explorations of the Jesuit Missionaries in New France, 1610–1791* (Cleveland: Burrows, 1900), 66: 123–28; Min. to Bégon, May 25, 1707, Archives des Colonies, B 29, f. 259–59v.

39. Min. to Dartaguiette, June 20, 1707, Archives des Colonies, B 29, f. 284–85.

40. Interrogatoire des habitants, Feb. 25, 1708, Archives des Colonies, C13A, 2, f. 263–69.

41. Min. to Bienville, Archives des colonies, B 29, f. 263; Richebourg G. McWilliams, ed., *Fleur de Lys and Calumet* (Baton Rouge: Louisiana State University Press, 1953), 119–31.

42. La Vente [to Brisacier], July 4, 1708, Archives du Séminaire de Québec, Lettres, R 83.

43. La Salle to Min., Sept. 8, 1706, Archives des Colonies, C13A, 1, f. 545–47; Gregory C. Spies, *Retracing the Bounds of Old Mobile* (Mobile: Archaeotechnics Publishing Co., 1993).

44. Dartaguiette to Min., June 20, 1711, Archives des Colonies, C13A, 2, f. 643–44.

45. Giraud, *Histoire de la Louisiane Française,* 172–73.

46. Ibid., 173–74, 258; Plan de la ville et du Fort Louis, sur la Mobile, Archives Nationales, Section Outre-mer, DFC, 120B.

47. Bienville to Min., June 20, 1711, Archives des Colonies, C13B, 1, No. 11, f. 1–3.

2. Colonial Mobile, 1712–1813

1. Mathé Allain, *"Not Worth a Straw": French Colonial Policy and the Early Years of Louisiana* (Lafayette, La.: Center for Louisiana Studies, University of Southwestern Louisiana Press, 1988), 21.

2. Gwendolyn Midlo Hall, *Africans in Colonial Louisiana: The Development of Afro-Creole Culture in the Eighteenth Century* (Baton Rouge: Louisiana State University Press, 1992), 11.

3. O'Neill, *Church and State,* 91.

4. Allain, *"Not Worth a Straw,"* 67.

5. O'Neill, *Church and State,* 113.

6. Patricia Dillon Woods, *French-Indian Relations on the Southern Frontier, 1699–1762* (Ann Arbor, Mich.: UMI Research Press, 1980), 42.

7. Ibid., 92–93.

8. Carl A. Brasseaux, "The Moral Climate of French Colonial Louisiana, 1699–1763," *Louisiana History* 27 (winter 1986): 37.

9. Daniel H. Usner Jr., *Indians, Settlers and Slaves in a Frontier Exchange Economy: The Lower Mississippi Valley before 1783* (Chapel Hill: University of North Carolina Press, 1992), 94.

10. Woods, *French-Indian Relations,* 83–86.

11. Peter H. Wood, "The Changing Population of the Colonial South: An Overview by Race and Region, 1685–1790," in *Powhatan's Mantle: Indians in the Colonial Southeast,* ed. Peter H. Wood, Gregory A. Waselkov, and M. Thomas Hatley (Lincoln: University of Nebraska Press, 1989), 58.

12. Usner, *Indians, Settlers, and Slaves,* 60.

13. Woods, *French-Indian Relations,* 36.

14. Usner, *Indians, Settlers, and Slaves,* 65. On page 86 he adds, "By encouraging presentation of enemy scalps for rewards, colonial officials in North America actually helped transform a practice traditionally used by Indian warriors to display their individual courage and to acquire power from the enemy into an economic incentive to kill as many enemies as possible."

15. Ibid., 246; South Carolina in the 1730s and 1740s shipped an average of one hundred thousand skins a year. Katherine E. Holland Braund, *Deerskins and Duffels: The Creek Indian Trade with Anglo-America, 1685–1815* (Lincoln: University of Nebraska Press, 1993), 97–98; Hall, *Africans in Colonial Louisiana,* 11–12.

16. Usner, *Indians, Settlers, and Slaves,* 257–58.

17. Woods, *French-Indian Relations,* 88, 115–16; Jean-Bernard Bossu, *Jean-Bernard Bossu's Travels in the Interior of North America, 1751–1762,* trans. and ed. Seymour Feiler (Norman: University of Oklahoma Press, 1962), 127 (quotation).

18. Usner, *Indians, Settlers, and Slaves,* 89–90; Patricia Galloway, "'The Chief Who Is Your Father': Choctaw and French Views of the Diplomatic Relation," in *Powhatan's Mantle,* 254–78; Woods, *French-Indian Relations,* 163.

19. Hall, *Africans in Colonial Louisiana,* 6.

20. Ibid., 7; Usner, *Indians, Settlers, and Slaves,* 33, 35 (quotation).

21. Usner, *Indians, Settlers, and Slaves,* 33.

22. Ibid., 49.

23. Hall, *Africans in Colonial Louisiana,* 8.

24. Ibid., 26–27; Marcel Giraud, *A History of French Louisiana,* vol. 1, *The Reign of Louis XIV, 1698–1715,* trans. Joseph Lambert (Baton Rouge: Louisiana State University Press, 1974).

25. Milo B. Howard Jr. and Robert R. Rea, "Introduction," *The Memoire Justificatif of the Chevalier Montault de Montberaut* (Tuscaloosa: University of Alabama Press, 1965), 21–22, 89–90.

26. Usner, *Indians, Settlers, and Slaves,* 54.

27. Bossu, *Bossu's Travels,* 127.

28. Usner, *Indians, Settlers, and Slaves,* 222, 224.

29. Ibid., 59.

30. Ibid., 50, 55.

31. Allain, *"Not Worth a Straw,"* 86–87. One French visitor in the 1730s gossiped that Mobile's women were barren because of the local water and that they recovered on moving west. Le Page du Pratz, *The History of Louisiana,* ed. Joseph G. Tregle Jr. (1774; reprint, Baton Rouge: Louisiana State University Press, 1975), 152; Brasseaux, "Moral Climate," 34–37. On Louisiana Creole, see Hall, *Africans in Colonial Louisiana,* 187–200.

32. Usner, *Indians, Settlers, and Slaves,* 191–218.

33. Robert R. Rea, *Major Robert Farmar of Mobile* (Tuscaloosa: University of Alabama Press, 1990), 35.

34. J. Barton Starr, *Tories, Dons, and Rebels: The American Revolution in British West Florida* (Gainesville: University of Florida Press, 1976), 9.

35. Farmar acquired substantial holdings while he was governor and engaged in an unseemly battle for Dauphin Island with Montfort Browne. At his death he had fifty-seven slaves. Robin F. A. Fabel, *The Economy of British West Florida, 1763–1783* (Tuscaloosa: University of Alabama Press, 1988), 47.

36. Starr, *Tories, Dons, and Rebels,* 27.

37. Usner, *Indians, Settlers, and Slaves,* 130.

38. Rea, *Farmar,* 35.

39. Ibid., 35–36, 44, 46; Bernard Bailyn, *Voyagers to the West: A Passage in the Peopling of America on the Eve of the Revolution* (New York: Knopf, 1986), 477.

40. Robin F. A. Fabel, *Bombast and Broadsides: The Lives of George Johnstone* (Tuscaloosa: University of Alabama Press, 1987), 49.

41. Rea, *Farmar,* 41.

42. Fabel, *Bombast,* 33.

43. Rea, *Farmar,* 42.

44. Fabel, *Economy,* 13.

45. Fabel, *Bombast,* 52 (quotation); see also Usner, *Indians, Settlers, and Slaves,* 112; Gordon's estimate from Fabel, *Economy,* 18.

46. Starr, *Tories, Dons, and Rebels,* 48; Usner, *Indians, Settlers, and Slaves,* 112; Fabel, *Economy,* 15.

47. Mark Van Doren, ed., *Travels of William Bartram* (New York: Dover, 1955), 323.

48. Robert R. Rea, "Planters and Plantations in British West Florida," *Alabama Review* 29, no. 3 (July 1976): 230 (first quotation); Fabel, *Economy,* 19 (second quotation).

49. Fabel, *Economy,* 24, 26, 43.

50. Usner, *Indians, Settlers, and Slaves,* 137.

51. Ibid.

52. Fabel, *Bombast,* 27; Fabel, *Economy,* 48.

53. John D. Born, "Charles Strachan in Mobile: The Frontier Ordeal of a Scottish Factor, 1764–1768," *Alabama Historical Quarterly* 27 (1965): 23–42.

54. Starr, *Tories, Dons, and Rebels,* 23.

55. Fabel, *Economy,* 112–16; Usner, *Indians, Settlers, and Slaves,* 120.

56. Rea, "Planters," 231–32.

57. Ibid., 233–34.

58. Usner, *Indians, Settlers, and Slaves,* 119.

59. Rea, *Farmar,* 37.

60. Robert Rea, "Outpost of Empire: David Wedderburn at Mobile," *Alabama Review* 7 (July 1954): 223–25.

61. Usner, *Indians, Settlers, and Slaves,* 124–25.

62. Ibid., 127.

63. Ibid., 129.

64. Ibid., 143; Starr, *Tories, Dons, and Rebels,* 45.

65. Starr, *Tories, Dons, and Rebels,* 102–5. Starr adds that there is no evidence to support the claim that Willing was captured in Mobile.

66. Ibid., 133–34.

67. Ibid., 167.

68. Jack D. L. Holmes, "French and Spanish Military Units in the 1781 Pensacola Campaign," in *Anglo-Spanish Confrontation on the Gulf Coast during the American Revolution,* ed. William S. Coker and Robert R. Rea (Pensacola: Gulf Coast History and Humanities Conference, 1982), 146.

69. Starr, *Tories, Dons, and Rebels,* 169–71.

70. Ibid., 173.

71. Eric Beerman, "José de Ezpeleta: Alabama's First Spanish Commandant during the American Revolution," *Alabama Review* 29, no. 4 (October 1976): 253.

72. Ibid., 253.

73. Usner, *Indians, Settlers, and Slaves,* 144; David J. Weber, *The Spanish Frontier in North America* (New Haven: Yale University Press, 1992), 278–80.

74. William S. Coker and Thomas D. Watson, *Indian Traders of the Southeast Spanish Borderlands: Panton, Leslie and Company and John Forbes and Company, 1783–1847* (Pensacola: University of West Florida Press, 1986), 8–9, 12.

75. Ibid., 58.

76. Ibid., 60; David H. White, "The Indian Policy of Juan Vicente Folch, Governor of Spanish Mobile, 1787–1792," *Alabama Review* 28, no. 4 (October 1975): 270.

77. Coker and Watson, *Indian Traders,* 134, 365.

78. Ibid., 180; Thomas Marc Fiehrer, "The Barón de Carondelet as an Agent of Bourbon Reform: A Study of Spanish Colonial Administration in the Years of the French Revolution" (Ph.D. diss., Tulane University, 1977), 462.

79. Coker and Watson, *Indian Traders,* 157.

80. Ibid., 200; Fiehrer, "Barón de Carondelet," 536.

81. Coker and Watson, *Indian Traders,* 201.

82. Ibid.

83. Peter J. Hamilton, *Colonial Mobile* (Tuscaloosa: University of Alabama Press, 1976), 322; Fiehrer, "Barón de Carondelet," 571–72.

84. Lois Virginia Meacham Gould, "In Full Enjoyment of Their Liberty: The Free Women of Color of the Gulf Ports of New Orleans, Mobile, and Pensacola" (Ph.D. diss., Emory University, 1991), 39, 332; Jack D. L. Holmes, "The Role of Blacks in Spanish Alabama: The Mobile District, 1780–1813," *Alabama Historical Quarterly* 37 (spring 1975): 8.

85. Hamilton, *Colonial Mobile,* 332; Holmes, "Role of Blacks in Spanish Alabama," 6; see the map in Hamilton, *Colonial Mobile,* 435.

86. Hamilton, *Colonial Mobile,* 502.

87. Andrew Ellicott, *The Journal of Andrew Ellicott* (Chicago: Quadrangle Books, 1962), 211; Hamilton, *Colonial Mobile,* 501–10.

88. Hamilton, *Colonial Mobile,* 509.

89. Jack D. L. Holmes, "Alabama's Forgotten Settlers: Notes on the Spanish Mobile District, 1780–1813," *Alabama Historical Quarterly* 33 (summer 1971): 89, 90–91, 96.

90. Holmes, "Role of Blacks," 10.

91. Hall, *Africans in Colonial Louisiana,* 317–74.

92. Virginia Gould, "In Defense of Their Creole Culture," *GCHR* 9 (fall 1993): 30–31; Holmes, "Role of Blacks," 17; Virginia Gould, "The Free Creoles of Color of the Antebellum Gulf Ports of Mobile and Pensacola: A Struggle for the Middle Ground," in *Creoles of Color of the Gulf South,* ed. James H. Dormon (Knoxville: University of Tennessee Press, 1996), 28–46.

93. Gould, "Free Creoles of Color," 10–11.

94. Ibid., 15.

95. Frank Lawrence Owsley Jr. and Gene A. Smith, *Filibusters and Expansionists: Jeffersonian Manifest Destiny, 1800–1821* (Tuscaloosa: University of Alabama Press, 1997), 9, 23, 61.

96. Ibid., 12, 63.

97. Ibid., 65.

98. In Hamilton, *Colonial Mobile,* 404–7.

99. Owsley and Smith, *Filibusters and Expansionists,* 88–91; Henry DeLeon Southerland Jr. and Jerry Elijah Brown, *The Federal Road through Georgia, the Creek Nation and Alabama, 1806–1836* (Tuscaloosa: University of Alabama Press, 1989), 22–50.

100. Southerland and Brown, *Federal Road,* 22–50.

101. Ibid., 95; Coker and Watson, *Indian Traders,* 278, 284, 326.

3. Cotton City, 1813–1860

1. This essay comes from Harriet E. Amos [Doss], *Cotton City: Urban Development in Antebellum Mobile* (Tuscaloosa: University of Alabama Press, 1985). Citations to primary and secondary sources are included here in notes; *Niles' Register* 22 (1822): 96; *Mobile Regis-*

ter, February 7, 1822; Solomon Mordecai to Ellen Mordecai, August 20, 1829, Mordecai Family Papers, Southern Historical Collection, University of North Carolina, Chapel Hill, North Carolina (hereafter SHC UNC).

2. Karl Bernhard, *Travels through North America during the Years 1825 and 1826* (Philadelphia: Carey and Lea, 1828), 2: 39.

3. Clarence E. Carter, ed., *The Territorial Papers of the United States,* vol. 18, *The Territory of Alabama, 1817–1819* (Washington, D.C.: Government Printing Office (hereafter GPO), 1952): 124; Adam Hodgson, *Remarks during a Journey through North America in the Years 1819, 1820, and 1821, in a Series of Letters,* ed. Samuel Whiting (New York: Samuel Whiting, 1823), 1: 151–52.

4. Hamilton, *Colonial Mobile,* 410–13.

5. Ibid., 478–81.

6. Amos, *Cotton City,* 16.

7. [Edouard Delius], *Wander eines jungen Norddeutschen durch Portugal, Spanien, und Nord-Amerika in den Jahren 1827–1831,* ed. Georg Lotz (Hamburg: Heroldschen Buchhandlungen, 1834), 4: 111; Thomas Hamilton, *Men and Manners in America* (Philadelphia: Carey, Lea and Blanchard, 1833), 328; Carl David Arfwedson, *The United States and Canada in 1832, 1833, and 1834* (London: Richard Bentley, 1834), 2: 44; *Mobile Register,* quoted in *Niles' Register* 45 (1833): 165.

8. Amos, *Cotton City,* 17.

9. Ibid.

10. Ibid., 18, 20.

11. Charles S. Davis, *The Cotton Kingdom in Alabama* (Montgomery: Alabama State Department of Archives and History [hereafter ADAH], 1939), 42–43, 25.

12. Robert Greenhalgh Albion, *The Rise of New York Port [1815–1860]* (New York: Charles Scribner's Sons, 1939), 105.

13. Amos, *Cotton City,* 22.

14. *Hunt's Merchants' Magazine* 13 (1845): 417–18; 19 (1848): 593.

15. Joseph Holt Ingraham, ed., *The Sunny South, or, The Southerner at Home, Embracing Five Years' Experience of a Northern Governess in the Land of the Sugar and the Cotton* (Philadelphia: G. G. Evans, 1860), 502; John W. Oldmixon, *Transatlantic Wanderings, or, A Last Look at the United States* (London: George Routledge, 1855), 152; J. W. Hengiston [Siras Redding], "Mobile, Pensacola, and the Floridas: Cotton Barque to Cape Cod, along the Gulf Stream," *New Monthly Magazine* 98 (1853): 366; John S. C. Abbott, *South and North or, Impressions Received during a Trip to Cuba and the South* (New York: Abbey and Abbot, 1860), 91–92.

16. James C. Parker, "The Development of Port of Mobile, 1819–1936" (master's thesis, Auburn University, 1968), 44–45; Hamilton, *Colonial Mobile,* 473; *Hunt's Merchants' Magazine* 13 (1845): 417; 24 (1851): 266; T. C. Fay, *Mobile Directory or Strangers' Guide for 1839* (Mobile: R. R. Dade, 1839); *Directory for the City of Mobile, 1859* (Mobile: Farrow and Dennett, 1859); Peter Joseph Hamilton, *Mobile of the Five Flags: The Story of the River Basin and Coast about Mobile from the Earliest Times to the Present* (Mobile: Gill Printing Co., 1913), 270.

17. *Hunt's Merchants' Magazine* 24 (1851): 266; Parker, "Development of Port of Mobile," 46–47.

18. Ralph W. Haskins, "Planter and Cotton Factor in the Old South: Some Areas of Friction," *Agricultural History* 39 (1955): 1; Duke Goodman Circular, June 7, 1832, Singleton Family Papers, SHC UNC.

19. David R. Goldfield and Blaine A. Brownell, *Urban America: From Downtown to No Town* (Boston: Houghton Mifflin, 1979), 129–30; Robertson and Barnewall to Ogden Day and Co., May 11, 1821, Peters and Stebbins to Ogden Day and Co., March 14, April 7, 1821, R. Stebbins and Co. to Ogden Ferguson and Co., April 10, 1830, Ogden Ferguson and Day Papers, New York Historical Society, New York; Brown Brothers and Co. to John Boyd and Co., July 26, December 19, 1826, N. W. Collet to Stewart Brown, September 10, 1858, Brown Shipley and Co. to Brown Brothers and Co., May 12, 1859, Brown Brothers and Co. Letter Book, Brown Brothers Harriman and Co. Historical File, New York Historical Society; John R. Killick, "Risk Specialization and Profit in the Mercantile Sector of the Nineteenth Century Cotton Trade: Alexander Brown and Sons 1820–1880," *Business History* 16 (1974): 5; John R. Killick, "The Cotton Operations of Alexander Brown and Sons in the Deep South, 1820–1860," *Journal of Southern History* 43 (1977): 181; Edwin J. Perkins, *Financing Anglo-American Trade: The House of Brown, 1800–1880* (Cambridge: Harvard University Press, 1975), 97; Davis, *Cotton Kingdom in Alabama,* 153; R. G. Dun and Co. Credit Reports, Alabama, 17: 230, 180, 66, Baker Library, Graduate School of Business Administration, Harvard University.

20. William Garrett, *Reminiscences of Public Men in Alabama for Thirty Years* (Atlanta: Plantation Publishing Company Press, 1872), 726–27; Thomas McAdory Owen, *History of Alabama and Dictionary of Alabama Biography* (Chicago: S. J. Clarke Publishing Co., 1921), 4: 1790, 3: 78–79; Bernard Reynolds, *Sketches of Mobile, from 1814 to the Present Time* (Mobile: B. H. Richardson, 1868), 38.

21. Amos, *Cotton City,* 34–38.

22. Margaret Hall, *The Aristocratic Journey: Being the Outspoken Letters of Mrs. Basil Hall Written during a Fourteen Months' Sojourn in America, 1827–1828,* ed. Una Pope-Hennessy (New York: G. P. Putnam's Sons, 1931), 245–46; *Rowan's Mobile Directory and Commercial Supplement for 1850–51* (Mobile: Strickland and Benjamin, 1850), 17; *Niles' Register* 49 (1835): 241; James S. Buckingham, *The Slave States of America* (London: Fisher, Son, 1842), 1: 283; *Mobile Register,* April 6, 1836, February 28, 1840, November 23, 1842, August 1, 1843, November 8, 1845; Francis S. Bronson, *Bronson's Travelers' Directory, from New York to New Orleans, Embracing All the Most Important Routes, with a Condensed Outline of the Country through Which They Pass* (La Grange, Ga.: American Star Book Store, 1845), 20; J. G. Wariner to Edward A. Greene, March 13, 1842, Mobile Letters, SHC UNC; Alexander Mackay, *The Western World, or, Travels in the United States in 1846–47* (London: Richard Bentley, 1849), 3: 281; *Mobile Advertiser,* July 20, August 15, October 2, 1850; *Rowan's Directory 1850–51,* 22; Oldmixon, *Transatlantic Wanderings,* 153.

23. *Mobile Register,* December 13, 1852 (quotations), May 13, 1859; February 3, 1853, January 5, 1858; *Mobile Advertiser,* October 15, 1853.

24. *Mobile Register,* August 14, 1840; *Alabama Tribune* (Mobile), September 27, 1849.

25. Wayne Dean, *Mardi Gras: Mobile's Illogical Whoop-De-Doo, 1704–1970* (Chicago: Adams Printing Co., 1971), 9–10, 13–15, 27, 29, 220, 222; Solomon Mordecai to Ellen Mordecai, January 2, 1824, Mordecai Family Papers, SHC UNC; Jones Fuller to Anna Thomas, January 1, 1846, Mrs. Jones Fuller to Mrs. Ann Thomas, January 8, 1852, Fuller-Thomas Papers, Fuller Division, William R. Perkins Library, Duke University, Durham, North Carolina; Eliza Carolina (Burgwin) Clitherall Books, 3: 42–43, SHC UNC; *Mobile Register,* December 31, 1852, January 4, 1847; *Alabama Planter,* January 4, 1847; *Mobile Advertiser,* January 3, 1851. The custom of gentlemen calling on ladies of their acquaintance on New Year's Day was transplanted from New York City to Mobile.

26. Erwin Craighead, *From Mobile's Past: Sketches of Memorable People and Events* (Mobile: Powers Printing Co., 1925), 141; Corine Chadwick Stephens, "Madame Octavia Walton Le Vert" (master's thesis, University of Georgia, 1940), 81; Thomas Cooper De Leon, *Belles, Beaux, and Brains of the 60's* (New York: G. W. Dillingham, Co., 1907), 183; Louis Fitzgerald Tasistro, *Random Shots and Southern Breezes, Containing Critical Remarks on the Southern States and Southern Institutions, with Semi-Serious Observations on Men and Manners* (New York: Harper and Brothers, 1842), 1: 232; Thomas Low Nichols, *Forty Years of American Life* (London: J. Maxwell, 1864), 1: 225; Caldwell Delaney, *Remember Mobile,* 2d ed. (Mobile: Haunted Book Shop, 1969), 189–90; Frederika Bremer, *The Homes of the New World: Impressions of America,* trans. Mary Howitt (New York: Harper and Brothers, 1853), 2: 215; Virginia Tatnall Peacock, *Famous American Belles of the Nineteenth Century* (Philadelphia: J. B. Lippincott, 1901), 110–11.

27. Ingraham, *The Sunny South,* 507–8; Charles Mackay, *Life and Liberty in America, or, Sketches of a Tour in the United States and Canada, in 1857–8* (New York: Harper and Brothers, 1859), 180; Hiram Fuller, *Belle Brittan on a Tour, at Newport, and Here and There* (New York: Derby and Jackson, 1858), 112.

28. Amos, *Cotton City,* 47.

29. Ibid., 48.

30. Michael H. Frisch, *Town into City: Springfield, Massachusetts, and the Meaning of Community, 1840–1880* (Cambridge: Harvard University Press, 1971), 33–34; Erwin Craighead, *Mobile: Fact and Tradition, Noteworthy People and Events* (Mobile: Powers Printing Co., 1930), 355; *Mobile Register,* May 4, 1829.

31. Amos, *Cotton City,* 70, 75.

32. William H. Willis, "A Southern Traveler's Diary, 1840," *Publications of the Southern History Association* 8 (1904): 136–37.

33. Amos, *Cotton City,* 78–79.

34. Ibid., 79.

35. Ibid., 80.

36. *Mobile Advertiser,* November 29, 1851.

37. *Alabama Planter,* February 13, 1854; Robert C. Reinders, "Slavery in New Orleans in the Decade before the Civil War," in *Plantation, Town, and Country: Essays on the Local History of American Slave Society,* ed. Elinor Miller and Eugene D. Genovese (Urbana: University of Illinois Press, 1974), 370; Amos, *Cotton City,* 85.

38. Frederic Bancroft, *Slave-Trading in the Old South* (Baltimore: J. H. Furst, 1931), 298;

Charles S. Davis, *The Cotton Kingdom in Alabama* (ADAH, 1939), 76; James Benson Sellers, *Slavery in Alabama* (Tuscaloosa: University of Alabama Press, 1950), 160–61, 153–54; Hamilton, *Mobile of the Five Flags,* 284; Richard C. Wade, *Slavery in the Cities: The South, 1820–1860* (New York: Oxford University Press, 1964), 205.

39. Laura A. White, "The South in the 1850's As Seen by the British Consuls," *Journal of Southern History* 1 (1933): 38; Emma Langdon Roche, *Historic Sketches of the South* (New York: Knickerbocker Press, 1914), 71–72, 94–97; Harvey Wish, "The Revival of the African Slave Trade in the United States, 1856–1860," *Mississippi Valley Historical Review* 27 (1941): 584–85; Craighead, *Mobile: Fact and Tradition,* 357; National Archives Branch Depository, East Point, Ga., RG 21, Records of the District Courts of the United States, Final Record Book for the Southern District of Alabama, 1859–1860 (S-23), 270–74, and Box 46, Mobile, Mixed Cases, 1820–1860 (case no. 2619, *United States v. John M. Dabney,* and case no. 2621, *United States v. William Foster*). See also Roy Hoffman, "Search for a Slave Ship," *Mobile Register,* January 25, 1998.

40. Slave ownership for 1830, 1840, and 1860 was computed by the author from Bureau of the Census, *Fifth Census,* Slave Schedule, Alabama, microcopy, 19, roll 33, 361–71; Bureau of the Census, *Sixth Census,* Slave Schedule, Alabama, microcopy, 432, roll 22, 1–81; Bureau of the Census, *Eighth Census,* Slave Schedule, Alabama, microcopy, 653, roll 33, 25–74. For this study the number of individual slave holders was divided by the total free population to determine the extent of slave ownership. Calculations for 1850 are those of Alan Smith Thompson, "Mobile, Alabama, 1850–1861: Economic, Political, Physical, and Population Characteristics" (Ph.D. diss., University of Alabama, 1979), 306. His 8.6 percent is lower than Richard Wade's 11 percent in his *Slavery in the Cities,* 20.

41. Amos, *Cotton City,* 88–89.

42. Thompson, "Mobile," 255.

43. Dorman, "Free Negro," 23–24; Sellers, *Slavery in Alabama,* 383–86; Ira Berlin, *Slaves without Masters: The Free Negro in the Antebellum South* (New York: Pantheon Books, 1974), 108–9, 131–32, 278; Marilyn Mannhard, "The Free People of Color in Antebellum Mobile County, Alabama" (master's thesis, University of South Alabama, 1982), 5–6; Diane Lee Shelley, "The Effects of Increasing Racism on the Creole Colored in Three Gulf Coast Cities between 1803 and 1860" (master's thesis, University of West Florida, 1971), 22; Melvin Lee Ross, Jr., "Blacks, Mulattoes, and Creoles in Mobile, during the European and American Periods" (master's thesis, Purdue University, 1971), 45–46.

44. Amos, *Cotton City,* 94–95.

45. Ibid., 112–13.

46. Ibid., 116–17.

47. Ibid., 123–24.

48. Aldermen's Minutes, April 3, 1841, Local History and Genealogy, Mobile Public Library, Mobile, Alabama (hereafter MPL).

49. Amos, *Cotton City,* 135–36.

50. Harry A. Toulmin, *A Digest of Laws of the State of Alabama* (Cahawba, Alabama: Ginn and Curtis, 1823), 790; Alexander McKinstry, *The Code of Ordinances of the City of Mobile, with the Charter and an Appendix* (Mobile: S. H. Goetzel, 1859), 29.

51. Amos, *Cotton City,* 166–67.

52. Ibid., 167.

53. David R. Goldfield, "The Urban South: A Regional Framework," *American Historical Review* 86 (1981): 1021, 1025.

54. Amos, *Cotton City,* 168.

55. Ibid., 169–70; McKinstry, *Code of Ordinances of Mobile,* 152–53.

56. *Mobile Register,* September 4, 1835, January 30, 1850; Eliza Horton to Gustavus Horton Jr., April 25, 1852, Horton Family Papers, in the possession of Miss Edith Richards, Mobile.

57. Amos, *Cotton City,* 172–76.

58. *Mobile Register,* January 15, 1850.

59. Amos, *Cotton City,* 176–78.

60. Ibid., 179–88.

61. School Commissioners' Minutes, October 30, 1852, May 3, 1854 (quotation), November 18, 1852, January 5, 1853, January 5, 1859, Barton Academy, Mobile, Alabama (hereafter BA).

62. School Commissioners' Minutes, December 8, 1852, February 2, 1853, June 4, 1856, August 18, 1856, September 3, 1856, March 7, 1860, BA; Francis Butler Simkins and Charles Pierce Roland, *A History of the South,* 4th ed. (New York: Alfred A. Knopf, 1972), 174; Berlin, *Slaves without Masters,* 305–6.

63. School Commissioners' Minutes, October 9, 1852, October 24, 1856, November 3, 1858, June 1, 1859, BA; Oscar Hugh Lipscomb, "The Administration of Michael Portier, Vicar Apostolic of Alabama and the Floridas, 1825–1829, and First Bishop of Mobile, 1829–1859" (Ph.D. diss., Catholic University of America, 1963), 328, 251; *Eighth Census,* Free Population Schedule, Alabama, microcopy 653, roll 17, 117–20; *Mobile Register,* March 21, 1858.

64. Amos, *Cotton City,* 191–92.

65. Ibid., 193.

66. Ibid., 195–96; *Hunt's Merchants' Magazine* 19 (1848): 580; *Mobile Register,* November 27, 1847.

67. Clement Eaton, *The Growth of Southern Civilization, 1790–1860* (New York: Harper and Brothers, 1961), 210; Allan Pred, *Urban Growth and City-Systems in the United States, 1840–1860* (Cambridge: Harvard University Press, 1980), 45–47, 116.

68. Amos, *Cotton City,* 207.

69. Ibid., 207, 209.

70. *Alabama Planter,* October 27, 1851.

71. *Alabama Tribune,* March 25, 1849; *Mobile Advertiser,* June 12, 1850; *Alabama Planter,* September 25, 1852.

72. Amos, *Cotton City,* 211–12; *Alabama Tribune,* May 3, 1849, June 8, 1850; *Mobile Register,* December 6, 1850; *Mobile Advertiser,* November 29, 1851; *Alabama Planter,* May 29, 1852, January 17, 1853; *DeBow's Review* 22 (1857): 111; *Mobile Advertiser,* May 30, 1850, September 26, 1851.

73. Amos, *Cotton City,* 216, 218.

74. Ibid., 221.

75. Ibid.

76. Ibid., 222.

77. Ibid., 222–23.

78. Ibid., 225–26. Figures compiled from "An Indexed Catalogue of Minute Entries Concerning Naturalization in the Courts of Mobile County, Alabama, 1833–1907," prepared from the original records by the Municipal Court Records Project of the Works Progress Administration, MPL.

79. Thompson, "Mobile," 167.

80. Aldermen's Minutes, 1852, 265; 1854, 463, 489–91, 507, MPL; Lipscomb, "Administration of Michael Portier," 261–63, 265. The Sisters of Charity then founded their own hospital, Providence Infirmary.

81. Amos, *Cotton City,* 226–29; W. Darrell Overdyke, *The Know-Nothing Party in the South* (Baton Rouge: Louisiana State University Press, 1950), 63; *Mobile Advertiser,* April 22 and 24, 1855, May 16 and 17, 1855, July 6 and 20, 1855, July 21 and 25 and August 1 and 7, 1855, December 4, 1855; *Mobile Register,* December 4, 1855; William M. Dowell to F. I. Levert, December 8, 1855, Levert Family Papers, SHC UNC; *Mobile Advertiser,* November 9, 1855; McKinstry, *Code,* 292.

82. Lewy Dorman, *Party Politics in Alabama from 1815 through 1860* (Wetumpka, Alabama: Wetumpka Printing Co., 1935), 126; Overdyke, *The Know-Nothing Party,* 125; Aldermen's Minutes, July 15, 1856, MPL; *Mobile Register,* July 2 and 16, 1856, December 1, 3–4, 1858.

83. Amos, *Cotton City,* 230.

84. *Mobile Register,* February 5, 1858.

85. Paul Ravesies, *Scenes and Settlers of Alabama* (Mobile: n.p., 1885), 37.

86. Amos, *Cotton City,* 232.

87. Ibid.

88. Ibid., 239.

4. Secession, War, and Reconstruction, 1850–1874

1. Thompson, "Mobile," 134–40; James H. Beam, "Mobile and the Southern Question: Public Debate over the Slavery Controversy of 1850" (master's thesis, University of South Alabama, 1994), 62–63.

2. J. Mills Thornton, *Politics and Power in a Slave Society: Alabama, 1800–1860* (Baton Rouge: Louisiana State University Press, 1978), 254–58.

3. *Mobile Daily Register,* November 23, December 4, 1850; Robert Saunders Jr., *John Archibald Campbell: Southern Moderate* (Tuscaloosa: University of Alabama Press, 1997), 97; Beam, "Mobile and the Southern Question," 63.

4. Beam, "Mobile and the Southern Question," 41–46.

5. *Mobile Daily Register,* December 7, 1850.

6. Beam, "Mobile and the Southern Question," 66–67.

7. By 1860 almost 75 percent of the unskilled work force in Mobile consisted of Irish

immigrants. This growth had begun in the late 1840s. Amos, *Cotton City,* 92; Thompson, "Mobile," 263; Ira Berlin and Herbert G. Gutman, "Natives and Immigrants, Free Men and Slaves: Urban Workingmen in the Antebellum American South," *American Historical Review* 88 (December 1983): 1177–81.

8. Josiah Nott, "An Essay on the Natural History of Mankind Viewed in Connection with Negro Slavery: Delivered before the Southern Rights Association, 14th December, 1850" (Mobile: Sage, Thompson and Co., Printers, 1851); Reginald Horsman, *Josiah Nott of Mobile: Southerner, Physician, and Racial Theorist* (Baton Rouge: Louisiana State University Press, 1987), 122–26; George M. Fredrickson, *The Black Image in the White Mind: The Debate on Afro-American Character and Destiny, 1817–1914* (Hanover, N.H.: Wesleyan University Press, 1971), ch. 3.

9. Thompson, "Mobile," 150–51; Beam, "Mobile and the Southern Question," 57; Fredrickson, *Black Image in the White Mind,* ch. 3.

10. For a thorough analysis of these ideas in the regional context see Laurence Shore, *Southern Capitalists: The Ideological Leadership of an Elite, 1832–1885* (Chapel Hill: University of North Carolina Press, 1986), ch. 2.

11. Thornton, *Politics and Power,* 355.

12. Augusta Jane Evans, *Macaria, or, Altars of Sacrifice* (Baton Rouge: Louisiana State University Press, 1992), 220. Samuel Cummins, who was in Mobile in 1855, described politics in the city as "native against foreign." Cummins to William T. Lewis, July 1855, Lewis Papers, ADAH.

13. *Mobile Daily Register,* November 8, 1855.

14. Ibid., February 19, April 24, 1856.

15. *Ordinances of the City of Mobile, 1859;* Thompson, "Mobile," 170–71.

16. Thompson, "Mobile," 174–75; Amos, *Cotton City,* 230–33.

17. Amos, *Cotton City,* 236. A few historians have equated anti-Breckenridge votes with anti-secessionist sentiment. In the case of Mobile, it was true that opponents of secession under any circumstances voted for Douglas or Bell. Future events indicate, however, that although the majority hoped Lincoln would be defeated and the need for secession thereby removed, they also saw Lincoln's election as sufficient cause for secession.

18. William L. Barney, *The Secessionist Impulse: Alabama and Mississippi in 1860* (Princeton: Princeton University Press, 1974), 216, 252–53 (all quotations).

19. Amos, *Cotton City,* 235–38.

20. William R. Smith, *The History and Debates of the Convention of the People of Alabama* (1861; reprint, Spartanburg, S.C.: Reprint Co., 1975), 223–26.

21. Shorter to P. Hamilton, May 4, 1863, Shorter to A. Powell, May 12, 1863, both in Shorter Papers, ADAH; Arthur W. Bergeron Jr., *Confederate Mobile* (Jackson: University Press of Mississippi, 1991), 45–91.

22. Bergeron, *Confederate Mobile,* 47.

23. Ibid., 92–101.

24. W. C. Corson, *Two Months In the Confederate States: An Englishman's Travels through the South,* ed. Benjamin H. Trask (Baton Rouge: Louisiana State University Press, 1996),

52–56. Comparisons of southerner and northerner emphasizing northern materialism found their way into numerous editorials and letters to the editor. Some examples may be found in the *Mobile Advertiser and Register,* October 6, 13 and November 11, 26, 1863. See also Drew Gilpen Faust, *The Creation of Confederate Nationalism: Ideology and Identity in the Civil War South* (Baton Rouge: Louisiana State University Press, 1988), 44.

25. *Acts of the General Assembly of Alabama,* 2d sess., 1862.

26. *Mobile Advertiser and Register,* June 26, 1863.

27. Bergeron, *Confederate Mobile,* 101–2; Malcolm C. McMillan, *The Disintegration of a Confederate State: Three Governors and Alabama's Wartime Homefront, 1861–1865* (Macon: Mercer University Press, 1986), 45–46.

28. *Mobile Advertiser and Register,* October 1, 1863; Bergeron, *Confederate Mobile,* 102.

29. *Mobile Advertiser and Register,* November 14, 1863. Bergeron states that needs were met (Bergeron, *Confederate Mobile,* 102).

30. *Mobile Advertiser and Register,* October 30, 1863.

31. Ibid., October 6, 1863.

32. Ibid., October 28, 1863 (quotations). Faust argues that criticism of speculation revealed the strength of premarket values and their influence on opposition to the war. The thrust of the discussion in Mobile does not seem to reflect premarket values so much as differences over how markets should operate, the extent to which the distribution of goods in the community should be governed by market forces alone, and the responsibility of the government in eliminating "monopolies." Faust, *Creation of Confederate Nationalism,* 52. The debate was very much a part of Jacksonian America; see Lawrence Frederick Kohl, *The Politics of Individualism: Parties and the American Character in the Jacksonian Era* (New York: Oxford University Press, 1989), ch. 5; John Ashworth, *Slavery, Capitalism, and Politics in the Antebellum Republic,* vol. 1, *Commerce and Compromise, 1820–1850* (Cambridge: Cambridge University Press, 1995): 307–15.

33. *Mobile Advertiser and Register,* November 1, 1863.

34. Ibid., November 15, 19, 24, 26, 27, 1863.

35. Ibid., November 1, 1863.

36. Shorter to T. A. Hamilton, February 28, 1863, Shorter Papers, ADAH; *Acts of the General Assembly,* 3d sess., 1863; *Mobile Advertiser and Register,* November 1, 1863.

37. Shorter to Lt. General John Pemberton, February 28, 1863, Shorter Papers, ADAH; *Mobile Advertiser and Register,* October 30, November 15, December 14, 1863.

38. *Mobile Advertiser and Register,* January 5, 1864.

39. Ibid., March 20, 1864.

40. Evans, *Macaria;* Drew Gilpin Faust, *Southern Stories: Slaveholders in Peace and War* (Columbia: University of Missouri Press, 1992), 168.

41. For the best detailed account of the Battle of Mobile Bay see Bergeron, *Confederate Mobile,* ch. 11.

42. Don H. Doyle, *New Men, New Cities, New South: Atlanta, Nashville, Charleston, Mobile, 1860–1910* (Chapel Hill: University of North Carolina Press, 1990), 62.

43. Ibid.

44. Russell E. Belous, "The Diary of Ann Quigley," *GCHR* 4 (spring 1989): 96–97; Bergeron, *Confederate Mobile,* 192.

45. David Roediger, *The Wages of Whiteness: Race and the Making of the American Working Class* (New York: Verso, 1991), 68, 145.

46. Belous, "Diary of Ann Quigley," 97–98; Walter Lynwood Fleming, *Civil War and Reconstruction in Alabama* (Gloucester, Mass.: Peter Smith, 1949), 437–38; Michael W. Fitzgerald, *The Union League Movement in the Deep South: Politics and Agricultural Change during Reconstruction* (Baton Rouge: Louisiana State University Press, 1989), 178–79.

47. Joseph Edgar Brent, "No Surrender: Mobile, Alabama during Presidential Reconstruction, 1865–67" (master's thesis, University of South Alabama, 1988), 26–27.

48. Ibid., 23–26.

49. Ibid., 18–27.

50. Ibid., 35–39.

51. *Mobile Nationalist,* March 15, 1866; Fleming, *Civil War and Reconstruction,* 379–82; Laura Edwards, *Gendered Strife and Confusion: The Political Culture of Reconstruction* (Urbana: University of Illinois Press, 1997), 43–53.

52. *Mobile Nationalist,* January 18, March 8, 1866.

53. There are several variations in the spelling of Chief Slac's name. Doyle, *New Men, New Cities,* 250–51; Robert Overton, "The Volunteer Fire Companies' Role in Redemption" (seminar paper, University of South Alabama, 1996), 7.

54. Fleming, *Civil War and Reconstruction,* 636–52; John Calametti, "The Catholic Church in Mobile during Reconstruction, 1865–1877" (master's thesis, University of South Alabama, 1993), 73–85 (quote 73).

55. Calametti, "Catholic Church in Mobile," 84–85; Fleming, *Civil War and Reconstruction,* 458–61.

56. *Mobile Nationalist,* March 15, 1866; Peter Joseph Hamilton, *The Reconstruction Period,* vol. 16 of *The History of North America* (Philadelphia: George Barrie and Sons, 1905), 121. Hamilton was a resident of Mobile during Reconstruction and here reported events he witnessed.

57. Eric Foner, *Reconstruction: America's Unfinished Revolution, 1863–1877* (New York: Harper and Row, 1988), 276.

58. Fitzgerald, *Union League,* 178–79; Brent, "No Surrender," 60, 242.

59. *Mobile Advertiser and Register,* April 20, 21, 1867.

60. Quote is from Brent, "No Surrender"; Fitzgerald, *Union League,* 180–81.

61. Brent, "No Surrender," 63–66; Fitzgerald, *Union League,* 182–83.

62. *Mobile Advertiser and Register,* May 5, 7, 1867.

63. Brent, "No Surrender," 72–73.

64. Ibid., 74–75; Fitzgerald, *Union League,* 184.

65. Billy G. Hinson, "The Beginning of Military Reconstruction in Mobile, Alabama, May–November, 1867," *GCHR* 9 (fall 1993): 65–69; Harriet E. Amos [Doss], "Trials of a Unionist: Gustavus Horton, Military Mayor of Mobile during Reconstruction," *GCHR* 4 (spring 1989): 139–41; Fitzgerald, *Union League,* 189.

66. Amos, "Trials of a Unionist," 142–43.

67. Ibid., 143; Fleming, *Civil War and Reconstruction;* Billy Hinson, "The Rise and Fall of the Republicans in Mobile, Alabama, May–November, 1867," paper in the possession of the author.

68. Michael W. Fitzgerald, "Railroad Subsidies and Black Aspirations: The Politics of Economic Development in Reconstruction Mobile, 1865–1879," *Civil War History* 39 (1993): 242–49.

69. Ibid., 251–54.

70. Ibid., 253. On Democratic strategy see Michael Perman, *The Road to Redemption* (Chapel Hill: University of North Carolina Press, 1984), 76–79.

71. *Mobile Daily Register,* July 25, 1874.

72. Ibid., July 4, 1874. On fears of miscegenation see Peter W. Bardaglio, *Reconstructing the Household: Families, Sex and the Law in the Nineteenth Century South* (Chapel Hill: University of North Carolina Press, 1995), 176–85.

5. The New South Era in Mobile, 1875–1900

1. House, *Affairs in Alabama,* 43d Cong., 2d sess., 1875, Report No. 202 (Washington, D.C.: GPO, 1875).

2. Ibid.

3. Thomas M. Owen, *History of Alabama and Dictionary of Alabama Biography* (Spartanburg, S.C.: Reprint Co., 1978), 2: 876; *Mobile Weekly Register,* August 11, 1877; *Mobile Daily Register,* August 12, 1877.

4. Doyle, *New Men, New Cities,* 70.

5. *Mobile Register,* June 11, 1905.

6. Ibid.

7. Peter J. Hamilton, *The Charter and Code of Ordinances of 1897 of the City of Mobile* (Mobile: City of Mobile, 1897), 402–4.

8. Nicholas H. Holmes Jr., "Mobile's City Hall," *Alabama Heritage* 6 (fall 1987): 2–15.

9. *Mobile Register,* June 11, 1905.

10. Ibid.

11. Owen, *History of Alabama,* 3: 139.

12. *Mobile Register,* December 6, 1877.

13. Owen, *History of Alabama,* 2: 512; *Mobile Register,* January 11, 1977.

14. Doyle, *New Men, New Cities,* 70; *Mobile Register,* December 6, 1877; Charles G. Summersell, *Mobile: History of a Seaport Town* (Tuscaloosa: University of Alabama Press, 1949), 45.

15. *Mobile Register,* January 13, 1879.

16. Ibid., June 11, 1905.

17. *Acts of the General Assembly of Alabama,* session of 1878–1879, 381–92; *Mobile Register,* June 11, 1905.

18. *Mobile Register,* June 11, 1905.

19. Ibid.

20. Ibid., January 24, 1879.

21. Ibid., February 19, 1879.

22. Ibid., March 3, 12, 1879.

23. Ibid., March 18, 20, 1879.

24. Owen, *History of Alabama,* 3: 1310.

25. *Mobile Register,* February 15, 1879.

26. Ibid., June 11, 1905.

27. Ibid.

28. Ibid.

29. Ibid.; Alma E. Berkstresser, "Mobile, Alabama, in the 1880s" (master's thesis, University of Alabama, 1951), 21–27.

30. Berkstresser, "Mobile, Alabama," 21–27.

31. Ibid.

32. Ibid.

33. Ibid., 34–35.

34. Ibid.; Owen, *History of Alabama,* 2: 1024.

35. Owen, *History of Alabama,* 4: 1435.

36. George H. Ewert, "Old Times Will Come Again: The Municipal Market System of Mobile, Alabama, 1888–1901" (master's thesis, University of South Alabama, 1993), 1–9.

37. Ibid., 40.

38. Ibid., 42–45.

39. Ibid., 66–71.

40. Ibid., 104.

41. Berkstresser, "Mobile, Alabama," 84–86.

42. Charles E. Mathews, *Highlights of 100 Years in Mobile, 1865–1965* (Mobile: First National Bank of Mobile, 1965), 35–37.

43. Ibid.

44. Ibid.

45. *Mobile Register,* August 21, 1889.

46. Ibid.

47. Ibid.

48. Ibid.

49. Inez P. Langham, "Politics in Mobile County from 1890 to 1900" (master's thesis, University of Alabama, 1947), 88.

50. Ibid., 104–10.

51. Summersell, *History of a Seaport Town,* 45–46.

52. Doyle, *New Men, New Cities,* 68.

53. Berkstresser, "Mobile, Alabama," 112–19; Mathews, *Highlights of 100 Years,* 37–38.

54. Melton McLaurin and Michael Thomason, *Mobile: The Life and Times of a Great Southern City* (Woodland Hills, Calif.: Windsor Publications, Inc., 1981), 80.

55. Summersell, *History of a Seaport Town,* 47–49.

56. Berkstresser, "Mobile, Alabama," 199–201.

57. McLaurin and Thomason, *Mobile,* 82–83, 95.

58. Ibid., 81; Doyle, *New Men, New Cities,* 249–59.

59. Doyle, *New Men, New Cities,* 249–59.

60. *Mobile Register,* September 1, 1910; *The Alabama Negro, 1863–1946* (Mobile: Gulf Publishing Co., n.d.)

61. Berkstresser, "Mobile, Alabama," 96–98.

62. Ibid., 92–96.

6. Progress versus Tradition in Mobile, 1900–1920

1. The most detailed study of Mobile in this period is David E. Alsobrook, "Alabama's Port City: Mobile during the Progressive Era, 1896–1917" (Ph.D. diss., Auburn University, 1982). This first-rate study laid the foundation for much of the analysis in my essay, and I owe a debt to Alsobrook for his thorough research.

2. Bureau of the Census, *Thirteenth Census of the United States, 1910, vol. 2, Population Reports by States* (Washington, D.C.: GPO, 1913), Alabama Table 1, and Bureau of the Census, "Fourteenth Census: Preliminary Assessment of Population," undated, RG 6, Records of the Commission Government, 1911–1985, Series 79 (United States Government), File 2185, Mobile Municipal Archives, Mobile, Alabama (hereafter MMA).

3. Doyle, *New Men, New Cities,* 113.

4. *Mobile Register,* September 26, 1906.

5. The petition and a short commentary about it can be found in Tennant S. McWilliams, "Petition for Expansion: Mobile Businessmen and the Cuban Crisis," *Alabama Review* 28, no. 1 (January 1975): 58–62.

6. *Mobile Register,* April 22, 1898; Alsobrook, "Alabama's Port City," 94.

7. C. Vann Woodward, *Origins of the New South, 1877–1913* (Baton Rouge: Louisiana State University Press, 1951), 125; Robert Wolley, "The Development of Gulf Ports," *American Review of Reviews* (February 1906), 192–93. For biographical information see Owen, *History of Alabama,* 3: 88–92.

8. Wolley, "Development of Gulf Ports;" Alsobrook, "Alabama's Port City," 290.

9. *Mobile Register,* September 1, 1904. Suburban development was segregated during this period.

10. For the best brief biography see Tennant S. McWilliams, "The City of Mobile, the South, and Richard V. Taylor," *Alabama Review* 46, no. 3 (July 1993): 163–79 (quotation 166).

11. Ibid., 172, 177.

12. "The Oldest Institution in Mobile," unpublished manuscript, "The Tablet," April 1961, and "Brief History of the Mobile City Hospital," unpublished manuscript, Mobile-Hospitals-City Hospital File, MPL. The dispensary closed in 1920.

13. Alsobrook, "Alabama's Port City," 45.

14. *Mobile Register,* February 2, 1910.

15. Mathews, *Highlights of 100 Years,* 60, 69.

16. Ibid., 69; *New York Times,* September 29, 1906, 1; *Mobile Register,* October 2, 1906; "Mobile Panics," unpublished manuscript, Mobile-Panics File, Vertical Files, MPL.

17. *Mobile Register,* June 16, 1910, September 1, 1911. In 1912, after a merger with other groups, the group renamed itself the Mobile Chamber of Commerce and Business League.

18. David E. Alsobrook, "Mobile's Forgotten Progressive: A. N. Johnson, Editor and Entrepreneur," *Alabama Review* 32, no. 3 (July 1979): 188–202; Alsobrook, "Alabama's Port City," 203.

19. Alsobrook, "Mobile's Forgotten Progressive," 189; Christopher M. Scribner, "Nashville Offers Opportunity: *The Nashville Globe* and Business as a Means of Uplift, 1900–1917," *Tennessee Historical Quarterly* 54, no. 1 (spring 1995): 54–67.

20. *Southern Watchman,* May 11, 1901; Alsobrook, "Alabama's Port City," 199, 208.

21. Alsobrook, "Alabama's Port City," 118, 128–29.

22. Ibid., 143–51; *Mobile Register,* November 5, 1902. For a similar story in another city see Scribner, "Nashville."

23. Alsobrook, "Alabama's Port City," 158.

24. Bureau of the Census, *Twelfth Census of the United States, 1900, Vol. 2, Population, Pt. 2* (Washington, D.C.: GPO, 1902), Table 55; *Thirteenth Census, Vol. 2,* Alabama Table 1; Bureau of the Census, *Fourteenth Census, Vol. 2, Population General Report* (Washington, D.C.: GPO, 1923), Table 19. Also see "Brief History," MPL.

25. Emmet J. Scott, "Additional Letters of Negro Migrants of 1916–1918," *Journal of Negro History* 4 (October 1919): 446.

26. Alsobrook, "Alabama's Port City," 180–93.

27. Ibid., 72, 315.

28. Don H. Doyle, "Urbanization and Southern Culture" (paper read at the Southern Historical Association, St. Louis, Mo., 1978); Mayor to Frederick Rex, August 31, 1917, RG 6, Series 35 (Entertainment), File 1863, MMA.

29. Unidentified news clipping, March 10, 1918; *Mobile Press,* October 13, 1972, January 26, 1930; *Mobile Press Register,* July 26, 1976; Gary Higginbotham, "Bears," unpublished manuscript, all in Mobile-Sports-Baseball File, Vertical File, MPL.

30. In 1890 Catholics made up one-fourth of church members in the city (and more than 40 percent of white churchgoers). In 1920 this had declined to about one-third of white churchgoers, still a substantial minority. The city had about ten thousand Catholics, who attended nine churches. Bureau of the Census, *Report on Statistics of Churches in the United States at the Eleventh Census: 1890* (Washington, D.C.: GPO, 1894), 112–13; Bureau of the Census, *Religious Bodies 1926: Summary and Detailed Tables* (Washington, D.C.: GPO, 1930), Table 31.

31. *Mobile Register,* December 24, October 8, 1910.

32. Other provisions stipulated that Alabama's governor would appoint two of the first three commissioners; their elections would be staggered; they would serve for two years; and voters could use the preferential ballot.

33. *Mobile Register,* June 7, 1911.

34. Harry Pillans to Price Williams, October 21, 1915, and Laz Schwarz to Morris Metz, October 27, 1915, RG 6, Series 21 (Commissioners Correspondence), File 684, MMA.

35. "150 Year Celebration of the U.S. Marine Hospital," County Board of Health—Mobile File, Vertical Files, MPL.

36. *Mobile Register,* September 1, 1911; unidentified newspaper clipping in Mobile-Women File, and "The Oldest Institution in Mobile," Mobile-Hospitals-City Hospital File, Vertical Files, MPL.

37. Mayor to Jas. A. Reed, June 20, 1917, RG 6, Series 79, File 960, MMA.

38. Harry Pillans to John McDuffie, June 2, 1920, and Pat Lyons to War Labor Policies Board, November 26, 1918, RG 6, Series 79, File 960, MMA; Bureau of the Census, "Fourteenth Census."

39. See Bureau of the Census, *Thirteenth Census of the United States, 1910, Vol. 9, Manufactures* (Washington, D.C.: GPO, 1913), Table 1, and Bureau of the Census, *Fourteenth Census of the United States, 1920, Vol. 9, Manufactures* (Washington, D.C.: GPO, 1923), Table 31.

40. *Mobile Register,* undated, and Chairman to Harry Pillans, February 6, 1918, RG 6, Series 79, File 960, MMA. Hundreds of Mobilians served in the war, and seventy-one died in combat. Kenneth T. Jackson, *The Ku Klux Klan in the City, 1915–1930* (New York: Oxford University Press, 1967), 7, 83.

41. George Crawford to John McDuffie, June 1, 1920, RG 6, Series 79, File 2185, MMA.

42. Alsobrook, "Alabama's Port City," 294–97; Mayor to Wm. Redfield, September 3, 1917, and undated resolution in RG 6, Series 79, File 960, MMA.

7. Mobile during the Interwar Years

1. *Mobile Register,* January 1, 9, 10, 13, 20, 1920.

2. McLaurin and Thomason, *Mobile,* 105–8.

3. *Mobile Register,* section K, clipping in Mobile-History-1918-Present, Vertical Files, MPL.

4. Alabama State Docks, *Port of Mobile Handbook* (Birmingham: Vulcan Printing and Lithographing, 1964), 6.

5. *Mobile Register,* January 1, 1920.

6. McLaurin and Thomason, *Mobile,* 110.

7. Mathews, *Highlights of 100 Years,* 89; *Mobile Register,* September 19, 1923.

8. Alabama State Docks, *Port,* 6.

9. Summersell, *History of a Seaport Town,* 63.

10. Bennett A. Ryan et al., *An Economic History of Mobile: Selected Periods* (Mobile: University of South Alabama, 1974), 45, 60–61.

11. J. G. White Engineering Corporation, *Economic Survey of the State Docks, Port of Mobile: Report to State of Alabama Department of State Docks and Terminals, Mobile, Alabama, 1945* (New York: J. G. White Engineering Corporation, 1945), 58–60, 70.

12. Bureau of Business Research, *Mobile: An Economic Appraisal* (Mobile: Gill Printing Co., 1949), 19.

13. Maritime History, ADDSCO, History, Vertical Files, University of South Alabama Archives, Mobile, Alabama (hereafter USA).

14. Maritime History, Waterman Steamship Corporation, History, Vertical Files, USA.

15. Mathews, *Highlights of 100 Years,* 96–97.

16. Ryan et al., *Economic History,* 47.

17. First National Bank, *Highlights of 75 Years in Mobile* (Mobile: First National Bank of Mobile, 1940), 97, 115.

18. Ryan et al., *Economic History,* 46.

19. First National Bank, *Highlights of 75 Years,* 115.

20. *Mobile Register,* July 1, 2, 1925.

21. Mathews, *Highlights of 100 Years,* 95–96.

22. *Mobile Daily Register,* June 4, 15, 1927.

23. Mathews, *Highlights of 100 Years,* 95.

24. Jay Higginbotham, *The First National Bank of Mobile, 1865–1978* (Mobile: First National Bank, 1978), 114.

25. Mathews, *Highlights of 100 Years,* 95–96.

26. Higginbotham, *First National Bank,* 146–48.

27. Dianne Bryars, "Bankhead Tunnel Project Wasn't Pork-Barrel Fantasy," *Azalea City News and Review,* November 4, 1987.

28. Ryan et al., *Economic History,* 44, 53–54.

29. Bureau of Business Research, *Mobile,* 41; J. G. White Engineering Corporation, *Economic Survey,* 32, 33.

30. "Steady Gain In Tonnage Reflected in Auditor's Report," *Port of Mobile News* 13 (February 1939): 7.

31. Bureau of Business Research, *Mobile,* 47, 59–65, 82.

32. Jean King, ed., *Delchamps: 50 Golden Years, 1921–1971* (Mobile: Delchamps, 1971), 4–5, 7.

33. Higginbotham, *First National Bank,* 125; *Mobile Daily Register,* February 23, 1929.

34. Bernadette Kuehn Loftin, "A Social History of the Mid-Gulf South (Panama City-Mobile) 1930–1950" (Ph.D. diss., University of Southern Mississippi, 1971), 240–41; *Report of the Board of Commissioners of the City of Mobile for the Year Ending September 30, 1933,* 40, MMA; Loftin, "Social History," 241; Higginbotham, *First National Bank,* 125.

35. Mathews, *Highlights of 100 Years,* 102; *Mobile Daily Register,* August 26, 30, 1929.

36. Mathews, *Highlights of 100 Years,* 102–3, 106; Jay Higginbotham, *Mobile: City by the Bay* (Mobile: Azalea City Printers, 1968), 162–66; Loftin, "Social History," 241; Mathews, *Highlights of 100 Years,* 107; Bureau of Business Research, *Mobile,* 171.

37. Loftin, "Social History," 242.

38. McLaurin and Thomason, *Mobile,* 113.

39. *Mobile Daily Register,* October 25, 30, 1929; Loftin, "Social History," 224.

40. Loftin, "Social History," 235; Bureau of Business Research, *Mobile,* 34, 74.

41. *Mobile Register,* March 1–5, 1933; Mathews, *Highlights of 100 Years,* 109.

42. *Mobile Register,* March 9–10, 12, 15, 1933.

43. Loftin, "Social History," 225, 232–33.

44. South Central Bell Telephone Company, *Hello, Mobile: The History of Telephone Service in Mobile, Alabama, 1879–1979* (Mobile: South Central Bell, 1980), 2, 8, 10, 15, 22–24; *Mobile City Directory* (Richmond: R. L. Polk and Co., 1929), 13.

45. Bill Kirven, "Great Depression was Devastating to Mobile," newspaper clipping in Depression, Vertical Files, Caldwell Delaney Collection, University of Mobile, Mobile, Alabama (hereafter CDC UM); Loftin, "Social History," 259.

46. McLaurin and Thomason, *Mobile,* 114.

47. Armistead Leake to Mr. Harry Fisher, December 6, 1935, RG 23, Series 9, Box 1, MMA.

48. Commissioner Cecil F. Bates to Mr. L. C. Levine, May 2, 1936, and Armistead Leake, District Director, to Mr. Henry Hiden, Jr., Project Engineer, Works Project Administration, Mobile, Alabama, October 7, 1936, File 1349, Federal Grants, Community Centers, 1935–1940, RG 6, Series 38, Box 1, MMA.

49. J. A. Walker to Mr. Chas. A. Baumhauer, August 2, 1935, and Emma Roche to Honorable Cecil Bates, Mayor, March 20, 1940, and November 3, 1938, File 1349, Federal Grants, Art Projects No. 165–1–61–288, Work Project No. 6453, 1935–1943, RG 6, Series 38, MMA. The *Clotilda* actually arrived in Mobile in July 1860, and the Africans on board were not legally slaves, though they were treated as such.

50. Owen Moore, Superintendent, Work Project No. 4962, to Mr. Cecil Bates, May 1, 1939; Mrs. Eunice Howsman to Mayor Chas. A. Baumhauer, March 20, 1939; Commissioner to Mrs. Eunice Howsman, September 22, 1938; Mrs. Willie G. Smith, Sup't, Housekeeping Aide Project No. 4864, to Mr. Cecil Bates, March 29, 1939; Cecile De Ornellas to Hon. Chas. A. Baumhauer, April 10, 1939; Chairman E. Roy Albright, Mobile County Board, Department of Public Welfare, to Board of Commissioners, Mobile, January 25, 1937, all in File 1349, Federal Grants, Beautification Projects, 1937–1942, RG 6, Series 38, MMA; Mayor to Mrs. Eunice Howsman, September 19, 1939, File 1349, Federal Grants, Toy/Furniture Projects, 1939–1943, RG 6, Series 38, MMA; Kirven, "Great Depression"; *Mobile Press Register,* June 4, 1961; First National Bank, *Highlights of 75 Years,* 113–15; Robert Allen Kennedy, "A History and Survey of Community Music in Mobile, Alabama" (Ed.D. diss., Florida State University, 1960), 141.

51. E. B. Bowman, Director District No. 2, National Youth Administration, to Mr. Charles A. Baumhauer, April 27, 1937, File 1349, Federal Grants, Street Markers/Numbers, 1933–1942; Bess Brininstool, Executive Secretary YWCA, to Hon. Cecil F. Bates, May 2, 1935, File 1349, Federal Grants, YWCA: Tennis Courts, 1934–1938, RG 6, Series 38, Box 1, MMA; Kirven, "Great Depression"; Billy G. Hinson, "The Civilian Conservation Corps in Mobile County," *Alabama Review* 45 (October 1992): 244–45, 248.

52. *Mobile Register,* January 17, 1920; Higginbotham, *Mobile,* 142–43; Arthur Howington, "John Barley Corn Subdued: The Enforcement of Prohibition in Alabama," *Alabama Review* 23, no. 3 (July 1970): 224.

53. *Mobile Register,* January 2, 1927; Higginbotham, *Mobile,* 141–42.

54. *Mobile Register,* January 18, February 9, 1920; Loftin, "Social History," 227–28, 237; William J. Lovett Jr., *Mardi Gras In Mobile* (Mobile: Mobile Area Mardi Gras Association, 1980), 6, 10.

55. Caldwell Delaney to Mr. Mike Keough, November 15, 1991, "Baseball," Vertical Files, CDC UM; Gary J. Higginbotham, comp., "Mobile Professional Baseball Yearly Standings,"

unpublished manuscript, n.d., Vertical Files, MPL; Proclamation by H. Pillans, Mayor, April 7, 1920, File 1673, Mobile Baseball Association, RG 6, Series 35, Box 1, MMA; *Mobile Register,* April 14, 15, 1920; *Mobile Press Register,* October 21, 1993.

56. *Mobile Register,* clipping transcribed by Charles Dickson in Baseball, Babe Ruth/Hartwell Field, Vertical Files, USA; *Azalea City News and Review,* March 31–April 10, 1983.

57. C. E. Lanham to Mayor R. V. Taylor, Commissioner H. T. Hartwell, and Commissioner Geo. E. Crawford, April 9, 1923, File 1673; George H. Blalack to Mr. R. V. Taylor, January 24, 1922, and Commissioner Taylor to Mr. George H. Blalack, January 25, 1922, File 1741, Twilight Baseball League, both in Mobile Baseball Association, RG 6, Series 35, Box 1, MMA.

58. H. C. Farley to Mr. Harry T. Hartwell, October 1, 1921; Charles W. Greer to Mr. Cecil Bates, February 22, 1928; C. B. Arendall to Mayor Leon Schwarz, July 2, 1928; C. B. Arendall to the Board of Commissioners, May 10, 1928; Mayor to Paul Ford, February 10, 1921; Paul Ford to Savini Films, Feb. 10, 1921; Paul Ford to Commissioners, Feb. 11, 1921; Savini to H. Pillans, February 12, 1921; W. O. Mann to Honorable City Commissioners, March 7, 1921; and Resolution of Board of Commissioners, March 15, 1921, File 1683, Theaters: Motion Picture, RG 6, Series 35, Box 1, MMA; Emily Staples Hearin, *Downtown Goes Uptown* (Mobile: First Southern Federal Savings and Loan Association, 1983), 62, 64.

59. Frances Beverley, "Musical Mobile," in Mobile-Music (through 1949), Musicians, Vertical Files, MPL; Alabama Federation of Music Clubs, *Musical Alabama* (Montgomery: Paragon Press, 1925), 31, 35; Kennedy, "History of Community Music," 132–49.

60. Beverley, "Musical Mobile."

61. *Mobile Register,* March 6, 11, 1921.

62. *Mobile City Directory* (Birmingham: R. L. Polk and Co., 1920), 76; (1924), 8; (1926), 8; (1927), 10; (1939), 1053. According to a telephone interview of June 2, 1998, with Ben Jones, general manager of the Country Club of Mobile, the golf course was relocated to Springhill in 1914.

63. *Report of the Board of Commissioners of the City of Mobile for the Year Ending September 30, 1926* (Mobile: Wood Printing Co., 1926), 10; (1929), 23; (1931), 25.

64. John Hall Jacobs, "Historical Background and Legal Basis of the Mobile Public Library," unpublished manuscript, 1954, and "MPL History," unpublished manuscript, n.d., History, 1925–30, Vertical Files, MPL; *Mobile Register,* December 10, 15, 1925.

65. *Mobile City Directory* (1920), 65–66; (1933), 17; (1939), 1101.

66. Bama Wathan Watson, "The History of Barton Academy" (master's thesis, University of Alabama, 1949), 37; *Mobile Register,* January 14–15, 23, 1920, and January 23–24, 1923; School Commissioners' Minutes, March 10, 1920, March 22, 1922, April 12, 1922, BA; ibid., November 22, 27, 1922, December 19, 1922; ibid., November 22, 24, 1922, January 10, 29, 1923.

67. School Commissioners' Minutes, November 22 and December 19, 1922, August 1, 1923. For more details and evidence on the site dispute see the following school board minutes in 1923: July 25, August 1 and 8, September 12 and 26, October 24 and 31, and December 12, BA; *Mobile News-Item,* April 13, 14, 1923; School Commissioners' Minutes, June 25, 1924, BA; M. Aline Bright, ed., *Barton Centennial, 1836–1936* (Mobile: Heiter-Starke Printing Co., 1936), 20, BA.

68. "History of Murphy High School," unpublished manuscript, n.d., in Murphy High School Barton Academy, Vertical Files, BA; *Mobile Register,* April 13, 1926; Watson, "History of Barton Academy," 37, 39; *Mobile Register,* April 13, 1926.

69. Henry C. Williams, "A History of Mobile County Training School, 1859–1977" in African-American Education: Mobile County Training School, Vertical Files, USA.

70. Elisa Baldwin, "A Guide to the Papers of John L. LeFlore, 1926–1976," manuscript, 1996, USA, 3; J. L. LeFlore to Mr. Schuyler, Dec. 16, 1931; to Executive Department, Louisville and Nashville RR Co., January 6, 1930; to Roy Wilkins, March 2, 1936; to Walter White, March 11, 1936; to William Pickens, March 11, 1936; to James E. Gayle, April 14, 1936; to H. C. Ball, April 16, 1936; to Capt. Archie L. Weaver, April 18, 1936; to Walter White, January 13, 1934; to Stanton Curtis, January 5, 1935; to Chief Executive Officer, Southern Railway System, January 5, 1935, all in NAACP Files: Mobile Branch Correspondence, 1930–37; to George S. Schuyler, January 24, 1935, Personal Correspondence, 1935 July–December, John L. LeFlore Papers, USA; Loftin, "Social History," 252–53; "Background Information on Persons For Whom Our Schools Are Named," an unpublished compilation, March 1994, in Know Your Schools, Vertical Files, BA (last quotation).

71. Paulette Davis-Horton, *Avenue . . . The Place, The People, The Memories* (Mobile: Horton Inc., 1991), 126, 129, 151–53, 155, 163–65, 169, 179, 187, 235–36, 264.

72. A Resolution Certified by S. H. Hendrix, City Clerk, Mobile, July 3, 1928, Map Book 2, 30; Inspectors Certificate to the Judge of Probate of the County of Mobile, April 2, 1930, Deed Book 228, 12, Probate Office, Mobile County Court House.

73. C. A. Mohr, M.D., County Health Officer to Senator John Craft, July 8, 1927, Annexation: A-B, RG 6, Series 7, Box 1, MMA; *Mobile Register,* April 12, July 10, 19, 23, 27, 1931; Territory Proposed to Be Annexed to the City of Mobile, Map Book 3, 18, Probate Office; Map of Mobile, September 1931, MMA; Growth by Annexation Map, Urban Development Department, City of Mobile; *Acts of the Legislature of Alabama of Local and Special Character,* Session of 1931, Act No. 531 (Birmingham: Birmingham Printing Co, 1931), 255–56; *City Directory,* 1923, 1930, 1931, 1939; Mobile Chamber of Commerce, "Industrial Report of Mobile, Alabama," prepared for the Mobile Public Library by the Mobile Chamber of Commerce, 1931, 4.

8. Mobile and World War II, 1940–1945

1. Neil R. McMillen, ed., *Remaking Dixie: The Impact of World War II on the American South* (Jackson: University of Mississippi Press, 1997).

2. Edward Boykin, *Everything's Made for Love in This Man's World: Vignettes from the Life of Frank W. Boykin* (Mobile: n.p., 1973), 59.

3. George Pearce, "Pensacola, the Deep Water Harbor of the Gulf: Its Development, 1825–1930," *GCHR* 5 (spring 1990): 128–39; Harriet Amos [Doss], "From Old to New South Trade in Mobile, 1850–1900," *GCHR* 5 (spring 1990): 114–27; the state docks coal and bulk handling equipment could unload six hundred tons an hour. The port of Mobile had progressed from twenty-fifth to sixteenth busiest port in the country by 1941. See defense

industry issue of *Alabama: The News Magazine of the Deep South* 6 (December 22, 1941): 23–27, 41–43, 58–63; *Mobile Register,* December 30, 1945.

4. Alabama State Military Department, Office of the Adjutant General, *Quadrennial Report of the Adjutant General for the Four Year Period Ending September 30, 1942* (n.p., n.d.), 151–53; *Mobile Register,* September 17, October 16–17, 25, 30, 1940.

5. Frank Dixon to (Mississippi Governor) Paul Johnson, June 23, 1941, in Dixon Files, Selective Service System Organization, Regulations, ADAH.

6. *Mobile Register,* December 5, 1945; William Coker, lecture, Auburn University, April 11, 1991; Joseph Langan, telephone interview, January 3, 1992; E. B. Peebles, telephone interview, April 14, 1992.

7. Alabama Military Department, *Quadrennial Report,* 96.

8. Inventory, Frank William Boykin, 1885–1969, Alabama Congressman Collection, 1911–1973, ADAH. For many amusing Boykinisms, see Boykin, *Everything's Made for Love.* In the early 1960s, Boykin resigned from Congress upon his conviction for conspiracy to commit fraud and for violating conflict of interest laws. See Virginia Van der Veer Hamilton, *Alabama: A Bicentennial History* (New York: W. W. Norton, 1977), 35; *Mobile Register,* March 31, 1941.

9. Boykin, *Everything's Made for Love,* 102–3; *Birmingham Age-Herald,* September 21, 1940; *Mobile Register,* June 19, 1955. On a visit to inspect a prospective site for the Southeastern Air Depot, General Hap Arnold praised Representative Frank Boykin and Senator Lister Hill for bringing the advantages of the Mobile area to his attention. See account of Arnold's remark to a Rotary luncheon and to a Mobile Chamber of Commerce dinner in *Mobile Register,* December 8, 1939, July 18, 1950.

10. *Mobile Register,* September 10, October 4, 1940, November 16, 1941.

11. Telephone interview with W. J. (Bill) Lambard, Gainestown, Alabama, October 3, 1997; John Will, "John B. Waterman—He Loved Ships—Gave Spark That Started Port of Mobile's Growth," *Mobile Register,* December 16, 1945.

12. *Mobile Register,* October 19, 1940; ADDSCO files, USA; Cathalynn Donelson, *Mobile: Sunbelt Center of Opportunity* (Northridge, Calif.: Windsor Publications, 1986), 40–41; McLaurin and Thomason, *Mobile,* 124.

13. *Mobile Register,* January 10, February 21–22, 1941, April 19, 1944. The city of Mobile itself registered a 16 percent gain in population between 1930 and 1940 (from 68,202 to 78,720 residents). In the 1940s, Mobile's population soared to 129,009—a gain of 63 percent. Alabama Department of Public Health, Special Services Administration, Division of Vital Statistics, *Alabama's Population, 1930–1976* (n.p., 1977), 69.

14. *Mobile Register,* March 9, 1941; Bruce Nelson, "Organized Labor and the Struggle for Black Equality in Mobile during World War II," *Journal of American History* 80 (December 1993): 956; McLaurin and Thomason, *Mobile,* 126; John Dos Passos, *State of the Nation* (Boston: Houghton Mifflin, 1943), 92.

15. *Mobile Register,* September 15, December 21, 1940, August 16, 1941; Alabama Power Company, *Annual Report of Alabama Power Company for 1942* (Birmingham: Alabama Power Co., 1943), 5–6.

16. Nelson, "Organized Labor," 956; *Mobile Register,* August 3, 1941.

17. *Mobile Register,* January 2, 20, 1942, July 29, 1943.

18. Ibid., October 13, 1942.

19. Emily Staples Hearin and Kathryn Taylor de Celle, *Queens of Mobile Mardi Gras, 1893–1986* (Mobile: Museum of the City of Mobile, 1986), 26; Caldwell Delaney and Cornelia MacDuffie Turner, *Infant Mystics: The First Hundred Years* (Mobile: n.p., 1968), 47.

20. Albert Hirschberg, *Henry Aaron: Quiet Superstar* (New York: Putnam, 1969), 20–21; "Hammerin' Hank Aaron," *Mobile* 3 (spring 1974): 4–6.

21. *The Alabama Negro, 1863–1946* (Mobile: Gulf Informer Publishing, 1946).

22. *Mobile Register,* February 3, 1941.

23. Ibid., August 15, 1942; Nelson, "Organized Labor," 952–88.

24. Alabama State Military, *Quadrennial Report,* 89; *Mobile Register,* September 19, 1942.

25. *Mobile Register,* September 19, 1942.

26. Ibid., September 21, 1942.

27. Ibid., October 10, 1942; Mary Martha Thomas, "The Mobile Homefront during the Second World War," *GCHR* 1, no. 2 (spring 1986): 55–75.

28. *Mobile Register,* October 25, 1942.

29. Ibid., March 14, 1941, September 26, 1942 (quotation); Patricia G. Harrison, "Riveters, Volunteers and WACS: Women in Mobile during World War II," *GCHR* 1, no. 2 (spring 1986): 33–34; Thomas, "Mobile Homefront," 55–75; Mary Martha Thomas, "Rosie the Alabama Riveter," *Alabama Review* 32, no. 3 (July 1986): 196–212; Mary Martha Thomas, "Alabama Women on the Homefront, World War II," *Alabama Heritage* 19 (winter 1991): 2–23; Jessie Parkhurst Guzman, *Negro Yearbook: A Review of Events Affecting Negro Life, 1941–1946* (Tuskegee, Ala.: Tuskegee Institute Department of Records and Research, 1947), 56–75.

30. *Birmingham News,* June 14, 1944.

31. *Mobile Register,* September 13, 1942.

32. Ibid.

33. Thomas, "Alabama Women," 2–23.

34. Guzman, *Negro Year Book,* 233–34; Nelson, "Organized Labor," 978–82; Merl E. Reed, *Seedtime for the Modern Civil Rights Movement: The President's Committee on Fair Employment Practice, 1941–1946* (Baton Rouge: Louisiana State University Press, 1991), 117.

35. *Mobile Register,* May 31, 1943.

36. Reed, *Seedtime,* 120–21; Sheriff W. H. Holcombe to Governor Chauncey Sparks, June 3, 1943, Race Riots, ADAH.

37. *Mobile Register,* June 9, 1943.

38. Ibid., June 11, 1943; telephone interview with William Hearin, January 20, 1998.

39. *Mobile Register,* May 26, 1944; "Report of Anticipated Racial Trouble at Alabama Dry Dock and Shipbuilding Company, Mobile, Alabama, May 31, 1944," Sparks Papers: Race Problems, ADAH. This report was transmitted by George L. Cleere, adjutant general of the Alabama State Military Department, to Governor Chauncey Sparks on June 8, 1944.

40. *Mobile Register,* May 26, 1943.

41. Nelson, "Organized Labor," 959–60.

42. Agnes E. Meyer, *Out of These Roots: The Autobiography of an American Woman* (Boston: Little, Brown, 1953), 230.

43. *Mobile Register,* June 9, 1943.

44. Ibid., October 5–11, November 10, 1940.

45. Interview with Clarke Holloway, Auburn, Alabama, August 11, 1997; Nell Burks, "Opera Star Who Likes Turnip Greens Sings in Mobile Today," *Mobile Register,* April 18, 1942; *Mobile Register,* February 22, 1941, May 4, 1941, October 4, 1941, December 21, 1941.

46. *Mobile Register,* September 7, 1942.

47. "Early History of the Alabama State Docks," pt. 2: 1939–1940, Vertical File, Alabama State Docks, MPL.

48. *Selma Times Journal,* July 24, 1941; *Mobile Register,* March 3, 1941.

49. *Mobile Register,* April 1–3, 1941.

50. *Selma Times Journal,* July 21–24, 1941; *Montgomery Advertiser,* July 23–25, 1941; *United States v. Martini, et al,* No. 10701, District Court, Southern District Alabama, December 27, 1941, *Federal Supplement,* vol. 42, *Cases Argued and Determined in the District Courts of the United States and the Court of Claims* (St. Paul: West Publishing, 1942), 502–11; Carol Van Valkenburg, *An Alien Place: The Fort Missoula, Montana, Detention Camp, 1941–1944* (Missoula, Mont.: Pictorial Histories, 1995); James Brooke, "After Silence, Italians Recall the Internment," *New York Times,* August 11, 1997.

51. *Mobile Register,* June 14, 1941.

52. Telephone interview with Buford Perry, Chunchula, Alabama, September 30, 1997; *Mobile Register,* October 18, 20, 1941.

53. *Mobile Register,* October 22, 25, 1941.

54. Telephone interview with Quinton J. Pollard, Mobile, October 8, 1997.

55. Telephone interview with Nell Burks, Mobile, October 2, 1997; interview with Clarke Holloway, George Kenan, and Laverne Taylor Flanagan, Pebble Hill, Auburn University, July 31, 1997; special World War II issue of Alabama Beta Chapter (Auburn University), Phi Delta Theta, *Auburn Phi* (December 1991).

56. Interview with Clark and Mona Yarbrough, Pebble Hill, August 11, 1997; *Mobile Register,* April 16, 1968, November 4, 1977; Burks interview, October 2, 1997.

57. Interview with Lurie Sawada, Pebble Hill, March 24, 1998.

58. Telephone interview with Ben Sawada, Montgomery, August 14, 1997.

59. *Mobile Register,* June 27, 1942.

60. David Conwell, retired Alcoa captain, has described this event in an unpublished manuscript in the author's possession. Arthur R. Moore, *A Careless Word . . . A Needless Sinking: A History of the Tremendous Losses in Ships and Men Suffered by the U.S. Merchant Marine during World War II, 1941–1945,* rev. ed. (King's Point, N.Y.: American Merchant Marine Museum, 1990).

61. Samuel Eliot Morison, *History of United States Naval Operations in World War II,* vol. 1, *The Battle of the Atlantic, September 1939–May 1943* (Boston: Little, Brown, 1948), 142.

62. *Mobile Register,* May 8, 1942.

63. Allen Cronenberg, "U-Boats in the Gulf: The Undersea War in 1942," *GCHR* 5, no.

2 (spring 1990): 163–78; Melanie Wiggins, *Torpedoes in the Gulf: Galveston and the U-Boats, 1942–1943* (College Station: Texas A and M Press, 1995).

64. *Mobile Register,* May 16, June 13, July 1, 1942.

65. Alabama Defense Council Plans for Blackout, Alabama Governor (Frank Murray Dixon), Governor's Speeches, March 14, 1942, ADAH; *Mobile Register,* March 18, 1942; Major Gaines E. Maxwell, Fort McClellan, to Haygood Patterson, director of Alabama Civilian Defense, August 30, 1943, Alabama State Council of Defense, SG 19851, Folder 33: Dimouts, 1942–43, ADAH.

66. Alabama State Council of Defense, SG 19851, Folders 35–44: Program Administration File, 1942–1946—Mobile County Correspondence, 1942, ADAH.

67. Bob Zink to Allen Cronenberg, July 15, 1997.

68. Public Information Subject Files, Mobile County, SG6889, Folder 22: Bar Pilots, ADAH; *Mobile Register,* August 26, 1945.

69. Hallie Farmer, ed., *War Comes to Alabama* (Tuscaloosa: University of Alabama Press, 1946), 131; *Steel in the War* (New York: United States Steel Corporation, 1946), 39–41.

70. Charles C. Carr, *Alcoa: An American Enterprise* (New York: Rinehart and Co., 1952), 257.

71. *Mobile Register,* October 4, 1940.

72. William C. White (president, Alcoa Steamship Company) to I. W. Wilson (president, Aluminum Company of America), November 3, 1954; W. H. Trauth (manager, Washington office of Alcoa) to Irwin M. Heine (U.S. Maritime Administration), December 3, 1954; copies of letters, enclosures, and other documents furnished by Cecil S. Ashdown, New York, September 25, 1995; J. C. (Cecil) Huffmaster, phone interview, Saraland, Alabama, March 4, 1995; "Vessels Sunk by Enemy Action in U.S. Bauxite Trade during World War II," and "Vessels Sunk by Enemy Action in Canadian Bauxite Trade during World War II," unpublished manuscripts by Captain David M. Conwell, in possession of the author.

73. Public Information Subject Files, General, SG6592, Folder 568: Defense Program WW II, ADAH.

74. *Mobile Register,* November 25, 1945; Donelson, *Mobile,* 146; Earle L. Rauber, *The Alabama State Docks: A Case Study in State Development* (Atlanta: Federal Reserve Bank of Atlanta, 1945), 44–52; "Early History," Vertical File, Alabama State Docks, MPL.

75. *Mobile Register,* May 16, 1942, March 18, August 26, 1945; Navy Department, Office of the Chief of Naval Operations, *Dictionary of American Naval Fighting Ships,* vol. 4 (Washington, D.C.: U.S. Naval History Division, 1969), 401–2.

76. *Mobile Register,* June 7, 1944.

77. Ibid., May 9, 1945.

78. Eugene B. Sledge, *With the Old Breed at Peleliu and Okinawa* (Novat, Calif.: Presidio, 1981; reprint, New York: Oxford University Press, 1990).

79. In 1948, PFC John D. New's remains were returned from Peleliu and buried with military honors in Mobile's National Cemetery; United States Senate Committee on Veterans' Affairs, *Medal of Honor Recipients, 1862–1978* (Washington, D.C.: GPO, 1979), 641–42; George Werneth, "Home for a Hero," *Mobile Register,* August 16, 1997; Lee McCoy, *PFC John D. New: A Tribute* (Mobile: n.p., 1997).

80. Paul Fussell, *Wartime: Understanding and Behaviour in the Second World War* (New York: Oxford University Press, 1989), 292.

81. Sledge, *With the Old Breed,* 268, 312.

82. United States War Department, Bureau of Public Relations, *World War II Honor List of Dead and Missing: State of Alabama* (Washington, D.C.: GPO, 1946); U.S. Navy, *State Summary of War Casualties (Alabama)* (Washington, D.C.: GPO, 1946).

83. Ed Lee, "Lots of Clues are Given; Wreck Still Unidentified," *Mobile Press Register,* September 27, 1959; "Clippings Add Some Weight to Old German Sub Report," *Mobile Press Register,* April 19, 1964.

84. *Mobile Register,* December 29–30, 1945; Lt. Commander J. B. Casler, commanding officer, Ex-U-2513, to Mobile Mayor, October 6, 1946, RG 6, Series 79, Box 9, Navy Day, MMA.

85. *Mobile Register,* November 13, 1945; Mathews, *Highlights of 100 Years,* 128–29.

86. *Mobile Register,* April 13, 1945.

87. Ibid., May 24, 1945.

88. Alabama Department of Public Health, *Alabama's Population, 1930–1976* (Montgomery: Alabama Department of Public Health, Division of Vital Statistics, 1977), 65–68.

89. War Production Board, *War Industrial Facilities Authorized by State and County as of September 1943,* February 2, 1944; *Summary of War Supply and Facility Contracts by State, Industrial Area and County, Cumulative through June 1944,* August 24, 1944; *Alphabetical Listing of War Industrial Facilities Financed with Public Funds through June 30, 1944,* October 15, 1944; *State Listing of Major War Supply Contracts Active as of June 30, 1945,* August 6, 1945; *War Manufacturing Facilities Authorized through December 1944 by State and County,* vol. 1, *Alabama-New Hampshire,* June 15, 1945, Sparks Papers, ADAH; *Mobile Register,* July 8, 1943.

90. *Mobile Register,* August 5, 1945.

9. Politics and Civil Rights in Post–World War II Mobile

1. For a lengthy discussion of these early efforts, see Eric Duke, "A Life in the Struggle: John L. LeFlore and the Civil Rights Movements in Mobile, Alabama (1925–1975)" (master's thesis, Florida State University, 1998).

2. Austin Presnell Boyte, "The Impact of WWII on Race Relations in Mobile, Alabama, 1940–1948" (master's thesis, Atlanta University, 1972).

3. Melton A. McLaurin, "Mobile Blacks and World War II: The Development of Political Consciousness," in *Gulf Coast Politics in the Twentieth Century,* ed. Ted Carageorge (Pensacola Preservation Board, 1973), 47.

4. *Smith v. Allwright,* 321 U.S. 649 (1944); McLaurin, "Mobile Blacks," 49–50.

5. McLaurin, "Mobile Blacks," 49–50.

6. Ibid.

7. Ibid.

8. Duke, "Life in the Struggle," 89.

9. *Davis v. Schnell,* 81 F. Supp. 872.

10. McLaurin, "Mobile Blacks," 52.

11. For extensive discussion of this controversial amendment, see William D. Bernard, *Dixiecrats and Democrats: Alabama Politics from 1942–1950* (Tuscaloosa: University of Alabama Press, 1974), 59.

12. *Davis v. Schnell,* 879.

13. Bernard, *Dixiecrats and Democrats,* 71; *Davis v. Schnell,* 872–81.

14. *Davis v. Schnell,* 872–81.

15. Ibid.

16. Ibid., 878.

17. McLaurin, "Mobile Blacks," 54.

18. Patsy Busby Dow, "Joseph N. Langan: Mobile's Racial Diplomat" (master's thesis, University of South Alabama, 1993).

19. Duke, "Life in the Struggle," 12.

20. Dow, "Joseph N. Langan," 13–14.

21. David E. Alsobrook, "Mobile's Commission Government Campaign of 1910–1911," *Alabama Review* 44, no. 1 (January 1991): 36–60.

22. Endorsement letter from Citizens Committee for Good Government (September 12, 1953), LeFlore Papers, USA.

23. Ex parte National Association for the Advancement of Colored People, a corporation. In re: *State of Alabama, ex rel. John Patterson, Attorney General v. NAACP,* 91 So.2d 221 (1956).

24. Ibid., 109 So.2d 138 (1959), 139.

25. Court Reporter's Transcript, vol. 1, *Wiley L. Bolden et al v. City of Mobile,* Civil Action 75–297-P in the United States District Court for the Southern District of Alabama (1976), 208.

26. Duke, "Life in the Struggle," 102–3.

27. James E. Voyles, "An Analysis of Voting Patterns in Mobile, 1948–1970" (Ph.D. diss., North Texas State University, 1973), 57–61.

28. Non-Partisan Voters League, "Memorial and Anniversary Banquet Program, August 20, 1976," NPVL Papers, USA.

29. Ibid.

30. Supreme Court ruling: *Martin J. Wiman v. Willie Seals, Jr.,* 372 US 915 (1963); Appeals Court ruling: United States of America ex rel. *Willie Seals, Jr. v. Martin J. Wiman,* Warden, Kilby Prison, Montgomery, Alabama, 304 F.2d 53 (1962).

31. *Birdie Mae Davis, et al. v Board of School Commissioners of Mobile County, et al,* Civil Action No. 3003–63-H, United States District Court for the Southern District of Alabama (1963); *Birdie Mae Davis, et al v. Board of School Commissioners of Mobile County, et al,* 422 F.2d (1970), 1139; *Mobile Register,* March 1, 1997.

32. Interview with O. B. Purifoy, May 20, 1992, revealed that the league even bought luggage for Ms. Malone's trip to Tuscaloosa.

33. *Lelia G. Brown, et al v. John L. Moore, et al,* Mobile County Board of Commissioners and School Commissioners, Civil Action No. 75–298-P in the United States District Court for the Southern District of Alabama (1975); *Bolden v. Mobile* (1975); *Brown v. Moore,* 583 F. Supp. 391 (1984).

34. Dow, "Joseph N. Langan," 29.

35. Ibid., 27–31.

36. Voyles, "Analysis of Voting Patterns," 86–90.

37. Ibid., 93.

38. Ibid.; *Mobile Press Register,* August 18, 1965.

39. Voyles, "Analysis of Voting Patterns," 98; Dow, "Joseph N. Langan," 53–54.

40. Frederick Douglas Richardson, *The Genesis and Exodus of NOW,* 2d ed. (Boynton Beach, Fla.: Futura Press, 1996); Voyles, "Analysis of Voting Patterns," 98.

41. *Mobile Register,* August 17–18, 1969.

42. Voyles, "Analysis of Voting Patterns," 66–67; Richardson, *Genesis and Exodus,* 154.

43. *Mobile Register,* August 19, September 5, 1973.

44. Voyles, "Analysis of Voting Patterns," 156.

45. *Bolden v. Mobile,* 423 F.Supp. 384 (S.D. Ala. 1976); *Opinion and Order,* October 21, 1976, 1–2.

46. *Mobile Press Register,* May 13, 1990.

47. This information was obtained by the author in a confidential interview on February 15, 1991, with a high-level administrator of the federal District Court for the Southern District of Alabama.

48. *Bolden v. Mobile,* 423 F.Supp. 384 (S.D. Ala. 1976); *Opinion and Order,* October 21, 1976, 26.

49. *Opinion and Order,* October 21, 1976, 26.

50. *Mobile Press,* November 8, 1976.

51. *City of Mobile v. Bolden, et al,* 571 F.2D 238 (5th Cir. 1978).

52. Ibid., 446 U.S. 55 64 L. Ed. 2d 47, 100 S. Ct. 1490 (1980).

53. *Bolden, et al v. City of Mobile,* 542 F. Supp. 1050 (S.D. Ala. 1982); *Opinion and Order,* April 15, 1982, 5.

54. *Mobile Register,* August 18, 1981.

55. Peyton McCrary, "History in the Courts," in *Minority Vote Dilution,* ed. Chandler Davidson (Washington, D.C.: Howard University Press, 1984), 56.

56. *Bolden, et al v. Mobile,* Civil Action No. 75–297-P, *Notice of Proposed Compromise* (February 4, 1983), 2–7.

57. *Birmingham News,* July 3, October 6, 1985.

58. Alabama Law, Act No. 85–229, Section 28, 10. The only exception to the supermajority requirement is the city budget, which requires a simple majority for passage.

59. *Mobile Register,* May 13, 1992.

60. Ibid., September 24, 1997

10. Mobile since 1945

1. McLaurin and Thomason, *Mobile,* 127.

2. Ibid., 137–38.

3. Ibid., 139–40; Paul R. Cherney, *Civic Index Review: Milestones in Community Develop-*

ment, Mobile, Alabama, 1960–1994 (Mobile: Mobile United, 1995), 10; *Mobile Press Register,* January 3, 1946, January 5, 1947.

4. *Mobile Press Register,* December 28, 1947.

5. Ibid.

6. McLaurin and Thomason, *Mobile,* 144–45; *Mobile Press Register,* February 5, 1997 (quotation); Samuel Kinser, *Carnival, American Style: Mardi Gras at New Orleans and Mobile* (Chicago: University of Chicago Press, 1990), 278–79; Emily Staples Hearin, *Let the Good Times Roll: Mobile, Mother of Mystics* (Mobile: E. S. Hearin and W. B. Taylor, 1991); Samuel Eichold, *Without Malice: The 100th Anniversary of the Comic Cowboys, 1884–1984* (Mobile: R. E. Publications, 1984); Dean, *Mardi Gras.*

7. *Mobile Press Register,* January 4, 1946, January 5, 1947, December 28, 1947, January 1, 1950.

8. Ibid., December 28, 1947, December 26, 1948, January 2, 1950 (quotation); McLaurin and Thomason, *Mobile,* 141, 144.

9. McLaurin and Thomason, *Mobile,* 140; Cherney, *Civic Index,* 10; *Mobile Press Register,* January 2, 1950, December 31, 1950, December 30, 31, 1951, January 4, 1953, January 3, 1954.

10. *Mobile Press Register,* December 27, 1953, January 2, 5, 1955, January 1, December 31, 1956, January 2, 1957; Cherney, *Civic Index,* 13.

11. *Mobile Press Register,* January 1, 1956, December 30, 1956 (quotation), December 28, 1958.

12. Kennedy, "Survey of Community Music," 154–59, 168–69, 183n; *Mobile Press Register,* January 2, 1951, December 28, 1952, December 27, 1953, January 1, 1956, December 30, 1956, December 29, 1957, December 28, 1958, December 28, 1947 (quotation).

13. *Mobile Press Register,* December 28, 1947; Kennedy, "Survey of Community Music," 183–84 (quotations), 350–52.

14. Kennedy, "Survey of Community Music," 178–79; Cherney, *Civic Index,* 25; Kinser, *Carnival,* 15; *Mobile Press Register,* January 2, 1955, December 29, 1957, December 27, 1959.

15. *Mobile Press Register,* January 2, 1955, May 11, 1997; interview with John Dixon and Jean Lavender Fowler, April 2, 1997; McLaurin and Thomason, *Mobile,* 141.

16. Cherney, *Civic Index,* 11; *Mobile Press Register,* December 28, 1958 (quotation), December 29, 1957.

17. *Mobile Press Register,* December 29, 1957, December 28, 1958; McLaurin and Thomason, *Mobile,* 140.

18. McLaurin and Thomason, *Mobile,* 145; Cherney, *Civic Index,* 92–93; *Mobile Press Register,* January 1, 1956, December 27, 1959.

19. *Mobile Press Register,* December 29, 1957, January 3, December 28, 1958, January 1 (quotation), 4, December 27, 1959; McLaurin and Thomason, *Mobile,* 141.

20. Cherney, *Civic Index,* 13–14.

21. Ibid., 14–15, 31–32.

22. Ibid., 14–16, 32.

23. McLaurin and Thomason, *Mobile,* 142 (quotation); Cherney, *Civic Index,* 15.

24. Cherney, *Civic Index,* 23; Higginbotham, *Mobile,* 223 (quotation); *Mobile Press Register,* January 1, 4, December 31, 1961, December 30, 1962.

25. *Wall Street Journal,* July 18, 1963; Cherney, *Civic Index,* 17, 23; *Mobile Press Register,* December 30, 1962, December 29, 1963, December 27, 1964, January 3, 1965.

26. *Mobile Press Register,* December 27, 1959, January 1, December 31, 1961, December 30, 1962, December 29, 1963 (quotation), January 3, 1965.

27. McLaurin and Thomason, *Mobile,* 142; Cherney, *Civic Index,* 22, 23, 128; *Mobile Press Register,* December 29, 1963 (quotation).

28. William Warren Rogers Sr. et al., *Alabama: The History of a Deep South State,* 538; Cherney, *Civic Index,* 18, 25; *Mobile Press Register,* December 31, 1961, December 28, 1963, January 3, 1965.

29. McLaurin and Thomason, *Mobile,* 140.

30. Ibid., 139; Cherney, *Civic Index,* 11, 25; *Mobile Press Register,* December 30, 1962 (quotation), December 29, 1963, December 7, 1964, January 3, December 26, 1965.

31. McLaurin and Thomason, *Mobile,* 141; Higginbotham, *Mobile,* 200; *Mobile Press Register,* December 29, 1963, December 27, 30, 1964, January 3, December 26, 1965.

32. *Mobile Press Register,* December 30, 1956, December 30, 1962; interview with John Dixon and Jean Lavender Fowler, April 2, 1997.

33. *Mobile Press Register,* December 28, 1957 (quotations); McLaurin and Thomason, *Mobile,* 141; John Sledge, "Seeking a Future for the Past: Historic Preservation in Mobile," *Mobile Bay Monthly* (May 1992), 18–19.

34. *Mobile Press Register,* December 29, 1963, January 2, December 26, 1965, December 31, 1967; Cherney *Civic Index,* 20, 22, 24; Sledge, "Seeking a Future," 18–19.

35. Cherney, *Civic Index,* 25; McLaurin and Thomason, *Mobile,* 133, 142–43; *Mobile Press Register,* December 29, 1963, December 27, 1964 (quotation), December 21, 25, 1966, December 31, 1967, December 29, 1968.

36. *Mobile Press Register,* December 27, 1959, January 1, 1967, December 29, 1968.

37. *Mobile Press Register,* December 29, 1968 (quotation), December 28, 1969; Cherney, *Civic Index,* 29.

38. Cherney, *Civic Index,* 30–31; *Mobile Press Register,* December 29, 1968, December 28, 1969 (quotation).

39. McLaurin and Thomason, *Mobile,* 146–47; *Mobile Press Register,* January 1, 1967, December 27, 1970, December 31, 1971 (quotation).

40. Cherney, *Civic Index,* 28; *Mobile Press Register,* December 27, 1970.

41. *Mobile Press Register,* December 29, 1968, January 4, 1970, December 27, 1970, January 1, 2, 1972.

42. Cherney, *Civic Index,* 38 (quotations), 42; *Mobile Press Register,* December 28, 1969, December 27, 1970, December 26, 1971, January 1, 1972, January 1, 1974, January 1, December 28, 1975, January 1, 4, December 26, 1976, December 31, 1978, December 30, 1979; McLaurin and Thomason, *Mobile,* 139.

43. McLaurin and Thomason, *Mobile,* 140; *Mobile Press Register,* January 1, 1967, January 1, 1972, January 5, December 28, 1975, December 26, 1976, January 1, 1978.

44. Cherney, *Civic Index,* 23, 28, 38, 43, 51; Mark G. Stith, "Delightful Dauphin Street," *Southern Living,* April 1997, 30; *Mobile Press Register,* December 31, 1967, December 29,

1968, December 28, 1969, December 27, 1970, January 3, December 26, 1971, January 2, 1972, January 1, December 29, 1974, January 1, December 28, 31, 1975, January 4, December 30, 1979 (quotation).

45. Cherney, *Civic Index,* 45; *Mobile Press Register,* January 1, December 30, 1979, January 1, 1980 (quotations).

46. *Mobile Press Register,* December 27, 1981, January 1, 1982 (quotation); Cherney, *Civic Index,* 52.

47. Cherney, *Civic Index,* 56, 58, 62, 129; *Mobile Press Register,* December 27, 1970, January 1, 1985, January 1, 1987.

48. *Mobile Press Register,* December 27, 1970, January 2, 1972, January 1, 4, December 27, 1981, January 1, 1982, January 2, December 25, 1983, January 1, 1988, January 1, December 31, 1989; Cherney, *Civic Index,* 52, 56, 61–63, 77.

49. Cherney, *Civic Index,* 27, 64; *Mobile Press Register,* December 27, 1970, December 30, 1973, January 2, 1977, January 2, 1984.

50. *Mobile Press Register,* January 1, 1973, January 1, 1974, December 28, 1978, December 31, 1980.

51. Ibid., January 29, 1957, December 31, 1961, January 3, December 29, 1970, January 1, December 31, 1972, December 30, 1975, January 4, 1976, January 2, 1977.

52. Ibid., January 1, 1982, January 1, 1983, January 1, 1985, January 1, 1986; Cherney, *Civic Index,* 53.

53. Cherney, *Civic Index,* 21, 35, 38, 44, 52–54; *Mobile Press Register,* January 1, 1979, January 1, December 31, 1980, January 1, December 20, December 26, 1982; McLaurin and Thomason, *Mobile,* 142.

54. *Mobile Press Register,* December 28, 1983, January 1, 1984, January 1, 1988.

55. Cherney, *Civic Index,* 59; *Mobile Press Register,* January 1, 1985, January 1, 1986.

56. *Mobile Press Register,* December 28, 1983, January 1, 1986, January 1, 1988, January 1, 1989; Cherney, *Civic Index,* 62.

57. *Mobile Press Register,* January 1, December 27, 1981, January 1, 1982, January 1, December 28, 1984, January 1, December 25, 1985, January 1, 1986.

58. McLaurin and Thomason, *Mobile,* 141; *Mobile Press Register,* January 1, December 28, 1980, December 27, 1981, January 1, 3, 1982 (first quotation), January 1, 1984, January 1, 1985, January 1, 1990; Sledge, "Seeking a Future," 19–20 (second quotation).

59. Cherney, *Civic Index,* 62 (quotations), 71, 78–82, 84, 88; *Mobile Press Register,* January 1, December 21, 1989, January 1, 1990; McLaurin and Thomason, *Mobile,* 146.

60. Cherney, *Civic Index,* 13, 57, 65, 70, 88, 90, 91; *Mobile Press Register,* January 1, 1985.

61. McLaurin and Thomason, *Mobile,* 144–45; Cherney, *Civic Index,* 57–58; Kinser, *Carnival,* 12–13, 250, 262, 268–78, 307–8, 315; *Mobile Press Register,* December 26, 1982, January 1, 1987, February 5, 1997.

62. Cherney, *Civic Index,* 78, 80, 86, 88–89, 90.

63. Ibid., forward, 47–48, 75, 79, 92–93, 101; Stith, "Delightful Dauphin," 30; Sledge, "Seeking a Future," 20; *Mobile Press Register,* April 20, 1997; *Birmingham News,* February 24, 1997.

Bibliography

Books

Abbott, John S. C. *South and North, or, Impressions Received during a Trip to Cuba and the South.* New York: Abbey and Abbot, 1860.

The Alabama Federation of Music Clubs. *Musical Alabama.* Montgomery: Paragon Press, 1925.

The Alabama Negro, 1863–1946. Mobile: Gulf Publishing, n.d.

Alabama Power Company. *Annual Report of Alabama Power Company for 1942.* Birmingham: Alabama Power Co., 1943.

Alabama State Docks Department. *Port of Mobile Handbook.* Birmingham: Vulcan Printing and Lithographing, 1964.

Albion, Robert Greenhalgh. *The Rise of New York Port [1815–1860].* New York: Charles Scribner's Sons, 1939.

Allain, Mathé. *"Not Worth a Straw": French Colonial Policy and the Early Years of Louisiana.* Lafayette, La.: Center for Louisiana Studies, University of Southwestern Louisiana Press, 1988.

Amos [Doss], Harriet E. *Cotton City: Urban Development in Antebellum Mobile.* Tuscaloosa: University of Alabama Press, 1985.

Arfwedson, Carl David. *The United States and Canada in 1832, 1833, and 1834.* 2 vols. London: Richard Bentley, 1834.

Ashworth, John. *Slavery, Capitalism, and Politics in the Antebellum Republic.* Vol. 1, *Commerce and Compromise, 1820–1850.* Cambridge: Cambridge University Press, 1995.

Bailyn, Bernard. *Voyagers to the West: A Passage in the Peopling of America on the Eve of the Revolution.* New York: Knopf, 1986.

Bancroft, Frederic. *Slave-Trading in the Old South.* Baltimore: J. H. Furst, 1931.

Bardaglio, Peter W. *Reconstructing the Household: Families, Sex, and the Law in the Nineteenth Century South.* Chapel Hill: University of North Carolina Press, 1995.

Barney, William L. *The Secessionist Impulse: Alabama and Mississippi in 1860.* Princeton: Yale University Press, 1974.

Bergeron, Arthur W., Jr. *Confederate Mobile.* Jackson, Miss.: University Press of Mississippi, 1991.

Berlin, Ira. *Slaves without Masters: The Free Negro in the Antebellum South.* New York: Pantheon Books, 1974.

Bernard, William D. *Dixiecrats and Democrats: Alabama Politics from 1942–1950.* Tuscaloosa: University of Alabama Press, 1974.

Bernhard, Karl. *Travels through North America during the Years 1825 and 1826.* Philadelphia: Carey and Lea, 1828.

Bossu, Jean-Bernard. *Jean-Bernard Bossu's Travels in the Interior of North America, 1751–1762.* Translated and edited by Seymour Feiler. Norman, Okla.: University of Oklahoma Press, 1962.

Boykin, Edward. *Everything's Made for Love in this Man's World: Vignettes from the Life of Frank W. Boykin.* Mobile: N.p., 1973.

Braund, Katherine E. Holland. *Deerskins and Duffels: The Creek Indian Trade with Anglo-America, 1685–1815.* Lincoln: University of Nebraska Press, 1993.

Bremer, Frederika. *The Homes of the New World: Impressions of America.* Translated by Mary Howitt. 2 vols. New York: Harper and Brothers, 1853.

Bright, M. Aline, ed. *Barton Centennial, 1836–1936.* Mobile: Heiter-Starke Printing Co., 1936.

Bronson, Francis S. *Bronson's Travelers' Directory, from New York to New Orleans, Embracing All the Most Important Routes, with a Condensed Outline of the Country through Which They Pass.* La Grange, Ga.: American Star Book Store, 1845.

Buckingham, James S. *The Slave States of America.* 2 vols. London: Fisher, Son, 1842.

Carr, Charles C. *Alcoa: An American Enterprise.* New York: Rinehart and Co., 1952.

Casson, Lionel. *Ships and Seafaring in Ancient Times.* Austin: University of Texas Press, 1994.

Chan, Roman P. *The Olmec: Mother Culture of Mesoamerica.* New York: Rizzoli International Publications, 1989.

Cherney, Paul R. *Civic Index Review: Milestones in Community Development, Mobile, Alabama, 1960–1994.* Mobile: Mobile United, 1995.

Clayton, Lawrence A., Vernon James Knight Jr., and Edward C. Moore, eds. *The De Soto Chronicles.* 2 vols. Tuscaloosa: University of Alabama Press, 1993.

Coker, William S., and Thomas D. Watson. *Indian Traders of the Southeast Spanish Borderlands: Panton, Leslie and Company and John Forbes and Company, 1783–1847.* Pensacola: University of West Florida Press, 1986.

Corson, W. C. *Two Months In the Confederate States: An Englishman's Travels through the South.* Edited by Benjamin H. Trask. Baton Rouge: Louisiana State University Press, 1996.

Craighead, Erwin. *From Mobile's Past: Sketches of Memorable People and Events.* Mobile: Powers Printing Co., 1925.

———. *Mobile: Fact and Tradition, Noteworthy People and Events.* Mobile: Powers Printing Co., 1930.

Cumming, William P. *The Southeast in Early Maps.* Princeton: Princeton University Press, 1958.

Curren, Caleb. *Archeology in the Mauvila Chiefdom: Native and Spanish Contacts during the Soto and Luna Expeditions.* Mobile: Mobile Historic Development Commission, 1992.

Davis, Charles S. *The Cotton Kingdom in Alabama.* Montgomery: Alabama State Department of Archives and History, 1939.

Davis-Horton, Paulette. *Avenue . . . The Place, The People, The Memories.* Mobile: Horton Inc., 1991.

Dean, Wayne. *Mardi Gras: Mobile's Illogical Whoop-De-Doo, 1704–1970.* Chicago: Adams Printing Co., 1971.

Delaney, Caldwell. *Remember Mobile.* 2d ed. Mobile: Haunted Book Shop, 1969.

Delaney, Caldwell, and Cornelia MacDuffie Turner. *Infant Mystics: The First Hundred Years.* Mobile: N.p., 1968.

Delanglez, Jean. *El Rio del Espíritu Santo: An Essay on the Cartography of the Gulf Coast and the Adjacent Territory during the Sixteenth and Seventeenth Centuries.* New York: United States Catholic Historical Society, 1945.

De Leon, Thomas Cooper. *Belles, Beaux, and Brains of the 60's.* New York: G. W. Dillingham Co., 1907.

Delius, Edouard. *Wander eines jungen Norddeutschen durch Portugal, Spanien, und Nord-Amerika in den Jahren 1827–1831.* Edited by Georg Lotz. Hamburg: Heroldschen Buchhandlungen, 1834.

De Navarette, Martín Fernández. *Colección de los Viajes . . . III.* Madrid: N.p., 1825–27.

Donelson, Cathalynn. *Mobile: Sunbelt Center of Opportunity.* Northridge, Calif.: Windsor Publications, 1986.

Dorman, Lewy. *Party Politics in Alabama from 1815 through 1860.* Wetumpka, Ala.: Wetumpka Printing Co., 1935.

Dos Passos, John. *State of the Nation.* Boston: Houghton Mifflin, 1943.

Doyle, Don Harrison. *New Men, New Cities, New South: Atlanta, Nashville, Charleston, Mobile, 1860–1910.* Chapel Hill: University of North Carolina Press, 1990.

du Pratz, Le Page. *The History of Louisiana.* Edited by Joseph G. Tregle Jr. 1774. Reprint, Baton Rouge: Louisiana State University Press, 1975.

Eaton, Clement. *The Growth of Southern Civilization, 1790–1860.* New York: Harper and Brothers, 1961.

Edward, Laura. *Gendered Strife and Confusion: The Political Culture of Reconstruction.* Urbana: University of Illinois Press, 1997.

Eichold, Samuel. *Without Malice: The 100th Anniversary of the Comic Cowboys, 1884–1984.* Mobile: R. E. Publications, 1984.

Ellicott, Andrew. *The Journal of Andrew Ellicott.* Chicago: Quadrangle Books, 1962.

Evans, Augusta Jane. *Macaria, or, Altars of Sacrifice.* Baton Rouge: Louisiana State University Press, 1992.

Fabel, Robin F. A. *Bombast and Broadsides: The Lives of George Johnstone.* Tuscaloosa: University of Alabama Press, 1987.

———. *The Economy of British West Florida, 1763–1783.* Tuscaloosa: University of Alabama Press, 1988.

Farmer, Hallie, ed. *War Comes to Alabama.* Tuscaloosa: University of Alabama Press, 1946.

Faust, Drew Gilpen. *The Creation of Confederate Nationalism: Ideology and Identity in the Civil War South.* Baton Rouge: Louisiana State University Press, 1988.

———. *Southern Stories: Slaveholders in Peace and War.* Columbia: University of Missouri Press, 1992.

Favata, Martin A., and José B. Fernández, eds. *La "Relación" o "Naufragios" de Álvar Nuñez Cabeza de Vaca.* Potomac, Md.: Scripta Humanistica, 1986.

First National Bank. *Highlights of 75 Years in Mobile.* Mobile: First National Bank, 1940.

Fitzgerald, Michael W. *The Union League Movement in the Deep South: Politics and Agricultural Change during Reconstruction.* Baton Rouge: Louisiana State University Press, 1989.

Fitzhugh, George. *Cannibals All!, or, Slaves without Masters.* Edited by C. Vann Woodward. Cambridge: Belknap Press, 1988.

Fleming, Walter Lynwood. *Civil War and Reconstruction in Alabama.* Gloucester, Mass.: Peter Smith, 1949.

Foner, Eric. *Reconstruction: America's Unfinished Revolution, 1863–1877.* New York: Harper and Row, 1988.

Fredrickson, George M. *The Black Image in the White Mind: The Debate on Afro-American Character and Destiny, 1817–1914.* Hanover, N.H.: Wesleyan University Press, 1971.

Frisch, Michael H. *Town into City: Springfield, Massachusetts, and the Meaning of Community, 1840–1880.* Cambridge: Harvard University Press, 1971.

Fuller, Hiram. *Belle Brittan on a Tour, at Newport, and Here and There.* New York: Derby and Jackson, 1858.

Fussell, Paul. *Wartime: Understanding and Behaviour in the Second World War.* New York: Oxford University Press, 1989.

Galloway, Patricia K. "'The Chief Who Is Your Father': Choctaw and French Views of the Diplomatic Relation." In *Powhatan's Mantle: Indians in the Colonial Southeast,* edited by Peter H. Wood, Gregory A. Waselkov, and M. Thomas Hatley. Lincoln: University of Nebraska Press, 1989.

———, ed. *La Salle and His Legacy: Frenchmen and Indians in the Lower Mississippi Valley.* Jackson: University Press of Mississippi, 1982.

Garrett, William. *Reminiscences of Public Men in Alabama for Thirty Years.* Atlanta: Plantation Publishing Company Press, 1872.

Giraud, Marcel. *Histoire de La Louisiane Française: Le Règne de Louis XIV, 1698–1715.* Paris: Press Universitaires de France, 1953.

———. *A History of French Louisiana.* Vol. 1, *The Reign of Louis XIV, 1698–1715.* Translated by Joseph Lambert. Baton Rouge: Louisiana State University Press, 1974.

Goldfield, David R., and Blaine A. Brownell. *Urban America: From Downtown to No Town.* Boston: Houghton Mifflin, 1979.

Gould, Virginia M. "The Free Creoles of Color of the Antebellum Gulf Ports of Mobile and Pensacola: A Struggle for the Middle Ground." In *Creoles of Color of the Gulf South,* edited by James H. Dormon. Knoxville: University of Tennessee Press, 1996.

Guzman, Jessie Parkhurst. *Negro Yearbook: A Review of Events Affecting Negro Life, 1941–1946.* Tuskegee, Ala.: Tuskegee Institute Department of Records and Research, 1947.

Hakluyt, Richard. *Principall Navigations.* London, 1589.

Hall, Gwendolyn Midlo. *Africans in Colonial Louisiana: The Development of Afro-Creole Culture in the Eighteenth Century.* Baton Rouge: Louisiana State University Press, 1992.

Hall, Margaret. *The Aristocratic Journey: Being the Outspoken Letters of Mrs. Basil Hall Written during a Fourteen Months' Sojourn in America, 1827–1828.* Edited by Una Pope-Hennessy. New York: G. P. Putnam's Sons, 1931.

Hamilton, Peter J. *The Charter and Code of Ordinances of 1897 of the City of Mobile.* Mobile: City of Mobile, 1897.

———. *The Reconstruction Period.* Vol. 16 of *The History of North America.* Philadelphia: George Barrie and Sons, 1905.

———. *Mobile of the Five Flags: The Story of the River Basin and Coast about Mobile from the Earliest Times to the Present.* Mobile: Gill Printing Co., 1913.

———. *Colonial Mobile.* Tuscaloosa: University of Alabama Press, 1976.

Hamilton, Thomas. *Men and Manners in America.* Philadelphia: Carey, Lea and Blanchard, 1833.

Hamilton, Virginia Van der Veer. *Alabama: A Bicentennial History.* New York: W. W. Norton, 1977.

Hearin, Emily Staples. *Downtown Goes Uptown.* Mobile: First Southern Federal Savings and Loan Association, 1983.

———. *Let the Good Times Roll: Mobile, Mother of Mystics.* Mobile: E. S. Hearin and W. B. Taylor, 1991.

Hearin, Emily Staples, and Kathryn Taylor de Celle. *Queens of Mobile Mardi Gras, 1893–1986.* Mobile: Museum of the City of Mobile, 1986.

Herbert, Thomas. *A Relation of Some Yeares Travaile.* London, 1634.

Higginbotham, Jay. *Mobile: City by the Bay.* Mobile: Azalea City Printers, 1968.

———. *The First National Bank of Mobile, 1865–1978.* Mobile: First National Bank, 1978.

———. *Old Mobile: Fort Louis de la Louisiane, 1702–1711.* Tuscaloosa: University of Alabama Press, 1991.

Hirschberg, Albert. *Henry Aaron: Quiet Superstar.* New York: Putnam, 1969.

Hodgson, Adam. *Remarks during a Journey through North America in the Years 1819, 1820, and 1821, in a Series of Letters.* Edited by Samuel Whiting. New York: Samuel Whiting, 1823.

Holmes, Jack D. L. "French and Spanish Military Units in the 1781 Pensacola Campaign." In *Anglo-Spanish Confrontation on the Gulf Coast during the American Revolution,* edited by William S. Coker and Robert R. Rea. Pensacola, Fla.: Gulf Coast History and Humanities Conference, 1982.

Horsman, Reginald. *Josiah Nott of Mobile: Southerner, Physician, and Racial Theorist.* Baton Rouge: Louisiana State University Press, 1987.

Howard, Milo B., Jr., and Robert R. Rea. *The Memoire Justificatif of the Chevalier Montault de Montberaut.* Tuscaloosa: University of Alabama Press, 1965.

Ingraham, Joseph Holt, ed. *The Sunny South, or, The Southerner at Home, Embracing Five Years' Experience of a Northern Governess in the Land of the Sugar and the Cotton.* Philadelphia: G. G. Evans, 1860.

J. G. White Engineering Corporation. *Economic Survey of the State Docks, Port of Mobile: Report to State of Alabama Department of State Docks and Terminals, Mobile, Alabama, 1945.* New York: J. G. White Engineering Corporation, 1945.

Jackson, Kenneth T. *The Ku Klux Klan in the City, 1915–1930.* New York: Oxford University Press, 1967.

King, Jean, ed. *Delchamps: 50 Golden Years, 1921–1971.* Mobile: Delchamps, 1971.

Kinser, Samuel. *Carnival, American Style: Mardi Gras at New Orleans and Mobile.* Chicago: University of Chicago Press, 1990.

Kohl, Lawrence Frederick. *The Politics of Individualism: Parties and the American Character in the Jacksonian Era.* New York: Oxford University Press, 1989.

Leonard, Irving A. *Documentos inéditos de Don Carlos Sigüenza y Góngora.* Mexico City: Biblioteca Mexicana, 1963.

———, ed. *The Spanish Approach to Pensacola, 1689–1693.* Albuquerque: Quivira Society, 1939.

Lovett, William J., Jr. *Mardi Gras In Mobile.* Mobile: Mobile Area Mardi Gras Association, 1980.

McCoy, Lee. *PFC John D. New: A Tribute.* Mobile: N.p., 1997.

McCrary, Peyton. "History in the Courts." In *Minority Vote Dilution,* edited by Chandler Davidson. Washington, D.C.: Howard University Press, 1984.

McKinstry, Alexander. *The Code of Ordinances of the City of Mobile: With the Charter and an Appendix.* Mobile: S. H. Goetzel, 1859.

McLaurin, Melton, and Michael Thomason. *Mobile: The Life and Times of a Great Southern City.* Woodland Hills, Calif.: Windsor Publications, Inc., 1981.

McMillan, Malcolm C. *The Disintegration of a Confederate State: Three Governors and Alabama's Wartime Homefront, 1861–1865.* Macon: Mercer University Press, 1986.

McMillen, Neil R., ed. *Remaking Dixie: The Impact of World War II on the American South.* Jackson: University of Mississippi Press, 1997.

McWilliams, Richebourg G. *Iberville's Gulf Journals.* Tuscaloosa: University of Alabama Press, 1981.

———, trans. and ed. *Fleur de Lys and Calumet.* Baton Rouge: Louisiana State University Press, 1953.

Mackay, Alexander. *Travels in the United States in 1846–47.* 3 vols. London: Richard Bentley, 1849.

Mackay, Charles. *Life and Liberty in America, or, Sketches of a Tour in the United States and Canada, in 1857–8.* New York: Harper and Brothers, 1859.

Mathews, Charles E. *Highlights of 100 Years in Mobile, 1865–1965.* Mobile: First National Bank of Mobile, 1965.

Meyer, Agnes E. *Out of These Roots: The Autobiography of an American Woman.* Boston: Little, Brown, 1953.

Milanich, Jerald T. *Archaeology of Precolumbian Florida.* Gainesville: University Press of Florida, 1994.

———. "Original Inhabitants." In *The New History of Florida,* edited by Michael Gannon. Gainesville: University Press of Florida, 1996.

Mistovich, Tim S., and Vernon James Knight Jr. *Cultural Resources Survey of Mobile Harbor, Alabama.* Moundville, Ala.: OSM Archaeological Consultants, 1983.

Moore, Arthur R. *A Careless Word . . . A Needless Sinking: A History of the Tremendous Losses in Ships and Men Suffered by the U.S. Merchant Marine during World War II, 1941–1945.* King's Point, N.Y.: American Merchant Marine Museum, 1990.

Morison, Samuel Eliot. *History of United States Naval Operations in World War II.* 15 vols. Boston: Little, Brown, 1947–1962.

Nichols, Thomas Low. *Forty Years of American Life.* 2 vols. London: J. Maxwell, 1864.

Nott, Josiah. *An Essay on the Natural History of Mankind Viewed in Connection with Negro Slavery.* Mobile: Sage, Thompson and Co., Printers, 1851.

Oldmixon, John W. *Transatlantic Wanderings, or, A Last Look at the United States.* London: George Routledge, 1855.

O'Neill, Charles Edwards. *Church and State in French Colonial Louisiana: Policy and Politics to 1732.* New Haven: Yale University Press, 1966.

Overdyke, W. Darrell. *The Know-Nothing Party in the South.* Baton Rouge: Louisiana State University Press, 1950.

Owen, Thomas M. *History of Alabama and Dictionary of Alabama Biography.* 4 vols. Spartanburg, S.C.: Reprint Co., 1978.

Owsley, Frank Lawrence, Jr., and Gene A. Smith. *Filibusters and Expansionists: Jeffersonian Manifest Destiny, 1800–1821.* Tuscaloosa: University of Alabama Press, 1997.

Peacock, Virginia Tatnall. *Famous American Belles of the Nineteenth Century.* Philadelphia: J. B. Lippincott, 1901.

Perkins, Edwin J. *Financing Anglo-American Trade: The House of Brown, 1800–1880.* Cambridge: Harvard University Press, 1975.

Perman, Michael. *The Road to Redemption.* Chapel Hill: University of North Carolina Press, 1984.

Peypus, Frederick. *Praeclara Ferdiñandi Cortesü de Noua Maris Oceani Hyspanica Narratio.* Nuremberg, 1542.

Powel, David. *The Historie of Cambria.* London, 1584.

Pred, Allan. *Urban Growth and City-Systems in the United States, 1840–1860.* Cambridge: Harvard University Press, 1980.

Priestley, Herbert Ingram, trans. and ed. *The Luna Papers: Documents Relating to the Expedition of Don Tristán de Luna y Arellano for the Conquest of La Florida in 1559–1561.* 2 vols. De Land: Florida State Historical Society, 1928.

Rauber, Earle L. *The Alabama State Docks: A Case Study in State Development.* Atlanta: Federal Reserve Bank of Atlanta, 1945.

Ravesies, Paul. *Scenes and Settlers of Alabama.* Mobile: N.p., 1885.

Rea, Robert R. *Major Robert Farmar of Mobile.* Tuscaloosa: University of Alabama Press, 1990.

Reed, Merl E. *Seedtime for the Modern Civil Rights Movement: The President's Committee on Fair Employment Practice, 1941–1946.* Baton Rouge: Louisiana State University Press, 1991.

Reinders, Robert C. "Slavery in New Orleans in the Decade before the Civil War." In *Plan-*

tation, Town, and Country: Essays on the Local History of American Slave Society, edited by Elinor Miller and Eugene D. Genovese. Urbana: University of Illinois Press, 1974.

Relación que dio Alvar, nuñez cabeça de vaca. . . . Zamora, 1542.

Reynolds, Bernard. *Sketches of Mobile, from 1814 to the Present Time.* Mobile: B. H. Richardson, 1868.

Richardson, Frederick Douglas. *The Genesis and Exodus of NOW.* 2d ed. Boynton Beach, Fla.: Futura Press, 1996.

Roche, Emma Langdon. *Historic Sketches of the South.* New York: Knickerbocker Press, 1914.

Rogers, William Warren, Sr., Robert David Ward, Leah R. Atkins, and Wayne Flynt. *Alabama: The History of a Deep South State.* Tuscaloosa: University of Alabama Press, 1994.

Ryan, Bennett A. et al. *An Economic History of Mobile: Selected Periods.* Mobile: University of South Alabama, 1974.

Saunders, Robert, Jr. *John Archibald Campbell: Southern Moderate.* Tuscaloosa: University of Alabama Press, 1997.

Sellers, James Benson. *Slavery in Alabama.* Tuscaloosa: University of Alabama Press, 1950.

Shore, Laurence. *Southern Capitalists: The Ideological Leadership of an Elite, 1832–1885.* Chapel Hill: University of North Carolina Press, 1986.

Simkins, Francis Butler, and Charles Pierce Roland. *A History of the South.* 4th ed. New York: Alfred A. Knopf, 1972.

Sledge, Eugene B. *With the Old Breed at Peleliu and Okinawa.* Novat, Calif.: Presidio, 1981. Reprint, New York: Oxford University Press, 1990.

Smith, William R. *The History and Debates of the Convention of the People of Alabama.* 1861. Reprint, Spartanburg, S.C.: Reprint Co., 1975.

South Central Bell Telephone Company. *Hello, Mobile: The History of Telephone Service in Mobile, Alabama, 1879–1979.* Mobile: South Central Bell, 1980.

Southerland, Henry DeLeon, Jr., and Jerry Elijah Brown. *The Federal Road through Georgia, the Creek Nation and Alabama, 1806–1836.* Tuscaloosa: University of Alabama Press, 1989.

Spies, Gregory C. *Retracing the Bounds of Old Mobile.* Mobile: Archaeotechnics Publishing Co., 1993.

Starr, J. Barton. *Tories, Dons, and Rebels: The American Revolution in British West Florida.* Gainesville: University of Florida Press, 1976.

Steel in the War. New York: United States Steel Corporation, 1946.

Stephens, Thomas. *Madoc: An Essay on the Discovery of America by Madoc ap Owen Gwynedd in the Twelvth Century.* London: Longmans, Green, 1893.

Summersell, Charles G. *Mobile: History of a Seaport Town.* Tuscaloosa: University of Alabama Press, 1949.

Tasistro, Louis Fitzgerald. *Random Shots and Southern Breezes, Containing Critical Remarks on the Southern States and Southern Institutions, with Semi-Serious Observations on Men and Manners.* 2 vols. New York: Harper and Brothers, 1842.

Thomas, Mary Martha. *Riveting and Rationing in Dixie: Alabama Women and the Second World War.* Tuscaloosa: University of Alabama Press, 1987.

Thornton, J. Mills. *Politics and Power in a Slave Society: Alabama, 1800–1860.* Baton Rouge:

Louisiana State University Press, 1978.

Thwaites, Rueben Gold, ed. *The Jesuit Relations and Allied Documents: Travels and Explorations of the Jesuit Missionaries in New France, 1610–1791.* 73 vols. Cleveland: Burrows, 1900.

Toulmin, Harry A. *A Digest of Laws of the State of Alabama.* Cahawba, Ala.: Ginn and Curtis, 1823.

University of Alabama, Bureau of Business Research. *Mobile: An Economic Appraisal.* Mobile: Gill Printing Co., 1949.

Usner, Daniel H., Jr. *Indians, Settlers and Slaves in a Frontier Exchange Economy: The Lower Mississippi Valley before 1783.* Chapel Hill: University of North Carolina Press, 1992.

Valdés, Gonzalo Fernández de Oviedo y. *Historia General y Naturel de las Indias, Islas y Tierra-firme del Mar Océano.* 5 vols. Madrid, 1852.

Van Doren, Mark, ed. *Travels of William Bartram.* New York: Dover, 1955.

Van Valkenburg, Carol. *An Alien Place: The Fort Missoula, Montana, Detention Camp 1941–1944.* Missoula, Mont.: Pictorial Histories, 1995.

Wade, Richard C. *Slavery in the Cities: The South, 1820–1860.* New York: Oxford University Press, 1964.

Waselkov, Gregory A. *Archaeology at the French Colonial Site of Old Mobile.* Mobile: University of South Alabama, 1991.

Weber, David J. *The Spanish Frontier in North America.* New Haven: Yale University Press, 1992.

Weddle, Robert S. *Wilderness Manhunt: The Spanish Search for La Salle.* Austin: University of Texas Press, 1973.

———. *Spanish Sea: The Gulf of Mexico in North American Discovery, 1500–1685.* College Station: Texas A and M University Press, 1985.

———. *The French Thorn: Rival Explorers in the Spanish Sea.* College Station: Texas A and M University Press, 1991.

Wiggins, Melanie. *Torpedoes in the Gulf: Galveston and the U-Boats, 1942–1943.* College Station: Texas A and M University Press, 1995.

Williams, David. *Cymru ac America: Wales and America.* Cardiff: University of Wales Press, 1946.

Wood, Peter H. "The Changing Population of the Colonial South: An Overview by Race and Region, 1685–1790." In *Powhatan's Mantle: Indians in the Colonial Southeast,* edited by Peter H. Wood, Gregory A. Waselkov, and M. Thomas Hatley. Lincoln: University of Nebraska Press, 1989.

Woodward, C. Vann. *Origins of the New South, 1877–1913.* Baton Rouge: Louisiana State University Press, 1951.

Woods, Patricia Dillon. *French-Indian Relations on the Southern Frontier, 1699–1762.* Ann Arbor, Mich.: UMI Research Press, 1980.

Articles

Alabama: The News Magazine of the Deep South 6 (December 22, 1941): 23–27.

Alsobrook, David E. "Mobile's Forgotten Progressive: A. N. Johnson, Editor and Entrepreneur." *Alabama Review* 32, no. 3 (July 1979): 188–202.

———. "Mobile's Commission Government Campaign of 1910–1911." *Alabama Review* 44, no. 1 (January 1991): 36–60.

Amos [Doss], Harriet E. "Trials of a Unionist: Gustavus Horton, Military Mayor of Mobile during Reconstruction." *Gulf Coast Historical Review* 4 (spring 1989): 139–41.

———. "From Old to New South Trade in Mobile, 1850–1900." *Gulf Coast Historical Review* 5 (spring 1990): 114–27.

Beerman, Eric. "José de Ezpeleta: Alabama's First Spanish Commandant during the American Revolution." *Alabama Review* 29, no. 4 (October 1976): 253.

Belous, Russell E. "The Diary of Ann Quigley." *Gulf Coast Historical Review* 4 (spring 1989): 96–97.

Berlin, Ira, and Herbert G. Gutman. "Natives and Immigrants, Free Men and Slaves: Urban Workingmen in the Antebellum American South." *American Historical Review* 88 (December 1983): 1177–81.

Born, John D. "Charles Strachan in Mobile: The Frontier Ordeal of a Scottish Factor, 1764–1768." *Alabama Historical Quarterly* 27 (1965): 23–42.

Brasseaux, Carl A. "The Moral Climate of French Colonial Louisiana, 1699–1763." *Louisiana History* 27 (winter 1986): 37.

Bryars, Dianne. "Bankhead Tunnel Project Wasn't Pork-Barrel Fantasy." *Azalea City News and Review,* November 4, 1987.

Cronenberg, Allen. "U-Boats in the Gulf: The Undersea War in 1942." *Gulf Coast Historical Review* 5, no. 2 (spring 1990): 163–78.

Fitzgerald, Michael W. "Railroad Subsidies and Black Aspirations: The Politics of Economic Development in Reconstruction Mobile, 1865–1879." *Civil War History* 39 (1993): 242–49.

Fox-Genovese, Elizabeth. "The Anxiety of History: The Southern Confrontation with Modernity." *Southern Cultures* (Inaugural Issue 1993): 65–82.

Goldfield, David R. "The Urban South: A Regional Framework." *American Historical Review* 86 (1981): 1021, 1025.

Gould, Virginia M. "In Defense of Their Creole Culture." *Gulf Coast Historical Review* 9 (fall 1993): 30–31.

"Hammerin' Hank Aaron." *Mobile* 3 (spring 1974): 4–6.

Harrison, Patricia G. "Riveters, Volunteers and WACS: Women in Mobile during World War II." *Gulf Coast Historical Review* 1, no. 2 (spring 1986): 33–34.

Haskins, Ralph W. "Planter and Cotton Factor in the Old South: Some Areas of Friction." *Agricultural History* 39 (1955): 1.

Hengiston, J. W. "Mobile, Pensacola, and the Floridas: Cotton Barque to Cape Cod, along the Gulf Stream." *New Monthly Magazine* 98 (1853): 366.

Higginbotham, Jay. "The Battle of Mauvila: Causes and Consequences." *Gulf Coast Historical Review* 6 (spring 1991): 19–33.

Hinson, Billy G. "The Civilian Conservation Corps in Mobile County." *Alabama Review* 45 (October 1992): 244–48.

———. "The Beginning of Military Reconstruction in Mobile, Alabama, May–November, 1867." *Gulf Coast Historical Review* 9 (fall 1993): 65–69.

Holmes, Jack D. L. "Alabama's Forgotten Settlers: Notes on the Spanish Mobile District,

1780–1813." *Alabama Historical Quarterly* 33 (summer 1971): 89–96.

———. "The Role of Blacks in Spanish Alabama: The Mobile District, 1780–1813." *Alabama Historical Quarterly* 37 (spring 1975): 8.

Holmes, Nicholas H., Jr. "Mobile's City Hall." *Alabama Heritage* 6 (fall 1987): 2–15.

Howington, Arthur. "John Barley Corn Subdued: The Enforcement of Prohibition in Alabama." *Alabama Review* 23, no. 3 (July 1970): 224.

Killick, John R. "Risk Specialization and Profit in the Mercantile Sector of the Nineteenth Century Cotton Trade: Alexander Brown and Sons, 1820–1880." *Business History* 16 (1974): 5.

———. "The Cotton Operations of Alexander Brown and Sons in the Deep South, 1820–1860." *Journal of Southern History* 43 (1977): 181.

McLaurin, Melton A. "Mobile Blacks and World War II: The Development of Political Consciousness." In *Gulf Coast Politics in the Twentieth Century,* edited by Ted Carageorge. Pensacola: Historic Pensacola Preservation Board, 1973.

McWilliams, Tennant S. "Petition for Expansion: Mobile Businessmen and the Cuban Crisis." *Alabama Review* 28, no. 1 (January 1975): 58–62.

———. "The City of Mobile, the South, and Richard V. Taylor." *Alabama Review* 46, no. 3 (July 1993): 163–79.

Nelson, Bruce. "Organized Labor and the Struggle for Black Equality in Mobile during World War II." *Journal of American History* 80 (December 1993): 956.

Pearce, George. "Pensacola, the Deep Water Harbor of the Gulf: Its Development, 1825–1930." *Gulf Coast Historical Review* 5 (spring 1990): 128–39.

Rea, Robert R. "Outpost of Empire: David Wedderburn at Mobile." *Alabama Review* 7 (July 1954): 223–25.

———. "Planters and Plantations in British West Florida." *Alabama Review* 29, no. 3 (July 1976): 230.

Scott, Emmet J. "Additional Letters of Negro Migrants of 1916–1918." *Journal of Negro History* 4 (October 1919): 446.

Scribner, Christopher M. "Nashville Offers Opportunity: *The Nashville Globe* and Business as a Means of Uplift, 1900–1917." *Tennessee Historical Quarterly* 54, no. 1 (spring 1995): 54–67.

Sledge, John. "Seeking a Future for the Past: Historic Preservation in Mobile." *Mobile Bay Monthly* (May 1992): 18–19.

"Steady Gain In Tonnage Reflected in Auditor's Report." *Port of Mobile News* 13 (February 1939): 7.

Stith, Mark G. "Delightful Dauphin Street." *Southern Living,* April 1997, 30.

Thomas, Mary Martha. "The Mobile Homefront during the Second World War." *Gulf Coast Historical Review* 1, no. 2 (spring 1986): 55–75.

———. "Rosie the Alabama Riveter." *Alabama Review* 32, no. 3 (July 1986): 196–212.

———. "Alabama Women on the Homefront, World War II." *Alabama Heritage* 19 (winter 1991).

Thompson, Gunnar. "Counter Point: Egypt's Role in Ancient America." *Ancient American* 2, no. 8 (February 1995): 32–34.

White, David H. "The Indian Policy of Juan Vicente Folch, Governor of Spanish Mobile,

1787–1792." *Alabama Review* 28, no. 4 (October 1975): 270.

White, Laura A. "The South in the 1850's As Seen by the British Consuls." *Journal of Southern History* 1 (1933): 38.

Willis, William H. "A Southern Traveler's Diary, 1840." *Publications of the Southern History Association* 8 (1904): 136–37.

Wish, Harvey. "The Revival of the African Slave Trade in the United States, 1856–1860." *Mississippi Valley Historical Review* 27 (1941): 584–85.

Wolley, Robert. "The Development of Gulf Ports." *American Review of Reviews* (February 1906): 192–93.

Manuscript Collections

Alabama

Alabama State Department of Archives and History, Montgomery, Alabama

Alabama State Council of Defense. SG 19851, Folder 33: Dimouts Files, 1942–43.

Alabama State Council of Defense. SG 19851, Folders 35–44: Program Administration File, 1942–1946—Mobile County Correspondence, 1942.

Boykin, Frank William, 1885–1969, Alabama Congressman Collection.

"Defense Program WWII." Public Information Subject Files, General, SG6592, Folder 568. Frank M. Dixon Papers. Selective Service System Organization, Regulations and Governor's Speeches.

Lewis Papers.

Public Information Subject Files, Mobile County, SG6889, Folder 22: Bar Pilots. Race Riots.

Shorter Papers.

Sparks Papers. Race Problems.

Barton Academy, Mobile, Alabama

"Background Information on Persons For Whom Our Schools Are Named." Know Your Schools. "History of Murphy High School." Unpublished manuscript, n.d. Murphy High School Barton Academy.

School Commissioners' Minutes.

Caldwell Delaney Collection, University of Mobile, Mobile, Alabama

"Baseball." Vertical File.

Kirven, Bill. "Great Depression Was Devastating to Mobile." Newspaper clipping.

Mobile Municipal Archives, Mobile, Alabama

Record Group 6. Series 2.

Commissioners Correspondence.

———. Series 7. Box 1.
Annexation: A-B.
———. Series 21. File 684.
Commissioners Correspondence.
———. Series 35. File 1673 and 1741.
Mobile Baseball Association.
Theatres: Motion Picture.
———. File 1863.
Entertainment.
———. Series 38. File 1349.
Federal Grants. Beautification Projects (1937–1942).
———. Street Markers/Numbers (1933–1942).
———. Toy/Furniture Projects (1939–1943).
———. Box 1.
Federal Grants. Art Projects (1935–1943). Work Project No. 6453.
———. Community Centers (1935–1940).
———. YWCA: Tennis Courts (1934–1938).
———. Series 79. File 960.
Correspondence.
War Policies Labor Board.
———. File 2185.
Correspondence.
Thirteenth Census of the United States, 1910, Vol. 2, Population Reports by States. Washington, D.C.: 1913.
"Fourteenth Census—Preliminary Assessment of Population." Records of the Commission Government (1911–1985).
———. Box 9.
Navy Day.
Record Group 23. Series 9. Box 1.
Correspondence.
Report of the Board of Commissioners of the City of Mobile for the Year Ending September 30, 1933.
Resolution Certified by S. H. Hendrix, City Clerk, July 3, 1928, Map Book 2.
Territory Proposed to Be Annexed to the City of Mobile, Map Book 3. Probate Office; Map of Mobile, September 1931.

Probate Court Archives, Mobile, Alabama

Inspectors Certificate to the Judge of Probate of the County of Mobile, April 2, 1930, Deed Book 228, 12.

Local History and Genealogy Division, Mobile Public Library, Mobile, Alabama

"150 Year Celebration of the U.S. Marine Hospital." County Board of Health—Mobile

File.
Aldermen's Minutes.
Beverly, Frances. "Musical Mobile." Mobile-Music, Musicians.
"Brief History of the Mobile City Hospital." Vertical Files.
"Early History of the Alabama State Docks."
Higginbotham, Gary J., comp. "Mobile Professional Baseball Yearly Standings." Unpublished manuscript, n.d.
———. "Bears." Mobile-Sports-Baseball File.
"An Indexed Catalogue of Minute Entries Concerning Naturalization in the Courts of Mobile County, Alabama, 1833–1907." Prepared from the Original Records by the Municipal Court Records Project of the Works Progress Administration.
Jacobs, John Hall. "Historical Background and Legal Basis of the Mobile Public Library." Unpublished manuscript, 1954.
Mobile. History: 1918–Present.
Mobile. Music: Through 1949.
Mobile Chamber of Commerce. "Industrial Report of Mobile, Alabama." Prepared for the Mobile Public Library by the Mobile Chamber of Commerce, 1931.
"Mobile Panics." Mobile-Panics File.
"MPL History." Unpublished manuscript, n.d., History, 1925–30.
"The Oldest Institution in Mobile." Mobile-Hospitals-City Hospital File.
"The Tablet" and "Brief History of the Mobile City Hospital." Unpublished manuscripts. Mobile-Hospitals-City Hospital File.
Twelfth Census of the United States 1900, Vol. 2, Population, Pt. 2, Table 55.
Thirteenth Census, Vol. 2, Table 1.
Fourteenth Census, Vol. 2, Population General Report, Table 19.

University of South Alabama Archives, Mobile, Alabama

Alabama Dry Dock and Shipbuilding Company Files.
Baldwin, Elisa. "A Guide to the Papers of John L. LeFlore, 1926–1976." Manuscript, 1996.
Baseball. Babe Ruth/Hartwell Field. Vertical File.
LeFlore, John L. Papers.
Maritime History. ADDSCO History. Vertical File.
Maritime History. Waterman Steamship Corporation History. Vertical File.
Non-Partisan Voters League Papers.
Williams, Henry C. "A History of Mobile County Training School, 1859–1977." African-American Education: Mobile County Training School. Vertical File.

National Archives Branch Depository, East Point, Georgia

Record Group 21. S-23.
Records of the District Courts of the United States, Final Record Book for the Southern District of Alabama (1859–1860).
———. Box 46.
Mobile, Mixed Cases (1820–1860).

Massachusetts

Harvard University

R. G. Dun and Co. Credit Reports, Alabama. Baker Library, Graduate School of Business Administration.

New York

New York Historical Society

Brown Brothers and Co. Letter Book. Brown Brothers Harriman and Co. Historical File.

Ogden Ferguson and Day Papers.

North Carolina

William R. Perkins Library. Duke University, Durham, North Carolina

"Correspondence." Fuller-Thomas Papers.

Southern Historical Collection, University of North Carolina, Chapel Hill, North Carolina

Duke Goodman Circular. Singleton Family Papers.

Eliza Carolina (Burgwin) Clitherall Books.

Levert Family Papers.

Mobile Letters.

Mordecai Family Papers.

Foreign

Archives Nationales, Paris, France

Archives des Colonies.

Série B: Correspondence générale.

B29, f. 259–59, 263, 284–85.

Série C: Correspondence générale.

C13A—Louisiane. Registre 1, f. 545–47; 2, f. 263–69, 643–44.

C13B—Louisiane. Registre 1, 11, f. 1–3.

C13C—Louisiane. Registre 2–109.

Section Outre-Mer.

Plan de la ville et du Fort Louis, sur la Mobile, DFC, 120B.

Bibliothèque Nationale, Paris, France

Journal de Levasseur-Russouelle *[sic]* du fort des Billochies, 1700, FF, 21690, f. 310–21v.

Archivo General de Indias, Seville, Spain

Gobierno, Legajo 12.
Mexico, Legajo 616.
Mexico, Legajo 618.
Archives du Séminaire de Québec
Lettres, R 83

Theses and Dissertations

Alsobrook, David E. "Alabama's Port City: Mobile during the Progressive Era, 1896–1917." Ph.D. diss., Auburn University, 1982.

Beam, James H. "Mobile and the Southern Question: Public Debate over the Slavery Controversy of 1850." Master's thesis, University of South Alabama, 1994.

Berkstresser, Alma E. "Mobile, Alabama, in the 1880s." Master's thesis, University of Alabama, 1951.

Boyte, Austin Presnell. "The Impact of WWII on Race Relations in Mobile, Alabama, 1940–1948." Master's thesis, Atlanta University, 1972.

Brent, Joseph Edgar. "No Surrender: Mobile, Alabama during Presidential Reconstruction, 1865–67." Master's thesis, University of South Alabama, 1988.

Calametti, John. "The Catholic Church in Mobile during Reconstruction, 1865–1877." Master's thesis, University of South Alabama, 1993.

Dow, Patsy Busby. "Joseph N. Langan: Mobile's Racial Diplomat." Master's thesis, University of South Alabama, 1993.

Duke, Eric. "A Life in the Struggle: John L. LeFlore and the Civil Rights Movements in Mobile, Alabama (1925–1975)." Master's thesis, Florida State University, 1998.

Ewert, George H. "Old Times Will Come Again: The Municipal Market System of Mobile, Alabama, 1888–1901." Master's thesis, University of South Alabama, 1993.

Fiehrer, Thomas Marc. "The Barón de Carondelet as an Agent of Bourbon Reform: A Study of Spanish Colonial Administration in the Years of the French Revolution." Ph.D. diss., Tulane University, 1977.

Gould, Lois Virginia Meacham. "In Full Enjoyment of Their Liberty: The Free Women of Color of the Gulf Ports of New Orleans, Mobile, and Pensacola." Ph.D. diss., Emory University, 1991.

Kennedy, Robert Allen. "A History and Survey of Community Music in Mobile, Alabama." Ed.D. diss., Florida State University, 1960.

Langham, Inez P. "Politics in Mobile County from 1890 to 1900." Master's thesis, University of Alabama, 1947.

Lipscomb, Oscar Hugh. "The Administration of Michael Portier, Vicar Apostolic of Alabama and the Floridas, 1825–1829, and First Bishop of Mobile, 1829–1859." Ph.D. diss., Catholic University of America, 1963.

Loftin, Bernadette Kuehn. "A Social History of the Mid-Gulf South (Panama City-Mobile) 1930–1950." Ph.D. diss., University of Southern Mississippi, 1971.

Mannhard, Marilyn. "The Free People of Color in Antebellum Mobile County, Alabama."

Master's thesis, University of South Alabama, 1982.

Parker, James C. "The Development of Port of Mobile, 1819–1936." Master's thesis, Auburn University, 1968.

Ross, Melvin Lee, Jr. "Blacks, Mulattoes, and Creoles in Mobile, during the European and American Periods." Master's thesis, Purdue University, 1971.

Shelley, Diane Lee. "The Effects of Increasing Racism on the Creole Colored in Three Gulf Coast Cities between 1803 and 1860." Master's thesis, University of West Florida, 1971.

Stephens, Corine Chadwick. "Madame Octavia Walton Le Vert." Master's thesis, University of Georgia, 1940.

Thompson, Alan Smith. "Mobile, Alabama, 1850–1861: Economic, Political, Physical, and Population Characteristics." Ph.D. diss., University of Alabama, 1979.

Voyles, James E. "An Analysis of Voting Patterns in Mobile, 1948–1970." Ph.D. diss., North Texas State University, 1973.

Watson, Bama Wathan. "The History of Barton Academy." Master's thesis, University of Alabama, 1949.

Periodicals

Alabama Planter

Alabama Tribune

Azalea City News and Review (Mobile)

Birmingham Age-Herald

Birmingham News

Debow's Review (New Orleans)

Hunt's Merchants' Magazine (New York)

Mobile Advertiser

Mobile Advertiser and Register

Mobile Daily Register

Mobile Nationalist

Mobile News-Item

Mobile Press

Mobile Press Register

Mobile Register

Mobile Tribune

Mobile Weekly Register

Montgomery Advertiser

New York Times

Niles' Register (Baltimore)

Selma Times Journal

Southern Watchman (Mobile)

Wall Street Journal

City Directories

Directory for the City of Mobile, 1859. Mobile: Farrow and Dennett, 1859.
Mobile City Directory. Birmingham: R. L. Polk and Co., 1920.
Mobile City Directory. Richmond: R. L. Polk and Co., 1929.
Mobile Directory or Strangers' Guide for 1839. Mobile: R. R. Dade, 1839.
Rowan's Mobile Directory and Commercial Supplement for 1850–51. Mobile: Strickland and Benjamin, 1850.

Government Documents

Alabama Department of Public Health. Division of Vital Statistics. *Alabama's Population, 1930–1976.* Montgomery: Alabama Department of Public Health, 1977.
Alabama Legislature. *Acts of the General Assembly of Alabama.* 1862, 2d sess.
———. *Acts of the General Assembly of Alabama.* 1863, 3d sess.
———. *Acts of the General Assembly of Alabama.* Session of 1878–1879.
———. *Acts of the Legislature of Alabama of Local and Special Character.* Session of 1931, Act No. 531. Birmingham: Birmingham Printing Co., 1931.
———. Alabama State Military Department, Office of the Adjutant General. *Quadrennial Report of the Adjutant General for the Four Year Period Ending September 30, 1942.* N.p., n.d.
Carter, Clarence E., ed. *The Territorial Papers of the United States. Vol. 18, The Territory of Alabama, 1817–1819.* Washington, D.C.: GPO, 1952.
City of Mobile. *Report of the Board of Commissioners of the City of Mobile for the Year Ending September 30, 1926.* Mobile: Wood Printing Co., 1926.
U.S. Bureau of the Census. *Fifth Census, Slave Schedule, Alabama.* Microcopy, 19, roll 33.
———. *Sixth Census, Slave Schedule, Alabama.* Microcopy, 432, roll 22.
———. *Eighth Census, Slave Schedule, Alabama.* Microcopy, 653, roll 33.
———. *Thirteenth Census of the United States, 1910, Vol. 10, Manufactures.* Washington, D.C.: GPO, 1913, Table 1.
———. *Fourteenth Census of the United States, 1920, Vol. 9, Manufactures.* Washington, D.C.: GPO, 1923, Table 31.
———. *Religious Bodies, 1926: Summary and Detailed Tables.* Washington, D.C.: GPO, 1930, Table 31.
———. *Report on Statistics of Churches in the United States at the Eleventh Census, 1890.* Washington, D.C.: GPO, 1894.
U.S. Congress. House. *Affairs in Alabama.* 43rd Cong., 2d sess., 1875, Report No. 202. Washington D.C.: GPO, 1875.
———. Senate. Committee on Veterans' Affairs. *Medal of Honor Recipients, 1862–1978.* Washington, D.C.: GPO, 1979.
U.S. Department of Defense. Office of the Chief of Naval Operations. *Dictionary of Amer-*

ican Naval Fighting Ships. 4 vols. Washington, D.C.: U.S. Naval History Division, 1969.
———. U.S. Navy. *State Summary of War Casualties (Alabama).* Washington, D.C.: GPO, 1946.
———. War Department, Bureau of Public Relations. *World War II Honor List of Dead and Missing: State of Alabama.* Washington, D.C.: GPO, 1946.

Other Reference Works

Coker, William. Lecture delivered at Auburn University, April 11, 1991.
Conwell, David M. "Vessels Sunk by Enemy Action in Canadian Bauxite Trade during World War II." Manuscript in possession of Allen Cronenberg.
———. "Vessels Sunk by Enemy Action in U.S. Bauxite Trade during World War II." Manuscript in the possession of Allen Cronenberg.
Doyle, Don H. "Urbanization and Southern Culture." Paper read at the Southern Historical Association, St. Louis, Mo., 1978.
Hinson, Billy. "The Rise and Fall of the Republicans in Mobile, Alabama, May–November, 1867." Paper in the possession of Billy Hinson.
Overton, Robert. "The Volunteer Fire Companies' Role in Redemption." Seminar paper, University of South Alabama, 1996.
Phi Delta Theta. Special World War II issue of Alabama Beta Chapter (Auburn University). *Auburn Phi* (December 1991).

Illustrations

Black-and-White Photographs and Maps

Color Section One (Colonial Period through Civil War)

following page 126

Color Section Two (Post–Civil War to the Present)

Note: The illustrations were assembled and captioned by Elisa Baldwin.

Chronology of Key Events in the History of Moblile

1702	Mobile is founded by Jean Baptiste Le Moyne de Bienville and Pierre Le Moyne d'Iberville as capital of French Louisiana
1711	Mobile is moved to present site
1763	England acquires Mobile in Treaty of Paris
1780	Don Bernardo de Gálvez captures Mobile for Spain
1799	Ellicot survey stone is erected marking the thirty-first parallel boundary between the United States and Spain
1802	Spain returns Louisiana territory to France, but status of Mobile as part of the territory is ambiguous
1803	United States purchases Louisiana territory from France
1813	Mobile is occupied by U.S. Army, April 13; massacre occurs at Fort Mims, August 30; city population less than one thousand
1814	City of Mobile is incorporated by Mississippi Territory on January 20; is governed by board of commissioners
1819	Mobile becomes city in new state of Alabama; adopts mayor-alderman form of government; Creole Fire Company is established; first river steamboat arrives
1823	Fort Condé (Charlotte) is demolished
1827	Fire consumes two-thirds of business district; city starts to rebuild with brick
1830	Spring Hill College is founded
1830–31	Michael Krafft/Cowbellian de Rakin Society begins carnival tradition on New Year's Eve
1830–60	Cotton becomes increasingly important export; Mobile is second leading cotton exporter in South; population nears thirty thousand by 1860

1836	Barton Academy, Alabama's first public school building, is constructed
1839	Three great fires burn much of downtown
1840	Mobile adds common council as second legislative body
1843	Mobile experiences first city bankruptcy
1853	Most serious antebellum yellow fever outbreak occurs
1855–56	City Hall/Southern Market (now Museum of Mobile) is constructed
1859	Medical College of Alabama opens in Mobile
1861	State of Alabama passes secession ordinance, January 11; many Mobilians celebrate
1861–64	Blockade produces shortages; Mobile fortifies extensively against Union attack
1863	"Bread and Peace" riot occurs in September
1864	Battle of Mobile Bay puts lower bay in federal hands, August 5; port is completely closed
1865	Mobile surrenders to Union forces, April 12; Emerson Institute is opened in May by American Missionary Society as school for blacks
1866	Joe Cain parades as Chief Slackabamorinico on Shrove Tuesday
1867	Reconstruction Act passes; Republicans and freed blacks join forces; Republicans take control of city offices
1868	Order of Myths (OOM) first Mardi Gras parade occurs
1869	Infant Mystics first parade occurs
1874	Democrats regain political control of city
1879	City is in default of all obligations, state legislature passes act replacing City of Mobile with Port of Mobile to save money
1879–80	Telephone service begins
1880	Mobile County Training School for African American students opens
1886	Debt issue is solved, citizens lobby for more autonomy; state legislature passes bill establishing mayor–general council form of government
1888	Paid municipal fire department is established; Corps of Engineers deepens ship channel to twenty-three feet so oceangoing vessels can reach city docks on year-round basis

1893	Electric streetcars come to Mobile; Monroe Park opens
1897	Last yellow fever epidemic occurs
1900	Population of Mobile reaches forty thousand; forest products displace cotton as port's largest export
1901	New state constitution leads to hardening of racial customs and loss of civil and political rights for blacks
1905	Original Battle House burns; "new" Battle House opens three years later
1906	City is hit by hurricane and south Mobile County is devastated by the storm
1911	Mayor-council form of government is replaced with three commissioners
1913	Woodrow Wilson visits Mobile and speaks at the Southern Commercial Congress meeting at the Lyric Theater on October 27, pledging that the United States will not seek additional territory in the Americas
1916	Alabama Dry Dock and Shipbuilding Company (ADDSCO) is created; town of Chickasaw and Chickasaw shipyards are established by U.S. Steel; Mobile is hit by hurricane on July 4–5
1919	Fire destroys forty blocks of city south of Government Street
1920	Population of Mobile reaches sixty thousand; Mardi Gras resumes after two-year war interruption
1926	In April, eighteen hundred students from Barton Academy move to new Mobile High School (renamed Murphy High School two years later); chapter of the National Association for the Advancement of Colored People (NAACP) is reactivated (a first chapter in 1919 operated briefly); last hurricane to hit Mobile until 1979 occurs
1927	Alabama State Docks opens; Cochrane Bridge opens; first Alabama Deep Sea Fishing Rodeo is held
1932	Bellingrath Gardens opens
1936	State Teachers Branch Junior College (the "Branch"), originally a branch of Alabama State University, is established as a two-year college (now Bishop State Community College)
1939	Population of Mobile exceeds seventy thousand
1940	War in Europe generates local defense spending; army begins construction of Brookley Field; Department of Defense appropriates millions for shipbuilding
1940–45	Defense work opens up opportunities for women and African Americans

1941	Population of Mobile reaches 112,000; Bankhead Tunnel opens, February 20
1943	Population of city expands to 125,000; forty thousand workers are employed at shipyards, seventeen thousand at Brookley Field; Mobile builds an average of one ship per week and repairs and overhauls more than two thousand other vessels during war; race riot at ADDSCO occurs stemming from attempt to integrate workforce
1946	In response to a suit brought by John LeFlore in federal court, blacks are granted right to vote in Democratic Party primary; Mardi Gras resumes after four-year wartime suspension
1947	First postwar multistory building, the Waterman building (now Southtrust Bank building), is constructed
1951	First Senior Bowl game is played in Mobile
1954	In *Brown v. Board of Education,* U.S. Supreme Court rules segregation illegal; racial tensions increase in Mobile and across South
1956	Alabama prohibits NAACP from operating in state; Non-Partisan Voters League (NPVL), led by John LeFlore, becomes premier civil rights organization in Mobile area
1957	Annexation nearly triples size of city
1958	First Junior Miss pageant is held
1962	Mobile Historic Development Commission is established
1963	Segregated seating on city buses ends; Mobile County public school desegregation suit (*Birdie Mae Davis* case) is filed in U.S. district court and becomes one of the longest running desegregation cases in U.S. history, not being settled until 1999; University of South Alabama is founded, with first classes held in 1964
1964	Three black students are admitted to Murphy High School; Department of Defense announces closure of Brookley Field; Chamber of Commerce sets up Task Force 200 to attract new industries; Civic Center and art gallery open; Mobile College (later University of Mobile) is founded; DeTonti Square, Mobile's first historic district, is organized
1965	USS *Alabama* Battleship Memorial Park opens
1968	Neighborhood Organized Workers (NOW) emerges in Mobile as major civil rights organization
1973	Bayway and George C. Wallace Tunnel are completed
1974	Mobile Greyhound Park opens; City Hall/Southern Market building is designated a national historic landmark

1976	Judge rules in *Wiley L. Bolden v. City of Mobile* that Mobile's form of city government is discriminatory; city appeals; courts eventually uphold ruling; reconstructed Fort Condé opens in honor of America's bicentennial
1979	Hurricane Frederic slams into Mobile and Gulf Coast, with more than $2 billion in damages; first oil well is drilled in Mobile Bay
1982	I-65 link across Mobile–Tensaw Delta is completed
1984	Tennessee-Tombigbee Waterway opens
1985	City changes government to mayor-council form
1992	Government Street Presbyterian Church is designated a national historic landmark
1993	Arthur R. Outlaw Mobile Convention Center opens
1995	Mobile is named "All America City" by National Civic League; downtown historic revival accelerates; Government Plaza is constructed
1996	Bay Bears stadium is constructed, named for Mobilian Hank Aaron
1997	Cathedral Square opens
1998	Exploreum opens
1999	Frederick P. Whiddon resigns as president of the University of South Alabama after thirty-five years; Gordon Moulton is appointed successor
2000	City acquires Saenger Theater; Midtown, Mobile's eighth historic district, is established
2001–2	Mobile celebrates its tricentennial

Contributors

ELISA BALDWIN, who collected all of the illustrations for this volume, received her B.A. degree from Bryn-Mawr College, her M.A. from Yale University, and her M.L.S. from the University of Southern Mississippi. She is a senior librarian at the University of South Alabama and archivist with the University Archives. She is also the author of *Where the Wild Animals Is Plentiful: Diary of an Alabama Fur Trader's Daughter, 1912–1914* (1999).

RICHMOND F. BROWN received his B.A. from Spring Hill College and his M.A. and Ph.D. from Tulane University. Associate professor of history at the University of South Alabama, he is the author of *Juan Fermin de Aycinena: Central American Colonial Entrepreneur, 1729–1796* (1997).

ALLEN CRONENBERG received his B.A. and M.A. degrees from the University of North Carolina at Chapel Hill and his Ph.D. from Stanford University. He is an associate professor of history and director of the Auburn University Center for the Arts and Humanities. He is also the author of *Forth to the Mighty Conflict: Alabama and World War II* (1995).

HARRIET E. AMOS DOSS received her B.A. from Agnes Scott College and her M.A. and Ph.D. from Emory University. She is associate professor of history at the University of Alabama at Birmingham. She is also the author of *Cotton City: Urban Development in Antebellum Mobile* (1985).

GEORGE EWERT received his B.A. and M.A. degrees from the University of South Alabama. He is the director of the Museum of Mobile and has published articles in the *Gulf Coast Historical Review.* In addition, he frequently lectures on a variety of topics concerning the history of Mobile.

JAY HIGGINBOTHAM is founder and former director of the Mobile Municipal Archives. He is the author of numerous books and articles in journals, newspapers, and magazines, and his works have been translated into twenty-seven languages. Among his most noted books are *Old Mobile: Fort Louis de la Louisiane, 1702–1711* (1977), *Fast Train Russia* (1983), and *Autumn in Petrishchevo* (1987).

Billy Hinson received his B.S. and M.A. degrees from Northeast Louisiana University and his Ph.D. from the University of Mississippi. He is professor of history in the Department of Social and Behavioral Sciences at the University of Mobile and author of several journal articles.

Harvey H. Jackson III received his B.A. from Birmingham Southern College, his M.A. from the University of Alabama, and his Ph.D. from the University of Georgia. He is professor and head of the Department of History and Foreign Languages at Jacksonville State University. His books include *Lachlan McIntosh and the Politics of Revolutionary Georgia* (1979); *Rivers of History: Life on the Coosa, Tallapoosa, Cahaba, and Alabama* (1995); *Putting "Loafing Streams" to Work: The Building of Lay, Mitchell, Martin, and Jordan Dams, 1910–1929* (1997); and *Henry Goodrich: A Life of Business and the Business of Life* (1999).

Henry M. McKiven Jr. received his B.S. from Auburn University in Montgomery, his M.A. from Virginia Polytechnical Institute, and his Ph.D. from Vanderbilt University. An associate professor of history at the University of South Alabama, he is the author of *Iron and Steel: Race, Class, and Community in Birmingham, Alabama, 1875–1920* (1995).

Keith Nicholls received his B.A. and M.A. degrees from Memphis State University and his Ph.D. from Florida State University. He is professor of political science and the director of the University of South Alabama Polling Group. He has published a variety of journal articles.

Christopher MacGregor Scribner received his A.B. from Princeton and his M.A. and Ph.D. from Vanderbilt University. His revised dissertation, "Trying to Back Full Speed into the Future: Federal Funding and Change in Birmingham, Alabama, 1929–1979," will be published by the University of Georgia Press. He is the city hall reporter for the *Birmingham News.*

Michael V. R. Thomason received his B.A. from the University of the South (Sewanee) and his M.A. and Ph.D. from Duke University. He is professor of history and director of the University Archives at the University of South Alabama. He is the author of *Trying Times: Alabama Photographs, 1917–1945* (1985) and of *To Remember a Vanishing World: D. L. Hightower's Photographs of Barbour County, Alabama, c. 1930–1965* (1997) and is coauthor, with Melton McLaurin, of *Mobile: American River City* (1975), *The Image of Progress: Alabama Photographs, 1877–1917* (1980), and *Mobile: The Life and Times of a Great Southern City* (1981).

Index

(Note: Numbers in italics refer to illustrations.)